Force, Order, and Justice

FORCE, ORDER, and JUSTICE

By Robert E. Osgood
and Robert W. Tucker

THE JOHNS HOPKINS PRESS
Baltimore

The Johns Hopkins Press, Baltimore, Maryland 21218
The Johns Hopkins Press Ltd., London

ISBN-0-8018-0510-4 (clothbound edition)
ISBN-0-8018-1274-7 (paperback edition)

Originally published, 1967
Second printing, 1971
Johns Hopkins Paperbacks edition, 1971

To Arnold Wolfers

PREFACE

The importance of examining the role and rationale of force today needs no explanation, but the difficulty should not be underestimated. We are impressed by the difficulty of drawing firm conclusions on the basis of the very limited experience of the nuclear age, especially when major features of the familiar cold war seem to be rapidly changing. Yet it is none too soon to suggest salient implications of certain trends in the characteristics of military power and its uses for the problem of international order. To do this we found it necessary and illuminating to view the current status of military power in the perspective of its status before the nuclear age. For it is in the interplay of continuing, changing, and, in a few respects, really novel manifestations of force that one finds essential clues to understanding the present and speculating about the future.

This book is in two parts, the first by Robert E. Osgood and the second by Robert W. Tucker. It is the product of parallel and closely coordinated inquiries by the authors over a period of several years. It reflects the major interest of The Washington Center of Foreign Policy Research in identifying and interpreting significant trends in international politics with historical and philosophical insight.

Both parts were written with close attention to each other through a continual exchange of ideas, information, criticism, and editorial scrutiny. Neither part is complete without the other. We found it valuable, however, to preserve some overlapping of material in order to develop common themes in a complementary fashion without sacrificing the unity of either distinct part.

We wish to thank the following individuals for reading our manuscript in part or whole and giving us the benefit of their critical judgment on many matters of detail and substance: Leonard Bushkoff, Thomas I. Cook, William M. Franklin, Pierre Hassner, George Liska, Theodore Ropp, Kenneth N. Waltz, and Arnold Wolfers. We are particularly grateful to Naomi Schwiesow, John J. Weltman, and Patricia S. Winer for their scholarly research assistance. Miss Schwiesow, in addition to her scholarship and her fine critical faculty, devoted marvelous editorial talents to the first part of the manuscript at every stage of its development and devised the book's index. Her contribution has been indispensable.

For expert, unfailing secretarial performance we are indebted to Elaine Clark and Catherine B. Grover.

Finally, we want to acknowledge the invaluable stimulus provided by all our colleagues in the Center, not only as individuals but also through the Center's unique institution of weekly discussions in which we collectively scrutinize current international developments from the perspective of abiding issues of power and ethics.

CONTENTS

PART I
THE EVOLUTION OF FORCE

1

THE PERSISTENCE OF FORCE

1. The Fundamental Question

Is military power in the nuclear age obsolete, or does it remain an indispensable instrument of conflict and order among autonomous states? This is a fundamental question of our time. It is a recurrent question, which deserves to be taken more seriously than ever before because the destruction that could be swiftly inflicted—by at least two states now and probably by several more in the future—would nullify any rational purpose of war for either belligerent and inflict unconscionable damage on many other nations as well.

The question of military power includes more than the obsolescence or utility of war. By "military power" we mean the ability of states to affect the will and behavior of other states by armed coercion or the threat of armed coercion. It is equivalent to "force," broadly defined. Moreover, the threats of war with which we are concerned may be explicit or implicit, and may range from unqualified ultimatums, in which one state tries to compel another to comply with specific demands by open threats of war, to implied and ambiguous prospects of war, conveyed simply by the determined opposition of one state to another's policies.

By "obsolete" we mean more than "out of date." As generally used in reference to war or force, "obsolete" implies "dysfunctional." Therefore, to ask whether military power is obsolete is not necessarily to question its existence or the possibility of war but rather to pose the broader question of whether force can serve the functions of security, domination, status, and influence which it has served in the past.

The answer to this question has crucial implications for national policy and, more fundamentally, for the very nature of international politics. If nuclear weapons jeopardize civilization, our only salvation may be to get rid of them or perhaps to put all weapons under the

3

control of a supranational government. A number of observers of international politics who are by no means pacifists or utopians have reached conclusions as drastic as this.[1] Yet conventional wisdom and historical evidence suggest that in our time the prevailing system of autonomous states is quite unlikely to be transformed so as to eliminate war and the threat of war. And there are no examples of weapons being abolished, once developed. If there is no practical point in speculating about a visionary world, even if the familiar one is doomed, the best we can do is to try to ameliorate the hazards of the existing military and political realities and hope that the very prospect of catastrophe may foster the orderly control of force. Yet an international order based on the perpetual fear of sudden catastrophe leads to the possibility that either continual peace will undermine the credibility of a nuclear strike or continuing tension will sooner or later lead to nuclear war. In either case the basis of order would be destroyed.

Theoretically, there is a third possibility for avoiding catastrophe, one that involves no radical transformation of the international system. The incentives for avoiding war may be so overwhelming in the nuclear age that independent states could learn to wage their conflicts without reference to military power. International politics would continue, but regular war and the threat of war would wither away. This proposition strains the conventional imagination no less than the prospect of centralizing international force. Yet the seriousness of the problem it is intended to cope with should compel us to re-examine the basic premises about the relationship of force to politics upon which it rests. For if force is not a fundamental and inseparable aspect of international politics, the excesses of nuclear power may simply provide us with the necessary incentive to do something that has always been possible: to expunge it from international politics. But if force is essential to international politics, if it is as persistent as the international system itself, we cannot avoid the problems of coping with it, whatever we may think about the incompatibility of modern weapons with the system.

1. For example, Hans J. Morgenthau reaches this general conclusion without specifying the exact nature of the transformation that is required: "Instead of trying in vain to assimilate nuclear power to the purposes and instrumentalities of the nation-state, we ought to have tried to adapt these purposes and instrumentalities to the potentialities of nuclear power. We have refrained from doing so in earnest, because to do so successfully requires a radical transformation—psychologically painful and politically risky—of traditional moral values, modes of thought, and habits of action. But short of such a transformation, there will be no escape from the paradoxes of nuclear strategy and the dangers attending them." "The Four Paradoxes of Nuclear Strategy," *American Political Science Review*, LVIII (March, 1964), 35.

2. The Basic Motives of Force

The history of international politics gives us no reason to suppose that all major states with conflicting interests can pursue their interests without exploiting force and, occasionally, resorting to war. There is too much evidence of the pervasiveness of force and of the multifarious functions it has served in international—and, for that matter, intertribal and interprincipality—relations. One simply cannot comprehend the rise, spread, and decline of ancient civilizations and peoples, or the creation, unification, expansion, and protection of modern nation-states, except in relation to force. The boundaries of states, their external holdings and rights, their internal strength or weakness, their influence and status, the harmony or discord of their relations—in short, the very identity of states—have been decisively shaped by competition for military power and by the fortunes of war. Indeed, the whole astonishing explosion of modern Western civilization is linked with a distinctive bellicosity in its organized political life.[2]

Nevertheless, the central role of force in the past is not a conclusive forecast of the future if nuclear weapons constitute a radical qualitative change in the nature of military power. Furthermore, the fact that some states some of the time—indeed, most states most of the time in many periods of history—have contested their conflicts without war or even the threat of war makes it at least conceivable that all states could dispense with force all of the time. To determine whether force is a necessary element of international politics we must examine the basic reasons for its pervasiveness in the past and ask whether these reasons persist.

Some find these basic reasons in man's innate aggressiveness and pugnacity.[3] But these propensities, whether innate or socially condi-

2. William H. McNeill expounds this proposition throughout *The Rise of the West* (Chicago: University of Chicago Press, 1963). See, for example, pp. 569ff.

3. For analyses of the roots of war in pugnacity and aggressiveness, through the process of displacement and projection, see Sigmund Freud, *Civilization, War and Death* (London: Hogarth Press, 1953); E. F. M. Durbin and John Bowlby, *Personal Aggressiveness and War* (New York: Columbia University Press, 1939); William McDougall, *An Introduction to Social Psychology* (London: John W. Luce, 1915); and John Dollard *et al.*, *Frustration and Aggression* (New Haven: Yale University Press, 1939). For a short review of this approach, see Quincy Wright, *A Study of War* (Chicago: University of Chicago Press, 1942), I, 131–43. Analyses that emphasize the instinctual basis of war generally share with analyses that view war as a product of social conditioning the confidence that men are basically similar and good, that they can be masters of their social and political as well as their material environment, and that, having rationally ordered the conditions of their education and living, they can live harmoniously without resort to violence. For representatives of this school of behaviorism, see Mark A. May, *A Social Psychology of War and Peace* (New Haven: Yale University Press, 1943), and Edward C.

tioned, are no more conclusive than the historical record as a reason for thinking that war or even the threat of war must persist. Aggressiveness and pugnacity can be indulged in many ways other than armed coercion. Even those who regard war as a manifestation of biological instincts generally maintain that such instincts can be diverted into harmless or even constructive channels.[4] Regardless of whether these instincts are basic sources of violence among individuals, they need not lead to violence among states, since the functions of fighting within a community and among individuals are not the same as the functions of war between political units.[5]

But if the psychosocial roots of man's behavior do not conclusively establish that force is an integral part of international politics, the evidence of man's basic *political* behavior is more difficult to dismiss. Psychosocial analysts, like philosophers, properly probe beneath the historians' data to examine the roots of organized violence that lie in human nature. What most of them fail to appreciate, however, is that the persistence of force among states springs not only from individual psychic drives and social needs but from basic political imperatives that operate among all autonomous and interacting political units.

Like faithful children of the Enlightenment, they reject the state's concern with power and status as though it were a remnant of feudal society or aristocratic privilege which is now a needless obstacle to the common interests of all peoples in advancing their material and social welfare. Moreover, they may be so convinced of the primacy of the common interest of humanity over the conflicting interests of states that even the security of the state does not warrant, in their minds, the

Tolman, *Drives Toward War* (New York: D. Appleton-Century-Crofts, Inc., 1942). For a critical analysis of the psychological and sociological interpretations of the basic causes of war, see Kenneth N. Waltz's examination of the literature of modern behavioral science in *Man, The State, and War* (New York: Columbia University Press, 1954), chap. iii.

4. Konrad Lorenz, the noted Austrian student of ethology, takes a comparable position when he contends, in opposition to those who attribute aggression to environmental conditions and frustrations, that human beings, like animals, must act out the drama of their innate impulse for aggression without the benefit of their animal antecedents' instinctive or habitual restraints upon intraspecies fighting, yet concludes that men can channel their aggressiveness away from war by cultivating international competition in sports. *On Aggression*, trans. M. K. Wilson (New York: Harcourt, Brace & World, Inc., 1966).

5. Among others, the noted anthropologist Bronislaw Malinowski makes this point in "An Anthropological Analysis of War," *American Journal of Sociology*, XLVI (January, 1941), 521–50, reprinted in *War: Studies From Psychology, Sociology, and Anthropology*, eds. Leon Bramson and George W. Goethals (New York: Basic Books, 1964), pp. 245–68.

resort to force. Why, they ask, should men wage and threaten war if they are not somehow compelled to do so by instinct or cultural conditioning? Why, indeed, unless men entertain ends or values that can be secured only through the exercise of force? If, however, these ends are rejected, war or the threat of war must appear a useless atavism, an entirely dysfunctional institution that has somehow managed to survive an advanced stage in man's social and cultural progress.

On the basis of these assumptions it is understandable that behavioral scientists should view war as the result of abnormal international tensions caused by avoidable or remediable personal or social frustrations, maladjustments, biases, and stereotypes.[6] It is understandable that one analyst anticipates the eradication of war through the replacement of man's pugnacity by his instinct for "emulation," as manifested, particularly, in commercial competition, and that another concludes that since war has been learned, it can be replaced simply by learning "a new technique or way of life."[7]

A realistic view of political behavior, however, must reject the assumption that individuals have common interests so compelling as to obviate serious conflicts of interest among states or the need of states to support their interests through force. Given the reality of man's primary loyalty to autonomous states, the need for force springs from compelling functional needs—most fundamentally, from the need of states to rely primarily on self-help in order to secure the conditions of their survival and welfare. This functional need is not ephemeral or atavistic. The modern nation-state is, after all, the most inclusive, deep-seated popular institution of our time. It is the chief repository and guarantor of the very values that the deprecators of force exalt. Its overwhelming appeal, whether among the old and industrially advanced or the new and poor states, is, if anything, increasing. The social scientists who recognize that force has a deep-seated functional relationship to particular forms of social and political relations come closer to describing reality than those who stress psychological aberration. But when they compare the role of force among nations to the once-pervasive but now generally obsolete institution of duelling, let alone slavery and trial by ordeal, they mistakenly equate the mores of men in secondary social relationships with

6. This view is fully represented in the psychosocial analyses of international tension after World War II. See, particularly, Otto Klineberg, *Psychological Factors of Peace and War* (New York: Columbia University Press, 1950), and Hadley Cantril (ed.), *Tensions That Cause Wars* (Urbana, Ill.: University of Illinois Press, 1950).

7. The first view is presented by William McDougall, the second by Mark A. May, in their works previously cited.

the imperatives confronting men acting in behalf of political communities engaged in the competition for power.[8]

We can find clues to the *political* motives of organized violence in the elemental drives that appear to move men who act not merely from individual or social motives but from group-oriented motives—that is, in the purposes of men who exercise force in behalf of all sorts of political organizations that are outside the authority of central government.[9]

Among primitive tribes, survival and subsistence, material gain (land, food, cattle, slaves, and booty), sport and glory, the acquisition of women, and religious ritual are the primary motives.[10] Among some clans, as among medieval kingdoms, honor, adventure, and plunder have been the predominant drives behind war. Modern states, however, pursue more impersonal and explicitly rationalized ends: security, material and

8. Margaret Mead, for example, makes these comparisons in defining war as a social invention and concludes that just as duelling and trial by ordeal went out of fashion when methods more congruent with the institutions and feelings of the period were invented, so the ingrained habit of war can be replaced by a better invention, provided only that "the people must recognize the defects of the old invention, and someone must make a new one." Margaret Mead, "Warfare Is Only an Invention—Not a Biological Necessity," *Asia*, XL (August, 1940), 402–5, reprinted in Bramson and Goethals, *op. cit.*, p. 274. Duelling is analogous to force among states since it was a method of settling conflicts of interest and honor by violence. But it became obsolete and disappeared largely because the state assumed this function, whereas there is no foreseeable institution to replace the state in this respect. Moreover, individuals could protect their security and their interests without duelling, whereas eschewing force leaves a state defenseless. John G. Millingen, *The History of Duelling* (2 vols.; London: R. Bentley, 1841). See also Quincy Wright's discussion of war and duelling in Wright, *op. cit.*, Vol. II.

9. The distinction between motives sanctioned by a political group in external conflict with another such group and the motives behind sanctioned forms of privately initiated violence among individuals or lesser groups (as in the case of some feuds) is often unclear in the case of primitive groups with less highly organized central institutions and more individually oriented standards of political behavior than in modern states. In states, as in lesser political units, there are, of course, all sorts of personal motives for going to war, which may or may not correspond to the group-oriented motives; but to assume that these are preponderant is to ignore the determining reality of highly developed group allegiance.

10. On primitive warfare, see Wright, *op. cit.*, Vol. I, chap. vi; Maurice R. Davie, *The Evolution of War* (New Haven: Yale University Press, 1929); Leonard T. Hobhouse, Gerald C. Wheeler, and Morris Ginsberg, *The Material Culture and Social Institutions of Simpler Peoples: An Essay in Correlation* (London: Chapman & Hall, 1930); Harry Holbert Turney-High, *Primitive War: Its Practices and Concepts* (Columbia. S. C.: University of South Carolina Press, 1949); Max Gluckman, *Custom and Conflict in Africa* (Oxford: Basic, Blackwell, & Mott, 1959); Lucy Mair, *Primitive Government* (Baltimore: Pelican Books, 1962). Roger D. Masters examines the relevance of the literature on primitive war and politics to international relations in "World Politics as a Primitive Political System," *World Politics*, XVI (July, 1964), 595–619.

commercial gain, influence and dominion, status or prestige, and religious or ideological supremacy.

These motives, of course, do not in themselves compel the resort to war. They are values for which tribes, clans, kingdoms, and states may or may not fight. All of them—except sport, adventure, and glory—can be and often are pursued by persuasion and propaganda, purchase and barter, or institutional and legal arbitrament. Why is it, then, that they so frequently lead to violent conflict and repeatedly evoke the prospect of violence?

Undoubtedly, as the psychosocial interpretations perceive, the answer does lie partly in innate pugnacity and the gratifications of organized violence. Clearly, like primitive tribes, the governments and citizens of the most civilized nations manifest these proclivities, however rationalized or sublimated they may be. Indeed, once aroused, the martial spirit of the organized mass, especially in a democratic country, is the most intense and unrestrained form of bellicosity. Yet the notable difference between modern states and tribes—or, for that matter, medieval kingdoms—is the much greater extent to which states consciously regard force, and especially the uses of force short of war, from a utilitarian standpoint, that is, as power to be used, if necessary, for an explicit collective purpose after calculating costs, gains, and risks, rather than as merely a customary way of doing things, needing no specific justification.[11] This remains true even though the general stakes of international politics and war have become less tangible and more ideological since the French Revolution.

In modern states, sport, adventure, and glory may still be powerful *personal* motives for going to war.[12] Similarly, the desire of social and economic groups within the nation to improve their status has sometimes enhanced the militancy or bellicosity of states.[13] But, unlike the motives

11. Turney-High, *op. cit.*, p. 169.
12. The classic discussion—and exaggeration—of the "play" element of warfare is Johan Huizinga, *Homo Ludens* (Boston: Beacon Press, 1962). Hans Speier draws a useful distinction between "agonistic" war, which has the quality of play, and "instrumental" war. *Social Order and the Risks of War* (Cornwall, N.Y.: George W. Stewart, Inc., 1952), chap. xviii. Clearly, the agonistic element in modern state wars is subordinate to instrumental motives so far as those acting in behalf of governments are concerned.
13. On the nature, sources, and history of modern militarism, see Alfred Vagts, *A History of Militarism* (rev. ed.; Cleveland: Meridian Books, 1959). There is a huge body of literature ascribing military preparations and war to various class and economic motives. Since World War II, the popular version of this interpretation is represented in the U.S. most ably in C. Wright Mills, *The Power Elite* (New York: Oxford University Press, 1956), which contends that the growing emphasis on military policies in the U.S. reflects the preponderance among ruling groups of an alliance between business, military, and political elites. For a critical analysis of this

of men waging war in behalf of primitive tribes and medieval kingdoms, these personal and socioeconomic motives are readily distinguished from the determining, highly rationalized, officially sanctioned motives of nations and governments. Moreover, governments have grown notably more cautious, deliberate, and impersonal in contemplating war as the state has become dissociated from the rule of the monarch, as the prospect of war has confronted citizens emotionally involved in the affairs of state with a fearful sacrifice, as warfare has become more impersonal, and as the state's management of military power has become more complicated and systematic. It is principally *after* nations have reluctantly become engaged in war that honor, glory, and revenge, which were typically elements of a code restraining conflict in primitive and medieval societies, have acted as mass catalysts of unrestrained bellicosity. And now the memory of two world wars, not to mention the prospect of nuclear catastrophe, may finally have deprived modern war of these emotional indulgences.

3. *The Integral Role of Force in International Politics*

Pugnacity and the emotional satisfactions of war may help to explain why states are sometimes bellicose, but they do not explain why states that would obviously prefer to secure their ends, whether offensive or defensive, without war habitually find it necessary to resort to war or the threat of war. They do not explain why war is endemic in international politics. The chief explanation for this phenomenon lies in the nature of the international system. More specifically, it lies in the conflicts among autonomous but interdependent political units that are organized for their own protection and advancement but that are not subordinate to a central political authority and police force. In this anarchical system, as in others where the sovereign authority and capacity to use force reside in independent political entities, armed coercion necessarily has a distinct utility that persuasion, negotiation, adjudication, and even nonviolent forms of coercion lack.

As in serious conflicts of interest within a community, force is the final argument after appeals to reason, sympathy, or tradition have failed, since it promises to gain an objective by direct means—by compelling one will to comply with another rather than by inducing one

tenuous thesis, see Talcott Parsons, "The Distribution of Power in American Society," *World Politics,* X (October, 1957), 123–43.

mind to consent to another. If men had an unlimited capacity to accommodate each other by appeals to reason and sympathy or custom, there would be no need for force. In fact, however, without organized force to prod reason, sympathy, and custom—or to compensate for their absence—all but the most static and isolated societies would be in chaos.

Within a well-ordered political community the preponderant power of compulsion lies in the hands of a government commanding the consent of the governed. In such a government force provides the ultimate sanction for a system of orderly relations in which conflicts are normally resolved peacefully. In the relations of competing political groups independent of a central government, however, the power of compulsion must reside in each group. In this sense, therefore, wars occur between political groups simply because there is nothing to stop them.[14] In international politics, moreover, the role of force, though not necessarily the propensity to war, is accentuated by the ability of popular states to mobilize mass loyalties, by the diversity of their interests and circumstances in a rapidly changing civilization, by their growing psychological, if not economic, interdependence,[15] and by the great magnitude of the force they can marshal. Under these conditions the diffusion of force among a number of states in close communication with each other accentuates mutual suspicions and animosities and reinforces the need of every major state for its own armed force.

It is true that most wars are perpetrated by states who want something they do not have rather than by states that are content to defend what they already have. Hence the imprudence of defensive states neglecting their military power. On the other hand, even if all states were purely defense-minded—a utopian supposition—there would still be need for force. The very search for security in a system of politics without government compels reliance upon military self-help, which, in turn, fosters conflict and a competition for military power.[16] The expansion of the meaning and conditions of national security to embrace tangible and intangible assets beyond the territorial boundaries of states makes this especially true. Only if all nations sought no more than the protection of their boundaries and, if at the same time, there were no conflicting requirements of such protection, could the competition for military

14. This is the general conclusion that Waltz reaches in following Rousseau's views. *Op. cit.*, especially chap. viii.

15. For a discussion of the extent and significance of interdependence among contemporary states, see n. 2, p. 325.

16. See John Herz's exposition of the "security dilemma" in *Political Realism and Political Idealism* (Chicago: University of Chicago Press, 1951), chap. ii. Cf. n. 11, p. 256.

power be avoided.[17] But this prescription is a fantasy, if only because security has become so much broader a concept.[18]

Increasingly, major powers feel compelled to protect their territory at places beyond their boundaries. Quite apart from the expanding range of their interests, they realize that the growing material and psychological interdependence of states—in conventional metaphor, the "shrinking" of the world—requires them to extend their defenses farther and farther into the surrounding international environment.[19] To feel secure, they must guard against a variety of external developments that are far down the chain of threatening circumstances: developments affecting commercial and military lines of communication, the strength of friendly nations, the distribution of power, and the credibility of their will to use force.

Furthermore, the national entity that the governments of major powers are bound to secure transcends territory to include the protection of national rights and privileges, the maintenance of national prestige and honor, and even the vindication of political values in the world. The intangible quality of the ends encompassed in the concept of security is implicit in the identification of individual citizens with an abstract national personality for which they seek the gratifications once enjoyed only by monarchs. As the ends of monarchical states were broader and less tangible than the struggles for food, slaves, cattle, and women among primitive societies, so the ends of popular nation-states are broader and less tangible than those of kingdoms.

The broad nature of the ends of states generalizes the function of force in supporting those ends. But this is a mark of the integral role of force in international politics, not of its unreality or dispensability. In its most general function force is an asset that is desirable in itself:

17. Thus Rousseau believed that the ideal but probably unachievable solution to the problem of war lay in a world of states effectively insulated from each other: small, self-sufficient republics that would use military power only to defend their territories from attack. For an acute analysis of this and other aspects of Rousseau's thoughts on international politics and war, see Stanley Hoffmann, *The State of War* (New York: Frederick A. Praeger, 1965), chap. iii.

18. On the extended meaning of national self-preservation and security, see pp. 271ff.

19. On this point, see Arnold Wolfers' explanation of the protean scope of security and the distinction between territorial and environmental goals (which he calls "possession" and "milieu" goals) in his essay "National Security as an Ambiguous Symbol" and on pp. 73ff. in *Discord and Collaboration* (Baltimore: The Johns Hopkins Press, 1962). Also relevant to this point is Charles de Visscher's view that the notion of security is strongly connected with the distribution of power and, hence, leads to "balanced tensions" and "hegemonial tensions." *Theory and Reality in Public International Law* (Princeton: Princeton University Press, 1957), pp. 78–87.

desirable not from infatuation with power but from a purely utilitarian standpoint. For, like money, military power is an indispensable means for meeting future, unspecified, and largely unpredictable contingencies.[20] It is common currency in international intercourse. A nation's reputation for using force to support its vital interests is much more important to it than is an individual's reputation for solvency or wealth to him. Especially when security depends so much on deterrence, the importance of preserving this reputation against a challenge will usually exceed by far the intrinsic importance of the immediate and tangible point of contention.

On the other hand, military power and, even more, the will to use it are much more difficult than money to measure or to relate to the values they can acquire. Therefore the tests of sufficiency are far more subjective and varied. Moreover, since military power exerts its effects chiefly through compulsion instead of reward, the power that one state acquires tends to incite, through fear and distrust, the counter-acquisition of power by other states. Thus the practical utility of military power in international politics justifies coveting it with an intensity which, if applied to the private pursuit of money, could spring only from avarice or vanity.

For these reasons war and the threat of war are endemic in international relations. The fact that most states are at peace most of the time and some are at peace all of the time, the fact that many states with conflicts of interest do not arm against each other or raise the prospect of war, does not argue against the integral relationship of force to international politics.[21] Since there is no other way for states to pursue what they regard as vital interests when other states are determined to oppose them, force must be as essential to international politics in an anarchy as elections are to domestic politics in an organized democracy.

20. Many political theorists have dealt with the analogy of military power to money or credit. See, for example, Rousseau's exceptions to the analogy in *Jugement sur la Paix Perpetuelle de l'Abbé de Saint Pierre*; C. E. Vaughan, *The Political Writings of J. J. Rousseau* (Cambridge: Cambridge University Press, 1915), I, 391. For a contemporary exposition of the analogy between power and monetary credit, see Talcott Parsons' suggestive essay, "Some Reflections on the Place of Force in Social Progress," *Internal War*, ed. Harry Eckstein (Glencoe, Ill.: Free Press, 1964).

21. "War consisteth not in battle only, or the act of fighting, but in a tract of time, wherein the will to contend by battle is sufficiently known; and therefore the notion of *time* is to be considered in the nature of war, as it is in the nature of weather. For as the nature of foul weather lieth not in a shower or two of rain but in an inclination thereto of many days together, so the nature of war consisteth not in actual fighting but in the known disposition thereto during all the time there is no assurance to the contrary." Thomas Hobbes, *Leviathan*, chap. xiii.

4. The Thesis That Military Power Is Obsolete

The integral role of force, however, does not determine whether force in the *nuclear* age can serve as a tolerable instrument of policy. Let us suppose, as many assert, that the use of nuclear weapons in war would virtually destroy the very states to which they seem indispensable, and that any war involving the nuclear powers will almost certainly become a nuclear war. And let us suppose that all states know this terrible reality. Under this condition can war and the threat of war be rational instruments of policy? Or is the utility of force severely limited by the fact that it must sooner or later touch off a catastrophic war? Even short of a catastrophe, how can force serve policy when its actual use would probably be self-defeating? Can the prospect of war supplant war itself indefinitely? These questions compel us to reassess the utility of war in light of the novelty of nuclear weapons.

The novelty of nuclear weapons is said to lie in the magnitude of destruction they could inflict. With sufficient time and effort, however, proportionate destruction could have been inflicted upon helpless and defeated nations before the nuclear age. In ancient times there was less to be destroyed, but it is hard to imagine more complete destruction than Rome inflicted upon Carthage, Corinth, and Thebes, or than the Mongols of the thirteenth century inflicted upon the cities and peoples of Asia Minor, the Near East, and Eastern Europe.

The nuclear forces of the U.S. and the Soviet Union are uniquely destructive in two respects: (1) They might cripple, if not annihilate, either adversary quickly and directly without defeating the enemy's armed forces. (2) In an unrestricted nuclear war neither adversary could avoid the high probability of crippling devastation.[22] The first characteristic makes national devastation physically easier and psychologically more terrifying than ever before. It gives governments a power of tremendous devastation that is continually and instantly available, subject to a single decision compressed into a moment, a decision that could be executed swiftly, irrevocably, and almost automatically without further political deliberation. The second characteristic makes an unrestricted war between the two principal nuclear powers not only unprofitable but, in effect, probably self-defeating to the initiator as well as the victim of an attack.

Together, these characteristics have enhanced the role of implicit threats of nuclear war, but they have diminished, if not completely nullified, the utility of carrying out such threats. What is more, the

22. See n. 4, pp. 124–25.

terrible potentialities of nuclear weapons also cast doubt on the utility
of any nonnuclear war that might expand into a nuclear war because
it impinges on the interests of nuclear powers. Thus nuclear weapons
have created a strange situation that challenges the continuity of the
traditional functions of military power in international politics, at least
so far as the conflicts of the superpowers are concerned. For if the utility
of war is greatly diminished or nullified, it is difficult to imagine threats
of war indefinitely performing all the functions of war itself. It is difficult
because the avoidance of war among states that depend so greatly upon
manipulating the risks of war puts an extreme burden upon their accurate
and prudent reading of each other's mind, and because, in the long run,
a threat of senseless violence never carried out may lose its credibility.

These novel implications of nuclear weapons have led a number of
contemporary observers to claim that we are experiencing a revolutionary
change in the functions of military power. In its most extreme form
this claim holds that war, and therefore the whole system of power
politics that depends on the prospect of war—the "war system," as
Walter Millis calls it—is obsolete. In more qualified form it maintains
that traditional, as opposed to unconventional or revolutionary, warfare is
obsolete but that autonomous states can continue to conduct power
politics without reference to such war.

The thesis that nuclear weapons have made war obsolete is presented
most fully and explicitly by Walter Millis.[23] It is implicit in the copious
peace literature since World War II; for example, the writings of
Bertrand Russell, Charles Osgood, Erich Fromm, and Seymour Melman.
The idea, however, is not confined to the peace group. General Douglas
MacArthur, for example, declared that the science of destruction in the
nuclear age has transformed the abolition of war from a moral question
to a practical necessity.[24] President Johnson affirmed what every post-
World War II President and many other heads of state have said in
similar words when he declared:

> There is no real comparison between the attitudes of most of the
> world's governments today and twenty-five years ago on the role of
> warfare as an instrument of national policy. War is obsolete, obsolete
> because there can be no winner. War is obsolete because the progress in
> mankind's abilities and knowledge make possible and imperative a new
> measure of national greatness, the measurement of how men are served

23. See especially: Walter Millis, *An End to Arms* (New York: Atheneum Press,
1964); "The Uselessness of Military Power," in Robert A. Goldwin, ed., *America
Armed* (Chicago: Rand McNally, 1961); Millis *et al.*, *A World Without War*
(New York: Washington Square Press, 1961): Millis and James Real, *The Abolition of War* (New York: Macmillan, 1963).
24. "The Abolition of War," *Vital Speeches*, XXI (February 15, 1955), 1041–42.

by their system. The question is not whether the world can eliminate war. The question is when—when all nations will have the courage and the good sense to do so.[25]

This kind of hyperbole differs from the views of the peace group because it assumes that until war is eliminated by some unspecified means, the war system must go on the same as ever, except that states must be especially cautious to avoid wars with a high risk of becoming nuclear. But it shares the basic assumption that war is obsolete because it must entail cataclysmic costs that are grossly disproportionate to any conceivable gains. Millis states the assumption this way:

> A continuation of the present state of international affairs is bound sooner or later to produce a catastrophe in which most civilized values and all of the present warring value systems must perish. . . . [War] can no longer serve its greatest social function—that of *ultima ratio* in human affairs—for it can no longer *decide*. It can render the first judgment of Solomon—to slaughter the disputed infant—but cannot render the second, which was to award it alive and whole to one or the other of the claimants.[26]

The contemporary thesis about the uselessness of war is not moral pacifism, which opposes organized violence as a matter of principle, regardless of the consequences. Nor is it simply the historic belief—or hope—that the inhumanity of new weapons will make men recoil from war.[27] Rather, it is the contemporary version of the pragmatic antiwar sentiment that gained prominence shortly before World War I, as exemplified in the writings of Ivan Bloch and Norman Angell, who charged that modern industrial-technological war had become obsolete because it would be economically ruinous.[28]

25. White House Press Release, June 23, 1964.

26. *A World Without War*, pp. 54–55. Cf. James T. Shotwell, an influential peace advocate in the interwar period, who contended that rapid changes in military resources and the technology of destruction had made war "as uncertain in its direction as in its intensity, or its spread. It is no longer a safe instrument for statesmanship under such circumstances; it is too dangerous to employ. It is no longer our *ultima ratio* because it has lost its *raison d'être*. Victor and victim may suffer a common disaster. . . . In short, war which was once a directable instrument of policy has now changed its nature with the nature of modern society and ceases to be controllable in the hands of statesmen. *War As An Instrument of Policy* (New York: Harcourt, Brace & Co., 1929), p. 36.

27. For a critical discussion of the impact of destructive technology on humanitarian restraints, see pp. 204ff. and n. 13, pp. 258–59.

28. Norman Angell, *The Great Illusion* (London: William Heinemann, 1914); Ivan S. Bloch, *The Future of War*, trans. R. C. Long (Boston: Ginn & Co., 1902), the final volume of a six-volume work published in 1899. Angell and Bloch reasoned that if nations realized that modern war must be economically ruinous, they would not resort to war. They were refuting a popular supposition at the time, avowed in the writings of Foch and Von Der Goltz, that wars had become commercial enterprises. J. F. C. Fuller, *The Conduct of War, 1789–1961* (New Brunswick, N.J.: Rutgers University Press, 1961), pp. 124–25.

The thesis, however, rests upon more than pragmatism. It has philosophical antecedents in the views of the eighteenth century *philosophes* and the nineteenth century utilitarians, who believed that, since the true interests of all states—namely, the peaceful enjoyment of material progress and the promotion of unhindered commerce—are identical and complementary, power politics and war are senseless anachronisms.[29] It echoes the pervasive material and scientific optimism of the nineteenth century as propounded by Benjamin Constant, Auguste Comte, and Herbert Spencer, who contended that the effects of what we now call "modernization" were supplanting the functions of war in preindustrial society.[30]

In the contemporary version of the thesis that war is obsolete, nuclear

29. J. B. Bury, *The Idea of Progress* (New York: Macmillan, 1932); Carl L. Becker, *The Heavenly City of the Eighteenth Century Philosophers* (New Haven: Yale University Press, 1932); Hans J. Morgenthau, *Scientific Man vs. Power Politics* (Chicago: University of Chicago Press, 1946); Felix Gilbert, "The 'New Diplomacy' of the Eighteenth Century," *World Politics*, I (October, 1951), 1–38. Condorcet's statement of the *philosophe*'s view of international politics is hard to improve upon: "If one considers the relationships of one people to another, one may say that the national interest does not exist, in the sense that one supposes these interests to be opposed. . . . The common interest of peoples is to be well governed at home, to be just toward foreigners as toward one's own citizens, to preserve peace with neighboring nations. Wars of vanity, wars of ambition, wars of commerce are equally without reason. A people can never have an interest in attacking another, nor in interfering with its liberty, nor in monopolizing to its exclusion, a branch of commerce; and one may say in general, and in the same sense, that the interest of one nation is in accord with the common interest of all, as we have said that the interest of each individual, properly understood, is in accord with the interest of society." Condorcet, *Vie de M. Turgot* (London: 1786), pp. 247–48.

30. The radical opposition of the military and industrial spirits was first formulated by the Abbé de Saint-Pierre in the eighteenth century. Constant took a simple materialistic position in reasoning that commerce will replace war as material civilization advances because commerce is a more effective way of gaining the same ends that war serves. Benjamin Constant, *De l'esprit de conquête* (3d ed.; Paris: Le Normand et H. Nicolle, 1814); also *Benjamin Constant et la Paix* (réédition de *De L'esprit de conquête*; Paris: Delagrave, 1910). Comte saw industrialism replacing war through stages of history in a kind of Hegelian dialectic, in which the ascendance and growing unity of the working classes, who are presumed to feel a common need for peace and are ennobled by the positive religion, play a major role. Auguste Comte, *System of Positive Polity* (London: Longmans, Green & Co., 1875), Vol. I; first published in 1851. Spencer also saw society developing in stages through militarism to an industrial society. Industrialism would enable men to live a full and pleasant life by voluntary co-operation instead of by the discipline of militancy. Arnold Wolfers and Laurence W. Martin, eds., "Herbert Spencer," *The Anglo-American Tradition in Foreign Affairs* (New Haven: Yale University Press, 1956). None of these theorists, however, believed that power politics and war had yet ceased to be important elements in international politics. For an acute analysis of the general thesis about industrialism replacing war, with particular reference to Comte, see Raymond Aron, *War and Industrial Society* (London: Oxford University Press, 1958); reprinted in Bramson and Goethals, *op. cit.*, pp. 351–94.

terror plays the part of commerce and industrial progress. The same faith
in man's reason and common interest persists. The contemporary version relies heavily on the supposition that sooner or later the war system
must lead to a catastrophic war. Yet this supposition is not essential to
the thesis. Some are confident that recognition of war's dangers guarantees the avoidance of war. Others believe that the very enormity of the
prospect of nuclear war will make even the threat of war, and therefore
the military establishments upon which the threat depends, useless.

In 1961 Millis held:

> However difficult it may be to imagine a world without war, this
> task is now forced upon us. Two propositions are, I think, irrefutable:
> That a continuation of the present state of international affairs is bound
> sooner or later to produce a catastrophe in which most civilized values
> and all the present warring value systems must perish; and that no
> strategic inventions, no new "national security" policies, no jugglings
> with weapons systems and armaments are likely to alter this prognos-
> tication.[31]

By 1964, however, he had refuted the irrefutable. "It is not, I think, at
all unreasonable to predict today that the nuclear stalemate will continue indefinitely," he wrote.[32] Nevertheless, he continued to believe
that the uses of military power, other than maintenance of the nuclear
stalemate, were rapidly withering away and that it was essential and
would soon be possible to replace military deterrence with a "constitution for a de-militarized world to which the great weapons systems will
be irrelevant," including an international police force that would confine
the power struggle to nonviolent means.[33]

This prophetic note, which seemingly springs from insights that transcend current evidence, runs strongly through the writings of the peace
movement. Thus, although the thesis that war is obsolete does not
logically require its adherents to believe that states are actually eschewing
war and the threat of war, since governments may not understand or act
upon the reality of military obsolescence, the prophets of obsolescence,
in fact, assert that military power is rapidly declining as a factor in
international politics, even while they rebuke governments for not
recognizing this truth. Thus Millis declares:

> Thanks in part—but only in part—to the supergiant weaponry, we
> have achieved a substantially nonmilitary form of international politics,
> which has shown a remarkable capacity to deal with the problem of
> the power struggle. . . . This situation has come about, not only through
> the fear of war in its hypertrophied modern form, but also, somewhat

31. Millis *et al.*, *A World Without War*, pp. 54–55.
32. Millis, *An End to Arms*, p. 221.
33. *Ibid.*, pp. 226–27.

paradoxically, through the real security of the great modern states against it. It is a security deriving less from the strength of the colossal deterrents than from their irrelevance.[34]

Not all the proponents of the contemporary thesis about war's obsolescence share Millis's sweeping characterization of its irrelevance. Some distinguish between the uselessness of war and the continuing efficacy of deterrence. Some, including Millis, explicitly exclude from the category of obsolescence revolutionary wars and wars between small and less developed states.[35] They accept the necessity of these wars as a concession to war's traditional role as an instrument of change. They are reconciled to the necessity because they believe, wrongly, that the functions of unconventional war are purely internal and because they are confident, plausibly, that such wars are less likely to become unlimited. In general, however, the thesis that war is obsolete applies at least to all wars that involve both nuclear superpowers or their European allies. If the thesis were true only to this extent, it would still have momentous implications for international politics.

We can explore these implications by supposing that all the major nations and their governments were absolutely convinced that war among the advanced states is obsolete (which would be a logical fulfillment of the contemporary thesis). Would statesmen who were convinced that war is useless also believe that all kinds of threats of war are equally useless? Could the implied and declared intention of resorting to war still deter, persuade, and intimidate governments with conflicting

34. *Ibid.*, pp. 138–39.
35. Hannah Arendt argues that revolutionary wars, supplemented by the nuclear stalemate and the Cold War, may be about to replace interstate wars, which have become obsolete because they threaten total annihilation; and she anticipates this imminent development taking place "without a radical transformation of international relations and without an inner change of men's hearts and minds." *On Revolution* (New York: Viking Press, 1963), pp. 1ff. Millis expects the abolition of the war system to give larger scope to guerrilla warfare and civil disorders, but he asserts that the resulting chaos "would be orderly in comparison with the unutterable chaos with which the great weapons now threaten our civilization." (*A World Without War*, p. 106.) Such violence, Millis believes, is not only less dangerous to world peace but also more functional and more morally acceptable because it is essentially political rather than military in character. He recognizes the danger that internal war may grow into an international war because of external intervention, but he thinks that with an international police and no major military establishments, internal wars could be accepted much as the law-abiding community now puts up with murder. (*An End to Arms*, pp. 200ff.) Arthur J. Waskow goes further in advocating the deliberate cultivation of violent as well as nonviolent methods of popular resistance and internal war to supplant the defensive functions of orthodox warfare in a disarmed world. (*The Limits of Defense* [Garden City, N.Y.: Doubleday, 1962], pp. 89ff.) On the fallacy of basing the preference for internal over external war on its allegedly superior moral character, see the discussion on pp. 230–33.

interests and policies? Could military power reinforce diplomacy? In other words, would the war system continue to operate? If so, how could the possibility of war, which is inherent in the threat, be eliminated? If not, what kinds of power could supplant the functions of armed coercion in international politics?

Reflection upon these questions indicates that in order for the threat or prospect of war to become strictly obsolete—that is, useless and irrelevant—in the eyes of statesmen, several novel conditions would have to exist within the international system as we know it: All the major nations and governments with opposing interests would have to be absolutely convinced that war must be self-defeating. All these nations would have to be completely sure that their potential adversaries were similarly convinced. On the basis of this mutual understanding all of these nations would have to refrain from resorting to war under any circumstances. And all of them would have to be convinced that none of them would ever resort to war. For if any one of these conditions were lacking, any government that was not completely committed to military abnegation would have a decisive advantage in threatening or actually using force against others in the knowledge that they would not resort to war under any circumstances. And any government that doubted an opponent's complete abnegation could scarcely refrain from threatening the use of force to deter the suspected nation. Then potential adversaries would be engaged in threats and counterthreats despite their conviction that war must be self-defeating. To state the conditions under which the threat of war might be expunged from international politics suggests the fanciful nature of the proposition that military power is obsolete in the nuclear age.

To explore the fancy further: Even if the major states were convinced that war could not possibly serve their interests, how could they convince one another that they will always act on their belief by abjuring war? Many have suggested that it would be necessary for them to disarm to make military abnegation completely credible, but an examination of this proposition shows once more the inextricable connection between autonomous states and the war system.[36]

Let us make the most favorable case for this proposition by assuming that in a disarmed world there would be no danger of internal security and paramilitary forces supplanting regular forces on the scale of conventional war. And let us put aside the serious problem of enforcing

36. For a fuller discussion of the consequences of so-called "general and complete disarmament," see Robert E. Osgood, "Military Power in a Disarming and Disarmed World," in Arnold Wolfers et al., *The United States in a Disarmed World* (Baltimore: The Johns Hopkins Press, 1966). See also pp. 331–41.

far-reaching restrictions upon the internal affairs of sovereign states. If nations could demonstrate military abnegation by effectively depriving themselves of the capacity to use force against each other, would they not also eliminate the very condition that is supposed to make war obsolete; namely, the possession of weapons that make war self-defeating? Then, having eliminated the novel incentive for avoiding war, what would prevent nations from rearming when the first serious conflict of interests arose?

Perhaps the very fear of rearmament would deter rearmament, just as the threat of war deters war in the armed world. Even so, the prospect of war would be as implicit in the threat of rearmament as in the threat of fighting with existing arms—and probably much more provocatively so, since rearmament would be a more serious departure from the rules of mutual restraint in a disarmed world than are the many subtle ways of threatening war in the armed world. Consequently, catastrophic war would be at least as likely to result from the "rearmament system" as from the war system.

Nevertheless, let us suppose that the great states were somehow induced to abandon the threat of war as well as war itself, because they were all confident that each believed war is useless and because each was determined to avoid war at any price. Then how would international politics be conducted? How would conflicting interests be advanced, checked, or resolved?

Some conflicts that are now rooted in military competition or aggravated by threats of war, such as those springing from the arms race and local brink-of-war situations, might be ameliorated or eliminated by disarmament. But other conflicts would surely remain: conflicts springing from internal revolutions and disturbances, competition for political allegiance, local rivalries and grievances, disputes over territories, waterways, and resources, and the deeper contests for hegemony, a favorable international environment, and ideological supremacy. To suppose that autonomous states would unconditionally abjure all forms of force in trying to cope with every such conflict of interest is an unwarranted act of faith.

Furthermore, if states *did* employ only instruments of power other than war and the threat of war, this would probably intensify, not pacify, clashes of interest, since it would remove the restraints that come from having to anticipate forceful opposition. Nor could internal war substitute for the deterrent and other nonviolent uses of regular military establishments. Reliance upon subversion, coups d'état, and revolution as the sole instruments of military power would not only be ineffective; it would create a chaos of intervention and violence that would undermine the order within states as well as destroy the order among them. One may regard the resulting risk of international and internal disorder as a price worth paying to end the risk of catastrophic war; but, actually, there is no reason to suppose that the choice would exist, since it is extremely unlikely that amid such disorder states would forego the resort to force against external sources of intervention.

On what assumptions, then, can one logically envision nations abandoning the uses of military power? The proponents of this thesis make several crucial assumptions that presuppose either a radical change in national psychology or transformation of the international system.

One assumption is that the principal source of serious conflicts among nations is simply addiction to the war system—to the notion that military power is useful. Thus the concern with force is thought to be largely a product of unwarranted fears and suspicions created by the bad habit of thinking in terms of power politics. It follows that if nations would realize that the war system is obsolete, break the habit of power politics, and get rid of their useless arms, there would be no conflicts among the great powers that could not be resolved without resort to force. This assumption enables Millis and Real to contend that the cold war is now "an almost pure struggle for power for power's sake" and to conclude that, "Once the enormous weapons systems, with the fears and the insoluble issues of abstract power that surround them, have been eliminated, differences that will continue to arise between the great-power centers will surely be susceptible to resolution by existing negotiatory and arbitral processes, as they are now within the Western community."[37]

Related to this assumption is the view that international tension and military competition result primarily from irrational biases, escape mechanisms, stereotyped perceptions, mirror image apprehensions, and ethnocentric distortions. In reality, according to this view, nations are pretty much alike. Therefore, if nations would simply realize that the chief cause of their conflicts is an obsessive fear of each other, and that they all have an overwhelming common interest in getting rid of war, they could take the animus out of power politics by disarming themselves psychologically. Having disarmed psychologically, they could build mutual trust and solve the problem of force by applying behavioral techniques of tension control and reduction, leading, perhaps, to disarmament and the establishment of a supranational order with a police force.[38]

37. Millis and Real, *The Abolition of War*, pp. 128–29, 164.
38. The fullest exposition of this view appears in Charles E. Osgood, *An Alternative to War or Surrender* (Urbana: University of Illinois Press, 1962). See also

These two assumptions about the nature of international politics—that the war system and irrational insecurities are bad habits or delusions that can be overcome rather than inherent aspects of international politics—are closely associated with another assumption: that the legitimate ends of states and the real stakes of international politics are now largely unrelated to the traditional objectives of military power, such as territory; that they are of a general, intangible nature, like gaining political and ideological adherents and winning the favor of world opinion, to which force is irrelevant.[39] According to this view, only an intellectual lag—the persistence of the fiction that force is an instrument of policy—prevents statesmen from seeing that military power is no longer relevant to their goals. Divorced from the tangible but outmoded objectives of the past, military power becomes an abstract goal in itself and therefore, by implication, illusory and ephemeral.

Thus the proponents of military obsolescence represent the war system as an anachronism that lingers only because it provides certain psychic satisfactions to those who perpetuate it. They hope to overcome the habit with reason and trust, while finding moral equivalents for the historic goals of power politics through international competition in great constructive tasks. Just as all the liberal opponents of power politics since the *philosophes* have advocated economic enrichment and humanitarian works as substitutes for war, so their kindred spirits today hope to supplant competition in power with competition in good works, science, space exploits, or building modern nations in the underdeveloped areas.[40]

Erich Fromm, *May Man Prevail?* (Garden City, N.Y.: Doubleday, 1962). Judd Marmor, presenting the conventional psychiatric view of international politics, discusses the irrational and ethnocentric sources of power politics and recommends as the basis of a warless world the scientific psychological conditioning of children and adults to prefer co-operation instead of conflict and violence. "Psychological Problems of Warlessness," *A Warless World*, ed. Arthur Larson (New York: McGraw-Hill, 1962).

39. Thus Evan Luard asserts, "The fact is that activity of this sort [direct aggression] is entirely irrelevant to the sort of struggle in which the world has become absorbed. The real object of dominion in the present world struggle is to win not territories but human hearts. The end of governments is not to paint new colors across the atlas, but to win friends and influence people; not to secure submissive populations in specific territories but enthusiastic adherents all over the world." *Peace and Opinion* (London: Oxford University Press, 1962), pp. 38–39. Cf. pp. 227–30.

40. Fromm, *op. cit.*, p. 15. Seymour Melman, *The Peace Race* (New York: Ballantine Books, 1961), pp. 65–66, 137. On scientific discovery and exploits as a moral equivalent for power politics, see Morton Grodzins and Eugene I. Rabinowitch (eds.), *The Atomic Age: Scientists in National and World Affairs* (New York: Basic Books, 1963), and Warner R. Schilling, "Scientists, Foreign Policy, and Politics," in Robert Gilpin and Christopher Wright (eds.), *Scientists and National*

Yet prophets of military obsolescence do not necessarily rest their hopes entirely on the transformation of attitudes and the creation of moral equivalents for power politics. Many also see the need for far-reaching institutional reforms, amounting to the establishment of a world government that would enforce complete disarmament and keep order with its own police force. This view at least recognizes that the obsolescence of force, carried to its full logic, requires the transformation of the international system; that international conflict without the war system presupposes the absence of national sovereignty. Yet underlying this view is a conception of international politics that underestimates the essential connection between politics and force as badly as Walter Millis, who believes that a completely demilitarized international politics does not require a world government.

Regarding world government as impractical, Millis contends that no such political transformation is necessary in order for an international police force to preserve a demilitarized world. For this police force need "only" verify disarmament and guarantee that the national power struggle is confined to nonviolent forms. Being detached from political issues, it need not decide the world's multiple power problems. For, according to Millis, questions about what constitutes rearmament or preparations for aggression or about how the police force should deal with such threats to order can be handled as purely technical, administrative, or judicial questions.[41]

This is not the place to discuss the grain of truth or the mountain of illusion in the basic presuppositions of these writings. Suffice it to say that their misconception of the nature of political man, the significance of the nation-state, and the relationship of military power to the prevailing international system has a venerable ancestry, beginning with the more profound philosophers of rationalism and liberalism in the eighteenth century. The existence of nuclear weapons seemingly provides dramatic confirmation of contemporary views about the obsolescence and dispensability of force which, in fact, rest upon utopian premises antedating the emergence of modern arms.

Policy-Making (New York: Columbia University Press, 1964), pp. 152–63. William James made the classic statement of the thesis that peace requires moral substitutes for war in his essay "The Moral Equivalent of War," published in 1910; reprinted in Bramson and Goethals, *op. cit.* To provide a peaceful equivalent of the discipline and inspiration of the martial values, James advocated conscripting youth to labor on public works in a vast war against nature.

41. Millis, *An End to Arms*, pp. 208–10, 236–38. Arthur I. Waskow presents the same ideal but advocates developing "non-lethal equivalents" of war in order to take some of the peacekeeping burden off the international force. "Non-lethal Equivalents of War," *International Conflict and Behavioral Science: the Craigville Papers*, ed. Roger Fisher (New York: Basic Books, 1964).

5. *The Contemporary Relevance of Force*

Nevertheless, the thesis that military power is obsolete does point up some crucial aspects of reality. Unrestricted war between the nuclear superpowers could indeed be useless, because self-defeating. The general appreciation of this fact has affected the role of military power and the modes of international politics in significant ways, which this essay elucidates in Chapter III. On the other hand, even a cursory survey of the contemporary scene indicates that the effects of nuclear weapons have been neither so radical, so simple, nor so novel as the proponents of military obsolescence believe.

If military power is obsolete, why are the states with supposedly the most obsolete kind of power—nuclear weapons—so concerned with maintaining and managing it? Never before have such vast economic, material, and scientific resources been so systematically directed toward the continual pursuit in peacetime of an advantageous balance of military power. The organization of military planning, research, development, and production in the United States and the Soviet Union is now as comprehensive during peace as it has ever been in total war. To suppose that this vast mobilization of national energies springs from an illusion or from purely internal forces is naïve.

Even where the thesis of military obsolescence seems most convincing—namely, in denying the utility of war between the superpowers—it must be qualified. The utility of war between the superpowers is very doubtful, chiefly because it is doubtful whether such wars could be limited and controlled for a useful political purpose. Yet the practical question, aside from the problem of deterrence, is whether such wars are so unlikely to occur or so unlikely to be kept within rational limits if they do occur as to warrant not preparing to fight them as rationally as possible. Suffice it to state here that this question cannot be responsibly answered categorically, because one of the dominant characteristics of military power in the nuclear age is the conjunction of war's terrible potentialities with its immense uncertainties.

If one looks at the lower instead of the upper end of the spectrum of violence, however, there can be no reasonable doubt that war is far from obsolete. Since World War II local wars—civil, revolutionary, and between the organized armies of states—have been as pervasive and decisive an instrument of international politics as in any modern period.[42]

42. See pp. 160–61.

Yet the principal deficiency of the thesis of military obsolescence lies less in its depreciation of the utility of war than in its failure to appreciate the subtle and varied role of military power short of war. Whatever the utility or uselessness of actual war among the advanced industrial-technological states may be, every day demonstrates that the fearful prospect of war and the policies for using, deterring, controlling, and disarming armed forces in the shadow of this prospect play a decisive role in international politics. In many ways that role is more pervasive than in previous periods of history when war was less dangerous.

This is not surprising, for when states dare not resort to war, yet dare not renounce the resort to war, international politics is bound to depend heavily upon the threat or prospect of war. The prospect that any war involving nuclear powers might become an uncontrollable cataclysm engenders great uncertainty about the circumstances in which states might actually fight, but it does not exclude that possibility as long as states must depend upon self-help to support vital interests. Just because governments wish to avoid war, they must act *as if* they might use their armed forces; and this necessity gives a certain reality to a resolve that neither they nor their adversaries can afford to assume is pure bluff.

The unprecedented magnitude, decisiveness, and psychological impact of forces-in-being and forces-in-development have greatly enhanced the uses of military power short of war. Thus confrontations and crises, testing national will and nerve under the shadow of war, have become major modes of international politics. The art of coercion short of war and on the brink has never been as finely developed or as deliberately applied. Deterrence, now the first prerequisite of military security, has become a highly sophisticated calculus. But deterrence is only the most explicit form of nonviolent military pressure in a copious arsenal of dissuasion, persuasion, compulsion, and intimidation.

Military strategy now embraces not only the waging of war but all the uses of force as an instrument of policy short of war. In fact, it is itself a major instrument of policy in peacetime. Thus strategic pronouncements can have the impact of major diplomatic statements, and the strategic "dialogue" with one's allies can be as politically significant as the communication of strategic intentions to one's adversaries.

Novel inhibitions against using modern weapons have blurred the distinction between technical military and political issues. The political repercussions of the command and control of nuclear weapons in NATO illustrate the point. As in the case of strategy, highly technical matters that used to be the exclusive concern of military officers are now the subject of national and international controversy because they are suffused with political import.

Even the continual attention commanded by arms control and disarmament, far from indicating the obsolescence of military power, testifies to the preoccupation of statecraft with military concerns. The widespread belief that the spread of nuclear ownership will have major consequences for international politics belies the assertion by some of the most vigorous opponents of nuclear proliferation that military power—even when based on the most "useless" weapons—is obsolete.

The prophets of military obsolescence not only ignore the uses of force short of war, but with the same overly materialistic view of the military function, they underestimate its continuing relevance to the broad, intangible issues of politics. They contend that because international politics is now more concerned with ideology, status, and political influence and less concerned with territory—a proposition, incidentally, that requires considerable qualification—military power tends to be increasingly irrelevant.[43] Yet military power is in many ways inseparable from these issues.

Is the prestige of a great power at stake? Few things can affect its prestige more than its reputation for using armed force prudently and effectively or rashly and ineffectively, resolutely and flexibly or hesitantly and without restraint.

Is the political independence or the domestic political system of a nation the issue? Scarcely any of the important changes in these two matters in the last twenty years can be explained without reference to military power. Most of them were achieved through war or military occupation.

Is the issue winning the "hearts and minds of men"? The outcome of the Korean War, the Cuban or Berlin crises, or the war in Vietnam will have been every bit as fateful as economic aid, political competition, or the power of example in determining the orientation of hearts and minds. If one side abandoned the military contest, no one would doubt this point.

As always, the issues of power, status, and influence have an abstract

---

43. Clearly, the function of territory for advanced states has changed since the eighteenth century, when it was more directly related to tangible military and economic assets; and the forceful acquisition of territory has generally become more costly, materially, politically, and morally. But the defense of foreign territories and the contest for political or ideological primacy in them are, in many ways, at least as important features of international politics as ever. Klaus Knorr examines the declining value of territorial conquest with pertinent qualifications in *On the Uses of Military Power in the Nuclear Age* (Princeton: Princeton University Press. 1966), chaps. ii and iii.

quality. Their abstractness, however, does not divorce the contention surrounding them from tangible evidence of military strength and the will to use it. Most of these issues come to a head in specific conflicts of interest in which armed force plays a determining role. They are mightily affected by the capacity of states to convey an impression of power through exploitation of the enhanced psychological and political impact of awesome but unused military technology. Space exploits exert something of the same impact of advanced technology upon impressionable contemporary minds; but although their efficacy as propaganda gains much from their implication of military prowess, their psychological and political impact is no substitute for the almost morbid awe inspired by weapons of sudden obliteration. In comparison, the majesty of battleships in an earlier period seems almost quaint.

Military power, then, is not losing its relevance to international politics. Indeed, in some respects, its role has expanded. It has expanded, however, not in opposition to politics but *through* politics. Political and military factors have come to suffuse each other in a way that makes the conventional distinctions of previous eras irrelevant. As the historical analysis in Chapter II indicates, international politics have, in a sense, become militarized; but, at the same time, military power has become politicized.

6. *The Impact of Nuclear Weapons upon International Politics*

The continuing and pervasive role of military power in international politics leaves open the possibility that it may have changed so radically as to require or produce a transformation of international politics. The obsolescence of the prevailing system of international politics would be no less momentous than the obsolescence of war and the threat of war.

The view that nuclear weapons must transform international politics is common. Yet its proponents furnish scant supporting evidence. They base their view, first, on the novel capacity of nuclear weapons to inflict catastrophic civilian damage suddenly and at great distances. In interpreting the significance of this capacity they stress a number of its outstanding characteristics: the ability to destroy a nation without defeating its armed forces, the inability of states to protect their territory and its inhabitants from devastation, the "overkill" or superfluous destructive power available to the nuclear superpowers, the parity or mutually nullifying effect of their military power, or the disproportion between the relative military strength of the superpowers and their capacity to use or threaten to use it against weaker powers. To these special characteristics of nuclear power they attribute various fundamental changes in the nature of international politics: the obsolescence of the classical system of power politics, the "political obsolescence" of military alliances, or the equalization of the power of small and giant states.[44]

Significantly, however, the analyses of these changes generally note a disparity between the expected effects of nuclear weapons upon international politics and the actual state of affairs. They then attribute the disparity between logic and fact to an intellectual, political, or institutional lag, which, purportedly, will lead to disaster unless eliminated by some transformation of the international system. Since this kind of analysis depends more on logical speculation than on empirical observation, it is difficult to tell whether it is clairvoyant or merely a mode of exhortation. But even if its conclusions are correct, they are of little practical help when they demand transformations of international politics that are almost certainly unattainable in time to save us. Therefore, rather than jump to conclusions about the political consequences of contemporary military technology, it is incumbent upon us to seek instruction, if not solace, from history.

In order to judge the validity of the proposition that radically new weapons must lead to radically new politics, it seems reasonable to look first at the nature of the relationship between new weapons and international politics in the past. The historic interaction between military power and international politics provides some basis for judging more precisely what aspects of nuclear power are so radically new as to make prenuclear modes of international politics obsolete and what aspects are extensions of older trends in military power, which may continue to be assimilated to traditional modes of international politics.

Many of the changes in the relationship of military power to inter-

---

44. On the drastic implications of territorial vulnerability for international politics, see John Herz, *International Politics in the Atomic Age* (New York: Columbia University Press, 1959); his "International Politics and the Nuclear Dilemma," *Nuclear Weapons and the Conflict of Conscience,* ed. John C. Bennett (New York: Charles Scribner's Sons, 1962); and Kenneth E. Boulding, *Conflict and Defense* (New York: Harper & Row, 1962), chap. xvi. On the obsolescence of the classical system of power politics because of "overkill" see Max Lerner, *The Age of Overkill* (New York: Simon & Schuster, 1962), chap. i. On the political obsolescence of alliances, stemming from the alleged equalizing effect of nuclear weapons and the purported unwillingness of one nation to protect another at the cost of nuclear retaliation, see Hans J. Morgenthau, "The Four Paradoxes of Nuclear Strategy," *op. cit.,* pp. 23–25. A military rationale of this argument lies in the theory of proportionate deterrence, as expounded by Pierre Gallois in *Stratégie de l'Âge Nucléaire* (1960), considerably revised in *The Balance of Terror* (Boston: Houghton Mifflin, 1961) and in earlier articles in *Politique Étrangère.*

national politics—which the proponents of international political transformation attribute to the invention of nuclear weapons—are continua-
tions of trends that have been particularly significant since the latter
part of the nineteenth century. Others seem less the product of nuclear
weapons than of gradual changes in the stakes of international politics,
the climate of opinion, and the diffusion or concentration of power
among states.

There are, indeed, some characteristics of nuclear weapons that are
radically new and that cannot readily be assimilated to traditional modes
of power politics. Yet, for about three centuries these modes have shown
a notable flexibility in adapting to military innovations within the
modern international system. In this respect man's political ingenuity is
as remarkable as his technological inventiveness. We simply cannot know
whether his ingenuity will measure up to the task of assimilating nuclear weapons without touching off a catastrophic war, but there seems
to be no practical alternative to his trying. In fact, the effort has begun.

7. Force as an Instrument of Order

The task of adapting international politics to modern weapons so that
force will be a rational as well as an indispensable instrument of policy
is inseparable from the problem of international order. For order requires
the restraint of force, and among autonomous states the restraint of
force requires an equilibrium of military power among opposing states—
or an empire. But is a lasting equilibrium based on weapons of sudden
annihilation feasible?

The fact that military power is endemic in international politics does
not mean that it will be used recklessly and without restraint. Although
the fragmentation of sovereignty and power creates a Hobbesian tendency toward war, it does not compel states to live in that chaos of
unlimited insecurity and perpetual violence that Hobbes posited as the
intolerable fate of individuals without a government.[45] Correspondingly,
it does not mean that there *must* be a nuclear holocaust sooner or later.

45. In *Leviathan*, Hobbes said that sovereigns, in their relations with one another,
are in the same state of nature as individuals would be if they did not subordinate
their natural freedom to the common power of government, and that this condition
compels them to live in a world dominated by the disposition to enmity and war.
But he believed that the resulting war of all against all was not nearly so dangerous
and injurious among states as among individuals, chiefly because states can protect a
large part of their citizens from the worst ravages of war. The question now arises
whether states can continue to protect their citizens, given the nature of nuclear
technology and revolutionary warfare. Chapter III answers this question generally in
the affirmative.

Yet it does mean that the possibility of a nuclear holocaust is inherent in power politics. That is an ominous fact as long as international order must be based on the hitherto fragile foundation of force-checking-force.

To appreciate the contemporary problem of order it is essential, first, to recognize the difference, as well as the similarity, in the roles of force within and among states. Within, as well as among, states the power of armed coercion is indispensable to order, because it is the final arbiter of disputes and of conflicts of rights and interests which cannot be satisfactorily prevented, resolved, or redressed merely by inducements of law, reasoned persuasion, bargaining, and sympathy. It is the ultimate obstacle to the excesses of ambition and power that would otherwise destroy the balance of interests in a cohesive political system. It is the ultimate sanction behind the network of customs, laws, and procedures that enable a political system to operate routinely. Within a state, however, the central authority—the government—holds a virtual monopoly of armed coercion. With this monopoly it enforces generally accepted laws, and it guards procedures for conducting politics peacefully. Within states, but not among them, groups with competing interests and aims normally acquiesce peacefully even in the most unfavorable situations because of their loyalty to the general community and their interest in preserving a political system from which they generally benefit, and also, of course, because they lack the power of improving their situation by violence.

To be sure, even in the most stable states violence often occurs when disaffected or hostile groups despair of securing their special interests through regular, legal channels. Civil violence and the threat of civil violence continue to play a significant role in the U.S. Throughout the Western world in the last three centuries coups d'état, subversions, insurrections, and full-scale civil wars have been more numerous and sometimes more ruinous than wars between states. But the crucial difference is that these outbursts of violence mark a breakdown of the legitimate order of government, or in any case constitute attempts to challenge, coerce, or capture it; whereas in international politics wars and threats of war are viewed as a more or less legitimate extension of politics in a system *without* government. It follows that the conditions for preserving order among states—primarily the conditions of a balance of power—are not the same as those for preserving order within states.

It is sobering to realize that the peaceful cohesion of society is tenuous in many—perhaps in most—states, and that even in the most orderly states disarmament of the central authority would soon reveal the latent violence beneath the calm surface. Yet even in unstable states the major political contests are not customarily waged, as in interstate politics, by threats of violence. The struggle for power does not turn on a calculation of the relative will and capacity of adversaries to fight each other. In a democratic state the most direct and conspicuous guarantor of order is not the internal security forces but the interplay of parties, pressure groups, and governmental factions within the constitutional framework of authority and procedures. Even in dictatorships this routine interplay, this "informal government," sustains a fabric of order without which the government would be in a continual state of crisis. Among states, however, the stability and order of the political system as a whole depend *normally* and often quite conspicuously on the military power of some states checking the power of others. Crises that threaten to dissolve this order in violence are endemic because the primary instrument of order—armed force—is also the primary threat to security.

Yet the dismal recurrence of international strife and violence should not lead us to overlook the prevalence of substantial international order during many periods of modern history. Correspondingly, the consolidation of strong secular states after the Religious Wars did not prevent considerable civil strife and violence. The history of international politics does not tell us conclusively whether states in the future will be equal to the task of establishing a tolerable order on the basis of countervailing power. But we can derive some hope, at least, from what we know of the roots of man's political behavior.

The whole record of man's political life manifests a propensity for order that is as deeply rooted as his propensity for conflict and violence. "Order," said Pope, "is Heaven's first law." But what is this propensity for order? Most simply, it is the inclination to seek a safe, dependable, predictable political environment in which the competition for power is moderated sufficiently to permit men to achieve the essential values they seek. Psychologically, it is akin to man's sense of esthetic order— to his innate desire for harmony, system, and regularity—and to his craving for the serenity that comes from these qualities in his surroundings. Practically, the propensity for order springs from an almost instinctive realization that the welfare of one's own group depends upon reciprocal restraints between it and competing groups.

Within a community the sense of order is more than a reasoned calculation of self-interest. It includes an element of sociability, of sympathy for others—a certain emotional identification of one's own group with a larger community with whose fate one's own is interlocked. Whether among states a comparable sentiment of human solidarity can sustain international order is, of course, debatable. Yet the need for this supplement to reasoned self-interest is implicitly or explicitly acknowledged in almost every theory of order, including the rationalist, utilitarian, and positivist theories, which base their hope for order upon a harmony of selfish interest; for that harmony presupposes a basic element of human sympathy and solidarity among men, regardless of political divisions.[46]

The universality of man's propensity for order is manifest in all kinds of political life. It is notable, for example, in the fine network of reciprocal restraints that customarily limits the conduct of external relations and war among rival primitive groups.[47] It is at least suggested in the instinctive and habitual inhibitions upon aggression and fighting that govern the orderly use of territory among animals.[48] Among modern states, however, the propensity is both more consciously developed and more tenuously established. It is more conscious in that the conditions of order in a rapidly changing environment must depend less on custom and more on deliberately contrived restraints, while the ideal of order must be more explicitly rationalized. It is more tenuous in that the very complexity and dynamism of civilization that put a premium upon contrived, as opposed to customary, order also call into question its reality and permanence.

As a political norm the ordering function of force has been celebrated in the name of the balance of power, the Concert of Europe, collective security, and now the balance of terror (or stable bipolar mutual deterrence). But have these norms been transcendent principles actually

46. Emphasis upon the expediential and moral bases of order, however, is typical of the liberal, "bourgeois" theory and outlook, whereas the aristocratic ethic emphasizes man's need for form, hierarchy, and propriety. The instinctual basis of order in a sense of solidarity was stressed in the writings of Jacques Novicow, Peter Kropotkin, and others who set out to refute social and political Darwinism around the beginning of the twentieth century. Thus Kropotkin wrote, "Love, sympathy, and self-sacrifice certainly play an immense part in the progressive development of our moral feelings. But it is not love and not even sympathy upon which Society is based in mankind. It is the conscience—be it only at the stage of an instinct—of human solidarity. It is the unconscious recognition of the force that is borrowed by each man from the practice of mutual aid; of the close dependency of everyone's happiness upon the happiness of all; and of the sense of justice, or equality, which brings the individual to consider the rights of every other individual as equal to his own." *Mutual Aid* (New York: Alfred A. Knopf, 1919), p. 6; first published in 1902.

47. Davie, *op. cit.*, chaps. xiv, xv; Wright, *op. cit.*, I, 96ff.

48. For an imaginative discussion linking animal and human behavior in this respect, see Robert Ardrey, *African Genesis* (New York: Atheneum Press, 1961). Ardrey's central theme is that "Three fundamental drives, for territory, for status, and for organized society become evident in the primates, those creatures closest to ourselves. And behind all three looms the vague outline of a fourth force, deepset, unaccountable and perhaps unprovable: a mysterious need for order." (*Ibid.*, p. 110.) The reciprocal restraints on animal behavior are elaborated in Ardrey, *The Territorial Imperative* (New York: Atheneum Press, 1966), and Lorenz, *op. cit.*

governing the conduct of states, or have they been merely rationalizations of transitory national interests or simply glorifications of fortuitous circumstances? The only conceptions of order that correspond to reality have been based on force-balancing-force. And perhaps the most one can claim for these is that they have been idealizations of rudimentary systems of reciprocal restraint which have moderated the behavior of prudent states as long as the practical conditions of restraint did not contravene vital national interests. Certainly, such restraint has depended much more on a coincidence of enlightened state interests than on fidelity to a principle of order.

But what is it that enlightens the interests of states? Pure reason calculating the long-run consequences of short-run restraints? One must doubt that reason is that pure or self-sufficient in the behavior of states. The history of international order and its breakdown confirms the common supposition about political life within the state: that reason is a reliable instrument of order only when guided by norms, sentiments, and conventions that transcend a cold calculus of self-interest.

Yet the establishment of a tolerable international order under contemporary conditions does put a novel premium upon deliberate, systematic calculations of reciprocal interest in the disposition of power, especially on the part of the states primarily responsible for managing the military balance. For the complexity of military technology, its capacity for sudden destruction at great range, and the crucial importance of deterrence and the accurate communication of intentions to use force mean that the control and restraint of military power must be scrupulously contrived rather than left to inherent and fortuitous constraints upon the capacity of states to fight each other. The dependence of reciprocal restraint upon calculated self-interest is all the greater because the emotional, social, and cultural elements of international order are so weak. The intensity of national and ideological animosities in this era greatly weakens feelings of sympathy and solidarity among opponents, while the aristocratic ethic of propriety and honor has long since ceased to command respect.

At the same time, the yearning for international order, which in earlier centuries was chiefly the concern of statesmen and the ruling classes, has become widespread and intense now that the lives of an entire nation can be directly disrupted by international strife and war. It is understandable, therefore, that men should now place their hopes for order so largely upon one elemental interest that is presumed to be universally compelling on selfish grounds: the avoidance of nuclear war.

8. *The Expansion and Control of Force*

The effort to make nuclear weapons serve international order is part of man's larger effort to impose order upon conflict in a field of expanding power. Most markedly since the last quarter of the nineteenth century, this effort has led to a growing tension between an increasingly intensive production and exploitation of military energy on the one hand and, on the other hand, a more uneven attempt to moderate and control the competition for power because of its growing volatility and destructive potential. This tension between the expansion and control of military power parallels the equally striking tension between the expansion and control of private economic activity. The analogy is quite inexact, but it suggests the dimensions of the problem.

Both spheres of activity have been wrenched by an unprecedented explosion of technological innovation and mass production, which we can call, for convenience, the expansion of material energy. This expansion of energy distinguishes the past century of Western civilization from all others in the history of the world.[49]

In both spheres, however, there have also been unprecedented plans and efforts to control this material expansion by a systematic, organized ordering of the production and use of energy. For the very characteristics of modern Western civilization that have intensified conflicts among its members—rapid environmental change and the increased effects of one individual's, group's, or state's actions upon another—have also, through a mixture of expediency and idealism, inspired attempts to restrain these conflicts for the common welfare. If the control of power and goods has not been adequate to ameliorate the social and political dislocations caused by its expansion, this is not because men have completely resigned themselves to a fate determined by their own restless drive toward material proliferation. In both spheres innovations in control have been propounded and put into effect—with outstanding successes in the domestic civilian realm.

Yet the problem of control does not abate; for the indefinite expansion of material energy is a universally compelling standard of modern Western civilization and seemingly as inexorable as a law of nature. In both the civilian and military realms the colossal explosion of material energy has been fostered by the same profound developments: the emergence of a secular, rational, utilitarian approach toward life and material things; the establishment of internal order through centralized state control in the aftermath of feudalism; the creation and exploitation

49. McNeill, *op cit.*, pp. 567–729.

of a popular mass base of energy with the onset of democratic and nationalist revolutions; the growth of increasingly professional and specialized management groups dedicated to material progress; and, finally, the systematic stimulation and application of technological innovation and, later, of science for the proliferation of material goods, increasingly directed and supported by the state.

Correspondingly, the effort to control the expansion of material energy for the public welfare has followed a similar course of development in the civilian and military realms: a period of laissez-faire expansion by the exploiters and producers of material energy, following their release from feudal and aristocratic constraints; then, with the democratization of society, the mobilization of popular concern and conscience toward controlling this expansion in the interests of an ever-broader public; beginning with the industrial-technological explosion, the growth and spread of the conviction that the increasing interdependence of modern society compels collective restraints upon the production and use of energy; followed by the introduction of systematic state control over the producers and managers of energy in behalf of the general welfare; and, finally, efforts to introduce comparable international control over the state's management of power.

Underlying and justifying these efforts, man's profound desire to control the seemingly inexorable expansion of power has expressed itself in similar theories of order in the military and civilian realms. In both spheres of activity there have been theories of laissez faire envisioning the reconciliation of the independent pursuit of power with the welfare of the general community through the benevolent operation of a more or less automatic harmony of selfish interests. In both spheres theories of public control arose in opposition to laissez faire: on the one hand, the systemic or revolutionary theories, which contend that the only way to secure the general welfare is to transform the whole social and political basis of the system of production; on the other hand, regulatory theories that would only reform or ameliorate the system of production through tacit or formal restraints and through limited intervention by the collectivity.

Yet the analogy between the expansion and control of civilian and military energy is, in part, misleading. Some of the differences between the two are as important as the similarities.

Thus the increase of material goods for civilian life is generally acclaimed as an end in itself, whereas the increase of military power is generally deplored as an unfortunate necessity. Therefore the conventional objective of control and order in the military realm is not to maximize the quantity and distribution of material goods, but, first, to secure the individuality of the competing political units and, secondly, to do this at as low a level of military production as possible.

In both spheres material expansion results from the irresistible drive for technological and scientific progress—hence the notable interdependence of civilian and military progress. But in the civilian realm the expansion of energy arises in part from acquisitive competition and, much less, from motives of self-preservation; whereas the imperatives of security are compelling in the expansion of military energy, since one state's military power can jeopardize another's very survival.

What gives these differences special significance from the standpoint of control and order is that in the civilian realm society is generally thought to benefit from competition that eliminates the inefficient units; and the enrichment of one individual, firm, or even state generally tends to enrich all—many competitors included—as long as competition or public regulation safeguards the general welfare. In the military realm, however, the safety of all states, not the elimination of the weaker ones through military competition, is now generally assumed to benefit mankind; and the expansion of one state's power is apt to threaten the welfare of others, since international competition is full of zero-sum games, in which the gains of one party are the losses of another.

Consequently, regulatory methods of international order, unlike those of domestic order, cannot rely upon institutions of central control to maximize production or to increase competition in accordance with a just distribution of power and goods. Rather, they must look to reciprocal restraints, whether by formal agreement or by tacit and unilateral actions, which can make competition safer and, perhaps, less expensive, in accordance with an equilibrium of power.

The problem of ordering the competition for power among states is, therefore, much more difficult than the problem of ordering economic life within a state, if the standards of domestic order are applied. On the other hand, the standards appropriate to international order are not so demanding. If one measures order only by the minimum standards of reciprocal restraint, the problem of regulating military power is far from hopeless. The first prerequisite, however, is that states should recognize the *need* for careful regulation, while eschewing both laissez-faire indulgences and systemic utopias. There are some signs that the fearful prospect of nuclear war is driving home this lesson where the adversities of World War I failed.

In military affairs as in civilian economic life, there has been a marked disillusionment with traditional laissez faire. Another version of laissez faire has gained some favor: the idea that nuclear weapons in themselves guarantee the abolition of war and the obsolescence of military power.

But although the prophets of a nuclear utopia may depreciate the need for deliberate regulation of force, they do not, like the laissez-faire theorists of the eighteenth or nineteenth centuries, advocate that each state maximize its power. As a universal standard of national behavior, that idea has long since lost its appeal.

The two or three decades before World War I probably saw the peak of optimism concerning military laissez faire, as glorified in the misapplication of Darwinian theory to the international struggle for power and as practiced in the politically undisciplined pursuit of technical military strength by the general staffs of the major European states. The unanticipated adversities of World War I provoked a massive reaction against the prevailing war system, just as the depression of 1929 provoked a reaction to the prevailing economic system.

In the reaction to international laissez faire, however, systemic conceptions of order, from Wilsonian collective security to the outlawry of war, gripped the popular imagination. They preoccupied—indeed, paralyzed—the governments of the states that were interested in order, while regulatory theories were discredited by their dependence on a balance of power. Meanwhile, the aggressive states were permitted to exploit the uses of force short of war until general war could no longer be avoided.

In the cold war the major powers have not only achieved a remarkably stable equilibrium of power, with highly developed doctrines and practices; they have also made some tentative beginnings toward regulating power politics. One can discern these beginnings in unilateral measures for effective political control of nuclear weapons, in the refinement of explicit concepts of mutual deterrence and limited war, in concepts of arms control and crisis management, and in the systematic attempt of governments and managerial elites to put such concepts into practice.

If these hopeful beginnings lead to an international order based on the continuing utility of military power among autonomous states, it will be due to the extension of relatively limited and informal reciprocal restraints rather than to the kind of legal and institutional reforms that have promoted order within states. We are not doomed by the absence of comparable reforms in the international realm. There the problem of order is different and, in some ways, less difficult because the requirements of conducting power politics without catastrophic war are less demanding than solving the problems of social justice, peaceful change, representative government, and cohesion within modern states. The relatively greater interdependence of individuals and groups within nations and the infinitely more extensive network of binding obligations that men have devised to construct internal order have afflicted modern states with internal problems of controlling conflict that are more complicated and intractable than they will ever encounter in their relations with each other. Even by the standard of avoiding or moderating violence the external relations of states in some periods of history and in many parts of the world have been more orderly than their internal relations.

The foreboding obstacle to the prospects of a tolerable international order now is not that nuclear weapons may aggravate international tensions—they may well contribute toward unprecedented stability and moderation of conflict among major states—but that a *single* breakdown of that order in nuclear violence could be catastrophic. Since there is little prospect of military technology halting or reversing itself and no possibility of wiping out the knowledge of it, we are apparently doomed to live with the literally incalculable danger of a cataclysmic war even if that danger should be the indispensable basis of unprecedented order.

It is too early to judge what, if any, permanent significance the international regulatory experiments of the cold war will have. In the final analysis, the success or failure of regulation will depend more on the attitudes of governments and nations toward force than on any particular measures of control. There is some encouragement, therefore, in the fact that the leading military states in the world have spurned both military free enterprise and nonmilitary utopias. The professional managers of force are groping for operational concepts of regulation. To a large extent the interested publics in nations with major military responsibility have endorsed or, at least, accepted the studied mutual restraint of their governments. Yet so far as the future is concerned, this essay is content with reasoned hopes rather than confident predictions. It is more interested in explaining the nature of the problem of order and how it has arisen than in expounding either predictions or hopes.

Toward this end the next two chapters deal with three overlapping aspects of force in modern international politics: the expansion of military power, the political uses and effects of military power, and the resulting problems of international order. Among the countless factors affecting the evolution of force in these three respects, we shall concentrate on the interaction of the social and political bases of military power, the development of military technology and science, the structure and organization of power among states, the professional management of military power, the stakes of international politics, and the prevailing attitudes toward force.

In the historical interaction of these factors there are a number of dividing points at which key developments fundamentally altered the nature of military power and its role in international politics. The introduction of nuclear weapons into the military establishments of the U.S. and the Soviet Union is, of course, one of these dividing points, and one with which we are primarily concerned. But in the prenuclear era there are other dividing points of equal significance, which in many ways set the stage for the contemporary period. For example, the French Revolution and World War I stand out as seminal events, and equally important is a less sharply defined period in the last quarter of the nineteenth century, when the convergence of a number of factors foreshadowed the impact of rapid technological innovation and new imperatives of peacetime military preparedness upon the problems of force and order.

From another perspective the evolution of force can be divided into several phases. The first phase, during a period before modern interstate politics, one might call the "agonistic" phase, in which war was a way of life, suffused with personal adventure and social custom, rather than a calculated tool of statecraft. The second period, which became solidly established in the eighteenth century after the Religious Wars, can be called the "utilitarian" phase, when war became a rational, limited instrument of state policy. The third phase, foreshadowed in the Napoleonic Wars but postponed until certain military and political developments in the latter half of the nineteenth century took effect, is the "expansionist" phase. In this phase the dimensions, forms, and impact of force, both in war and short of war, were drastically altered, and many of the potentialities of modern military power for disorder but also for order became manifest.

The present phase, beginning with the end of World War II and the onset of the largely bipolar world-wide contest between nuclear powers, can be called (with as much conjecture as hope) the "regulatory" phase. In many ways this phase is a response to the culmination of all the major trends in the evolution of force in the earlier phases. It raises the question whether the very same developments that account for the expansion of military power and the tendency of this power to become an autonomous and disruptive force beyond political control may now enable states to bring force back under control as a rational instrument of policy and order under radically different conditions.

2

THE EXPANSION OF FORCE

THE TRANSFORMATION OF FORCE

1. Sources of the Expansion of Force

Between the full establishment of the modern military state in the eighteenth century and the dawn of the nuclear age, military power underwent a transformation as remarkable as its transformation in the nuclear age. As in the nuclear age, the chief impetus of this transformation came from the tremendous expansion in the destructive power available to the most advanced states; but the sources of expansion were rooted deeply in social and political changes.

Materially, this expansion of force began most conspicuously in the middle of the nineteenth century with a sudden acceleration of technological innovation, mass production, and applied science. But material expansion was the product of these developments interacting with the state's mobilization and exploitation of mass enthusiasm for military purposes, its peacetime conscription of manpower, and the co-ordinated utilization of all these human, economic, and technological resources under professional military staffs.

Politically, the expansion of military power resulted first from the state's consolidation of internal order and its development of an efficient administrative apparatus and second from the emergence of popular national governments following the American and French revolutions.

Socially, these political sources of expanding military power were associated with the breakdown of aristocratic privileges and the development of a politically conscious mass, which made possible a professional military leadership and the conscription of manpower from a broad national base instead of a military caste system and an outcast soldiery drawn from the dregs of society.

Psychologically and spiritually, the beginnings of modern military power must be traced to the erosion of esthetic, moral, and cultural constraints upon warfare under the impact of a secular, rational, utilitarian approach to force in international politics; to the more recent injection of popular national and ideological fervor into state policy; and to the depersonalization of warfare that has accompanied military specialization and bureaucratization, the increasingly technical nature of military management, and the increasing remoteness of the inflictors of great destruction from their victims.

One can sum up the sources of the expansion of military power in the following terms, arranged in the approximate chronological sequence of their initial impact upon international politics: the rationalization, centralization, popularization, professionalization, and modernization of military power.

In many ways these developments have fostered disorder and complicated the problem of controlling and restraining military power. But since they seem as irreversible as modern Western civilization, we must wonder whether they condemn us to novel and terrible destruction or whether they may provide the foundation of a new international order of unprecedented stability.

2. *The Rationalization of Force under the State*

The modern state, applying a rational, instrumental approach to power and war in the wake of the relatively disorganized conflict of the Middle Ages, became the primary agent of the expansion of force. Man's approach to war had been highly rationalized in relatively orderly periods before. It did not become entirely divorced from motives of glory, adventure, and mission in the eighteenth century. When transferred to the nation-state after the French Revolution, these motives were more compelling than during the Crusades. Nevertheless, a significant change in man's approach to war took place with the state's establishment of internal order in the eighteenth century. As military power became the instrument of state policy, the religious and messianic, the social or agonistic, and the personal motives of war became subordinate to a utilitarian approach oriented toward using power with studied efficiency. This rationalization of military power has become increasingly comprehensive, calculated, and technical since the last part of the nineteenth century. Although we take this approach for granted as part of our civilization, this was not always the prevailing attitude.

In the Middle Ages, from roughly the eleventh century through much of the fourteenth, war was more a way of life than a calculated instrument of policy.[1] It was virtually a continuous but small-scale activity that men took for granted.[2] The small scale resulted from the smallness of the armies, the short term of service, and the physical difficulty of keeping forces in the field for more than a few weeks at a time. Moreover, armies lacked the weapons and logistics to overcome the defensive advantage of castles and fortresses or to hold territory. The most successful commanders relied on maneuver, while generally avoiding pitched battles, where all might be lost in a day. Strategic direction was weak or entirely missing, although some commanders displayed great tactical skill.

Battles were, in effect, extensions of personal disputes arising primarily from the network of conflicting jurisdictions and loyalties involved in feudal obligations and dynastic claims. They needed no other justification. Except for the Crusades and the later years of the semi-national Hundred Years' War (1338–1452), wars were fought for the security, status, and enrichment of kings and for the emotional and economic gratification of the nobility.[3] They were permeated by the chivalric values of personal honor, glory, and vengeance. We need not enter the controversy over the extent to which these values—especially the gentler ones of magnanimity and fair play—were actually lived up to. There are many examples in the Middle Ages of the mutual observation of rules of fair contest and of ceremonial restraints in the conduct of warfare. There are also many examples of one or both sides violating such rules and restraints. The important point here is that social and personal motives were so pervasive that war was more like a

1. The fullest and most authoritative account of medieval warfare is Charles W. C. Oman, *A History of the Art of War: The Middles Ages from the 4th to the 14th Century* (2 vols.; 2d ed.; London: Methuen, 1924), and *A History of the Art of War in The Sixteenth Century* (New York: E. P. Dutton & Co., 1937). See also Hoffman Nickerson, "Warfare in the Roman Empire, the Dark and Middle Ages: to 1494 A.D.," in Oliver Lyman Spaulding, Hoffman Nickerson, and John W. Wright, *Warfare: A Study of Military Methods from the Earliest Times* (Washington: The Infantry Journal, 1937), chaps. v–viii. A good brief interpretation is T. F. Tout, *Medieval and Modern Warfare* (Manchester: Longmans, Green & Co., 1919). Johan Huizinga deals with chivalry and stresses the personal and "play" elements of warfare in *Homo Ludens* and *The Waning of the Middle Ages* (Garden City, N.Y.: Doubleday Anchor Books, 1954).

2. In perhaps the greatest battle of the Middle Ages, Bouvines (1214), the French had 11,000 cavalry and about 20,000 militia infantry, fighting a coalition with 11,000 cavalry and over 70,000 infantry. Spaulding *et al., op. cit.,* pp. 347–54.

3. Even in these two periods warfare bore little resemblance to the coherent, well-organized campaigns for an overriding collective purpose that appeared chiefly after the French Revolution and the rise of popular nationalism. R. C. Smail, *Crusading Warfare (1097–1193)* (Cambridge: Cambridge University Press, 1956); Edward P. Cheyney, *The Dawn of a New Era, 1250–1453* (New York: Harper & Bros., 1936), chap. v.

continuing enterprise or recreation than a recurrent political necessity. Consequently, boldness, vengeance, adventure, plunder, and sometimes even generosity frequently overrode tactical or strategic considerations. In the spirit of knight-errantry, kingdoms went to war in the most reckless and unpremeditated way; armies fought in the most amateurish and capricious fashion.[4]

Chivalry as a code of military conduct was largely destroyed during the fourteenth through sixteenth centuries by infantries with crossbows and longbows, by Swiss pikemen, gunpowder, and the growth of national allegiance. Still, the instrumental approach to war remained subordinate to its social or agonistic aspect. The chaotic Religious Wars of the sixteenth and seventeenth centuries dissolved what was left of the old codes of combat and injected a new intensity into warfare. Yet war did not become an instrument of policy in the modern sense.

War was scarcely under the effective control of rulers. Armies were often little more than undisciplined bands of marauders living off the land, since states lacked organizational control of them and were unable to provide logistical support. War was a clash of dynastic and religious sectarian allegiances. Above all, it was, in Sir George Clark's words, a "general melee," a "collision of societies."[5] Even in fifteenth- and sixteenth-century Italy, which saw the origins of modern diplomacy, the formation of military coalitions, and the consolidation of several fairly cohesive political units absorbed in Machiavellian competition, war was governed by feudal and dynastic interests rather than by the interests of nations or modern states.

In the second half of the seventeenth century, as the religious issues waned, monarchs began to construct internal order by establishing effective control over economic and political life. The growing internal power of governments facilitated their control of war and gave war

---

4. Thus Oman notes that the expedition Edward III led against France in 1346 was not the execution of a plan; rather, it had "the character of a chivalrous adventure, of a great raid of defiance pushed deep into France to provoke its king." *A History of the Art of War: The Middle Ages from the 4th to the 14th Centuries* (London: Methuen, 1898), pp. 599–600. A lack of planning and calculation continued to characterize warfare after the Hundred Years' War. For example, France's repeated costly military adventures in Italy in the sixteenth century were undertaken without any calculation of possible material gains and losses. Her expeditions against Naples were militarily impossible tasks undertaken with neither naval supremacy nor effectual control of Lombardy and central Italy. J. R. Hale, "Armies, Navies and the Art of War," *The Reformation: 1520–1559*, Vol. II of *The New Cambridge Modern History*, ed. G. R. Elton (Cambridge: Cambridge University Press, 1958), p. 501; Garrett Mattingly, *Renaissance Diplomacy* (London: Jonothan Cape, 1955), chap. xiii.

5. Sir George Clark, *War and Society in the Seventeenth Century* (Cambridge: Cambridge University Press, 1958), pp. 25ff.

political direction. In the coalitions formed against Louis XIV's drive toward Continental hegemony, diplomacy became absorbed in efforts to shape the configurations of state interest and power. Concomitantly, effective control of the military establishments, marked by improved military discipline, the formulation of military codes restraining plunder and piracy, and the creation of more efficient and larger standing armies, laid the foundation for the war system of the eighteenth century, in which force and the threat of force were to serve as instruments of state policy. Through these developments modern *Realpolitik*, foreshadowed in Renaissance Italy, emerged on a larger scale than ever before, backed by the organized power of the state.

In the eighteenth century kings became identified with modern sectarian states, yet states transcended the monarchy to encompass the people and the land as well. The development of centralized authority and of financial and bureaucratic structures capable of raising revenue enabled the state to create and control professional standing armies in order to enforce civil order and support external policies. In the aftermath of Louis XIV's failure to establish a European order based on French hegemony, the ambitions and rivalries of military states led to a pattern of calculated, circumspect relations based upon alignments of countervailing power. The stakes of politics were predominantly dynastic, turning largely upon marriages and inheritances, territory and commerce, but the common unit of political currency was now more clearly the power of the state to make war. This currency was freely exchanged in limited quantities for limited ends. Yet these limitations were, in a sense, the result of the weakness as well as the strength of the state.

3. The Constraints on Force

The rulers of eighteenth-century Europe lacked the mobility and firepower and the base of mass enthusiasm that were essential to wage Napoleonic war. Equally important, they lacked the political system and the administrative capacity to mobilize the whole nation and its resources for war. The expensive standing armies and artillery of the period imposed a severe strain on the limited capacity of governments to tax the people and finance protracted campaigns.[6] The stringencies upon seapower were even greater, since no state could afford to train seamen in time of peace, and the quantity and quality of seamen that could be dragged into the service by press gangs were not conducive to large-scale

6. John B. Wolf, *The Emergence of the Great Powers, 1685–1715* (New York: Harper & Row, 1951), pp. 8ff., chap. vii, emphasizes the economic and fiscal limitations on the conduct of war.

warfare.[7] Throughout the eighteenth century, war on land and at sea had to be attenuated or terminated because it threatened financial ruin, owing to the destruction of commerce at sea and to the expense of keeping armies and navies fighting.

These limiting conditions were in accord with the political necessities of the ruling classes. To have waged war for larger purposes with greater violence would have required popular states (whether autocratic or representative) and, therefore, the end of the Old Regime. Besides, the stilted tactics and clumsy logistics of warfare seemed appropriate to the social differences of the time. They reflected on the one hand the aristocratic and mercantilist outlook of the ruling classes, who liked their battlefield amenities and wished to limit the expenditure of life and money, and on the other hand the apathy and unreliability of the soldiery, who, having been drawn from the nonproductive segments of society and feeling little allegiance to the state, had to be disciplined to the stylized, drill-like maneuvers of the time in order to be kept reasonably efficient.[8]

Yet the social and political constraints upon war would not have been so limiting without the material and technological constraints, which, in fact, persisted for decades after the French Revolution. The military inventions of the eighteenth century did not notably increase the scope, tempo, or intensity of warfare. The important changes in weapons since the Middle Ages—notably the development of muskets and artillery, fortresses, and heavily armed sailing ships—were assimilated only very gradually. The relative strength of the defense continued to retard the pace of war. Indeed, the greater use of artillery further encumbered logistics; and material shortages, especially in metal, fuel, and saltpeter, hampered exploitation of the new technology. The nearest thing to a modern arms race was the competitive establishment and enlargement of standing armies, but this competition was not accompanied by comparable competition in weapons.[9]

7. On navies and seapower in the eighteenth century, see Walter L. Dorn, *Competition for Empire, 1740–1763* (New York: Harper & Bros., 1940), pp. 102–21.

8. Alfred Vagts, *A History of Militarism* (New York: Meridian Books, 1959), chap. i; Hans Speier, *Social Order and the Risks of War* (New York: George W. Stewart, 1952), chap. xix; Dorn, *op. cit.*, pp. 80ff.

9. Nevertheless, the competition in standing armies impressed some contemporary observers as a novel and disturbing feature of international relations. Thus Montesquieu complained, "A new disease has spread through Europe. It has attacked our princes and makes them maintain a disproportionate number of troops. . . . As soon as one state increases the number called into service, the others immediately do the same, with the result that nothing is gained thereby but the common ruin. Each monarch keeps in readiness as many armies as he would need if his people were in danger; and this condition of rivalry of all against all is called peace." *Réflexions*

European industry, still mainly dependent on craftsmanship, had not yet developed much standardization or mass production, either in civilian or military technology. Transportation and communication did not become significantly faster and cheaper. There was little or no pressure for innovations in military technology from monarchs, and there was considerable resistance to it on the part of the nobility and soldiery: the nobility, because innovations threatened their supremacy as a fighting class; the soldiery, because they feared the destructiveness of new weapons. Military inventions were not the product of a systematic response to military needs; they were largely a by-product of civilian technology. Science was not oriented toward practical invention, even for civilian uses; and scientists were generally hostile to the thought of applying their learning to military uses.[10]

These basic material, technological, political, economic, and social constraints enable us to speak of the eighteenth century before the French Revolution as a century of limited wars. The generalization is too sweeping, since these wars were not notably different from those of the seventeenth century in their number, frequency, scope, duration, intensity, and deadliness to combatants. Indeed, when the typical wars of maneuver and position were punctuated with pitched battles, the improved discipline of the armies, together with the continuing low level of medical science, produced extremely high casualty rates. In one important respect, however, the limited wars of the eighteenth century were comparatively moderate: they caused significantly less destruction of civilian life, property, and welfare, with the exception of the devastating Seven Years' War in Prussia.[11] This limitation distinguished them

---

sur la monarchie universelle en Europe, quoted in Albert Sorel, *Europe Under the Old Regime,* trans. Francis H. Herrick (Los Angeles: Ward Ritchie Press, 1947), p. 25.

10. For an account of military innovations, dealing with their social and cultural background and their relation to science and technology in the eighteenth and preceding centuries, see John U. Nef, *War and Human Progress* (Cambridge: Harvard University Press, 1950), Parts I and II, and Bernard and Fawn Brodie, *From Crossbow to H-Bomb* (New York: Dell Publishing Co., 1962), chaps. iii and iv. The Brodies distinguish science from technology in the following way: "The growth of science is . . . an inductive process, where new increments of knowledge round out or modify existing principles. The application of science to machines, on the other hand, is a deductive process; it begins with a principle and proceeds to a mechanism." *Ibid.,* p. 7. In the eighteenth century the sailing warship was technologically the most complicated military machine, but it remained substantially unchanged, and its effectiveness continued to depend on relative skill of operation rather than on technological advantage. Theodore Ropp, *War in the Modern World* (new rev. ed.; New York: Collier Books, 1962), chap. ii.

11. Although attempts to quantify the characteristics of warfare in any period of history are apt to be misleading and subject to inaccuracies, Quincy Wright's gen-

from the *grand mêlée* of the Religious Wars and made them a discriminating tool of statecraft.

In this respect kings and statesmen, anxious to avoid the excesses of
the Thirty Years' War and determined to employ no more force than
necessary to achieve modest and well-defined objectives, kept war limited.
Limited war in turn generally served them as a means of policy commensurate with their ends. Thus the limited scope of land warfare was
well suited to the limited territorial goals that states usually sought. War
at sea was frequently little more than commercial war with an admixture
of violence. Diplomatic bargains resolved what force could not decide.

4. Harbingers of Military Dynamism

Yet even in this century of limited war there were harbingers of a
new military dynamism. The rulers of Prussia, despite the many limitations on military power, demonstrated the capacity of the state to improve its relative position in the hierarchy of states by generating military
power. By the end of the seventeenth century Frederick William, the
Great Elector of Brandenburg-Prussia, had already shown the capacity
of an absolute monarch to utilize the material, human, and administrative resources of the state to build a superior standing army.[12] In the
eighteenth century his successors, Frederick William I and Frederick

---

eralizations and statistics on this subject are indispensable: A *Study of War* (Chi-
cago: University of Chicago Press, 1942), chap. ix, appendixes xix–xxi. See also
Gilbert W. Beebe and Michael E. De Bakey, *Battle Casualties: Incidence, Mortality,
and Logistic Considerations* (Springfield, Ill.: Thomas, 1952); Gaston Bodart and
Vernon L. Kellogg, *Losses of Life in Modern Wars* (London: Oxford University
Press, 1916); and Lewis F. Richardson, *Statistics of Deadly Quarrels* (Chicago:
Quadrangle Books, 1960). A study of the Historical Evaluation Research Organization (HERO) includes statistics on percentages of killed and wounded in battles
during significant wars from the sixteenth century to the present. The percentages
for the wars of Louis XIV and Frederick the Great are somewhat lower than for
the sixteenth century and the Thirty Years' War, but a great deal lower for the
defeated states. The percentages for the nineteenth century after the Napoleonic
Wars, however, are lower than the eighteenth century. The ratio of wounded to
killed (about 3.5 to 1) did not rise significantly until World War I. *Historical
Trends Related to Weapon Lethality* (Washington: HERO, 1964), Annex, III,
enclosure 2.

12. Sidney B. Fay, "The Beginning of the Standing Army in Prussia," *American
Historical Review*, XXIV (July, 1917), 763–77. The greatest organizer of an efficient standing army in the seventeenth century was Sweden's King Gustavus Adol-
phus, although great advancements in rationalizing military organizations were also
made by Richelieu in the army and by Colbert in the navy, under Louis XIV.
Whereas Gustavus had about 30,000 men under arms in 1631, Louis XIV is said
to have maintained a military establishment of 400,000, with field armies approaching 100,000—a size not to be duplicated until the French Revolution. HERO, *op.
cit.*, Annex, I, 43.

the Great, added limited military conscription, intensive tactical training, efficient artillery barrages, and skillful generalship to raise Prussia through conquests and diplomacy to the front rank of states, although France, Russia, and Austria had from ten to twenty times the population and corresponding advantages in wealth, resources, trade, and territory.[13]

England provides the other striking example of an eighteenth-century state capitalizing upon military superiority based on efficient use of natural and human resources. By concentrating on naval power and a merchant marine and keeping military adventures on the Continent to a minimum, England compensated for her scarce native material resources by using her strategic geographical position, her substantial population, and her financial and trading prowess to become the dominant commercial and colonial power, with hegemony on the seas.

As Prussia based its military ascendance on the army and the control of land, England based its hegemony on the navy and control of overseas commerce. Through its army Prussia acquired and controlled land and population, which in turn were major ingredients in strengthening the army. Through its navy England acquired colonies and controlled commerce, which in turn provided the money to hire soldiers and subsidize allies on land while supporting a navy that could strangle the commerce of adversaries.[14] Both were pre-eminent examples of states operating as successful military organizations, although the relatively unobtrusive impact upon domestic life of a standing navy, as compared to a standing army, helped England avoid the conspicuous militarism that arose in Prussia. Both provided impressive examples of the internal expansion of military power, which subsequent generations would emulate in the nineteenth century.

Moreover, in the rationalism of the eighteenth century there was also

13. Penfield Roberts, *The Quest for Security, 1715–1740* (New York: Harper & Row, 1947), p. 64. On the Prussian army, see Walter Dorn, *op. cit.*, pp. 90ff., and R. R. Palmer, "Frederick the Great, Guibert, Bulow: From Dynastic to National War," *Makers of Modern Strategy*, ed. Edward M. Earle (Princeton: Princeton University Press, 1943), pp. 49–62. In size of population, Prussia, with 2½ million, was twelfth among European states in 1740, but largely through conquest this population had doubled by 1786. The Prussian army under Frederick the Great grew to about 200,000, with a field army of about 53,000, at the beginning of the Seven Years' War (as compared to an average size of 47,000 among first-rank field armies in the eighteenth century). Four-fifths of Prussia's revenue went into the army.

14. On the interaction of economic and military power as exploited by England and other maritime states, see Dorn, *op. cit.*, pp. 6ff., and Admiral Sir Herbert Richmond, *The Navy as an Instrument of Policy*, ed. E. A. Hughes (Cambridge: Cambridge University Press, 1953). England's integrated system of military power, instituted in the seventeenth century and consolidated in the eighteenth, followed the doctrine of mercantilism. Eli Heckscher, *Mercantilism*, trans. Mendel Shapiro (London: G. Allen & Unwin Ltd., 1935), Vol. II.

a harbinger of the technological explosion that transformed the scale of military power in the half century before World War I. In this century modern materialism—faith in the inevitable progressive increase of man's mastery of inanimate things for practical ends—became a sacred standard. The standard eroded the remnants of medieval moral and esthetic constraints upon weaponry and lay the cultural foundation for the uninhibited advancement of military technology. The invention of more powerful weapons was presumed to be a mark of advancing civilization. The perfection of firearms, some hoped, would make wars so destructive that they would be quickly terminated or avoided altogether.[15] Thus Europe was being prepared for a revolution in military technology that would be the counterpart of the industrial revolution—that astonishing explosion of man's ingenuity and productivity ignited in England two hundred years ago.[16]

Yet before the rise of popular nationalism and the onset of the industrial-technological revolution, military power could not approach the volatility, dynamism, mass, and intensity it attained in the nineteenth and twentieth centuries. Consequently, the military managers of the eighteenth century were spared the problems of control which afflicted their successors and were permitted the illusion of mastering the still latent energy of destruction. In the hands of enlightened statesmen and generals, military establishments seemed to be calculable and safe instruments of policy.[17]

Confidence in the calculability of war was consonant with the stress on rigid tactical principles of maneuver and position and with elaborate rules of siege and surrender. It reflected the prevalent faith in the ability of men to rationalize all human activity by discovering the precise, mechanical laws of its operation. Some analysts foresaw a universal military science that would be so exact as to render war futile and unneces-

15. Nef, *op. cit.*, pp. 200–1, 300. Nef perhaps exaggerates the extent to which restraints upon technological progress before the nineteenth century were imposed by the fear of original sin and the love of beauty, but his work remains the most complete and convincing account of the moral and cultural environment of military power.

16. Among the civilian innovations of the eighteenth-century industrial revolution which transformed military technology in the latter part of the nineteenth were the steam engine, iron metallurgy, the shift from wood to coal for fuel, the rise of industrial chemistry, the establishment of a machine tool industry, and the beginnings of the science of electricity. Brodie, *op. cit.*, pp. 118ff.

17. "By and large a statesman in 1750 or 1815, if he possessed information on the size of armies, on the men who led them, and on the relative wealth of the rulers, probably had a better chance of estimating the power of a foreign state than he would have today. Much of the necessary information was actually common knowledge in the chancelleries of Europe." Edward V. Gulick, *Europe's Classical Balance of Power* (Ithaca: Cornell University Press, 1955), p. 28.

sary.[18] There was reason for such confidence, for although the outcome of war depended on many imponderables, the principal elements of military power were sufficiently ponderable to facilitate roughly accurate comparisons in advance of war. In war itself they remained fairly stable, and victory turned upon the most skillful use of largely unchanging weapons and tactical rules known to everyone.[19]

In reality, of course, war was not as precisely calculable as its theorists professed. The vicissitudes of physical environment and human skill on the battlefield and especially at sea, where weather and unreliable communications interfered more with command and control, repeatedly led to miscalculations. The chief significance of the limitations on armed forces was that, together with the rough equality of combinations of opposing forces, they rendered the consequences of miscalculations less serious.

Thus Frederick II, who was increasingly impressed by the role of chance in war and diplomacy as he gained experience, reflected upon the results of the War of the Austrian Succession (1740–48) with a certain melancholy satisfaction: "Since the art of war has been so well understood in Europe, and policy has established a certain balance of power between sovereigns, grand enterprises but rarely produce such effects as might be expected. An equality of forces, alternate loss and success, occasion the opponents at the end of the most desperate war, to find themselves much in the same state of reciprocal strength as at the commencement."[20]

The wars of the French Revolution and Napoleon's military adventures would reveal a dynamism and decisiveness in war that Frederick II could not have imagined. But this new dimension of force also created a new dimension of miscalculation—and new efforts to master force.

The wars of the French Revolution showed what unprecedented concentration of military energy the popularization of war could produce even before the technological transformation preceding World War I. Although Carnot, as Minister of War in 1799, directed the first concerted effort to mobilize scientific talent for war, Napoleon was indifferent to technological innovations. Nevertheless, Napoleon magnified the force of war tremendously by exploiting the new sources of organized violence

18. Hans Speier, *op. cit.*, pp. 240–1.

19. See Ropp's description of "neoclassical warfare," *op. cit.*, pp. 44ff.; Eric Robson, "The Armed Forces and the Art of War," *The Old Regime, 1713–1763*, Vol. VII of *The New Cambridge Modern History*, ed. J. O. Lindsay (Cambridge: Cambridge University Press, 1957), chap. viii, is a good summary of the characteristics and conditions of eighteenth-century warfare.

20. Frederick II, *The History of My Own Times* (London: G. G. J. & J. Robinson, 1789), I, Part II, 301.

released by popular nationalism and ideological fervor. Following the course of the revolutionary leaders who preceded him, he transformed warfare into a national crusade, involving not just tactical maneuver and attrition of the enemy's supply lines but annihilation of the enemy's forces, occupation of his territory, and even political conversion of his people. With universal military conscription and comprehensive material and economic mobilization, he created a "nation in arms." To the revolutionary tactics of offensive mobility, surprise, the concentration of overwhelming numbers on a single point, massed artillery fire, and destructive pursuit, he added the extravagant ambition of a bold field commander, to give war a terrible new impact and momentum.

Truly, "The wars of Kings were at an end; the wars of peoples were beginning."[21] The sheer scale of the resulting violence made the impact of war as unpredictable and uncontrollable as it was momentous. In Clausewitz's terms, it made war more nearly "a thing in itself."

Yet, although the potential autonomy and dynamism of popular, massive war had been revealed, the European wars of the following century, from 1815 to 1914, were relatively limited. Indeed, there were fewer significant wars in the European state system than in the period from the defeat of Louis XIV to the French Revolution.[22] There were none of the scope or duration of the Seven Years' War and only one, the Crimean War, that was a general war involving several major powers. In the Crimean and Franco-Prussian Wars the field armies were several times larger than those of the seventeenth and eighteenth centuries— in the hundreds of thousands instead of twenty or thirty thousand—but the percentage of combat casualties was not much different, and civilian

21. This is Marshal Foch's pronouncement occasioned by the famous cannonade at Valmy (1792), which marked the end of the Prussian offensive. Foch, *The Principles of War*, trans. Hillaire Belloc (New York: Henry Holt & Co., 1918), p. 29. Much earlier, Goethe and Clausewitz, among others, had interpreted the battle at Valmy as the end of the old warfare and the beginning of the new. Actually, Valmy was tactically insignificant, but it was strategically and politically significant because a citizen army withstood a model eighteenth-century army and permitted the Revolutionary forces to go on to future victories. For a discussion of the impact of the French Revolution and Napoleon upon warfare, see J. F. C. Fuller, *The Conduct of War, 1789–1961* (New Brunswick, N.J.: Rutgers University Press, 1961), chaps. ii and iii.

22. Of course, what one regards as a militarily and politically significant war is somewhat subjective. By our reckoning there were either nine or sixteen such wars in the eighteenth century and either seven or thirteen in the latter period, depending upon what criteria are used. However, the number of belligerents and the duration of wars were markedly greater in the eighteenth century. In the eighteenth century the period from 1763 to the French Revolution was generally peaceful in the sense that there was no more than one large war and only a few small wars. In nineteenth-century Europe the periods 1815–1854 and 1871–1914 were equally peaceful.

destruction was localized. The wars of this period are notable for their short duration and the small number of battles and participating states, as compared to the eighteenth or twentieth centuries.[23] They were fought and settled for limited objectives, they were localized, and they were quickly terminated. Only the Crimean War was a general war involving a number of states, but it did not approach the duration or economic and human devastation of the Seven Years' War. Only the Franco-Prussian War approached the Napoleonic Wars in intensity of battles and numbers of forces involved, but it was far more limited in geographical scope and duration.

The explanation of limited war in the period between the Napoleonic Wars and World War I, as in the eighteenth century, seems to lie in circumstances that were partly fortuitous, partly technological and economic, and partly the result of deliberate restraints upon the political objectives of war. Although the material and technical limits upon war were not so constraining as before the French Revolution, the destructive potential of armies was still sufficiently restricted to enable states to keep combat within bounds in the absence of a political occasion for fighting a general war of annihilation.

The Austro-Prussian War and the Franco-Prussian War were limited chiefly by Prussia's ability to bring superior force to bear quickly and by Bismarck's willingness to negotiate a limited victory consistent with a new equilibrium of power. The Russo-Japanese War of 1906 was limited chiefly by Japan's sudden naval victory, by its satisfaction with a local victory, and by the material incapacity of both belligerents to carry the war to the other's homeland. The Crimean War was limited by its location—the same war in Austria might well have become a world war—and by the incompetence and inefficiency of the belligerents. These and other wars in this period remained local largely because the European system of political alignments, as in the eighteenth century, was relatively fragmented and loosely knit before the emergence of the two great alliances that clashed in 1914.

5. *The New Management of Force*

Although war itself remained limited in the period after the Napoleonic Wars and before World War I, military power expanded greatly. The professionalization and modernization of military power in the latter half of this period created an unprecedented peacetime war potential. But the success of states in preserving a relatively peaceful and

23. Wright, *op. cit.*, Vol. I, appendixes xix–xxi.

orderly international system while greatly expanding its military basis concealed the latent dangers of the new military potential.

In the latter half of the nineteenth century, military power in Europe came under the systematic direction of a new class of specialists in military organization and planning. Professionally dedicated to maximum military efficiency, these specialists directed their nation's human, material, technological, and economic resources toward the creation in peacetime of military machines capable of inflicting maximum destruction upon the enemy's forces in war. The systematic training of these military specialists, with their highly developed staffs and administrative procedures, codes of professional conduct, formulation of war plans, conduct of war games, and development of strategic and tactical doctrine marked the application to the management of force of those methods of modern production that were transforming private industry.

The outstanding model of military management was the Prussian General Staff.[24] By capitalizing on two great new military resources, universal compulsory peacetime conscription and the railways-and-telegraph system, the Staff led Prussia to two rapid, stunning victories over Austria in 1866 and France in 1871.[25] The quickness and completeness of Prussia's destruction of the fighting capacity of the dominant military power in Europe was particularly remarkable. It convincingly demonstrated to the rest of Europe the necessity of systematically developing peacetime military potential under professional, scientific management. Thereafter all the major states on the Continent created general staffs, railway networks, and systems of universal peacetime military service.

As we shall see in examining the political consequences of the expansion of military power, the new military machines provided statesmen with a powerful political instrument; but, unfortunately, the statesmen permitted the machines to follow a logic of their own—the narrow logic

24. Walter Gorlitz, *History of the German General Staff, 1657–1945,* trans. Brian Battershaw (New York: Frederick A. Praeger, 1957); Gordon A. Craig, *Politics of the Prussian Army: 1640–1945* (Oxford: Clarendon Press, 1955).

25. The conscription system introduced by the Prussian military reformers enabled Prussia to combine a relatively small, highly professional standing army with a large military potential and thereby to join numbers with skill at a tolerable cost. The system entailed compulsory universal service for several years with the regular army and the regular reserve and then with a civilian militia. The military organization of the railways entailed first constructing a railway network, then mobilizing the army, transporting it with weapons and supplies to the right spot at the right time, and finally deploying the forces properly. Prussia made many mistakes in conscription and railway organization in the war with Austria, but the General Staff studied the experience and profited from it. Michael Howard, *The Franco-Prussian War* (New York: Macmillan, 1961), pp. 18–29. Howard's study shows how substantially Prussia's success depended upon superior organization of mobilization and railway utilization.

of military efficiency held by the professional managers. Thus instead of becoming a flexible instrument of policy short of war, the new peace-time military potential became, in effect, an independent force largely divorced from political control. Because the military machines were geared so strictly to fighting a war, they tended to foreclose new oppor-tunities for using force short of war.

This fatal deficiency was related to the inflexibility of strategic doc-trine. The growing need to concert and co-ordinate the increasingly diverse components of military power gave new importance to strategy. The increased importance of continual planning and the growing de-pendence of military power on industry and technology expanded the very meaning of military strategy. Strategy outgrew its traditional mean-ing: the plan for fighting a battle. It became the plan for utilizing all the nation's resources and instruments of war most effectively in order to exert force advantageously in future military contingencies, in the light of a potential adversary's intentions and capabilities. The opera-tional strategy of states in peacetime might have a determining effect upon the character and even the outbreak of war. Strategic doctrine could also become a primary political factor short of war, as we shall see in the case of airpower after World War I.

The expanded function of strategy called for a systematic integration of military plans with foreign policy. In the hands of military profes-sionals, however, strategy tended, on the one hand, to exalt the romantic emphasis of Foch on *will* and the all-out offensive and, on the other hand, to emphasize meticulous operational planning for military effi-ciency measured by the maximum force that could be brought to bear upon the enemy. The result was a kind of strategic monism that simpli-fied planning but did not serve policy.

Thus the war mobilization plans of the general staffs in the years of armed peace after the Franco-Prussian War seriously limited the oppor-tunities for diplomatic accommodation and committed governments in certain contingencies to an almost automatic shift into general war, as though their war machines had only one forward gear and no brakes.[26] The prevailing military assumption that a future war would be swift and decisive like the Franco-Prussian War and that a long war would ruin a nation's economy and incur the danger of revolution put a premium on striking first with superior forces. This requirement in turn led military staffs to commit their governments to plans for total mobili-zation only and to regard mobilization as an inevitable prelude to all-out

26. Alfred Vagts, *Defense and Diplomacy* (New York: King's Crown Press, 1956), chaps. v and x.

war. When mobilization began, diplomacy would stop. For the sake of military efficiency, military plans were directed toward meeting a single contingency with one kind of response. The whole machinery was inflexibly geared to the complicated, exacting logistics of the railway networks, with the object of concentrating the maximum force at a single military point as quickly as possible. Consequently, when Austria declared war against Serbia in 1914, Austria, Russia, and Germany forfeited the diplomatic opportunities for avoiding war that partial mobilization against each other might have afforded, lest they lose precious time in fully mobilizing for the war that their military staffs considered inevitable.[27]

Actually, despite their commitment to full mobilization, each of these governments, at the behest of statesmen, tried to resist and, except in Germany, temporarily succeeded in resisting the prescribed automatic response by undertaking partial mobilization so as not to provoke the potential adversary into war or draw others into war. In the end, however, the military, pleading military necessity, prevailed and full mobilization was instituted, thereby turning military foresight into a self-fulfilling prophecy. In this way the attempt to manage military power more precisely and calculably made it more autonomous and less subject to control.

Thus mobilization plans seriously limited opportunities for diplomatic accommodation and, once they had been put into effect, virtually assured general war. In the end, the ineffective political control of peacetime military preparations proved to be even more dangerous to international order than the tremendous increase of destructive power that accompanied the outburst of industrial and technological energy. On the other hand, the modernization and hence increasing complexity of military power created a far more serious problem of peacetime political control than had existed before.

6. *The Technological Revolution in Military Power*

Competitive arming in a dynamic military technology further enhanced the role of military power as an autonomous political force. The

27. Thus Dobrorolski, in charge of mobilization in Russia, insisted, "The whole plan of mobilization is worked out ahead to its end in all its details. When the moment has been chosen, one only has to press the button, and the whole state begins to function automatically with the precision of a clock's mechanism. . . . Once the moment has been fixed, everything is settled; there is no going back; it determines mechanically the beginning of war." Quoted in Sidney B. Fay, *The Origins of the World War* (2d ed. rev.; New York: Macmillan, 1930), p. 481.

modern arms race originated in an unprecedented surge of military invention in the last quarter of the nineteenth century.

The rifled gun barrel, together with improvements in gunpowder and firing mechanisms, led to tremendous improvements of range and accuracy. The development of breech-loading rifles and artillery, along with improved recoil mechanisms late in the century, greatly increased rapidity of fire. As significant as the accelerated rate of invention was the reduction of time between invention, mass production, and tactical assimilation of weapons, due to the effective co-ordination of economic and technological-scientific resources and to systematic battlefield experimentation and analysis.[28]

As land warfare was transformed by the utilization of railways and the telegraph, maritime warfare was transformed by the invention of the iron-hulled, steam-propelled warship. The rapid development of the battleship and the profusion of offensive and defensive naval technology to counter it were unprecedented in the history of military innovation.[29] This weapon system changed more in the latter half of the nineteenth century than it had in the preceding ten centuries.

The development of the battleship altered the distribution of power, stimulated far-reaching rivalries, and shaped new political alignments. More than ever before a single weapon became the pre-eminent test and symbol of national greatness.[30] It was integrally linked to foreign policy in the gospel of seapower according to Mahan. Mahan's great popularity as a strategist (particularly in England, Germany, and France) was based

28. HERO, *op. cit.*, chap. iv. Despite the increased rate of assimilation, the French, although they developed the machine gun shortly before the Franco-Prussian War, failed to exploit its potentialities because they used it like artillery instead of like rifles against infantry at close range. Improved models by the Americans Gatling and Browning and the Englishman Maxim were developed in the last half of the century, but the full significance of the machine gun was not demonstrated until World War I.

29. For accounts of the development of the battleship and naval competition in the latter part of the nineteenth century and up to World War I, see Bernard Brodie, *Sea Power in the Machine Age* (2d ed.; Princeton: Princeton University Press, 1943); Arthur J. Marder's *The Anatomy of British Sea Power* (New York: Alfred A. Knopf, 1940) and *From Dreadnought to Scapa Flow: The Royal Navy in the Fisher Era, 1904–1919* (2 vols.; London: Oxford University Press, 1961); E. L. Woodward, *Great Britain and the German Navy* (London: Oxford University Press, 1935); Ludwig Dehio, *Germany and World Politics in the Twentieth Century*, trans. Dieter Pevsher (New York: Alfred A. Knopf, 1959).

30. The longbow, which England developed in the thirteenth century and used to great advantage at Crécy (1346), Poitiers (1356), and Agincourt (1415), dominated the battlefield for 100 years and helped mightily to make England a great power. (Only the English mastered it, since only the English trained archers from childhood.) Yet the symbolic power of the British battleship, its peacetime uses, and its linkage with strategy and foreign policy had no counterpart in the longbow.

on his view that seapower was the royal road to national wealth and prestige. It would enable states to enlarge and protect overseas imperial holdings and commerce with an integrated system of colonies, bases, and merchant marine, supported by a fleet of line-of-battle ships designed to control the sea lanes, not merely to raid commerce and protect ports.[31]

The rapid improvement of battleships created the first modern technological arms races. The arms race is a somewhat misleading metaphor for a competitive advancement of the type, quantity, and quality of weapons between adversaries seeking an advantageous ratio of military strength. In the latter part of the nineteenth century it became a major form of power politics and greatly enhanced the role of military power in peacetime.[32]

From the 1850s through the 1880s France precipitated an arms race with Britain by attempting to offset numerical inferiority in warships with superiority in ironclad battleships, guns, and commerce-destroying torpedo boats and light cruisers, in accordance with the strategic concepts of the *Jeune École* navalists.[33] The resulting competition was most conspicuous in the contest between offensive guns and defensive armor. France eventually abandoned the competition without approaching naval equality chiefly because of disorder in French politics, growing fear of the German army, and friendlier political relations with Britain.

Germany launched another naval race with Britain in 1898, primarily to compete with her as a colonial world power. The British naval program, based on the famous two-power standard, had been designed to offset a Franco-Russian combination. Germany's program, coinciding with an alleviation of the Russian threat by virtue of the Anglo-Japanese Alliance and the Russo-Japanese War, shifted the focus of Britain's naval program to Germany. In October, 1905, Britain laid down the original *Dreadnought* and in February, 1906, launched it. The *Dreadnought* had greater speed and several times

31. Margaret T. Sprout, "Mahan: Evangelist of Sea Power," in Earle, *op. cit.*, chap. xvii.

32. The first, best, and still virtually the sole comprehensive analysis of the military and political aspects of arms races is Samuel P. Huntington, "Arms Races: Prerequisites and Results," *Public Policy*, eds. Carl J. Friedrich and Seymour E. Harris (Cambridge: Harvard Graduate School of Public Administration, 1958). See also C. B. Joynt, "Arms Races and the Problem of Equilibrium," in *The Year Book of World Affairs, 1964* (London: Stevens & Sons, 1964).

33. This school of navalists, echoing the old view of naval warfare as an extension of commercial warfare, did not anticipate starving England but only cutting off enough food and raw materials to cause an economic panic by raising insurance rates. The British decided to counter this danger by providing national insurance and devising new tactics to protect merchant vessels. Marder, *The Anatomy of British Sea Power*, chap. vi.

greater long-range firepower than previous battleships. Germany soon followed suit, and in 1912 First Lord of the Admiralty Churchill announced a British naval standard of 60 per cent superiority over Germany in dreadnoughts, while threatening to lay two keels for every one German keel unless Germany would reciprocally slow down or freeze construction without any political conditions. By 1914 the German government had abandoned this competition for fear of encouraging further British naval expansion and pressing German taxpayers too heavily, as well as because of more urgent demands imposed by military preparations on land.

The role of dreadnoughts foreshadowed the revolutionary role of submarines and airpower in that they were intended not merely to defeat the enemy's forces but to exert a far-reaching effect upon its livelihood and status. They would do this, moreover, not merely by harassing commerce directly but primarily by securing or denying control of sea lanes vital to a nation's welfare and greatness. What is more, they were admirably suited to sustaining in peacetime a world policy and position through the conspicuous representation of a nation's might in distant places. This had been the more or less conscious strategy of British seapower since the latter part of the eighteenth century, but Mahan made it explicit and popularized it, and the modern battleship dramatized its efficacy.

The development of steamships with screw propellers relieved sea maneuvers from dependence on the vagaries of the wind and currents and completely outmoded sailing vessels. It greatly enhanced the defensive strength of advanced industrial nations, especially such insular powers as Japan and the U.S. It also greatly enhanced the geographical extension of the power of nations that could develop coaling bases and colonies. Therefore it became the mainstay of the great imperial contests and the virtually global struggles for hegemony that agitated international politics in the two decades or so preceding World War I.

In these ways the dreadnought exemplified the momentous impact of technological innovation upon international politics. It demonstrated the growing impact of armed forces, as well as their growing dependence, upon the nation as a whole.

It also posed the question of whether the new technology could be controlled. This question was posed in one form by the new factor of uncertainty in warfare and military planning, injected by the accelerated rate of technological innovation. The dreadnought complicated the calculation of relative military power and made more difficult the control and prediction of the outcome of war. To integrate the new battleships into war plans and production programs, certain assumptions had to be made about their military function. The assumption that a surprise attack with naval forces-in-being would be decisive provided the strategic impetus for naval competition, just as the assumption that the army that struck first with the most firepower would have a decisive advantage impelled the arms race in land weapons. Yet forces-in-being at the moment of a hypothetical war would depend not only on existing weapons but, equally, on future weapons produced by the building programs in the shipyards—programs that were complex and, in the case of challenging states, shrouded in secrecy.

In 1909 official and private British sources indicated that Germany might build 17 or even 21 dreadnoughts by 1912 instead of the officially announced 13. This estimate turned out to be wrong. It was based on information concerning an increase in German shipbuilding capacity; an increase in Krupp's capacity to produce gun mountings; the secret accumulation of nickel for use in guns, armour, and mountings; and an acceleration of contracts for ships. In effect, the alarmists based estimates of production on their view of Germany's capabilities, whereas more moderate advocates of a naval build-up credited Germany's announced intentions.[34] England, unlike Germany, did not keep production details secret. The details of its naval program were publicly debated in Parliament and in the press. On the other hand, the public debate was often a confusing guide to those concerned with estimating the future of England's naval program.

The secrecy, complexity, and dynamism of building programs meant that naval programs had to be based on uncertain estimates not only of an adversary's relative capacity but also of its *intentions* to increase the quantity and quality of its navy. Yet the adversary's intentions could be affected by many imponderable internal and external considerations, including its estimate of one's own capacity and intentions. Therefore one state might try to alter the other's intentions by threatening and bargaining with a construction program and, perhaps, by linking this game with political proposals.

After some controversy, the British built the more powerful dreadnoughts, although they knew that this would lead to expensive and possibly dangerous competition with Germany in a weapon in which British superiority would not be as great as in pre-dreadnought battleships. The decisive argument for doing so was simply that Britain's refraining from building dreadnoughts would not prevent Germany from building them but only give Germany a head start. After competitive building started, however, the British tried to induce the Germans to

---

34. Marder, *From Dreadnought to Scapa Flow*, Vol. I, chap. vii.

agree to a reciprocal reduction of the tempo of competition or at least to an exchange of construction information in order to mitigate exaggerated suspicions of rates of construction. But the German government was unwilling thus to concede British superiority without some political *quid pro quo*, such as British neutrality in the event of a Franco-German war. The British government, on the other hand, was unwilling to break the Anglo-French entente. Winston Churchill, First Lord of the Admiralty, tried in vain to get German agreement to proportional reductions or to a joint holiday in construction of dreadnoughts while threatening, otherwise, to outbuild Germany by a precise ratio or number of ships. In the end, Germany defeated its political purpose by driving Britain closer to France. At the same time, it had to concede British superiority in the naval competition.

The difficulties of using the new peacetime power of weapons as a finely calculated instrument of policy were demonstrated in the failure of Admiral Tirpitz's too-clever "risk" strategy, which foundered on miscalculations of British policies and capabilities. Tirpitz developed his "risk theory" as a strategy for advancing Germany's political status and security vis-à-vis Britain by improving its relative naval power without obtaining naval equality. According to this strategy England would prefer to make concessions to Germany in the colonial field or possibly even enter a military commitment with Germany rather than risk a clash with a smaller German navy, if, in the event of such a clash, that navy were strong enough to leave England inferior in the face of a Franco-Russian naval combination. The underlying assumptions of this strategy, if they ever had any merit, were invalidated by the Anglo-Russian entente, the Anglo-French rapprochement, the Admiralty's decision to concentrate the British fleet in the North Sea, and England's decision to build dreadnoughts. But the German government continued to pursue Tirpitz's strategy and brought about the very political result— consolidation of the Triple Entente—that it was intended to prevent, while inciting Britain to enter a competition Germany could not win.

As the Anglo-German naval competition illustrates, the nature of the new technology gave arms races a kind of self-generating impetus based on the interaction of opposing military capabilities and intentions, real and estimated. This interaction produced a mode of peacetime power politics that resembled the maneuvering and bargaining of eighteenth-century wars, except that the stakes of the game were larger, the rules less reliable, and the whole game more volatile and subjective.

Moreover, because the game was expensive, because it impinged upon national pride and affected international tensions and the prospect of war, and because even nondemocratic governments felt the need to elicit popular consent for arms policies, arms races were also deeply involved in the vagaries of public opinion and internal politics—an involvement which the armed services and the armaments manufacturers stimulated and exploited. Thus during both the Anglo-French and Anglo-German naval races there were a number of naval scares in England, causing widespread, although unwarranted, fears of sudden naval attack and invasion. News of French and German naval increases created considerable public apprehension and touched off controversies with political overtones in the government and press. There were lively public disputes over future German naval strength and the proper number of ships to be built in the British program.[35]

In England, as elsewhere, it was widely assumed that the outcome of crises like the two in Morocco depended upon naval superiority. Therefore all governments that could afford a navy, as well as some that could not, pointed to the navy as a symbol of national might and pride. The involvement of the public in military policies through arms races, demonstrations of military prowess, and crises added a further dimension of subjectivity and incalculability to the use of military power short of war.

The difficulties of planning in peacetime for the effective use of military power in war were no less severe. For in addition to all the other complicating factors in arms races, the new high rate of technological innovation and obsolescence deprived the military managers of one of the crucial, though increasingly inadequate, criteria for determining military requirements: wartime experience. Thus the London *Times* of November 19, 1895, noted: "A modern navy is a totally untried weapon of warfare. It is the resultant of a host of more or less conflicting theories of attack and defense. The seaman, the gunner, the torpedoist, the engineer, and the naval constructor each has his share in the creation of the modern man-of-war, each presses the paramount claim of his own department, and the result is a marvel of theory, compromise, and complication."[36]

To some extent, formulation of strategic doctrine, conduct of war games, and mathematical calculations of projected operations compensated for lack of experience,[37] but they also tended to foster a dan-

35. Richard Cobden, a critical observer of this phenomenon, wrote a classic liberal account of the role of naval officers, organized naval boosters, and the shipbuilding industry in the Anglo-French naval scares in "The Three Panics," *Political Writings* (London: T. Fischer Unwin, 1903), Vol. II. On the internal pressures for arms races, see Vagts, *A History of Militarism*, pp. 360–64.

36. Quoted in Marder, *The Anatomy of British Sea Power*, p. 9.

37. War games, however, often led to false conclusions. Thus the British Royal Navy's maneuvers of 1892 supported the belief that torpedo boats had little chance

gerous illusion of precision and predictability. The meticulous planning and rehearsal of complex military operations and the single-minded pursuit of maximum wartime efficiency tended not only to overlook the contingent and unpredictable elements of war; equally important, the inflexibility of military plans had unexpected and often quite adverse political consequences. Germany's Schlieffen Plan, before World War I, is the most notable case in point.[38]

Under Chief of Staff Von Schlieffen's command, this plan followed his predecessor Waldersee's crucial assumption that a full-scale two-front war with France and Russia was inevitable. The elder Moltke had planned a quick war and a settlement with Russia in the East while offering France neutrality or fighting her with a holding action if necessary. But Waldersee, coming into office after the formation of the Franco-Russian Alliance, planned a full-scale war against Russia, preceded by a quick knockout blow against France. This foreclosed the possibility of keeping a Balkan war localized, since even if a war with the Russians were to originate in the Balkans, Germany would have to strike first against France. Moreover, the Schlieffen Plan envisaged an attack through Belgium even if, as proved to be the case, France were to refrain from invading Belgium first and England were to regard the invasion of Belgium as requiring her intervention.

Strategic prognostications in other countries showed the same lack of foresight. On the eve of World War I the general staffs of the major European antagonists were universally convinced that their forces, with the help of allied forces, would be victorious and that victory would come from a quick, decisive contest like the Prussian victory over France in 1871.[39] They believed in Marshal Foch's mystical doctrine of *l'offen-*

---

of success against fleets at sea. *Ibid.*, p. 166. But the first real example of this new technology in battle, provided by Japan against Russia in the war of 1904–5, contributed much to Japan's astonishing victory when torpedo boats attacked the Russian squadron in Port Arthur and sank a Russian flagship and three other ships in the decisive Battle of Tsushima.

38. Gerhard Ritter, *The Schlieffen Plan: Critique of a Myth*, trans. Andrew and Eva Wilson (New York: Frederick A. Praeger, 1958).

39. The Elder Moltke and Joffre were exceptions in foreseeing a war of attrition, but neither undertook preparations for such a war. Only Lord Kitchener, who became war minister after war was declared, urged preparations for a long war of attrition. England's War Council, however, regarded his views as extravagant whimsy. Sir Philip Magnus, *Kitchener* (New York: E. P. Dutton & Co., 1959). The most detailed and well-reasoned prophecy of a war of attrition was made by Ivan S. Bloch in his six-volume work, *The Future of War in Its Technical, Economic, and Political Relations* (1897–99), which predicted that the increased firepower of guns would force entrenchment and stalemate. However, Bloch shared the consensus that modern war would be economically and socially catastrophic, or "impossible," as he put it. Ivan S. Bloch, *The Future of War*, trans. R. C. Long (Boston: Ginn & Co., 1902); Fuller, *op. cit.*, chap. vii.

sive brutale et à outrance.[40] Foch's stress on offensive action went along with his advocacy of "absolute" or total war, in opposition to the eighteenth-century limited wars of maneuver and position. It was associated with his belief in the decisiveness of the moral factor in war: the will to victory. It was in accord with the widespread belief that a modern war of attrition would be such a severe strain on industrial economies that nations would have to end a war quickly rather than face bankruptcy and revolution.[41]

The military staffs were, therefore, completely unprepared for the war of stalemate and attrition that ensued when the devastating firepower unleashed by the new weapons, unaccompanied by comparable innovations in tactical mobility, drove troops into the trenches and exacted unimagined casualties for negligible advances.[42]

7. World War I

In World War I the principal object of war was conceived to be the annihilation of the enemy's forces. Yet the British blockade and the German submarine campaign put whole nations under siege as never before. In the end Britain was bankrupted, France and Britain had lost a terrible portion of their youth, Italy was on the brink of political chaos, Russia and Germany were racked with revolution, the Austro-Hungarian Empire had vanished, and the Ottoman Empire was dismembered. Only the American Civil War, the first conflict to reveal fully the momentous destructive power generated by modern technology and the popularization of war, could have prepared the world of 1914 for the protracted, profligate expenditure of lives, homes, and money; but the lessons of that war were largely ignored in Europe.

Thus, contrary to the illusion of precision and calculability conveyed by advanced professional management—but contrary also to the conviction that sheer morale and the will to victory would be decisive—total war proved to be far more intractable to intelligent direction than the managers expected. This was partly the result of unwarranted faith in the simple military axioms that led armies into massive assaults in the expectation of quick, decisive victories and partly the result of the enormous dimensions of force and the immense complexity of military

40. Ferdinand Foch, *Principles of War*, trans. Hillaire Belloc (New York: Henry Holt, 1920); see Etienne Mantoux's analysis of Foch's ideas in Earle, *op. cit.*, chap. ix.

41. Vagts, *Defense and Diplomacy*, chap. ix.

42. Ropp, *op. cit.*, chap. viii. According to the official French history of the war, *Les Armées Françaises dans la grande guerre* (1922–25), French casualties in the month of August alone amounted to about 300,000 out of a field army of 1,600,000.

establishments, which multiplied the frequency and repercussions of unanticipated developments.

World War I precipitated a torrent of technological innovations, fostered for the first time by a comprehensive mobilization of scientific talent. These innovations included not only the improvement of previous weapons but also the introduction of new weapons: the airplane, the tank, poison gas, and the submarine.[43] Each of these weapons and the interaction of all of them with other weapons, with tactical innovations, and with new factors of logistics and materiel affected the conflict in unexpected ways. The submarine, which had been only an ineffective novelty in previous wars, came close to being a truly decisive weapon.

Of course, all these innovations provided only a faint foretaste of the proliferation of decisive technology in World War II,[44] in which the participants were as unprepared for mechanized, mobile, blitzkrieg warfare as they had been unprepared for trench warfare in 1914. In the interwar period mechanized mobile warfare had been espoused by a few prophets in England and France—notably, Fuller, Liddell Hart, and De Gaulle—but only the Nazis put it into practice.

The fact that the marvelous ingenuity of technology and military management resulted in such unexpected destruction of life and property produced a deep agony and revulsion in the world, in many ways deeper than that created by World War II. The unprecedented loss of life and the massive devastation of material civilization, compressed into a few years, intensified the psychological shock caused by the sharp contrast with prewar expectations of a quick, decisive, exhilarating contest. The wholesale inhumanity and suffering inflicted by modern nations geared to war seemed like a cruel refutation of the general optimism in the preceding decades that industrial-technological and sociopolitical progress marched together.

It is true that if one measures the destructiveness of war by economic and demographic statistics covering the immediate postwar period of recuperation as well as the war itself, World War I seems much less pernicious as a whole than its reputation—indeed, almost beneficent in some countries. For the same factors of modern civilization that made massive violence possible also facilitated a rapid restoration of population

43. On the role of science and technology in World War I, see Brodie, *op. cit.*, chap. vii.

44. In World War II the mobilization of scientific and engineering talent for military purposes was especially comprehensive and effective in England. The British program grew into a gigantic co-ordinated international effort including Canada and the U.S. A great part of this effort went into the perfection of weapons developed in previous wars; but new inventions—most notably radar, the proximity fuse, and the atomic bomb—played an even more significant role than in World War I.

and national incomes.[45] But this measurement, of course, is irrelevant to the lasting psychological and political effect of an immense, violent upheaval in modern civilization inflicted by man's own monstrous military machines running amuck.

8. A New Dimension of Force

Man's enthusiasm for war and the whole war system was deeply shaken by World War I, yet his underlying confidence in technological solutions to warfare was not undermined. On the contrary, the war aroused hope that some single new weapon might prove overwhelming, that some technological breakthrough might simplify the problem of exerting calculable, decisive force. This hope centered above all on the strategic bomber, which promised to attain victory by striking directly at the enemy's homeland, avoiding massive, inconclusive encounters on the ground and obviating the travails of attrition.[46]

Actually, although the development of strategic airpower greatly enhanced the peacetime effects of force, it showed as dramatically as World War I the difficulty of controlling the wartime effects of the volatile new technology. Indeed, the very characteristic of strategic airpower that enhanced its political impact short of war complicated its control in war: its capacity to inflict sudden punishment directly upon civilians at a range far beyond the battlefield. This characteristic, although analogous to the indirect punitive effect of the naval blockade, distinguishes airpower from all other kinds of military power.

In the midst of the stalemate during World War I, the development of the military airplane inspired a small but influential group of advocates to propound a doctrine of strategic bombing long before the bomber was technically capable of playing its purported role. The doctrine promised victory by inflicting decisive damage on the basic civilian

45. Raymond Aron makes this point in *The Century of Total War* (Garden City, N.Y.: Doubleday, 1954), pp. 74–83. The generalization is equally true of World War II, as the rapid recovery and dramatic prosperity of Western Europe demonstrate.

46. On the origins of the doctrine and organization of strategic bombing in Britain, Italy, and the U.S., see Harry H. Ransom, "The Politics of Air Power—A Comparative Analysis," *Public Policy*, eds. Carl J. Friedrich and Seymour E. Harris. A full account of the development of strategic bombing in Britain is given by Charles K. Webster and Noble Frankland, *The Strategic Air Offensive Against Germany, 1939–1945* (London: Her Majesty's Stationery Office, 1961), I, Part I. Bernard Brodie deals with the evolution of air strategy before World War II in *Strategy in the Missile Age* (Princeton: Princeton University Press, 1959), Part I. George H. Quester, *Deterrence Before Hiroshima* (New York: John Wiley & Sons, 1966), examines the development of the strategy and practice of strategic bombing from the beginning of the twentieth century, with special attention to precursors of strategic ideas and problems of the nuclear age.

sources of enemy power without having to defeat the enemy's armed forces or occupy his territory.

In April, 1918, British political leaders, over the opposition of the highest ranking military officers, succeeded in establishing a separate Royal Air Force in their search for an alternative to sending the flower of British manhood to "chew barbed wire in Flanders," as Churchill put it. The public shock over the German attacks on London with Zeppelins, and later Gotha bombers, provided the immediate impetus.[47] The prevailing strategic doctrine at the time contemplated the use of bombers against military targets directly related to the war on the ground, but the general impression that punitive air raids on cities could exert great psychological effects injected a significant ambiguity in the nascent doctrine of airpower. The heavy casualties inflicted by the day-light raids on undefended London raised great popular and professional expectations about the efficacy of strategic bombing. On the basis of these casualties it was calculated that in a future war London might be made almost uninhabitable in the first weeks of bombing. Furthermore, the one-sided emphasis on offensive uses of airpower in World War I fostered the conviction that there was no effective defense against such devastation except bombing the enemy's bases and factories and inflicting reprisal damage upon his cities. These assumptions and the strategic doctrine that was based upon them had a powerful effect upon international politics after World War I.

In the years after the war the writings of the Italian prophet of air-power, Giulio Douhet, broadcast the doctrine of victory-through-strategic-bombing throughout Europe and beyond.[48] In essence this doctrine held that victory depended first on obtaining "command of the air," which in turn depended on destroying air bases and air factories, and then on shattering the enemy's will to fight by inflicting maximum damage on his cities, transportation centers, and industries. The doctrine assumed that war among major powers must aim at annihilating the enemy before he annihilates you, that there would be no defense against the bomber, and that victory would come quickly (and, incidentally, therefore humanely) to the force that could strike first by surprise and inflict the greatest damage in the shortest time. The logical defense against this danger would be either to strike first in a pre-emptive or preventive attack or else to depend on the threat of reprisal to deter the enemy from striking first.

47. Webster and Frankland, *op. cit.*, I, 36ff.
48. The essence of Douhet's strategy is contained in his first book, *The Command of the Air* (New York: Coward-McCann, Inc., 1942), published in Italian in 1921.

As in the case of a prospective naval or ground attack, the supposition that a sudden first strike from the air could be decisive added an element of tension to international conflict and a new danger of preemptive or preventive attack. It also gave states a mighty instrument of intimidation and deterrence. With the integration of airpower into military establishments, the whole nation became the direct object as well as the source of military power—in peacetime as well as in war. In short, strategic bombing put the nation-in-arms in the front line. This further complicated the problem of calculating and controlling military power.

Success in exploiting military power for its psychological and political effects short of war depended heavily on the credibility of a government's and, indirectly, a whole nation's will to use its power of devastation, especially when the enemy was assumed to have the power of counter-devastation. But what determined credibility? It depended partly on the relative material capabilities of opposing air forces; but, because of the subjective nature of governmental and national will, the relation of capabilities to credibility was less direct and more complicated than in the case of weapons that exerted their effect only against armed forces.

Moreover, the estimate of air capabilities was also uncertain. Not only was the efficacy of untried weapons in doubt, but, as in the case of naval competition, plans and preparations for weapons that would be produced only years hence were a crucial factor in capabilities; yet these plans and preparations were obscured by secrecy and the diffuseness of the production process. Thus after the British decided in 1934 to seek air "parity" as a "deterrent" to German aggression, they discovered not only that parity was difficult to define in quantitative and qualitative terms but that attaining it required a rearmament effort based on quite uncertain and fallible estimates of Germany's rate of production, which in the early stages of German rearmament depended heavily on such obscure auxiliary preparations as the manufacturing of machine tools. In May, 1935, Prime Minister Baldwin publicly confessed that his government had completely underestimated the rate of German rearmament. Britain's task then became to expand her aircraft industry and rate of production so as to obtain parity with the air force that Germany was expected to have by 1940.[49]

Britain's whole air rearmament program was based on the assumption

---

49. Webster and Frankland, *op. cit.*, I, 66ff., and John F. Kennedy, *Why England Slept* (New York: Wilfred Funk, 1940), pp. 94–99. Actually, British intelligence estimates of German air production were exaggerated, especially with respect to long-range bombers; but Hitler and Goering encouraged exaggeration in order to intimidate the British.

that Germany could deliver a knockout blow against England. Baldwin's pronouncement that "the bombers will always get through" was taken as axiomatic. The fact that the Germans had no intention, plan, or capability for such an attack did not change the significance of the British assumption. Indeed, Germany capitalized on this psychological reality by encouraging British apprehensions of a knockout blow and by exploiting them to paralyze British diplomatic and military resistance to piecemeal aggression. Consequently, Britain's strategic doctrine stressed the deterrent effect of a capability for offensive reprisals against Germany, and her rearmament program stressed heavy bombers. Nevertheless, when the government belatedly discovered the magnitude of Germany's air superiority after 1938, it shifted from a strategy of massive civilian bombing to one of confining bombing to military objectives in the hope that Germany would spare British cities. Then, shortly before the war, the Air Staff, having previously failed to base air strategy on operational possibilities, discovered the limited penetration ability of bombers; so it shifted the strategic priority to defending France on the ground, although there were no concerted plans to fulfill this priority.

War itself was the great school of strategy and tactics, but wartime trial and error provided unexpected lessons. Strategic bombing turned out to be even more volatile and less subject to foresight and control than the contest between massive armies had been in World War I. At first both sides confined bombing to tactical and industrial targets. The air war demonstrated that both sides had unprecedented incentives for contrived reciprocal restraints. And for a while such restraints were practiced.[50] But, contrary to claims of great precision, the inaccuracy of bombing and the collateral civilian damage, combined with the unexpected vulnerability of bombers engaged in precision bombing, eventually broke down reciprocal restraints and led to raids designed chiefly to inflict terror and reprisals upon civilians and things of civilian value, culminating in the senseless bombing of cities like Dresden.[51]

The actual effect of such bombing upon civilian morale and the na-

50. In view of common assumptions about Hitler's "irrationality," it is interesting to note that he felt special incentives to avoid city bombing, such as the fear of the adverse effect of British retaliatory bombings on his domestic support; and that he was generally more anxious to preserve reciprocal restraints than the British. Quester, *op. cit.*, pp. 151ff.

51. Webster and Frankland, *op. cit.* *The United States Strategic Bombing Survey*. Wesley F. Craven and James L. Cate, *The U.S. Army Air Forces in World War II* (7 vols.; Chicago: University of Chicago Press, 1948–1955). Kent R. Greenfield, *American Strategy in World War II: A Reconsideration* (Baltimore: The Johns Hopkins Press, 1963), chap. iv. David Irving, *The Destruction of Dresden* (London: William Kimber, 1963).

tional will to fight proved to be almost negligible in Germany, as in England, although similar attacks on Japanese cities were apparently more effective in helping to induce surrender. But in both cases civilian bombing signified that an ultimate stage had been reached in the expansion of military power—a stage in which the whole nation had become a direct target of psychological pressure and physical punishment. Before the nuclear age airpower revealed both the possible utility of modern force short of war and its potential uselessness in war.

9. *The Politics of Limited War*

We have seen that the expansion of military power before the nuclear age gave the armed forces of major states a potential mass, scope, and intensity, as well as a dynamism and volatility, that greatly complicated the control of force as an instrument of policy in both war and peace. These characteristics of force together with the growing impact of military power as an independent influence upon international politics, raised the need for more deliberate methods of control and restraint. By examining more specifically the effects of expanding military power upon international politics—that is, upon the interplay of national interests, aims, alignments, and commitments—we can appreciate the new dimensions of the problem of political control.

The contrast between the relationship of force and politics in the eighteenth century and after the expansion of military power in the nineteenth is revealing. The eighteenth century was notable for the fusion of war and diplomacy and the subordination of the former to the latter. The harmony of force and politics reflected three related factors: the limited objectives of conflict among states, the flexibility of military alliances, and the limited force available to states.

Limited objectives. The principal stakes of international politics were territory and commerce. As determining, operational objectives of power politics, these stakes were generally limited and tangible. They seldom threatened the survival of the major states or even seriously challenged their administrative integrity or prestige.[52] Although the

52. To what extent this restraint was due to inadequate power is another question. Ultimate, as opposed to determining, intentions were not always so limited. Thus in 1745 and 1755 Austria tried to form alliances that would lead to the partition of Prussia, although its plans failed diplomatically and militarily. Dorn, *op. cit.*, pp. 157, 297–98. The partitions of helpless Poland showed what extensive ends statesmen might pursue when they had undisputed military superiority.

survival and integrity of weaker states might suffer in the contest among the larger ones, they were in no position to protest. They were passive instruments of the main diplomatic game. In any case, the general indifference of their populace to a change of rule made the disposal of their territory much less disturbing to international relations and, incidentally, much more profitable for conquerors than it would become when intense national feelings developed all over Europe during the nineteenth century.

In pursuit of these limited stakes, the noncoercive instruments of diplomatic bargaining and accommodation (dynastic marriages, treaties of succession, subsidies, exchanges of territory and of commercial benefits) mingled harmoniously with the coercive instruments (military alliances, threats of force, and war itself). It was taken for granted that rulers might with little moral compunction resort to war in order to gain additional leverage and that in war the political relations of states would not be much different from their relations at any other time. Indeed, diplomacy was often more active during wars, especially in the winter months when fighting customarily ceased.[53] Thus Clausewitz scarcely exaggerated when he described war in the eighteenth century as "only diplomacy somewhat intensified, a more forceful way of negotiating, in which battles and sieges were the diplomatic notes."[54]

Flexible alliances. Following the end of Louis XIV's bid for European hegemony, international politics settled into a complex configuration of interests and power in which disciplined armed forces backed endless diplomatic maneuvers for marginal advantages within a constraining equilibrium of power. Military power was fairly evenly distributed among five major states (England, France, Austria, Prussia, and Russia) competing in an arena of politics in which several secondary states (Spain, Sweden, Turkey, the United Netherlands, and, until partitioned, Poland) played peripheral roles and scores of small states and principalities were primarily pawns or onlookers. The interests of the major states converged and diverged in patterns of international conflict that kept opposing combinations of power in a rough equilibrium, which discouraged extreme ambitions and exploits.

In the constant pursuit of aggrandizement and of security against the aggrandizement of others, military alliances were the principal dynamic

53. See, for example, the detailed account of diplomacy during the War of the Austrian Succession in Sir Richard Lodge, *Studies in Eighteenth Century Diplomacy, 1740–1748* (London: John Murray, 1930), and the exhaustive description of the intermingling of war and diplomacy in Richard Waddington, *La guerre de sept ans* (5 vols.; Paris: Firmin-Didot & Cie, 1899–19-).
54. Karl von Clausewitz, *On War*, trans. O. J. Matthijs Jolles (New York: Random House, 1943), p. 580.

means of supporting state interests with power. For the strength of armed forces was relatively inflexible. The strength of opposing states and combinations of states was so nearly equal that no state could safely move without some assurance about the conditions under which other states might fight or abstain. To gain this assurance states sought commitments that would pledge other states to use or not use their armed forces in specific circumstances for specific objectives, usually in return for some exchange of benefits. Since *raison d'état*, commonly measured by the most expedient way of maximizing state power, was the determining consideration in making such commitments, military alliances were quite responsive to changing configurations of power and interest. They were therefore the dynamic instrument of power, the function of which was to arrange the relatively static pieces, the armed forces, into favorable relationships on the international chess board.

The typical military alliance in the eighteenth century was formed for specific, limited objectives. Many were made during a war or in anticipation of a war, after which they were terminated or became inoperative. They usually involved one or several of the following kinds of commitments: a subsidy to support another state's troops; a guarantee to fight in behalf of another state (often with a specific number of troops) if it should become engaged in war in stated circumstances; a pledge of nonintervention or mutual abstention from war in the event that one or both of the signatories should become engaged in war with other states; a division of the territorial and other spoils of war.

The fulfillment of these commitments in war often imposed heavy demands on the limited armies and resources of states, but it did not require keeping up burdensome long-term military coalitions in peacetime. For states did not need to make extensive military preparations or sustain the peacetime co-ordination of allied forces and strategies. Military operations and even alliances could be safely improvised during war.[55] As William L. Langer notes, "The easy-going nature of warfare made advance arrangements quite unnecessary, and the slowness of communication made it inadvisable to enter commitments of binding character.[56] And furthermore, long before alliances could consolidate into politically homogeneous coalitions and aggregate their armed forces,

55. Thus in 1740 Frederick II invaded Silesia, his major territorial ambition and the greatest permanent territorial conquest in the history of modern Europe to that time, with no well-conceived political plan and against the advice of his foreign ministers and generals, hoping that he could improvise an alliance with France or England. Dorn, *op. cit.*, p. 138.

56. *European Alliances and Alignments, 1871–1890* (2d ed.; New York: Alfred A. Knopf, 1950), p. 6.

some state would probably decide to go to war, if only to anticipate an attack upon itself. For the inhibitions against war were minimal, and neither public apprehensions nor the risks of devastation were sufficient to put the premium upon military deterrence and other uses of force short of war that became manifest in the latter half of the nineteenth century.

There were a few peacetime defensive military alliances designed to guarantee and stabilize a particular political and territorial status quo by military deterrence,[57] but there were scores of offensive alliances intended to acquire territory and other tangible assets by war. Indeed, most of the ostensibly defensive alliances were intended to assure peace in one area in order to facilitate war in another.[58]

Of course, alliances often exerted a deterrent effect by dissuading states from pursuing acquisitive goals in the face of a disadvantageous balance. But, just as often, the formation of an alliance was a deliberate prelude to war or, by threatening to upset the delicate balance of power to the disadvantage of some state, an unintentional provocation to war. Even more often, a dynastic marriage or death would so disturb the equilibrium that only war could restore it; hence, the wars of the Spanish, Polish, and Austrian successions.

Both offensive and defensive alliances aimed as often at restraining

---

57. The Third Barrier Treaty (1715), between England, Austria, and the Netherlands, was intended primarily to guarantee the Austro-Netherlands frontier provinces against French attack. The Triple Alliance (1717), between England, France and the Netherlands, confirmed and guaranteed the settlement at Utrecht. The Quadruple Alliance (1718), formed by England, France, Austria, and the Netherlands to check Spain, was in part a treaty of mutual defense and guarantee. When it was threatened in 1725 by Spain's alliance with Austria, the Alliance of Hanover between England, France, and Prussia (with the later accession of Sweden, Denmark, and the Netherlands) was instrumental in deterring a general war and helped localize the Spanish-British conflict over Gibraltar in 1727, although Prussia withdrew in 1726. The Triple Alliance (1788), between England, Prussia, and the Netherlands, guaranteed the settlement of Dutch affairs that England and Prussia had forcefully compelled France to accept in 1787 and pledged England and Prussia to defend each other.

58. Thus, with some reason, Frederick II believed that the secret clauses of the Russo-Austrian defensive treaty of 1746, which his espionage system discovered, were aimed at making war on Prussia at the first suitable moment. Vergennes' policy of making defensive treaties to pacify the Continent was intended to free France to defeat Britain overseas, although the other signatories did not have the same defensive purposes in mind. The Treaty of Versailles (1756) with Austria was defensive from France's standpoint, but the Austrians considered it a blank check for French support in an offensive war against Prussia. The Austro-Russian defensive alliance against the Turks (1781) was viewed by the Russians as an instrument facilitating the partition of the Ottoman Empire's European territories. The Austrians viewed it as support for their designs against Prussia and the United Provinces.

an ally, by limiting his political options and deflecting him from an opposing alliance, as at aggregating military power. The ideal of eighteenth-century alliance policy was to get as much support, or at least assurance of nonhostility, from an ally as possible in return for the most limited and least binding commitment to him. It was common practice to make secret military-political agreements, often as unpublished clauses in open alliances, not only in order to conceal aggressive designs but also in order to increase diplomatic options by making deals with one state without giving offense to another ally, which might otherwise have reason to charge duplicity. For example, during the Franco-Prussian campaigns against Austria in the War of the Austrian Succession, Frederick made the secret convention of Kleinshchnellendorf with Austria (1742), permitting the Austrians to march against the French in return for the cession of Silesia. Soon compelled to repudiate this treaty, he continued the war against Austria, only to make a separate peace in return for Silesia several months later.

It is understandable, therefore, that the secrecy of military commitments should have excited suspicions and fostered miscalculations of political and military intent among states. Although few secret clauses or alliances remained completely unknown, they often remained unknown long enough, or their substance remained sufficiently in doubt, to permit diplomatic surprises. And the fact that they were common practice incited suspicions even when suspicions were unwarranted. Thus, although Prussia's alliance with England in the convention of Westminster in 1756 was not hostile to France, Frederick's neglect to inform France about it in advance, together with his reputation for secretiveness and duplicity, enabled Kaunitz of Austria to broadcast rumors that the convention contained secret clauses concealing offensive intentions. France's indignation provoked her to make an alliance with Austria, which led directly to the Seven Years' War. This war was, therefore, precipitated by a diplomatic development that neither Prussia nor France had expected and that might very well have been avoided had diplomacy been more open, considering the basic interest of France in pacifying the Continent.

Thus the *ad hoc*, offensive, and secret nature of alliances accentuated the delicacy of the international equilibrium. In some respects this delicacy has been exaggerated, as in the common portrayal of the eighteenth-century equilibrium as a diplomatic minuet in which states continually changed partners. The period is, indeed, notable for the large number of military alliances that were formed and unformed, but the dominant hostilities and amities revolving around England, France,

Austria, and Prussia were as lasting as in any similar span of modern history. Hence, the shock of the Diplomatic Revolution in 1756.[59]

The significant point about eighteenth-century alliances is not their quantity or rate of change but the fact that they were of a limited nature and were readily adapted to shifting interests with little regard for the later constraints of sentiment and ideology or the imperatives of building a military coalition in peacetime. Consequently, they were readily susceptible to control as limited instruments of policy, leaving states free to form countervailing combinations of power that prevented any single state or group of states from gaining territory and other assets at the expense of the basic security and independence of any major state. The flexibility of military commitments also made them susceptible to miscalculations leading to war; but when war was more often the immediate purpose of alignment than was the deterrence of war, flexibility seemed more valuable than continuity of commitments.

Limited war. It must be emphasized, however, that the constructive function of flexible alliances as instruments of international order depended on the utility of war as a limited and controllable instrument of policy. For the chief object of alliances was not to defend states by dissuading adversaries from taking hostile military actions but rather to achieve a favorable distribution of power, and war was the principal method of implementing that objective.

The pragmatic rulers of eighteenth-century states naturally preferred to gain their objectives without war if possible, but this did not stop them from pursuing objectives that they knew could be attained only through war. By the same token, they did not go out of their way to

59. The aftermath of the Utrecht settlement (1713), until about 1731, was a period of warfare and fluidity of alignments. During this period England and France combined against Spain; Austria abandoned her alliance with England and France to join Spain; and these two combinations broke down. By 1731–33 basic alignments had crystallized. Before 1756 the basic alignments to which military alliances conformed were France with Prussia and England with Austria, reflecting two basic sets of hostilities: France vs. England, and Prussia vs. Austria. Russia was allied with Austria. The Diplomatic Revolution was the product of a chain reaction of realignments, in which Austria's opposition to Prussia's ascendance merged with Anglo-French hostility. It began with the Anglo-Russian subsidy treaty, which led to the convention of Westminster between England and Prussia. This convention in turn led to the Austro-French alliance together with the Austro-Russian treaty and Russia's accession to the Austro-French alliance. After the Seven Years' War Russia realigned herself with Prussia. Until the wars of the French Revolution these alignments continued to be reflected in military alliances, with the exception of the reversal of alliances in 1781, when Russia once more allied with Austria. Throughout the period from the aftermath of Utrecht to the French Revolution, the Dutch were aligned with France. The alliances of these three second-rank states generally conformed to the alliances of England and France, respectively.

exert force by methods short of war. Nor did they make studied efforts to establish the credibility of their will to resort to war. The possibility of war was always implicit in the incessant diplomatic intriguing and bargaining. No one doubted that a state unable to attain its objectives diplomatically would resort to war if it could arrange a favorable alliance and mobilize the proper resources. States repeatedly launched wars for modest objectives with slight assurance of victory and a large risk of failure.

Because war was taken for granted, there was no need for brinkmanship. The line between war and peace was often ambiguous, as in the virtually bloodless confrontation and bargaining between Prussia and Saxony in the War of the Bavarian Succession (or the Potato War) of 1778–79. And there were some instances of states exerting diplomatic pressure through military demonstrations and maneuvers short of war.[60] But only military weakness, not fear of retaliatory destruction, kept the participants in such crises from waging regular war. Diplomatic crises that stopped at the brink of war generally turned upon a resolution of substantive issues, not upon displays of military strength and determination. Armies were occasionally mobilized in order to convey a threat of war for a political purpose, but this was a relatively inconsequential gambit compared to the diversified and massive preparations for war that became possible at the end of the nineteenth century. Similarly, the ultimatum, demanding a political concession under threat of war, lacked utility in an age in which the distinction between war and peace was less dramatic and the fear of war less compelling. It was generally no more than a formality, not an instrument of policy.

The reason is clear. Before the creation of popular governments, states could not so readily play upon broad national, as opposed to merely official, fears and ambitions concerning war and peace. But equally important, states lacked the war potential, the military mobility and range, and the communications systems to undertake the calculated tests of will and nerves and the pointed measures of deterrence and intimidation under the shadow of war which characterized the crises of the nineteenth and twentieth centuries. Consequently, one is struck by the political utility of war and the underdevelopment of the uses of force

60. Perhaps the most complicated and serious crisis of this sort was Austria's conflict with the Dutch in 1784. Austria backed certain demands by running two naval ships on the diplomatically closed Scheldt. The Dutch defied Austria and stopped the ships. The subsequent agitation kept Europe on the brink of war for over a year, until France, with Prussian and Russian diplomatic support, mediated a settlement, reaffirmed the closure of the Scheldt, but secured certain advantages to Austria. Eugene Hubert, "Joseph II," *The Cambridge Modern History* (Cambridge: Cambridge University Press, 1934), VI, 643–46.

short of war in the eighteenth century, as compared to later periods in which the popularization and modernization of military power exerted their impact upon international politics.

The inability of states to launch sudden, massive assaults with decisive results, the slow pace and the restricted scope and intensity of war, permitted—one might almost say, necessitated—heavy reliance on diplomacy during war. Since major states could not be suddenly occupied or destroyed, and since they had continual recourse to diplomatic bargaining and realignments even during the most intensive wars, they could afford to keep political considerations foremost in the pursuit of victory. The limited, tangible objectives of war were partly enforced by the physical incapacity of states to pursue more ambitious ends; but, considering the limited value of these objectives, there was little incentive to exert violence to the full bounds of which states were capable.

Clausewitz made the classic statement about the political significance of this interaction between the ends and means of war:

> The greater and more powerful the motives for war, the more they affect the whole existence of the nations involved, and the more violent the tension which precedes war, so much the more closely will war conform to its abstract conception. The more it will be concerned with the destruction of the enemy, the more closely the military aim and the political object coincide, and the more purely military, and the less political, war seems to be. But the weaker the motives and the tensions, the less will the natural tendency of the military element, the tendency to violence, coincide with the directives of policy; the more, therefore, must war be diverted from its natural tendency, the greater is the difference between the political object and the aim of an ideal war and the more does war seem to become political.[61]

Yet Clausewitz's emphasis on the controlling effect of the ends of war over its dimensions overlooks the effect of the destructive capacity of armed forces. Although he was acutely aware of the effect of popular nationalist and ideological motives upon war—a phenomenon he had observed in the Napoleonic Wars—he did not anticipate the comparable effect that the professionalization and modernization of military power would exert in the latter part of the nineteenth century.

The wars of the French Revolution and of Napoleon revealed the mutually stimulating effect of extreme ends and extreme violence when war was liberated from the political and social constraints of the Old Regime. The mobilization of patriotic enthusiasm in the name of a universal political mission during the French Revolution gave warfare a zeal and dynamism that could not be evoked by *raison d'état*. The

61. *On War*, p. 17.

momentous scale of violence in turn incited an extension of the war's objectives, since a popular war demanded spiritual rewards commensurate to popular sacrifice.

Thus at the outset the French National Assembly proclaimed a war of pure self-defense against Austria and renounced any war of "conquest" or of "nation against nation." But after the national armies tasted their first big victories, the National Convention reformulated French war aims, swearing that France would not "lay down its arms until the sovereignty and independence of the people whose authority the troops of the Republic shall have entered shall be established, and until the people shall have adopted the principles of equality and founded a free and democratic government." Eventually the expansive missionary nationalism unleashed by the French Revolution and directed by Napoleon toward European hegemony aroused nationalistic resistance in France's opponents. War approached what Clausewitz called its "absolute form": violence pushed to the utmost. Diplomacy was replaced by a contest of national survival. Politics could regain control of power only after violence had run its unpredictable course—in this case, only after the complete defeat of France's armed forces.

10. *From Fragmentation to Aggregation* *of Military Power*

Thus at the beginning of the nineteenth century the world was given an awesome glimpse of the magnitude of modern war. Yet not until World War I were the full potentialities of the popularization of war made manifest. On the other hand, the role of peacetime force increased greatly during the nineteenth century. The political control of force in peacetime became as crucial as the control of force in war. The growing significance of force short of war reflected the aggregation of military power—the development of great military potential, the maintenance of large forces-in-being, and the formation of military coalitions—following the collapse of Bismarck's system of fragmented power.

After 1815 the European states, reacting to the excesses of the French Revolutionary and Napoleonic Wars, combined their military power to protect their common interest in preventing France or any other power from seeking hegemony and to nip in the bud any democratic-nationalist revolutions that might again disturb the international order. The Concert of Europe, however, was undermined by differences of national interest, especially with respect to suppression of the liberal and nationalist revolutions in the first half of the century. After 1822, when the British left the Quadruple Alliance because they refused to support the military suppression of revolutions, the concept of collective force survived only in sporadic great-power consultations during crises. The military power of states was again fragmented, except for shifting alignments, which reflected rapidly changing patterns of interests.

In the period of general peace from 1822 to 1854, international politics was not concerned with national crusades or bids for hegemony. Nor was it dominated by the drive of states to expand their territory and commerce. It was absorbed in limited territorial disputes, the old Russo-Turkish rivalry, and the unsettling effects of the revolutions of 1830 and 1848 upon the European equilibrium. The desire to avoid another European war was widespread among governments and deeply rooted in popular opinion. Aside from the distasteful memory of the Napoleonic Wars, the domestically conservative states (Russia, Austria, and Prussia) feared war because they feared revolution, especially if they had to fight a liberal state; while in Britain and France liberal bourgeois sentiment opposed the deflection of attention and expenditures from domestic to military purposes, thereby enforcing military retrenchment.

Yet the desire for peace was not so strong as to exclude the ready resort to war for limited ends. After 1848 the liberal states could count on strong patriotic support for demonstrations of military strength and determination. Consequently, there were repeated crises in which military maneuvers and threats of force brought states to the brink of war, where rulers and diplomats bargained a peaceful resolution.

In this mode of international politics the flexibility of alignments played a central role. Although Europe was divided ideologically between the Eastern conservative powers and the Western liberal powers, members of both groups freely crossed ideological lines to support each other against members of their own group. Neither ideology nor *raison d'état* inspired anything like the numerous formal military commitments that characterized international politics before the French Revolution. States were not preoccupied with the arrangement of advantageous combinations of military power in anticipation of wars for territory. If there was any guiding principle of their foreign policies, it was not Frederick the Great's axiom that states must continually seek to maximize their power but rather that no state should expand its holdings without the consent of others. Therefore, states concerted their power chiefly by ententes, rapprochements, and diplomatic alignments rather than by treaties formalizing detailed military commitments. The great fluidity of the resulting combinations, together with the willingness of states to use force to protect an equilibrium, served the modest ends of states well.

Yet this international equilibrium was far from foolproof. Although the system of fluid alignments and diplomatic resolutions on the brink of war enabled statesmen to surmount a number of crises, the major states of Europe were unable to improvise the proper configurations of power and interest, to hit upon the right combinations of military threats and diplomatic bargains, to prevent the international crisis precipitated by a Russo-Turkish dispute from erupting into the unintended and useless Crimean War (1853–56).

In the period after this war until the Franco-Prussian War (1870–71), England and Russia withdrew from active intervention in European affairs: England, in liberal reaction to the Crimean fiasco; Russia, because of internal troubles and preoccupation with redressing her losses. This development upset the dynamic equilibrium and seriously weakened constraints against the acquisitive uses of force. It gave Bismarck, Cavour, and Napoleon III irresistible opportunities to capitalize upon liberal nationalist ferment in their pursuit of aggressive national ambitions. Again, as in the eighteenth century, offensive, *ad hoc*, military alliances became a major instrument of policy.[62]

Taking advantage of the lack of concerted opposition, Bismarck backed his political designs with limited wars and the threat of war to acquire limited territory at the expense of Denmark and Austria. England, Russia, and France all tried to obstruct his designs with diplomatic protests and mediation efforts backed by military threats and demonstrations, but Bismarck correctly estimated that they were not prepared to combine to fight a general war against German forces for the sake of the limited stakes at issue. Rather, they preferred peaceful acquiescence in Bismarck's limited victories.[63]

Capitalizing upon Napoleon III's inept truculence and France's diplomatic isolation, Bismarck rounded out united Germany's boun-

62. The most important offensive alliances were the secret agreement of Plombières (1858), followed by a Franco-Sardinian treaty in which France and Sardinia plotted to provoke war with Austria and cede Savoy and Nice to France; the secret Franco-Russian alliance in 1859, in which Russia agreed to remain neutral in a Franco-Austrian war in return for French assistance in revising the Crimean settlement of 1856; the Austro-Prussian alliance (1864) for the purpose of war against Denmark in order to annex Schleswig-Holstein; and the Italo-Prussian alliance of 1866, in which Italy promised to join Prussia in the event that an Austro-Prussian war occurred within three months, in return for the cession of Venetia.

63. This was partly because Russia was preoccupied with Poland while France was preoccupied with Napoleon III's ambitions. Britain, which could have turned the balance of power against Prussia in a war, was reluctant to become involved on the Continent and saw a strong Germany as a counter to Russia. Moreover, both Britain and Russia wanted Germany as a counter to French adventurism. Werner E. Mosse, *The European Powers and the German Question, 1848–1871* (Cambridge: Cambridge University Press, 1958), chaps. vi and viii.

daries with a surprisingly rapid victory in the Franco-Prussian War. This achievement was entirely consistent with the rules of the game as Frederick the Great, Kaunitz, or any of the leading statesmen of the eighteenth century understood them. Indeed, it was not generally viewed as upsetting the balance of power or threatening international order.[64] Yet the formidable force with which Bismarck played the game was to change the game itself before the end of the century.

The sudden success of Bismarck's superior military machine undermined one important condition of the fluid, fragmented political system that facilitated his victories: the expectation that the pace of war would be sufficiently slow, and its intensity sufficiently moderate, to permit diplomatic maneuvers and military and political improvisations to be brought to bear upon its outcome. The suddenness and decisiveness of Prussia's victories and the efficacy of its advance preparations—particularly, the conscription system, the use of railroads, and the professional staff planning and direction—persuaded all governments that national security demanded a high level of peacetime preparedness. The game would be won or lost by what went on before the war.

Prussia's victories also seemed to show that preparedness would not be sufficient unless one could count on the military co-operation of other states; hence, the need for reliable allies before war became imminent. For in the crisis preceding the Franco-Prussian War, France was not only deluded about its military strength; with less justification it miscalculated its political support. It had counted on Austria and Italy becoming allies and on Russia giving support in the event of war with Prussia. But Russia, anticipating with equanimity a French victory, concentrated on keeping Austria-Hungary out of the war and to this end arranged reciprocal neutrality, while Austria intended to remain neutral in any case—at least until French military success should provide the opportunity of joining the war in order to restore the Hapsburg position in southern Germany.[65]

Of course we cannot know whether Napoleon III would have gone to war if he had known that France would lack allies, or Bismarck, if France had enjoyed a credible alliance with Austria-Hungary and Italy

64. In England the general view was that Germany's replacement of France as the leading Continental power would check dangerous French adventurism, contain Russia, and remove a source of unrest and war by consolidating Germany. The Russians hoped that Franco-German animosity would stalemate these two powers while Russia settled accounts with Austria. Austria was reconciled to abandoning its ambition for hegemony over Germany in alliance with France and turned to Bismarck for an accommodation. A. J. P. Taylor, *The Struggle for the Mastery of Europe, 1848–1918* (London: Oxford University Press, 1954), pp. 212–19.

65. *Ibid.*, pp. 206–13.

and the declared assurance of Russian support in advance of war. Perhaps Bismarck would have refrained from war if England had intervened diplomatically to that end, but England lacked both the requisite military power and the will to use it. The significant point, however, is not merely that the ambiguity of military alignments may have contributed to the outbreak of war, but that in this period states viewed alliances primarily as means of gaining support in war rather than as instruments of deterrence. Consequently, the lesson that contemporaries drew from the Franco-Prussian War related not to the conditions of deterrence but to the conditions of victory. Nevertheless, this lesson implied a transition from the military politics of the eighteenth century, when most alliances were formed in anticipation of specific wars waged for offensive purposes, to the politics of the nineteenth century, when alliances came to be regarded as defensive precautions against hypothetical surprise attacks and swift victories.

In another way, too, Bismarck's victory in the Franco-Prussian War undermined the system of fluid alignments from which he had profited. The successful operation of that system depended on the ability of governments to shift their power from the support of one state to another without much regard for emotional or ideological biases toward nations, and it presupposed the possibility of limited victories without inveterate animosities. But the French reaction to Germany's acquisition of Alsace-Lorraine indicated that thereafter *Realpolitik* would have to reckon with popular sentiment, that wars and alliances would be increasingly affected by national amities and enmities that were more volatile yet less tractable than the reasons of state that had governed the traditional politics of force. The annexation of Alsace-Lorraine would have been a normal part of the game in the eighteenth century; but, coming after the democratic and nationalistic revolutions of the nineteenth century, it engendered a smoldering sentiment of revenge that could not be extinguished until consumed in the conflagration of 1914.[66]

Finally, Bismarck undermined the prevailing politics of force by fashioning a complicated network of peacetime defensive alliances designed to protect Germany's enhanced position with a stalemate between opposing combinations of power. Against his original preference

66. As Michael Howard has written, "A century earlier the transfer of such provinces to the sovereignty of a victorious prince had been commonplace. A century later it would have been completed by the brutal surgery of transfer of populations. To the nineteenth century, with its growing belief in national self-determination and its plebiscitary voting, the process, carried out in defiance of the wishes of the populations, seemed an open flouting of that public law on whose development Europe was beginning to pride itself." *Op. cit.*, p. 449.

for *ad hoc*, flexible alignments, he helped create and consolidate a pattern of balanced antagonisms in which crisis diplomacy was increasingly subordinated to the imperatives of organizing military power in peacetime.[67]

After playing "honest broker" at the Congress of Berlin (1878), which tried to ameliorate the intractable Eastern question but aroused Russian resentment, Bismarck was more than ever haunted by the fear of a Franco-Russian alliance, which would threaten Germany with war on two fronts. He was equally anxious to prevent a Balkan war between Austria-Hungary and Russia, which would confront Germany with either the defeat of Austria or the prospect of war with Russia. Consequently, in 1879 he initiated a system of defensive alliances by arranging a secret treaty with Austria-Hungary which committed the signatories to assist each other against a Russian attack and to remain at least neutral if either should be attacked by another power (meaning France). In 1887 he balanced this with the secret Reinsurance Treaty with Russia, in which the signatories promised to remain neutral in the event that either became involved in war with a third power, except in the case of a German attack against France or a Russian attack against Austria. These alliances were supplemented by several others: the secret Alliance of the Three Emperors (1881), in which Germany, Russia, and Austria-Hungary agreed to certain political and territorial arrangements in the Balkans and promised to maintain friendly neutrality in the event that one power should become involved in war with a nonsignatory, except Turkey (in which case other conditions of consultation and belligerency were specified); the Triple Alliance (1882), between Germany, Austria-Hungary, and Italy, stating the secret conditions under which the signatories would aid each other if attacked by other states (France); and two Mediterranean Agreements (1887), engineered by Bismarck, between Britain, Italy, Austria-Hungary, and Spain, pledging the signatories to maintain the status quo in the Mediterranean area (against Russia and France) or to agree beforehand to changes.

From Bismarck's standpoint these alliances were intended to restrain as well as protect allies, while preventing a war. For example, they were intended to keep Austria-Hungary from attacking Russia in the Balkans by providing it with security from a Russian attack and implicitly threatening to withdraw German support in the event of an Austrian attack on

---

67. The most complete analyses and descriptions of Bismarck's alliance system and how it changed come from two admiring scholars: A. J. P. Taylor, *op. cit.*, and William L. Langer, *op. cit.* For a more critical account, see W. N. Medlicott, *Bismarck, Gladstone, and the Concert of Europe* (London: The Athlone Press, 1956).

Russia; and they were intended to keep Austria-Hungary from making an alliance with France by giving it an alternative ally. Similarly, they were intended to restrain Russia by distracting it from forming an alliance with France and by checking its ambitions in the Balkans and the Near East with opposing military combinations. Bismarck's alliances were not intended to establish a united military bloc in order to deter a single external threat. The configurations of interest were too complicated for that. Moreover, the secrecy of the key commitments, when their generally defensive purpose would seem to have warranted publication, reflected the traditional diplomatic search, not for the needs of military deterrence, but for flexibility.[68]

Nevertheless, the effect of Bismarck's alliance system was to foster two opposing alliances, which, although far from being united military camps, tended, under the growing pressure of military preparedness and the arms competition, to polarize the pattern of international conflict and bind allies in a way he had always tried to avoid. Bismarck's successors certainly accelerated this process, but it is doubtful that either his ingenuity or Germany's leverage on events could have prevented a development that was so largely inherent in the search for military security under the political and military conditions of the time. Be that as it may, his successors' failure to renew the Reinsurance Treaty provided the immediate impetus for the secret Franco-Russian alliance (1894), which began the replacement of Bismarck's multipolar system of balanced antagonisms with a more rigid confrontation of defensive military coalitions.

Significantly, in terms of the increased concern for military preparedness, France, which took the initiative, viewed the agreement with Russia chiefly as an arrangement for military co-ordination. Not until eighteen months after a military convention (1892) had been worked

68. All the associated military conventions and understandings were secret. Even the existence of the Reinsurance Treaty, the Alliance of the Three Emperors, the Triple Alliance, and the Franco-Russian alliance was supposed to be secret. In all cases except the Alliance of the Three Emperors (which did not become known until after World War I) and the Reinsurance Treaty (which became known in 1896), the existence of these treaties was known almost immediately and the general alignment they formalized and specified was perceived. But their exact provisions remained unknown or in doubt and therefore subject to misapprehension. Thus Bismarck felt it was necessary to assure France that the Austro-German Alliance of 1879 was not directed against France, and later to publish the treaty in order to prove its defensive intentions when confronted with intimations in the Hungarian parliament that the alliance might provide German support in a war against Russia. The Russians first learned the actual provisions of this treaty and the fact that it was directed exclusively against them when Bismarck revealed the text to them during the negotiation of the Reinsurance Treaty.

out did the two states sign a full military-political alliance, intended to remain in force as long as the Triple Alliance.[69] This alliance became part of a Triple Entente when the Anglo-Japanese Alliance, signed in 1902 and modified in 1904, freed Britain to return to an active diplomatic role in Europe. In the Anglo-French Entente (1904) the two powers settled all their colonial differences. In the Anglo-Russian Entente (1907) the signatories settled differences in Persia, Afghanistan, Tibet, and the Straits.

The Anglo-French and Anglo-Russian parts of the Triple Entente were not, in form, military alliances, but they established the political conditions for military staff conversations. In 1906 Sir Edward Grey, without informing the cabinet, authorized conversations between the British and French general staffs (there had already been naval conversations) on the ground that without co-ordinated plans Britain would not be able to help France if she should decide to go to war as an ally. The subsequent conversations and informal understandings constituted, in effect, a military alliance, although the British government insisted that they created no obligation. Similar arrangements with Russia were made in the Anglo-Russian naval convention of 1912.

The Triple Alliance and the Triple Entente were far from tight alliances diplomatically, particularly as long as colonial rivalries stimulated fluid, interlocking alignments and political compensations among the leading European powers. They did, however, provide the political frameworks within which military commitments were consolidated. The consolidation of military commitments in turn tightened the alliances. Thus alliances, which in Bismarck's heyday had been a means of fragmenting military power, became a means of aggregating military power. This transition reflected the emergence of the peacetime development of arms as a primary force in international politics.

11. The Politics of Military Coalitions

The increasing dependence of national security upon the military co-operation of allies and the tightening of political commitments in order

69. The Convention of the Franco-Russian alliance provided: (1) If France were attacked by Germany, or by Italy supported by Germany, Russia would employ all available forces against Germany; if Russia were attacked by Germany, or by Austria supported by Germany, France would employ all available forces against Germany. (2) In case the forces of the Triple Alliance, or of any one power a member of it, mobilized, France and Russia should mobilize without delay. (3) Other articles provided for the number of troops to be employed, for specific plans of the general staffs, the co-ordination of mobilization, etc. The agreement was supplemented by a naval convention in 1912.

to insure this co-operation tended to increase allied solidarity at the expense of diplomatic accommodation. The polarization of military alignments impeded the kind of accommodations that had kept the peace from 1815 to 1854. It fostered the rigidity of commitments exemplified in Germany's "blank check" to Austria, which practically assured a general war when Austria declared war on Serbia.[70] Yet in the final analysis it was primarily the nature of military plans and only indirectly the polarization of alliances which foreclosed diplomatic opportunities and set off the chain reaction leading to World War I. In fact, under other conditions the consolidation of defensive alliances, combined with the build-up of military power, could have promoted peace by strengthening military deterrence—by convincing adversaries that hostile action would lead to war. For this aggregation of military power clarified the question of who would defend whom, made credible the readiness of states to resist attacks with war, and minimized the chance of a major shift of alliance, which had so often upset the equilibrium and led to war in the eighteenth century.[71] Indeed the consolidation of military coalitions, although raising international tensions, may in fact have promoted peace. After all, as long as the great powers were determined to avoid war in Europe (if only because they felt that their military preparations were incomplete or because they were preoccupied with imperial rivalries), they managed to surmount one crisis after another by diplomatic accommodation, and they kept the Russo-Turkish War and the two Balkan wars local and limited. The triggering of general war resulted from the war between Austria-Hungary and Serbia, a state outside the two alliances. Therefore if the consolidation of al-

70. After the Anglo-Russian Entente the German chancellor Von Bülow, in deference to Austria's adherence to the alliance with Germany, gave Austria-Hungary a so-called diplomatic blank check, promising to mobilize if Russia mobilized and to support Austria-Hungary in a war with Russia, contrary to Bismarck's consistent policy of not pledging support to Austria unless Austria were attacked. In 1914, when Austria-Hungary declared war on Serbia, the Kaiser gave it assurance that Germany would intervene if Russia intervened. Since France was pledged to mobilize if Germany or Austria mobilized against Russia and to assist Russia if it were attacked by Germany or by Austria supported by Germany, Germany's commitment to support Austria played a major role in triggering a general war when Austrian moves against Serbia were resisted by Russia.

71. The question of who would defend whom under what circumstances was not completely clarified. It was not absolutely clear to Germany and Austria-Hungary that Russia would go to war in support of Serbia in an Austrian-Serbian war. Nor was it certain in Germany's view or even, for that matter, in France's that Britain would intervene against Germany in a Continental war, even if Belgium were invaded. The significant fact, however, is that the states that took military action first were quite willing to take that action on the supposition that a general war would result. Therefore, the element of doubt about Russian or British reactions did not lead to a war that would otherwise have been avoided.

liances contributed to the outbreak of war, it was only indirectly, by making the Triple Alliance susceptible to what has come to be called "catalytic war," a war in which one state becomes engaged somewhat against its will because of the actions of another.

In any event it would be reading too much of the present into the past to say that military deterrence failed, for it was not really put to the test. The guiding purpose of military-political commitments before World War I was not deterrence but preparation for war and, secondarily, restraint of allies. Thus the British, the least alliance-minded of the major powers, might contemplate entering alliances or ententes to prevent a hostile Continental coalition from forming, to reduce the political options of an ally, or to secure imperial spheres of influence. But as long as they felt that their navy and insular position would afford adequate protection in a war, they viewed military alliances suspiciously as a commitment to war, not hopefully as a means of deterrence. Thus Britain's original interest in an entente with France, like her interest in an entente with Germany, was in part to prevent the formation of a Continental coalition of France, Germany, and Russia, which would upset the balance of power on the Continent and threaten British security in a war. When Germany's naval policy and William II's blustering convinced the British of the threat of war with Germany, they sought an entente and military understandings with the French because they feared that the fall of France would imperil England. They did not publish their entente as a deterrent.

Deterrence, moreover, presupposes that the avoidance of war is a primary object of military commitments. The fact is that by 1914 the avoidance of war was not an overriding concern of governments. The general staffs were almost all resigned to the prospect of a general war and all confident of victory. The civilian administrations and statesmen largely accepted the primacy of assuring military success over arranging diplomatic accommodations. The general public, with a mixture of patriotic fervor and complacency, acquiesced.

But if the consolidation of alliances was not inconsistent with mutual deterrence and contributed only indirectly to the outbreak of war, it did assure that any war involving more than one member of the two alliances would become a general war by involving all. When that happened, the irreversible momentum of the military machines foreclosed any chance of limiting the war except by an early victory or political settlement. Yet an early settlement was precluded by the public passions the very magnitude of violence aroused, since only a war for the most extreme ends could justify such a massive conflict in the eyes of nations whose military power was rooted in mass support. Under the circumstances it is quite doubtful that even an early German victory at the Marne would have ended the war. Consequently, World War I fulfilled the potential of total war revealed by the French Revolution but largely obscured by the age of Bismarck.

12. *The Politics of Force Short of War*

The popular shock and disillusionment caused by such a lethal war at the dawn of what seemed to be an era of unexampled peace, order, and progress had a powerful effect on the politics of force. Liberal opinion drew the lesson that military alliances were a primary cause of war and that war could be eliminated by eschewing alliances and arms races in favor of a universal league of nations and disarmament. Ironically, this lesson impeded the defensive nations from concerting their military power just when international order and their own security demanded a united military effort to deter the expansion of Hitler's Germany.

Hitler engineered another one of those periodic bids for European hegemony, which ought to have called forth a military coalition like those that had checked previous bids; this time, however, the expansion of military power made it essential to thwart hegemony *in advance* of a general war. Countering Hitler's ambitions required forming a tight multilateral military alliance and actively engaging in an arms race in order to confront the aggressor with united military and political resistance. There was a genuine prospect of effective deterrence by these means, but that prospect was forfeited. The failure to deter Hitler was part of the general failure of defensive states to compete successfully with offensive states in exploiting the new utility of force short of war, although its defensive utility was probably greater than ever before.

The enhanced utility of force short of war sprang from a number of developments accompanying the popularization and modernization of force. Among psychological and political developments, the following were especially significant: the mobilization of mass support for foreign policies; stronger inhibitions against war, springing from the reaction to the Napoleonic Wars, the fear of revolution, the fear of modern war's destructiveness, and the growth of liberal pacific sentiment (especially in England); and, particularly important for the defensive use of force, the increased costs of conquering territory due to the activation of nationalist sentiment. Some of the material developments enhancing the utility of force short of war were faster and more extensive communications between governments, between governments and armed forces in the field and at sea, and between governments and their citizens; larger forces-in-being capable of striking suddenly and, it was thought, decisively; the new imperatives of preparing for war in advance of an imminent war; concomitantly, the new importance and political impact of mobilization plans and strategic doctrine; the growing capacity of states to alter their military power by weapons competition; the superior power and mobility of the modern battleship and its great capacity to project the impression as well as the physical reality of national power abroad; and, finally, the emergence of the doctrine and weapons of strategic bombing, oriented toward direct punitive civilian damage.

All these developments, combined, gave governments better access to foreign nations as a whole and enhanced the threat value of armed forces on a continuing basis in peacetime. Given the requisite will on the part of the major status quo powers to defend not only their own territories but those of smaller countries, this enhanced threat value might have readily contained totalitarian expansionism without a general war. But in the political climate of the 1930s the threat of general war became a devastating instrument of intimidation in the hands of the expansionist powers.

One manifestation of the enhanced role of force short of war that developed around the end of the nineteenth century was the increased number of diplomatic crises in which international friction and the prospect of war were intense yet the underlying political conflict was settled or pacified without war. In such crises there were usually explicit or implicit threats of war, sometimes accompanied by military confrontations or demonstrations, leading to growing international tension and talk of war and eventuating in active diplomatic maneuvering, often involving a number of states, followed by a *détente* and ending with some sort of political settlement. The period 1818–54 was full of such crises, but they lacked the degree of patriotic excitement and latent military explosiveness that agitated the crises of 1871–1914.[72] For in the earlier period national alignments were neither so clear nor so firm, nor national security and prestige so acutely involved. Neither was the capacity of states to make a show of strength so great before the develop-

---

72. In this latter period the most important crises in which there was thought to be a serious prospect of war among major powers or in which public or private threats of war were issued were Bismarck's "war in sight" crisis (1875), the Russian-Turkish conflict preceding the Congress of Berlin (1878), the Russian-Bulgarian crisis of 1887–88, Germany's Kruger telegram and threat of a Continental league against Britain in 1896, the Anglo-French confrontation at Fashoda (1898), the first Morocco crisis at Tangier (1905), leading to the conference at Algeciras (1906), the Bosnian crisis (1908–9), and the second Morocco crisis at Agadir (1911). Of these, the Bosnian and the second Moroccan crises were actually the most likely to have resulted in war.

ment of the modern battleship, arms races, and modern mobilization.[73]

Enhancement of the power of arms short of war was an aspect of the growing distinction between war and peace. By the end of the century this distinction was much more dramatic and portentous than it had been in the eighteenth century. By then it was presumed that a war resulting from the conflicts of major powers in Europe would be a general war during which diplomacy would be suspended until one or the other side had achieved a decisive victory. Shifts of alignment and diplomatic deals would be too risky under these conditions, and they would be incompatible with the mobilization of public sentiment for victory. Anyway, the pace and intensity of war would leave no time for such leisurely devices.

Even limited military encounters between major powers in peripheral areas came to seem too dangerous to be regarded casually or as mere extensions of diplomacy. And it was feared that the limited wars of lesser powers—the Russo-Turkish war of 1877–78, to some extent the Greco-Turkish war of 1897, and especially the two Balkan wars (1912–13)—might involve the great powers in an unwanted general war if they were not careful to isolate them and bring them to a settlement.

Therefore governments sought new methods of pressing their political positions with force short of war. Before World War I the language of diplomacy still conveyed fine shadings of national displeasure, resolve, and threat, but governments did not yet fully exploit the propaganda of words and actions that was foreshadowed in World War I and mastered by the revolutionary and revisionist states after the war.[74] In this period naval power came closest to playing the role that strategic airpower played much later.

73. Germany used single and smaller warships to demonstrate its political purpose in both of the Moroccan crises. The British reinforced diplomacy with naval deployments or preparations in all the crises in which they were directly involved. For example, after the Kruger telegram they organized a "flying squadron" ready to go to any part of the world. The Bosnian and second Moroccan crises were conducted with the Anglo-German naval race in the background. During the first Balkan War Austria-Hungary mobilized some forces and Russia failed to dismiss some conscripts that were due for release; but, in general, mobilization was considered too dangerous as a demonstration device, since it was regarded as a prelude to general war. Nevertheless, on the brink of World War I partial mobilization was resorted to as a deterrent, and it failed.

74. One interesting attempt at such propaganda was Bismarck's war of nerves against France in 1875, when he capitalized upon rising tension between the two countries to inspire a press campaign based upon the slogan, "Is war in sight?", accompanied by a halt in the export of horses from Germany and by other signals of preparation for war. Bismarck's exact political purpose—perhaps an entente with France—is unclear. In any case his tactic miscarried when the French exploited his agent's indiscreet private remarks defending the doctrine of preventive war in order to alarm Britain and Russia. Taylor, *op. cit.*, pp. 225–26.

The naval demonstration, as a symbol of national power and determination, was only a faint harbinger of more subtle methods of showing the flag which developed in the age of airpower.[75] The utility of naval force short of war depended upon the fact that no one doubted that states would use the weapons in war. Naval power, looming in the background of colonial competition, played a crucial role in local confrontations and tests of will, which served as substitutes for overt clashes of arms. But there was a direct relationship between the threat value and the war value of naval weapons. On the basis of this relationship, navies became highly prestigious symbols of world power. Thus states that wished to be world powers, but also states that wanted simply to impress the world or to gain a military advantage over a local rival,[76] sought conspicuous naval power—often at considerable economic sacrifice.

The Anglo-German naval race demonstrated most dramatically the political impact that an arms program might exert. It was the military basis of what contemporaries called a "dry war," which did much to polarize the prewar alliances. Although Germany intended to use its construction of dreadnoughts as a political lever to gain colonial concessions, a pledge of neutrality, or even an alliance from England, its naval program actually did more than any other development in Anglo-German relations to drive England into closer military alignment with France, since the British assumed that a program jeopardizing the military foundation of their national survival and status must originate in hostile intentions. Nevertheless, Germany's larger and vaguer political purpose—to assert her right to be a world power—was in some measure achieved, even if at the expense of alarming and antagonizing rivals. Whether wisely or foolishly used, the arms race revealed itself as a powerful and dynamic political instrument, no less influential than alliances as a means of altering the configurations of power and playing upon the will of nations.

Strategic airpower, as we have noted, added a new dimension to the peaceful uses of military power by inspiring fears of direct civilian damage and fostering a doctrine of punitive deterrence. In the decade before World War II Hitler was the chief beneficiary of this new power through his exploitation of Britain's unwarranted fears of strategic bombing. His exploitation of airpower, however, was only one aspect—

75. Alfred Vagts examines the use of both amicable and admonitory naval demonstrations during the nineteenth century and the period before World War I in *Defense and Diplomacy*, chap. vii, pp. 237–55.

76. For example, considerations of prestige and security led Argentina and Chile into a naval race in 1891–1902. The race did not end until rising tensions brought about a political and disarmament settlement, which was facilitated by the fact that both states had bought their battleships in Europe.

and not one to which he gave much forethought—of his general strategy of using the threat of force for far-reaching political and psychological effects.

With an uncanny sense of how and when to exploit the weaknesses and divisions of potential opponents, Hitler gradually rearmed Germany and by piecemeal aggression improvised an almost bloodless expansion. His successes depended on shrewd intuition about the unwillingness of other governments to use force. He capitalized on the widespread revulsion toward general war, as well as on the purported inequity of the Versailles settlement, to confront the democratic powers with a series of limited aggressions, none of which seemed worth resisting at the price of general war. Alternating menacing with conciliatory gestures, he placed the burden of undertaking another world war on nations that were neither materially nor morally prepared to accept it.

Sometimes he bluffed a determination to make war if Germany were not given its way, as in the case of the remilitarization of the Rhineland and in playing up to British fears about Germany's nonexistent capacity to devastate England from the air. Sometimes, as at the time of the Munich settlement of 1938, he was on the brink of going to war when concessions from the opposition saved him the trouble. At other times he was ready to fight a local war with confidence that there would be little or no united resistance. In all instances his tactical skill lay in disarming and isolating the opposition with the prospect of war.[77] His techniques of conveying the threat of war and testing the will and nerves of potential opponents were varied: military pageantry, calculated private conversations and inspired rumors about Germany's military intentions and capabilities, troop concentrations and maneuvers, exaggerated claims of military strength, ultimatums, political demands, studied hints of war, and, above all, an arsenal of diplomatic tactics aimed at alternately or simultaneously rattling the sword and waving the olive branch.

Time after time, even as late as the Munich settlement, Germany would have been unable to withstand united French and British military opposition. Repeatedly Hitler's generals protested that Germany was not militarily prepared to contend with such opposition: Germany never did undertake the "rearmament in depth" that Hitler's technical ad-

---

77. Military considerations in Hitler's mind and the role of the military in his regime are dealt with in J. W. Wheeler-Bennett, *The Nemesis of Power: The German Army in Politics* (New York: Macmillan, 1953), and E. M. Robertson, *Hitler's Pre-War Policy and Military Plans, 1933–1939* (London: Longmans Green & Co., 1963). A. J. P. Taylor's *The Origins of the Second World War* (Greenwich, Conn.: Fawcett Publications, 1961), despite its misguided insistence upon Hitler's lack of far-reaching and hostile motives in an effort to stress his opportunistic and stumbling actions, is a perceptive account of Hitler's diplomacy and military thinking.

visers urged as essential for general war. But conventional considerations of relative military capabilities finally came to seem of only secondary importance to a man who, with considerable justification, was so sure of his ability to gauge the intentions—that is, the political and military will—of governments.

Yet Hitler was not blind to constraints imposed by relative military strength. He was not irrational or capricious in assessing political and military intentions. And he was not uncalculating in his decisions to act. Therefore his very sensitivity to the will and nerve of governments should have enabled his opponents to discourage his aggressions with the threat of force. The same characteristics of twentieth-century military power which enabled Hitler to expand gave status quo nations new power to deter. These nations were not inferior in their capacity to arm and form reliable military commitments in peacetime. Moreover, they were not unique in their deep reluctance to go to war. Indeed, Hitler's fear of domestic disaffection in a general war matched the democratic countries' moral and emotional aversion to such a war.

Before World War I, and especially before the Napoleonic Wars, only a clear preponderance of military power could be counted on to deter an offensive war. After World War I, only an assured preponderance— or assured lack of opposition—could warrant the risk of undertaking an offensive war. The importance of an aggressor correctly calculating the will of defensive states to use force was, therefore, greatly enhanced; but even an ambiguous risk of opposition might deter offensive military action, given relatively equal military capacities.

Japan's decision to attack Pearl Harbor in order to thwart American opposition to its expansion in Asia indicates that one major power might still find it profitable to fight another for offensive territorial goals when it enjoyed a substantial military advantage, and that it might be provoked to do so when its advantage was dwindling. The generalization must be qualified in light of Japan's misapprehension that war with the U.S. would be a short and limited preventive action, yet the qualification is not decisive because before the nuclear age a great power might still expect to wage even a general war without paying an unacceptable price for victory. It is difficult, however, to draw any lessons about the efficacy or inefficacy of military deterrence in this case, because the threat of general war was scarcely enforced against Japan. The U.S., despite its well-known opposition to Japanese designs, its military and economic gestures to back diplomatic warnings, and its belated military build-up, did not undertake a systematic effort to convey its will and capacity to resist Japanese expansion with war. For until quite late in the game it simply was not prepared, either politically or militarily, to wage a major war to contain Japan as long as Japan did not attack American territories,[78] and later it came to consider war as inevitable while imposing clearly unacceptable demands on Japan.[79] Under the circumstances, American nonmilitary sanctions (especially the oil embargo), belated military preparations, and militant demands only accelerated Japan's attack on Pearl Harbor. By that time only a demonstrable American will and capacity to retaliate directly against the Japanese homeland might have deterred the attack;[80] but, lacking the capacity, the U.S. was in no position to employ this deterrent.

The ascendance of Hitler's Germany, however, truly marked a failure of military deterrence, because deterrence was not only imperative but feasible and tried; yet Germany's succession of bloodless victories finally led Hitler to launch a war against Poland from which Britain could no longer abstain. Here at least Hitler was clearly warned, but he decided to go to war anyway. The result was a general war that he and all other statesmen had hoped to avoid.

Deterrence failed, in the first place, because Britain and France failed to form a firm military alliance in order to convince Germany that aggression would be met by united resistance.[81] Until Hitler occupied Czechoslovakia, there was no question in his mind or in the minds of his generals that France and Britain combined, especially in conjunction with the strong Czechoslovakian forces, would be a formidable foe in a war with Germany and Italy.[82]

78. Herbert Feis, *The Road to Pearl Harbor* (Princeton: Princeton University Press, 1950).

79. Paul W. Schroeder, *The Axis Alliance and Japanese-American Relations, 1941* (Ithaca: Cornell University Press, 1958). One would conclude from Schroeder's analysis that a determined deterrent effort might have dissuaded Japan from moving southward in Indochina, but that probably no American military threat could have persuaded Japan to meet American demands to pull out of China.

80. In 1941 the U.S. developed plans for punitive air attacks against Japan. The Japanese military, government, and public were conscious of this threat. The hasty movement of bombers to the Philippines in the last months of 1941 contributed to Japan's decision to attack in December rather than later. Quester, *op. cit.*, pp. 131–35.

81. The postwar divergencies of British and French security policies are fully explained and interpreted in Arnold Wolfers, *Britain and France between Two Wars* (New York: Harcourt, Brace & Co., 1940), and W. M. Jordan, *Great Britain, France, and the German Problem, 1918–1939* (New York: Oxford University Press, 1943).

82. In September, 1938, much to Hitler's surprise, Britain, France, and Czechoslovakia rejected an ultimatum demanding that Czechoslovakia turn over Sudetenland areas to Germany. Czechoslovakia had ordered full mobilization, France had undertaken partial mobilization, and Britain was reported to have sent its fleet to sea. After further Anglo-French concessions, it became clear that there would be general war if Hitler carried out Operation Green for the invasion of Sudetenland. Under pressure from his own military chiefs, influential German civilians, and Mussolini, Hitler decided to cancel the invasion plans. Robertson, *op. cit.*, pp. 143–49.

The French government was eager to form an alliance because it was convinced that Germany would rearm, gain military supremacy on the Continent, and try to achieve hegemony unless it were kept disarmed and deterred by a military coalition. The British, however, did not feel that the threat to their security on the Continent was sufficient to require a military commitment in advance of war, contrary to England's traditional policy, or an invasion of the Lowlands. Furthermore, they took the position that the way to prevent a resurgent and expansive Germany was not to revert to the discredited alliance system or to try to impose unilateral disarmament, but rather through conciliation and universal disarmament to bring Germany back into the family of nations as a responsible equal within a system of Wilsonian collective security, in which all states through the medium of the League would deter aggression by any nation.

When France failed to get political and military guarantees from Britain and the U.S. in 1919–20, it entered the Little Entente with Czechoslovakia, Rumania, and Yugoslavia. This defensive entente, however, was doomed to fail as a deterrent because it was not supported by a French military strategy or capability consistent with its political commitments. France needed a sizable standing professional force capable of intervening against aggressions beyond its borders and of coming to the assistance of its Eastern allies in an offensive action across Germany. But after World War I the French government was as convinced of the military advantage of the defense, symbolized in the Maginot Line, as it had been convinced of the efficacy of the offense before. The economic drain of the war, popular antimilitary sentiment, and leftist preferences for militia reinforced defensive strategic propensities by compelling the government to build a military establishment largely dependent on reserves and short-term conscripts, with only a small professional contingent. Consequently, to fight a major power France would have had to undertake general mobilization. Yet only an imminent general war seemed to warrant mobilization, and only an invasion of France would justify a general war—at least in the absence of assured British support. This meant that France was not psychologically or strategically prepared to threaten war against limited aggressions. Lacking an offensive strategy, France was unable to promise credible military support to her Eastern allies and became unable to carry out such a promise in any case after Germany rearmed and reoccupied the Rhineland. Thus France no less than Britain was wedded to a narrow concept of military defense which fatally underestimated the real political and military conditions of security.

Nevertheless, even without an alliance, a timely full-scale rearmament by France and Britain, joint declarations of their determination to resist limited aggressions, and impressive military maneuvers and mobilization measures would probably have been sufficient to deter Germany's piece-meal expansion at least as late as the Munich settlement. In the absence of such measures Hitler had reason to discount the words and actions that Britain and France hoped would deter him. When Britain started rearming seriously in 1936, it was too little, too late, and only spurred Germany to accelerate its rearmament. By the time Britain undertook a concerted policy of military deterrence, Hitler was more impressed by the restraints intended to avoid provocation and reward Germany for good behavior than by warnings and preparations. When Britain, the least disposed to make a prewar alliance, finally guaranteed Poland in order not to repeat its futile concessions at Czechoslovakia's expense, Hitler was not sufficiently convinced of Britain's willingness to engage in general war over Danzig to refrain from attacking Poland.[83]

Thus the age of deterrence began with a failure. Yet it was a failure from which men drew lessons that would dominate the deterrence of Communist expansion after World War II.

FORCE AND ORDER

13. The Classical Balance of Power

We have observed that the expansion of force complicated yet made more essential the calculated political control of military power in war and peace and that such control could be especially useful to states interested in deterring forceful changes in the territorial status quo. We must now explore the relationship of this imperative to the changing conditions of international order.

The prerequisite of order among autonomous states is that force be restrained by countervailing force within a balance (or equilibrium) of power. The various meanings and uses of the ambiguous concept of balance have been fully explored elsewhere.[84] Here the phrase refers

83. The Anglo-Polish treaty caused Hitler to postpone the invasion of Poland. But although Hitler's subsequent attempts to detach Britain and France from war on Poland's behalf brought little tangible results, he believed that the Western democracies would not intervene or that, if they did, they would merely fight a token war. *Ibid.*, chap. xvii.

84. See particularly Hans J. Morgenthau, *Politics Among Nations* (2d ed.; New York: Alfred A. Knopf, 1954), chaps. xi–xiv; Ernst B. Haas, "The Balance of Power: Prescription, Concept, or Propaganda?" *World Politics*, V (July, 1953), 442–77, and "The Balance of Power as a Guide to Policy-Making," *Journal of Politics*, XV (August, 1953), 370–98; Inis L. Claude, Jr., *Power and International Relations* (New York: Random House, 1962), chaps. ii and iii; Arnold Wolfers, *Discord and Collaboration*, chap. viii; Herbert Butterfield and Martin Wight,

simply to a distribution of military power among potential adversaries that places significant restraints on their use of force at the expense of the vital interests of other states.

Few would deny that the balance of power in this minimal sense has been at least a periodic historical reality. Among the proponents of a balance the fundamental question underlying different views of its characteristics and demands is whether states should deliberately seek it as a principle of collective welfare for the sake of their long-run interest in international order or whether a balance of power can be no more than the natural result of states pursuing their immediate interests in the competition for power.[85]

According to the first conception (which we shall call "comprehensive") the balance of power requires continual maintenance of a fairly stable distribution of power, whereas the latter conception (which we shall call "limited") is consistent with the view that the balance requires only combined opposition to periodic drives for hegemony or preponderance. The limited conception has repeatedly been put into practice in modern European history. The comprehensive conception was often invoked to justify preventive military or diplomatic intervention, an equitable division of spoils, and territorial compensations; but it was also expounded by genuine proponents of a more stable order among states.[86] The ultimate expression of the comprehensive conception re-

---

Diplomatic Investigations: Essays in the Theory of International Politics, eds. Butterfield and Wight (Cambridge: Harvard University Press, 1966), chaps. vi and vii.

85. A good selection of extracts from balance-of-power theorists and their critics is *The Balance of Power and Nuclear Deterrence*, ed. Frederick H. Gareau (Boston: Houghton Mifflin, 1962). See also extracts from Viscount Bolingbroke, David Hume, and Richard Cobden in *The Anglo-American Tradition in Foreign Affairs*, eds. Arnold Wolfers and Laurence W. Martin. Among many useful examinations of equilibrium are Edward V. Gulick, *Europe's Classical Balance of Power*, and Per Maurseth, "Balance of Power Thinking from the Renaissance to the French Revolution," *Journal of Peace Research*, I, No. 2 (1964), 120–36. For extended prescriptions or criticisms of the balance of power I have relied on François Fénelon, *Écrits et lettres politiques*, ed. Charles Urbain (Paris: Editions Bossard, 1920), and *Oeuvres*, XX and XXII (Paris: J. A. Lebel, 1824); various writings of Condorcet in *Oeuvres*, eds. A. Condorcet-O'Conner and M. F. Arago (12 vols.; Paris: Didot, 1847–49); Gould Francis Leckie, *An Historical Research into the Nature of the Balance of Power in Europe* (London: Taylor and Hessey, 1817); Friedrich von Gentz, *Fragments on the Balance of Power* (London: M. Peltier, 1806); and Charles Dupuis, *Le Principe d'équilibre et le Concert Européen de la Paix de Westphalie à l'Acte d'Algesiras* (Paris: Perrin et Cie, 1909).

86. Thus Leckie proposed a wholesale rearrangement of European states, state boundaries, and laws of succession in order to "divide the continent of Europe into portions, though not all equal yet bearing a certain proportion to each other, and to fix these separate portions irrevocably, so that no disputes should be permitted,

sembles the Wilsonian ideal of collective security. It posits that all states
have an obligation, transcending their immediate interests, to counter
any disturbance to the balance of power.[87]

The two conceptions also underlie different views about the automaticity of the balancing process. Automaticity, however, is a matter of
degree. The common characterization of the balance as an automatic
or self-regulating mechanism was really a manner of speaking intended
to emphasize the regularity of compensating adjustments in a dynamic
equilibrium, not a literal description of a system operating without relation to human will. It suggested that the balance was preserved not
because states aimed for a balance but simply because their pursuit of
immediate national interests happened to produce a balance.[88]

The British generally avowed the limited conception; and Continental
Europeans in the eighteenth century, the comprehensive conception,
of the balance of power. In periods of the eighteenth and nineteenth centuries, however, there was a running argument in England,
corresponding to the argument about the proper extent of Continental
involvement, over whether England should take military and diplomatic
countermeasures regularly in order to preserve continual equilibrium or

---

and no two should be under one head; many causes of wars within Europe would
be obviated." Leckie, *op. cit.*, pp. 243–44. In its general concept of a static equilibrium, Leckie's European order bears a certain resemblance to what Bismarck
wanted to accomplish by a network of alliances after the Franco-Prussian War.
But in its emphasis upon a reconstruction of Europe based upon greater equality
among states, it is closer to the Grand Design for a confederation ("une seule
forme de république") of fifteen European states which was proposed by the duc de
Sully, a minister of Henry IV. *Nouvelle Collection des Mémoires pour servir à
l'histoire de France, depuis le XIIᵉ siècle jusqu'à la fin du XVIIIᵉ*, eds. Michaud
and Poujoulat, Series II, Vols. II and III (Paris: Didot frères et Cⁱᵉ, 1837); and
André Puharré, *Les projets d'organization Européenne d'après le Grand Dessein de
Henri IV et de Sully* (Paris: Union Féderaliste Inter-Universitaire, 1954).

87. For example, in the middle of the nineteenth century Lord Brougham, expounding the principles of the balance of power, asserted that "all particular interests, prejudices, or partialities must be sacrificed to the higher interest, indeed the
paramount duty, of uniting against oppression or against the measures which appear
to place the security of all in jeopardy," since a threat to the security of one country would be a threat to all. Gareau, *op. cit.*, p. 72. For a lucid discussion of the
similarity and difference between theories of the balance of power and of collective
security, see Claude, *op. cit.*, pp. 75–149, especially pp. 123ff.

88. This view appears in the oft-quoted passage from Rousseau's "Extrait du
projet de paix perpétuelle de M. l'Abbé de Saint Pierre," reprinted in Gareau, *op.
cit.*, pp. 22–23. See also Lord Henry Brougham's analogy of the balance of power
to the motions of planets, *ibid.*, p. 66. Rousseau's position was intended to support
his argument that the confederation of states in Saint Pierre's plan would not be
dominated by the hegemony of one state. But elsewhere in the *Extrait* and in other
writings he stressed the precarious, tumultuous, and violent nature of the balance of
power system, however necessary it might be.

only occasionally, when a Continental state or alliance obviously threatened traditional British interests, such as the independence of the Lowlands. Either position could be reconciled with the familiar view of Britain as an impartial holder of the balance, adding to one scale or the other as the equilibrium required. But Continental observers wryly noted that British advocacy of this role applied only to the Continent, not to Britain's involvement overseas, where dominance, not balance, seemed to be the goal.

Eighteenth-century theorists, in the popular Newtonian mathematical and mechanical metaphors of the time, were particularly given to figurative exaggerations of the orderliness of the balancing process. Even proponents of the limited conception of the balance of power claimed a regularity, precision, and efficacy for the balancing process which raised it to the status of a general operating principle in political affairs.

Not surprisingly, advocates of both the limited and comprehensive conceptions were inclined to see a close correspondence between their own nation's interest in the balance and the good of all states. If the self-serving uses to which equilibrium theory was put make it suspect, the evidence of the actual behavior of states compels skepticism toward any but the most modest claims for it as a description of reality. In practice, one must regard the balance of power principle as a laissez-faire theory of international order, since it has been adduced to justify the pursuit of immediate national interests rather than their subordination to a universal interest. The prevailing assumption has not been that states either should or consciously do seek a balance of power between themselves and rivals, but that they normally do and should seek to maximize their power for territorial and commercial aggrandizement or for security. The resulting opposition of competing drives for power, not the abstract preferences of states for equilibrium, was supposed to result in a mutually restraining balance. Each state, simply by following its selfish inclinations, would work for the benefit of all, as long as it remained perpetually vigilant, diplomatically flexible, and ready to intervene against any disturbance of the equilibrium which threatened its interests. Thus the balance of power was a prescription for free enterprise in international politics. To be sure, the preservation of the balance was often effectively invoked as a principle requiring military intervention beyond the needs of security and as a principle governing territorial compensations and an equitable division of the spoils of conquest, as in the partitions of Poland; but, except to moderate aggrandizement, it was not invoked as a dictate of self-denial or reciprocal restraint.

Significantly, the balance of power was often invoked as a justification for war but was not acclaimed as a deterrent to war. Its principal contributions to international order were held to be the maintenance of the independence and integrity of at least the half-dozen or so major states and the prevention of any major state's gaining too much at the expense of another. Although equilibrium theorists might deplore the wastefulness and inhumanity of war and argue its growing futility, they generally regarded even preventive war as a necessary instrument of politics among autonomous states and therefore as an essential means of preserving the balance of power.[89] For the balance of power was viewed as a dynamic and very delicate state of affairs that might be upset by a slight increase of power, a realignment, or a royal death, marriage, or succession. Therefore preservation of the balance depended on continual attention to shifts of power and interest and on perpetual readiness to act with force as well as with diplomacy. No exponent of the balance of power expected that in the prevailing diplomatic turmoil an equilibrium could be maintained by peaceful means alone.

But, equally significant, before the French Revolution none thought that war would be so intense and volatile as to disturb the international order greatly. Even decades after the French Revolution, Lord Brougham, taking note of the many wars and conquests the balancing system had produced in the last century, could write,

> But had it not been for that wholesome jealousy of rival neighbors, which modern politicians have learned to cherish, how many conquests and changes of dominion would have taken place, instead of wars, in which some lives were lost, not, perhaps, the most valuable in the community, and some superfluous millions were squandered! How many fair portions of the globe might have been deluged in blood, instead of some hundreds of sailors fighting harmlessly on the barren plains of the ocean, and some thousands of soldiers carrying on a scientific, and regular, and quiet system of warfare in countries set apart for the purpose, and resorted to as the arena where the disputes of nations might be determined![90]

89. Note, for example, Fénelon's justification of preventive war: "One must count on what is real and happens every day, which is that each nation seeks to prevail over all the others that surround it. Each nation is therefore obliged to be unceasingly watchful in order to prevent the excessive enlargement of each neighbor, for his own safety. To prevent the neighbor from being too powerful is not at all to do evil; it is to protect oneself from slavery and likewise to protect one's other neighbors. In a word, it is to work for liberty, for tranquility, for the public well-being; for the aggrandizement of a nation beyond a certain limit changes the general system of all the nations that have a connection with it. . . . Thus each prince is justified and obliged to prevent in his neighbor that increase in power which throws his people and all the other neighboring peoples in an immediate danger of slavery without remedy. . . . This attention to maintaining a kind of equality and equilibrium among neighboring nations is what assures their common peace." Fénelon, "Supplément à l'examen de conscience," in *Écrits et lettres politiques*, pp. 80–81, 83.

90. Gareau, *op. cit.*, pp. 62–63.

Before the Napoleonic Wars it was generally assumed that military power was so limited, so evenly distributed among states, and so readily balanced by alliances that warfare was becoming progressively more inconclusive, if not altogether useless. Thus Montesquieu, writing in 1734, reasoned that no nation could gain dominance in Europe because: (1) new discoveries equalized the power of all nations; (2) a military advantage could no longer gain the benefits of conquest, since international law forbade sacking, looting, and otherwise exploiting captured territory; (3) wars were fought by so many men that countries were exhausted by them; (4) prosperity depended on trade and industry, not on conquest.[91]

Similarly, Rousseau argued against the possibility of preponderance.

All conquerors who have instigated great upheavals have always opposed with unexpectedly great forces, or with foreign and differently armed troops, disarmed, divided, and undisciplined peoples. But where could a European prince obtain the unexpected forces to crush all the other princes, since the most powerful among them is such a small part of the whole, and since by mutual consent they are so vigilant? Will he have more troops than all the others? He cannot, or he will be only ruined the sooner by it, or the troops would be inferior because of their large numbers. Will he have better disciplined troops? He would then have proportionally fewer troops. Moreover, discipline is everywhere about the same, or it soon becomes so. Will he have more money? The sources of it are common to all, and money has never won great conquests. . . .

If we consider the waste of men, money, and forces of all kinds and the exhaustion which the most successful war causes any state and compare these losses with the benefits which are derived from it, we shall find that war often results in losses when one believes that it has resulted in gains and that the victor, always weaker than before the war, has only the consolation of seeing the vanquished weaker than himself. This advantage is less real than apparent, because the superiority which the victor achieves over his adversary is at the same time lost in respect to neutral powers, which without changing their condition, are strengthened in respect to the victor by every diminution of his strength.[92]

Thanks to the inherent constraints on force, the balance of power did operate in a limited way. Throughout most of the eighteenth and nineteenth centuries, there really was a sufficiently effective opposition of military power among competing states to preserve the independence of the great states while restricting their ambitions and preventing any of them from attaining preponderance. Moreover, in a sense this was the

91. *Réflections sur la monarchie universelle en Europe.*
92. "Extrait du projet de paix perpétuelle de M. l'Abbé de Saint Pierre," as quoted in Gareau, *op. cit.*, pp. 22, 24.

unintended, though not strictly speaking automatic, result of states pursuing their special interests within a system of international politics that translated the selfishness of all into the general welfare. For governments ordinarily sought superiority over opponents and would often have preferred to partition or otherwise eliminate their competitors but were constrained by countervailing power to accept the conditions of equilibrium and, at times, to make a virtue of necessity.

The operation of the balance was far from perfect or precisely mechanical. Thus the role of balancer, to which the British laid special claim, was from time to time played by several different states, but by no means consistently according to the ostensible rule of supporting the weaker side of the scale.[93] Yet contrary to a common contention of skeptics, the difficulty of measuring exactly the relative power of states did not invalidate the concept. The limited conception of the balance of power required only that states react to opposing power with sufficient perception to recognize a threat to their vital interests and with sufficient vigilance to restrain it with countervailing power. In dividing the spoils of conquest and making a formal settlement of war, it required only that states agree upon a configuration of territory and alignments that would prevent one party or another from gaining too great an advantage. These were not tasks beyond the comprehension or ingenuity of statesmen.

Nevertheless, the generally successful operation of the balance of power (measured by its two principal objectives, the independence and the mutual restraint of major states) was due as much to the fortuitous limitation and distribution of power as to the acumen of statesmen. The play of chance was as marked as the designs of states. Until the consolidation of alliances after the Franco-Prussian War, the balance of power was an unstable equilibrium, extremely susceptible to minor disturbances by unanticipated developments. It was accompanied by continual diplomatic turmoil, by frequent miscalculations of the configurations of power and interests and how they would be affected by moves on the international chessboard, by repeated shifts of alignment, and, in the eighteenth century, by chronic succession crises, all of which

93. For example, under Palmerston's leadership Britain supported the power in the strongest position to help special British interests, aligning with France against the autocratic powers in the Belgian crisis and in the Iberian peninsula during the 1830s but lining up with the autocratic governments against France in the Near East settlement in 1840. During the Bismarckian period Britain associated itself with the Triple Alliance, which dominated the Continent. In the last part of the nineteenth century, fearing an opposing Continental combination, Britain viewed with disfavor the Franco-Russian Alliance, although this alliance established an equilibrium that left England at the theoretical fulcrum.

took governments by surprise and precipitated chains of compensatory moves. The balancing process generated a pervasive mutual suspicion and distrust, perpetual uncertainty, and, especially in its eighteenth-century heyday, profound frustration among those who aspired to master the diplomatic maze.

Thus Frederick the Great, who sought to rationalize politics into a science, became sadly resigned in his later years to the continual interference of chance—frequently in the form of dynastic successions, deaths, or marriages—with his diplomatic stratagems and alliances.[94] In his Political Testament of 1768 he complained, "A frequently deceptive art of conjecture serves as foundation for most of the great political designs. One takes as one's point of departure the most certain factor one knows of, combines it, as well as one can, with other factors, but imperfectly known, and draws therefrom the most correct conclusions possible." Citing instances in which a variety of unforeseen events had upset prospective diplomatic bargains, he declared, "A similar uncertainty, although every time in another form, dominates all operations of foreign policy so that great alliances have often a result contrary to the one planned by their members."[95] It is not surprising that Count Kaunitz of Austria, who boasted of an "arithmetical method" of diplomacy—a "political algebra"—which would enable him to eliminate surprise and reduce political risk to negligible proportions, failed in his major diplomatic project: the recovery of Silesia. He failed partly because of diplomatic miscalculations preceding the Seven Years' War and partly because of fortuitous circumstances, particularly the death of Tsarina Elizabeth, which broke the Austro-Russian alliance against Prussia.[96]

As long as war was generally taken for granted as a method of coping with shifting interests and power, as long as states were willing to use force for limited ends when the margins of relative power were slight and the promise of victory uncertain, diplomatic surprises and ambiguities were ripe with the prospect of violence. Furthermore, the balance of power preserved international order not only at the price of diplomatic turmoil and warfare but also at the price of continual intervention in the internal affairs of states—intervention by bribery, subsidies, coups, and subversion, as well as by armed invasions. In addition, territorial compensations at the expense of the small states in Europe

94. Frederick II, *History of My Own Times*, and Friedrich Meinecke, *Machiavellism* (London: Routledge & Kegan Paul, 1957).
95. Quoted in Morgenthau, *Politics Among Nations*, p. 187.
96. Peter R. Rohden, *Die Klassische Diplomatie, von Kaunitz bis Metternich* (Leipzig: Koeler & Amelang, 1939). See also Dorn, *op. cit.*, pp. 137, 296–97.

and the nations and peoples outside Europe were one of the principal devices for preserving the major power balance.

Perhaps international politics would have been still more tumultuous and violent if there had not been a certain sense of kinship and cultural affinity among the ruling classes of Europe—a feeling that Europe was a single society. Remnants of such a sentiment survived the nationalist revolutions and lingered even until World War I. Yet if one assesses the actual operation of the balance of power in the period from Utrecht to World War I with an unnostalgic view, one must give more credence to the contemporaneous skeptics and critics of the system than to those who attributed the degree of prevailing international order to a transcendent sense of community or to the beneficent workings of an unseen hand.

Much of this period, including the years just before the wars of the French Revolution and just before World War I, seemed like a time of unexampled order to many contemporary observers. But this was primarily because the consolidation of the internal power of the state fostered domestic order and permitted immense material and considerable social and political progress, and because the impact of crises and warfare upon the lives of the citizenry was moderated by the limited nature of military power, the fairly even distribution of power among several major states, the facility with which alliances were made and unmade for reasons of state, and the natural tendency, under the circumstances, of the pursuit of power to result in mutually restraining counterpoises. Under these conditions the constant flux and agitation of international politics and the assumption that war was a normal extension of politics fostered a vigilance, a constant concern for the active management of power, that was crucial to the maintenance of a restraining equilibrium. Correspondingly, when peace and tranquility seemed to emerge as a normal state of affairs during the period from 1871 to 1914—when successive crises were readily surmounted with a flurry of diplomatic notes and mere hints of force—the very confidence in stability contributed to its breakdown in general war.

14. Deterrence as a Basis of Order

If the desire for peace had been less popular during the period of defensive alliances from 1871 to 1914, the international order would have been less stable; if the fear of war had been more compelling, peace might better have been preserved. World War I showed that in the age of modern military power the maintenance of international order put a new premium on the avoidance of war. Yet the period of Fascist ascent after World War I showed that the prerequisite of order remained the conspicuous will, backed by the capacity, to make war.

Both the avoidance of war and the will to make war imply a scrupulous political control over military power and a deliberate skill in exploiting its political and psychological uses. After World War I the defensive powers lacked the acumen and determination to master the uses of force short of war. They failed to grasp the full implications of military deterrence until after a second world war.

The expansion of military power at the end of the nineteenth century, by giving new significance to military deterrence, also altered the function of alliances in maintaining international order. The eighteenth century had been a period of acquisitive politics and offensive alliances not of deterrent alliances, but it was a period in which war could still be regarded as a normal means of preserving an equilibrium. The alliance policies that served the ends of states under these conditions were less compatible with equilibrium when the changing political and military environment in the decades immediately before and after World War I put a premium upon defensive security and the avoidance of war. Furthermore, the popularization of military power undermined the political and psychological conditions of the relatively flexible alliance system that could flourish when reason of state needed little or no public justification.

Even before the post-Bismarckian decades, however, a reaction to the eighteenth-century system of alliances had set in. The several treaties arranging the settlement following the defeat of Napoleon marked a deliberate effort by the victorious coalition powers to combine the eighteenth-century conception of equilibrium, as manifested in the territorial-political settlements and the Quadruple Alliance, with a quite different conception of the organization of countervailing power. This was the conception of a multilateral group of states pledged to concert power in order to preserve an international order—in this case, to preserve the order implicit in the Holy Alliance against liberal and nationalist revolutionary disturbances. Yet events soon demonstrated a political truth that would be underlined by the experience of the League of Nations and the United Nations after two other general wars: The interests of several major states are not likely to be sufficiently homogeneous to sustain for long an alliance capable of policing the world with preponderant power.

British foreign ministers Castlereagh and Canning assumed the chief burden of opposing the Holy Alliance by refusing to join the collective suppression of revolutions in Spain, Italy, Greece, and Latin America. Regardless of British policies, however, it would soon have become apparent that there was no political consensus among the great powers capable of supporting a collective guardianship of the European order. Therefore the return of the great states of Europe to a fragmented structure of power, in which order depended upon the improvisation of counterweights by alignments among states with divergent interests, was only a reaffirmation of political realities that had been temporarily obscured in some quarters by the reaction to the Napoleonic Wars.

The period from 1818 to 1856 saw a significant modification of laissez-faire politics in the general observation of the principle that all the major states, by virtue of their power, interdependence, and common interest in a modicum of order, have a responsibility to preserve an equilibrium—at least to the extent of consulting in advance of unilateral changes. But even this germ of international regulation expired in the emergence of a new system of alliances.

For a while after the Congress of Vienna, flexibility of alignments, together with the habit of international consultation, contributed to the peaceful resolution of crises. But we have seen how Bismarck's quick, decisive victories against diplomatically isolated Austria and France led to the breakdown of his own delicate system of balanced antagonisms and to the consolidation of defensive military alliances. This tended to harden enmities and increase tensions, and it entailed a greater risk of a catalytic war precipitated by an ally demanding military support. Yet when the balance of power came to depend more upon what is now called military deterrence and crisis management, the clarification and stability of commitments resulting from the consolidation of alliances was, on the whole, more compatible with order than the diplomatic flux and ambiguity of an earlier period would have been.

Unfortunately, however, the governments of Europe, still under the spell of traditional military politics, were less concerned with deterrence than with getting ready to fight. Worse still, the military plans and policies they adopted tended to foreclose opportunities for avoiding general war. Yet these deficiencies were not inevitable. They were eminently avoidable. Fundamentally, the trouble was that governments were preoccupied with a strategic doctrine and a concept of military efficiency that were oriented wholly toward gaining a rapid victory through the application of maximum offensive force. Further, they were dazed by an associated military bravado and romanticism when they should have been attending to the growing need for systematic control and limitation of the new military potential, in peacetime as well as in war. It was all the more tragic, therefore, that, in the face of the far more obvious need for military deterrence imposed by postwar Fascist expansionism, the prewar alliance system was widely regarded as the principal enemy of international order while the real lessons of peace-time military planning and deterrence were neglected.

Peacetime military competition, disparaged by the designation "arms races," shared the unjustified ill repute of military coalitions. To be sure, competitive armament, like all forms of competition in military power, including the forming and disbanding of alliances, tended to create insecurities and provoke countermeasures that might lead to war. But it was also well suited to the maintenance of a restraining balance of power short of war. Arms races were particularly well adapted to mili-tary deterrence, since they enabled potential adversaries who wished to avoid war to compete by internal means without the unsettling effects of shifts of alignment, territorial compensations, domestic interventions, and preventive war. When one or both sides reached a point at which the expense, domestic strain, or external political costs exceeded the expected value of continuing the race, the competition would tend to level off, or one side would abandon the competition. There was as-sumed to be a danger point at which the state being challenged might resort to preventive war rather than lose its superiority,[97] but in fact this danger was exaggerated, as was the danger that a technological break-through would tempt one side or the other to launch a war.

Undoubtedly the British naval competition with France and with Germany before World War I, and to a lesser extent the postwar naval rivalry of Britain, the U.S., and Japan, accentuated international ten-sions. But they did not lead to war. In the first two cases they led to amicable informal cessations of competition, and in the latter case, to a peaceful settlement through disarmament and political accommoda-tion. It was not an arms race but the failure of Britain and France to engage in an arms race soon enough that contributed so much to the failure of deterrence after World War I and the outbreak of World War II.

In the interwar period, as before, the prerequisite of international order in the face of an expansionist power seeking hegemony was the formation of a military coalition capable of checking that power. But the difference was that in the twentieth century the organization of such countervailing power required a peacetime defensive alliance and a steady competition in arms, without which the states interested

97. Thus Admiral Tirpitz reasoned that during Germany's naval expansion there would be a "danger zone" in which the British would have a special temptation to undertake a preventive war rather than see Germany achieve the ratio posited in his "risk theory." Indeed, there was talk of such action in Britain, especially among the military, but it never gained popular or official support. On the notion and practice of preventive war at this and other times, see Vagts, *Defense and Diplomacy*, chap. viii.

in order lacked the prerequisites of deterrence and the effective peace-time management of force. Above all, a salutary equilibrium required governments to maintain effective control of military plans, policies, and forces; to manage military power with the constant attention to mutual restraint that statesmen in the eighteenth century devoted to the immediate conditions of aggrandizement and security; and to regard their military establishments warily as potentially uncontrollable instruments of excessive violence, which must nevertheless serve an indispensable role short of war.

15. Regulatory and Systemic Concepts of Order

With the wisest control of military power and under the most favorable circumstances, there is bound to be a fortuitous element in any balance of power. The danger that some unanticipated imbalance will lead to war is implicit in any international order that rests on the power of some states checking the power of others and in which the only governing principle of state action is the independent pursuit of immediate interests.

One way to mitigate this danger is to temper laissez faire with what might be called "regulatory" methods of controlling military power—that is, with contrived tacit and formal reciprocal restraints on armaments and their use. The age in which states could safely rely upon purely inherent limits on force to preserve a tolerable international order passed with the emergence of modern military power at the end of the nineteenth century. The effective regulation of military power, however, cannot spring from a simple antimilitarism. It demands continual studied attention to the development, control, and use of force. Unfortunately, in the aftermath of World War I the popular search for order led in the opposite direction—toward systemic concepts of order purporting to downgrade or eliminate military power and to transform the political system within which it operates.

The most influential systemic concept was Wilsonian collective security. In theory this might be regarded as a concept of military deterrence, designed to confront any bid for domination with an overwhelming concert of power.[98] As actually applied, however, the concept

98. A British general, Sir Frederick Maurice, compared the deterrent efficacy of collective security with the balance of power systems in these terms:
The efforts of European statesmen (formerly) were directed to securing peace by organizing a balance of military power sufficiently exact to make the risk of attack by the group in one scale upon the group in the other prohibitive. This procedure failed. . . . The Covenant of the League of Nations endeavors to find a better guarantee against war by substituting for the small group of Powers a

was a substitute for the indispensable condition of deterrence—military alliance and preparedness. Advocates of collective security held that international order depended on the replacement of the bankrupt balance-of-power system with a community of power in which all states would deter war and aggression by pledging themselves to bring their collective power to bear against any state that used force against the rules of the community. They stressed the need for a universal, permanent international commitment of force against unspecified enemies, as opposed to haphazard alliances among particular friends against specific adversaries. Yet they generally ignored the problem of backing up such a sweeping commitment with the organized force of arms. They hoped that the moral pressure of public opinion, supplemented by the threat of economic sanctions, would be a sufficient deterrent to aggression.[99]

The efficacy of collective security depended in reality on the credibility of a pledge by all the great states to fight any aggressor, regardless of the implications of aggression for their immediate interests. But the deterrent effect of any such pledge was nullified by the requirement that states subordinate their own military interests to an imaginary supranational consensus and by the impossibility of states with conflicting interests reaching a common definition of "aggression."[100] It was equally nullified by the revulsion toward and depreciation of organized force

---

single group so large that its authority cannot be challenged with impunity. The Balance of Power is replaced by the Concert or Concentration of Power.

The guarantees . . . promise to make an attempt by any one state or group of states to win by force the power to dominate its neighbors far more dangerous to its originators than it has been in the past. The war of nations which was a development arising out of the balance of power, will tend under the concentration of power to become less and less possible and may eventually become impossible.

A *History of the Peace Conference of Paris*, ed. Harold Temperly, VI (London: 1924), 525, 533, as quoted in Claude, *op. cit.*, p. 112.

99. There had been many advocates of a league, as in the wartime League to Enforce Peace, who rejected a supranational concept and held a realistic view of the role of force; see Ruhl J. Bartlett, *The League to Enforce Peace* (Chapel Hill: University of North Carolina Press, 1944). But after President Wilson adopted the league idea as a war aim, his views carried the day among the league supporters in the U.S. and abroad. On President Wilson's concept of the league and the fallacy of interpretations representing him as a covert balance-of-power advocate, see Robert E. Osgood, "Woodrow Wilson, Collective Security, and the Lessons of History," *The Philosophy and Policies of Woodrow Wilson*, ed. Earl Latham (Chicago: University of Chicago Press, 1958). See also Laurence W. Martin, *Peace Without Victory: Woodrow Wilson and the British Liberals* (New Haven: Yale University Press, 1958), and Henry R. Winkler, *The League of Nations Movement in Great Britain, 1914–1919* (New Brunswick, N.J.: Rutgers University Press, 1952).

100. The futile attempt to define aggression in the League and the United Nations and the political reasons for it are examined in Julius Stone, *Aggression and World Order* (Berkeley: University of California Press, 1958).

which dominated the international outlook of the most ardent advocates of collective security. Consequently, although the concept of collective security, especially in England, served as an excuse for not forming military alliances or keeping up in the arms competition, it did not deter the disturbers of international order. Quite the contrary.

The depreciation of countervailing force as an instrument of order was also manifested in popular support for disarmament.[101] In theory, disarmament was perfectly compatible with a regulatory concept of controlling military power. Actually, when specific international agreements were under consideration, governments did approach disarmament as arms regulation rather than international reform, although they were also eager to exploit arms negotiations for propaganda and political warfare. Governments were interested in limiting arms in order to save money and yet maintain their military security, or, if they could get away with it, even improve their military position. Yet, like collective security, disarmament had the aura of a panacea promising to transform the role of force. As one of the pillars of a new international order, it was widely regarded as a crucial test of the League's success.[102] Moreover, its idealistic appeal was supplemented by its popularity, in the economic straits of the postwar period, as a means of holding down taxes. Therefore governments deferred to popular sentiment and presented disarmament as a painless way to achieve peace by doing away with arms. In taking this position, they became in varying degrees the victims of their own rhetoric.[103]

101. Disarmament is used here as a generic term to include all measures taken by formal international agreement to control, limit, reduce, or eliminate the development, manufacture, deployment, transfer, possession, or use of weapons and military facilities, resources, and personnel. Disarmament projects, proposals, negotiations, and even a few agreements occur throughout the period since the Peace of Westphalia; but disarmament was not adopted as a major program by peace movements until the latter part of the nineteenth century and was not in the forefront of diplomacy as a governmental as well as a popular concern until the two Hague conferences and after World War I. For the early history of disarmament, see Hans Wehberg, *The Limitation of Armaments* (Washington: Carnegie Endowment for International Peace, 1921), and Merze Tate, *The Disarmament Illusion* (New York: Macmillan, 1942).

102. The history of the disarmament effort under the auspices of the League is dealt with in Francis P. Walters, *A History of The League of Nations* (2 vols.; London: Oxford University Press, 1952).

103. Disarmament sentiment was strongest in the U.S. and Britain, where liberal international reform movements and the sense of insular security thrived. At the outset there was a division of opinion between states advocating direct disarmament (principally Britain), who claimed that arms were a principal cause of international tension and should be reduced before political guarantees and alliances were formed, and states advocating the indirect approach (chiefly France and other Continental countries that felt vulnerable to an attack by Germany), who maintained that insecurity was the cause of armaments and should be overcome with political guar-

The contribution of disarmament to international order would not have been promising anyway, considering its inherent limitations and the determination of the totalitarian powers to gain military superiority for aggressive ends. Nevertheless, it was reasonable, given the new volatility and magnitude of military power and the new importance of arms competition, to suppose that states might reciprocally limit this instrument of policy to their mutual advantage. There were precedents for this in the Rush-Bagot Treaty (1817), limiting warships on the Great Lakes, and in the Argentine-Chilean naval agreement of 1902, not to mention a number of treaties restricting or prohibiting arms, armed forces, and military installations in sensitive zones.[104]

The Washington Naval Treaties (1921–22) scarcely deserve the onus they acquired in a later period of disillusionment.[105] Unlike the two Hague Conferences in 1899 and 1907, which originated in purely national and tactical considerations and turned into farcical encounters of incompatible purposes poorly concealed by pious pretensions,[106] the

---

antees as a condition of disarmament. The League's Temporary Mixed Commission on disarmament reached a compromise, stating that guarantees to assist any Continental nation attacked should come into effect when arms reductions were made. However, the assembly did not endorse this compromise, and a Treaty of Mutual Assistance submitted to states in and out of the League was accepted only by France and Italy among the major states. France then felt free to go ahead with her alliance policy, and the League's Preparatory Commission for the Disarmament Conference, responding to popular pressure, pursued the direct approach to disarmament.

104. The Rush-Bagot Treaty, actually an exchange of notes between British Minister Bagot and Secretary of State Rush, which was later approved by the Senate, set quantitative and qualitative limits on warships on the Great Lakes, prescribed the dismantling of other vessels, and prohibited building or arming other ships on the lakes. On the circumstances preceding the agreement and its subsequent history, see Charles H. Levermore, "The Anglo-American Agreement of 1817 for Disarmament on the Great Lakes," *World Peace Foundation*, Vol. IV (June, 1914), pamphlet No. 4. The Argentine-Chilean Treaty pledged the two powers not to acquire new naval vessels, including those being built; to reduce their fleets within one year to a just balance; not to increase naval armaments for five years without giving eighteen months' notice; and to prohibit fortification of coasts and ports, as well as the construction of submarines or other vessels designed to defend them. It also provided for the adjustment of all disputes by arbitration.

105. The Washington Naval Treaties included the Five-Power Treaty (U.S., Britain, Japan, France, and Italy), establishing a ten-year holiday on the construction of new capital ships and a 5:5:3:1.75:1.75 ratio in capital ship tonnage; Article XIX, prohibiting new fortifications or bases in the Pacific; the Four-Power Treaty, superseding the Anglo-Japanese Alliance with a multilateral agreement in which the three great naval powers and France agreed to respect each other's rights in insular possession in the Pacific and to consult on disputes between any two signatories; and the Nine-Power Treaty reaffirming the Open Door principle.

106. On the first Hague Conference, see Calvin DeArmond Davis, *The United States and the First Hague Peace Conference* (Ithaca: Cornell University Press, 1962). On the second Hague Conference, see Merze Tate, *op. cit.*, chap. xv.

Washington Conference was a serious effort to accommodate conflicting interests and stabilize spheres of influence in the Pacific while avoiding expensive and provocative naval expenditures. The U.S. conceded nothing that it would not have granted anyway. Even the fortification of Guam and the Philippines, which Congress was not prepared to undertake, would not have enabled the U.S. to uphold the Open Door against determined Japanese opposition. With sufficient vigilance, a willingness to build up to prescribed limits as well as to compete in unrestricted weapons, and a readiness to meet violations with countermeasures, the U.S., in close co-operation with Britain, might have extended the useful life of this arrangement—but only as a supplement to, not a substitute for, an active program of deterrence. Yet the nation, having embraced the agreement on antimilitary grounds and isolationist assumptions, was in no mood to involve itself in the active management of military power to preserve a Pacific balance. Consequently, Japan was permitted to exploit disarmament so as to advance its special Asian interests at the expense of American and British interests in the Far East and, eventually, at the expense of American security and world peace.[107]

A more sober view of disarmament as a supplement to military security would have served international order better, but it would also have recognized that the utility of disarmament is limited by substantial obstacles to mutually acceptable agreements.

One obstacle is simply that mutually advantageous restrictions are rare between states whose antagonisms have led to an arms race, since the conflicting interests that occasion their competition are likely to be more compelling than any common interest in stopping it. This is not to say, as a familiar criticism of disarmament holds, that the prerequisite of disarmament is necessarily a resolution of the political conflict underlying the competition in arms. In the first place, the arms competition may itself be the major obstacle to accommodation because it is the major medium, if not the fundamental cause, of the political conflict, as in the case of the competitions that led to the Rush-Bagot agreement, the Argentine-Chilean agreement, and the London Naval Treaty of 1930. In the second place, arms agreements may initially reflect only a partial accommodation, not a resolution, of underlying conflicts of interest, as in the case of the Washington Naval Treaties and virtually every other arms agreement. The chief obstacle to mutually advantageous disarmament is simply that, typically, one side or both believe that they can obtain a more advantageous ratio of power through unrestricted

107. For an extended exposition of this interpretation of the Washington Naval Treaties, see Robert E. Osgood, *Ideals and Self-Interest in America's Foreign Relations* (Chicago: University of Chicago Press, 1953), pp. 333–46.

competition and are therefore unwilling to forego this advantage, except perhaps in return for political compensations, which the competitor is apt to be unwilling to grant.

Even if two signatories are agreed upon a satisfactory ratio of power between them, they may fear that the limitation will disadvantage them in relation to a nonsignatory. Yet to find a common ground for restrictions among all states with related military ratios is only to compound the difficulty of accommodating the interests of two.

Furthermore, to try to fix a satisfactory ratio of power that depends on many related weapons and forces and upon continual technological innovations and improvements is either to undertake the unmanageable task of restricting all significant present and future weapons systems or else to take the easier path of restricting only a portion of the total armaments at the risk that continued innovations and competition in related weapons will upset the intended balance. Thus the limitation on battleships in the Washington Naval Treaties helped channel naval expenditures into cruiser competition, which threatened to upset the balance underlying the specified big-three naval ratios. Similarly, the construction of submarines and destroyers threatened to nullify the effects of battleship limitations.

This difficulty was greatly accentuated by the increasing complexity and diversity of interrelated weapons, the high rate of military inventions and improvements, the growing fusion of civilian and military technology, and the greater importance of research and development, production capacity, and military training. Interwar disarmament efforts did not begin to cope with these various aspects of modern military power.

There was widespread fear in the 1920s of the secret development of decisive new weapons, especially poison gas. Yet aside from the protocol to the Geneva Disarmament Convention (1925) forbidding the use of poisonous and asphyxiating gases and bacteriological weapons (ratified by forty states but not by Japan and the U.S.), there was practically no effort between the two world wars to apply disarmament to the problem of technological innovations.

The difficulty of distinguishing civilian from military technology was particularly great with respect to chemical weapons and airplanes. Germany's illegal rearmament in the 1920s capitalized on the difficulty of distinguishing private and commercial activities from military weapons, training, production, and development.[108]

108. Germany used civilian flying (especially gliding) clubs to train military pilots, only thirty-six of whom were permitted by the Versailles Treaty. After 1926, when Germany was permitted to have commercial aviation, the heavily subsidized

Disarmament proposals did not come to grips with the problem of military resources that could be developed in war (called "war potential") in the interwar period, as opposed to forces-in-being (called "peace potential"). Germany argued that France's large peacetime forces gave it an unfair advantage, but France argued that Germany's small peacetime forces enabled it to enhance its superior war potential, based on a more numerous population, new machine tools, and other advantages. Both arguments were reasonable yet purely tactical, since Germany was determined to rearm and France was determined to preserve its military superiority.

All these obstacles to arms agreements are related to another one, which has also grown increasingly formidable with the modernization of military power: the fundamental ambiguity of the relationship of specific weapons and forces to military security and other national interests. When does a state have sufficient military power in relation to a rival? The ultimate test of sufficiency is successful combat; but as the components of military power became more numerous, as more new weapons untried in battle were introduced, and as the potential intensity and volatility of warfare increased, the relative strength of a nation's armed forces in combat became harder to calculate and the penalties of miscalculation more severe. That the test of military power was increasingly dependent on the political and psychological uses of force short of war only complicated the problem of measuring sufficiency by introducing into technical calculations the obscure interactions of many imponderable factors that might affect the behavior of states facing the risks of war.

Given the ambiguity of military sufficiency, statesmen were naturally reluctant to commit their countries in a solemn treaty to an estimate that might turn out to be wrong—or at least look wrong. Furthermore, an arms agreement, by revealing and prescribing armaments, might hinder governments from capitalizing upon the ambiguity of their military power in the eyes of other governments in order to gain some increment of security, influence, or prestige that the realities of power did not justify. In any case, governments faced with doubts about the sufficiency of their military power were understandably inclined to seek

---

Lufthansa was set up. By 1927 it had 6 training schools organized on military lines turning out 100 trained pilots annually. Similarly, tractors served as prototypes for tanks. Many factories that were converted to civilian manufacture could be readily reconverted. Hans W. Gatzke's writings are particularly informative on German rearmament: *Stresemann and the Rearmament of Germany* (Baltimore: The Johns Hopkins Press, 1954), and "Russian-German Military Collaboration During the Weimar Republic," *American Historical Review*, LXIII (April, 1958), 565–97.

a compensatory margin of safety in disarmament that others were, for the same reason, unwilling to grant. Therefore, governments that might be quite content with a particular ratio of power which they were free to alter unilaterally without regard to a treaty were reluctant to sign an agreement formally limiting themselves to this ratio.

In the almost continual but largely futile disarmament negotiations between the two world wars, the ambiguity of military power was most conspicuous in the technical difficulty of comparing the power of one state with that of another in commensurate and equitable terms. To be sure, this technical difficulty was exaggerated by the form of the disarmament dialogue, since states commonly cloaked their interests in technical arguments in order to convey a high-minded concern for disarmament while putting the onus of opposing it on the other side.[109] But, political tactics aside, the technical obstacles were genuine enough.

Battleships and cruisers, in contrast to land and air forces, were peculiarly susceptible to agreed criteria of measurement and comparison. Their technology had become fairly stable. Their military efficacy was believed to be relatively independent of other weapons. There was general agreement about their military function and tactics, the utility of a given number of ships, and the significance of a relatively few decisive components that determined their military strength. Nevertheless, even between Britain and the U.S.—neither of which was armed against the other, both of which agreed upon "parity," and both of which wanted to reduce naval expenditures—agreement on cruiser limitations proved inordinately difficult because technical complexities exacerbated considerations of prestige.[110]

109. The classic account of the propagandistic and tactical aspects of the interwar disarmament discussions is Salvador de Madariaga, *Disarmament* (New York: Coward-McCann, Inc., 1929).

110. One of the principal difficulties was that, because of different fleet requirements, the British thought they needed more six-inch-gun cruisers than the U.S. needed of eight-inch-gun cruisers, whereas the U.S. wanted an equal number of cruisers. Various formulas based on tonnage, numbers, gun calibers, age, replacement age, etc., were offered to resolve this difficulty. Eventually, at the London Naval Conference of 1930, the U.S. concept of a "yardstick" for measuring the combat strength of cruisers and comparing fleets on the basis of "equivalent naval values" became the basis of a compromise setting limits on both eight-inch and six-inch cruisers. Nevertheless, when the naval limitation treaty came before the Senate for approval, testifying admirals disagreed with each other on the relative combat strength of different kinds of ships and on the military implications of various ratios, and most of them argued that Britain's bases and merchant vessels gave it an advantage under the yardstick formula. The background and substance of the London Naval Treaty of 1930 are examined in Raymond G. O'Connor, *Perilous Equilibrium: The United States and the London Naval Conference of 1930* (Lawrence: University of Kansas Press, 1962).

The technical problems of measuring and comparing the strength of land weapons were insurmountable. These problems resulted from the many different weapons involved, their extensive interdependence, the many determinants of the combat strength of particular weapons, the dynamic nature of the technology, the decisive importance of the method of using land forces, and the fact that the same weapons served different tactical and strategic functions for different states. The importance of military personnel and the difficulty of measuring and comparing the combat strength of various categories of personnel—standing forces, reserves, professionals and conscripts, forces with different periods of training, officers and enlisted men, police and irregular forces, logistical and auxiliary forces—posed a special problem. Moreover, land weapons were particularly subject to a difficulty of all arms reductions: An equal numerical or equal percentage reduction usually changes the military significance of a given ratio of forces.

In an effort to by-pass these problems, budgetary limitations were suggested and discussed, but the U.S. and others objected that budgetary limits would not control production, that they could be easily violated, and that they were contrary to constitutional procedures. Germany protested that budgetary limits discriminated in favor of France, which already had large stocks of war materiel. The U.S. claimed a special inequity by virtue of its high rate of pay to soldiers. Besides, budgetary methods, it was discovered, varied too much from government to government to permit acceptable bases of comparison. At the World Disarmament Conference in 1932 a distinction between offensive—which implied aggressive—and defensive weapons was introduced; but this only obscured the problem of measurement and comparison, as each delegation strained its ingenuity to formulate definitions that would favor the weapons in which its country was strongest or most needy.

The limitation of air vehicles suffered the added difficulties that military aircraft was a particularly fast-changing technology and that nations had scarcely any relevant wartime experience with it. In the Hague Conferences the delegates readily adopted, on humanitarian grounds, a prohibition against dropping explosives from air vehicles, since no one saw any military value to balloons, nor did they grasp the importance of strategic bombing. By the time of the Washington Conference of 1922, however, it was generally recognized that aircraft were important weapons in their infancy and that major unpredictable advances lay ahead. Admiral Lord Fisher in Britain and Admiral Sims in the U.S. thought that the battleship was doomed to obsolescence by the development of aircraft as well as submarines, and airpower enthusiasts like General William Mitchell would make this supposition an article of faith. Consequently, no agreement upon limiting aircraft was possible, although various criteria of combat strength were discussed, from numbers of vehicles, their horsepower and lift tonnage, to numbers of personnel. The League disarmament study commissions grappled in vain with the problem of distinguishing civilian from military aircraft. But throughout the protracted discussions of naval limitations, including restrictions on aircraft carriers, there was no attempt to take into account the possible impact of aircraft upon naval strength.

All the political and technical obstacles to mutual agreement on arms restrictions—in which, it should be noted, the problem of inspection (or "supervision," as it was called) hardly figured—were roughly proportionate to the diversity of weapons systems, the complexity of their interdependence, the rate of technological innovation, and the absence of relevant battlefield experience. And each of these complicating factors was accentuated in the interwar period. Consequently, although the hypothetical utility of disarmament as a supplement to military security may have increased, so did the practical obstacles to disarmament. Before the modernization of military power, when the reciprocal limitation of arms would have been relatively easy, the incentive was negligible. With the expansion of military power after the middle of the nineteenth century, when the incentive became great, the practical difficulty was immense.

Yet, ironically, the chief trouble with disarmament efforts in the interwar period was not the technical-political difficulties that seemed to preoccupy governments but the overriding fact that arms limitation, in the absence of an effective concerted military deterrent to totalitarian expansion, only encouraged the breakdown of an international order for which disarmament was supposed to be indispensable. The British policy of so-called "unilateral disarmament," intended to persuade others to disarm by the power of example, struck the wrong target: the U.S. and France, instead of Germany.[111] By the time this was realized, it was too late to build a deterrent without hastening a war.

As a result, the reciprocal limitation of arms was temporarily discredited by World War II, somewhat as the balance of power and military alliances had been discredited by World War I. In reality, however, the detractors of disarmament and the critics of alliances exaggerated

---

111. Between 1926 and 1931 Britain claimed to be the only major power to have reduced its arms. "Unilateral disarmament" became an article of policy, reinforcing the public impression that Britain was leading the way to peace by her example. On British interwar disarmament policy, see Rolland A. Chaput, *Disarmament in British Foreign Policy* (London: Unwin Bros., 1935). John F. Kennedy's *Why England Slept* is still worth reading on the popular and political background of British disarmament policy, especially as it affected airpower.

the adverse effects of these instrumentalities because they misconceived their proper functions. This misconception, in fact, was the root of the interwar failures of policy. It lay in an approach to force which, having rejected laissez faire and embraced systemic reform (if only in theory), had not yet come to terms with the imperatives of regulating force in an age of rapidly expanding military power.

16. The Changing Attitude Toward Force

In the whole melancholy tale of misadventures accompanying the expansion of force through the period of two world wars, perhaps something as simple yet as imponderable as the prevailing attitude toward force and war affected international order more decisively than the structure and organization of power or the nature of military technology —although, of course, these factors were closely related.

The prevailing attitude toward force did not change as dramatically or as uniformly as military technology; yet there is a tremendous gap between the attitude of the eighteenth century and that of the period following World War I. In the eighteenth century, when the instruments of force were inherently quite limited and power politics was no concern of national publics, war was largely taken for granted as a normal recourse of statecraft. Those who deplored war did so more for its wastefulness, its control by the aristocracy, its cruelty, and its irrationality than for its material destruction of civilian life and its threat to national survival.

The Napoleonic Wars undermined confidence in the orderliness of a supposedly self-regulating balance of power system under the rational direction of enlightened despots and introduced the idea of a concert of power into practical politics. Yet in a decade the wartime concert had given way to the re-establishment of a fluid balance of power system, with the useful addition of customary international consultations.

The Crimean and Franco-Prussian Wars revealed again, in different ways, the fragility of the traditional balance of power system and began another reorientation of attitudes toward force. For one thing, the reaction to these two wars, intensified by the spread of popular education, literature, and the newspaper, greatly strengthened the organized peace movement.[112] Yet this movement had negligible influence on governments until the end of the century. It was dominated on the one

112. On the emergence of the peace movement in the nineteenth century and its change of content, tactics, and impact, see Hinsley, *op. cit.*, chaps. vi and vii; A. C. F. Beales, *The History of Peace* (New York: The Dial Press, 1931); and Frank M. Russell, *Theories of International Relations* (New York: D. Appleton-Century-Crofts, Inc., 1936), chaps. xii and xiv.

hand by advocates (largely confined to the Continent) of improbable schemes of European federation and on the other hand by liberal and pacifist groups (particularly in England) who rested their hopes for peace on popular government, free trade, or the rising voice of workers. Since governments were suspect in the eyes of international reformers, it relied on direct appeals to the public and to parliaments rather than on the more indirect methods of influencing governments.

During the last quarter of the nineteenth century governments became very receptive to an influential group that exalted war, the military virtues, and national expansion. In a kind of reversion to preindustrial attitudes and in reaction to the rising spirit of bourgeois liberal pacifism, this movement extolled international conflict and war as instruments of progress and expressed a strong preference for "total" war and the all-out offensive in contrast to unheroic and inconclusive limited wars.[113] But it is important to note that this glorification of war and the war system still assumed that war was either so quick and decisive as to be moderate in its destructiveness or else so intense as to be increasingly rare. Von der Goltz was typical in basing his identification of total war with progress on the premise that modern wars could be won by destroying only a small portion of armies, since the new intensity of firepower would bring victory by operating on the will of nations; and that, consequently, each new invention that made weapons more destructive would also end wars more rapidly and humanely.[114]

The romanticization of the military ethic reached its ultimate political expression in imperialism, rationalized by the Darwinian doctrine of the survival of the fittest through constant struggle.[115] Yet political Darwinism was really the dying, though vociferous, gasp of laissez faire in international theory. While the militant spirit continued to grow more popular and vocal, the liberal opposition to war and power politics also grew stronger. By the beginning of the twentieth century, the organized peace movement, now appealing directly to governments, had become

113. See, for example, Baron Colmar Von der Goltz, *The Nation in Arms*, trans. Phillip A. Ashworth (London: Hugh Rees, Ltd., 1913); Jacob Burckhardt, *Force and Freedom: Reflections on History* (New York: Pantheon Books, 1943), pp. 259–62; and the writings of Maurras in France, Treitschke in Germany, Carlyle in England, and Lea in the U.S. The resurgence of miltary romanticism represented, in part, an effort by the nobility, church, and military officer classes to use mass nationalism against the appeals of the liberal intelligentsia to the newly enfranchised classes.

114. Von der Goltz, *op. cit.*, pp. 8–13.

115. William L. Langer, *The Diplomacy of Imperialism 1890–1902* (New York: Alfred A. Knopf, 1935), chap. iii. A. P. Thornton, *The Imperial Idea and Its Enemies* (London: Macmillan, 1959). Jacques Barzun, *Darwin, Marx, Wagner: Critique of a Heritage* (Boston: Little, Brown & Co., 1941), chap. v. Richard Hofstadter, *Social Darwinism in American Thought* (Boston: Beacon Press, 1955), pp. 170ff.

a powerful voice in political life and diplomacy—witness the two Hague disarmament conferences and the active concern of governments with arbitration treaties. The argument about war's wastefulness and irrationality (by then called "obsolescence") had gained new force with the spectacular advance of industrialism and commerce and the growing interdependence of military preparedness and the civilian economy.

To be sure, on the eve of World War I public spokesmen could still rattle the national sword with an exuberant spirit of military adventure and glory without being considered eccentric or evil. The patriotic thirst for military pageantry and excitement reached its height. Nations could face war with unabashed crusading zeal, exulting in the prospect and then in the reality with a passion more intense than was ever attained in the real Crusades. Yet this was probably the final spasm of massive military enthusiasm in the advanced democratic states. World War I killed the romance in war—except in a tragic or personal sense—and destroyed man's confidence in the beneficence of military laissez faire. The Fascist glorification of war was an evil aberration and seemed so at the time.

One should not depreciate the practical significance of the spreading popular aversion to force and the declining legitimacy of acquisitive war, which has been voiced so conspicuously since World War I, simply because of the continuing discrepancy between the ideal and reality of international politics.[116] The widespread revulsion against the Religious Wars and the Napoleonic Wars probably had more to do with the moderation of war and politics in the eighteenth century and the resolution of crises short of war in the nineteenth than any of the so-called objective factors of international politics. Similarly, the widespread revulsion against war, international laissez faire, and military preparedness after World War I had a decisive impact upon international order. Its impact, unfortunately, was largely negative because it was accompanied by an aversion to the calculated management of force as an instrument of policy.

In the nuclear age preoccupation with the avoidance of war between nuclear powers and their allies has tempered the aversion to war with a novel respect for deterrence and the contrived control of force. It remains to be seen whether it has also created a more stable international order, or only the complacent illusion of self-sustaining order that has eventually proved the nemesis of every other period of equilibrium.

116. For an interesting discussion of the causes and consequences of the growing antipathy to war in the advanced industrial states during the last century, see Klaus Knorr, *On the Uses of Military Power in the Nuclear Age* (Princeton: Princeton University Press, 1966), chap. iii. We examine the moral and practical limits of the view that war is illegitimate except in self-defense throughout Part II.

3

THE CONTROL OF FORCE

1. Nuclear Optimism and Pessimism

Unlike any other weapon in history, the atomic bomb, from the moment of its first use, was expected to exert such a radical impact upon warfare as to alter the character of international politics and determine the prospects of war and peace. Yet throughout an astounding succession of developments in nuclear weapons, the specific consequences of nuclear energy have remained in doubt and controversy.

The tremendous destructive capacity of nuclear energy has focused attention on its implications for international order, but the prevailing view on these implications has oscillated between pessimism and optimism. It has oscillated between apprehension on the one hand that a technological breakthrough, the inadvertent use of nuclear weapons, a crisis between the superpowers, a miscalculation of intentions, the expansion of local wars, or the spread of nuclear weapons to other states must sooner or later touch off a nuclear Armageddon, and confidence on the other hand that the prospect of nuclear terror, combined with a stable balance of overwhelming nuclear retaliatory capabilities, makes any clash of arms between the superpowers virtually impossible. This oscillation is especially marked in the U.S., where sensitivity to the political and military implications of a rapidly changing nuclear technology has been most profound and articulate.

At the outset American scientists, taking the lead in interpreting the consequences of their invention, declared that the atomic bomb portended a widespread nuclear arms race that would create unbearable international tension, drive cities underground, undermine democracy, and provoke a surprise attack leading to a catastrophic war.[1] This view

1. See, for example, the early issues of the *Bulletin of the Atomic Scientists*, which was first published in December, 1945, as a medium for expressing the inter-

underlay the Baruch Plan, which proposed the abolition of nuclear weapons, under international control, on the ground that, whatever short-run security advantages the U.S. might extract from its temporary monopoly in atomic weapons, the inevitable spread of nuclear weapons to the Soviet Union and beyond would undermine American security and lead to a nuclear holocaust. But this pessimistic attitude coexisted with less drastic assessments based on the reasoned hope that nuclear weapons would foster both American security and world peace by deterring general war with their tremendous retaliatory power.[2]

In various forms, with varying degrees of optimism at different times, the hopeful prognostication has continued in uneasy juxtaposition with the fear that the nuclear balance of terror, like other military balances, will eventually break down in war. This ambivalence lurks in the minds of all sensitive observers because the novel inhibitions against war depend on destructive potentialities that, if actually used, would be catastrophic. It persists simply because there is much evidence of both the pernicious and the beneficent influence of nuclear weapons and no way to determine which influence will predominate.

The task of the analyst is to cut beneath the shifting moods of the nuclear age in order to discover the underlying realities as far as reasoned inferences from inconclusive data permit, but these inferences are bound to be highly conjectural and subject to error. After all, our experience with international politics in the nuclear age is extremely limited. The political and technological factors, not to mention the fortuitous events, governing this experience continue to change in unpredictable ways.

---

national fears and hopes of scientists. See also Robert Gilpin, *American Scientists and Nuclear Weapons Policy* (Princeton: Princeton University Press, 1962), chap. ii.

2. In general, those who believed that arms and power politics are a menace to international harmony were most alarmed by the implications of nuclear weapons, while those who believed that arms and power politics are a necessary feature of international politics and the only basis of international equilibrium foresaw opportunities to build international order on deterrence. Some in the military establishment saw atomic weapons as only somewhat more powerful bombs that would not basically change strategy. After the invention of hydrogen warheads and long-range missiles, the traditionalists and the military became less confident about the prospects of assimilating nuclear weapons to a reasonably safe balance-of-power system, or at least more impressed by the complexity of preserving mutual deterrence, while some of the international reformers became confident that peace could be based on the fact that nuclear weapons made war and the balance-of-power system obsolete. Some of the most astute early prognostications about the military and political implications of nuclear weapons were made by social scientists with a realistic approach to power politics in *The Absolute Weapon*, ed. Bernard Brodie (New York: Harcourt, Brace & Co., 1946).

2. The Novelty of the Nuclear Age

Since the cold war began, a consensus has emerged that nuclear weapons have created a new kind of international order based primarily on the unprecedented common interest of all states in avoiding nuclear war. Such a nuclear order undoubtedly exists, however limited, fragile, or eventually disastrous it may be. To be sure, a comparable order might have existed in the absence of nuclear weapons, considering the reaction to World War II and the growing destructiveness of non-nuclear weapons. And of course the present military restraints rest on many factors in addition to the nuclear balance, some of which may be changing fundamentally—for example, the political and military preponderance of the U.S. and the Soviet Union. Nevertheless, the widespread assumption that nuclear weapons have been the primary factor determining the distribution and dynamics of countervailing power warrants our examining the prospects of order first in the nature of the new military technology.

The expansion of force in the nuclear age needs no detailed discussion. The essential facts are familiar: the quantum jump in the speed, range, war-readiness, and destructiveness of strategic weapons; the unprecedented rate of technological innovation; the great complexity and diversity of the American-Soviet arms race—actually an immense aggregation of many separate but interacting competitions in weapons, forces, logistics, communications systems, and so forth, in which a quantitative-qualitative rivalry feeds upon a rapid sequence of innovation and obsolescence in weapons and counter-weapons throughout a broad spectrum of technology.

In the U.S. and the Soviet Union the massive mobilization of human and material resources for research and production has created gigantic scientific, industrial, and military establishments. These complex and highly developed establishments embody by far the most extensive fusion of military and civilian technology in history—a fusion that is now, like some law of nature, irreversible, perhaps even under total disarmament. The profound impetus behind the indiscriminate expansion of military-civilian technology was signified at the inception of the nuclear age by the determination of the scientific community to pursue the material benefits of peaceful uses of nuclear energy although it recognized that this would vastly increase the difficulties of abolishing nuclear weapons, which it believed was essential to peace.[3] In the 1960s

3. Only after the failure of negotiations on the Baruch Plan and some disillusionment with the economic pay-off of peaceful nuclear energy did the proposal to ban peaceful nuclear production begin to receive much attention among scientists.

the spread of peaceful applications of nuclear energy throughout the world is rapidly creating opportunities for additional nuclear forces, yet in spite of widespread fears of the proliferation of nuclear weapons it seems almost unthinkable that governments should stop or obstruct the spread of peaceful uses of nuclear energy. Meanwhile it becomes increasingly difficult to distinguish civilian from military technology in nuclear energy, as in space and other realms.

The single most conspicuous feature of the expansion of military power in the nuclear age is the tremendous increase in the capacity of nuclear states to devastate one another directly and quickly without defeating armed forces, coupled with the incapacity of even the most powerful state to defend itself against such devastation. In this respect the novelty of nuclear weapons is one of degree; but the degree of prospective retaliatory damage may now be so great as to amount to a qualitative change, since it raises the ratio of potential loss to possible gain in an all-out exchange to the point of irrationality for *both* sides. In any case, this seems to be the operating assumption in the calculations of the superpowers. Long before the Soviet Union actually had the physical capacity to inflict overwhelming damage in a retaliatory blow, American as well as Soviet leaders were publicly warning in apocalyptic terms that a nuclear war would devastate their own country as well as the adversary's.[4]

See, for example, the memorandum of the Working Committee of the Association of Scientists for Atomic Education, Atlantic Region, reprinted in the *Bulletin of the Atomic Scientists*, IV (June, 1948), 183–84. The general argument against this idea, which easily prevailed in the pages of the *Bulletin*, was that the military applications of peaceful technology and science are unpredictable, that the progress of mankind depends upon the open spread of technology and the free pursuit of scientific truth, and that scientists cannot be responsible for the evil use of their knowledge.

4. In 1954 Malenkov declared that a thermonuclear war could result in "the destruction of world civilization." *Pravda*, March 13, 1954. Subsequent Soviet leaders and military writers revoked the application of this assessment to Communist society but continued to paint a picture of terrible mutual devastation. American leaders commonly spoke of a nuclear war as being virtually as disastrous for the U.S. as for the Soviet Union. Thus in 1959 President Eisenhower declared, in connection with the Berlin crisis, that a thermonuclear war would be "self-defeating" and would bring about "the destruction of civilization as we know it." *The New York Times*, March 12, 1959. Indeed, Eisenhower made a similar statement in 1953, even before Soviet leaders explicitly claimed a capacity to attack the U.S. with nuclear weapons. *Ibid.*, December 9, 1953.

It is not clear that the Soviet Union had, at any time before obtaining quantities of missiles in the middle 1960s, the capacity to inflict deaths in the tens of millions upon the U.S. even on a first strike, let alone on a second strike. In the 1950s American fears were based on the prospect of a first strike by Soviet bombers, capable of one-way trips to the U.S. But although American intelligence, on the basis of misleading observations at Moscow on Aviation Day in July, 1955, ex-

This assumption has caused a qualitative change in the willingness of advanced military states to contemplate all-out war for any reason, but especially for reasons other than the defense of their own territory or that of indispensable allies. Before World War I the general expectation was that victory would come quickly and decisively to the side that struck first with the greatest mass and intensity. Before World War II a general war was expected to be total and protracted, but even the Continental states believed that the human and material costs would be clearly outweighed by the value of defeating the adversary.

The general expectation that the costs of nuclear war would outweigh the value of defeating a nuclear adversary has greatly reduced the willingness of states deliberately to take risks of such a war except for defensive reasons of the most compelling nature. This fact, together with the global extent of American and Soviet interests and the prospect that the involvement of one or both in even a small peripheral war might expand into a larger conflict, has extended inhibitions against the overt and direct use of force to all levels of violence and placed a novel emphasis on the carefully contrived limitation of war—at least as far as the superpowers and their allies are concerned.

The enormities of potential nuclear destruction go far to explain two outstanding characteristics of military power since World War II: (a) the limitation of warfare to local, non-nuclear, and "internal" conflict (that is, wars affecting international politics which take place largely within the boundaries of a single state, though supported from outside) and (b) the pervasive, highly developed exploitation of force short of war.

Thus in the nuclear age an excess of force has imposed upon warfare some of the constraints that resulted from an insufficiency of force in

---

pected the Soviet Union to acquire 600 to 700 intercontinental bombers by 1959, it evidently procured only a small fraction of this number. By 1965 the reliable Institute for Strategic Studies estimated that the Soviet Union had 200 intercontinental bombers and 200 ICBMs and that the U.S. had 625 bombers, 925 ICBMs, and 480 Polarises. *The Military Balance, 1965–66.*

In March, 1966, Secretary of Defense McNamara testified that by 1970, on the basis of existing defense programs, the Soviet Union would be able to inflict 130 to 135 million deaths in the U.S. on a first strike and 90 to 95 million if the U.S. were to strike first. Even with a full-scale antiballistic missile and civil defense program he saw little hope of reducing fatalities from a Soviet first strike below 50 million. Yet even if the Soviet Union by 1970 were to assign its entire missile force against American strategic forces, he estimated that the U.S. could still destroy about one-third of the Soviet population and half of its industrial capacity. *Statement of Secretary of Defense Robert S. McNamara before the House Armed Services Committee on the Fiscal Year 1967–71 Defense Program and 1967 Defense Budget,* pp. 48, 53, 55.

earlier periods of history, but it has also expanded the nonviolent uses of force. One aspect of this dual effect is that although the politically offensive use of force has become still less attractive (except perhaps when disguised as internal war), the potential defensive efficacy of force has increased so as to give states with the most advanced military technology a greater capacity to extend deterrence far beyond their own territory to cover foreign territories. As the range of effective military protection has increased, so has the scope of national interests that the superpowers have been able to support and contest.

The expansion of force in the nuclear age has created novel dangers of war as well as novel prospects of order. One might take more comfort from the diminished utility of an outright offensive use of force by the nuclear powers but for the fact that the extended defensive utility of force and the expanded arena of power contests in the shadow of war have further clouded the distinction between politically defensive and offensive military action (which, given the ambiguity of motivation in international conflicts, has never been clear). For when the major military confrontations do not spring from clear-cut threats of territorial conquest but take the form of contests of the comparative resolve of adversaries to support a variety of competing claims concerning the status of foreign territories or, even more ambiguous, rights of access to foreign territories (for example, Berlin), the distinction between offense and defense is as subjective as the legitimacy of the conflicting interests at stake. Although the first use of force carries a special onus in the nuclear age, contests of will and nerve in which nuclear adversaries try to maneuver each other into assuming that onus are bound to make the distinction between first and second use of force as meaningless and ambiguous as the legal distinction between aggressor and defender— and in fact largely irrelevant when competing threats of war remain below the threshold of an overt clash of arms. One consequence of the enhanced subjectivity of power contests waged by threats of war is a greater chance of war resulting from miscalculations of national interests, intentions, and resolve.

The technical characteristics of nuclear weapons also pose novel dangers. The complexity of modern military plans, which nuclear weapons necessitate, has multiplied the possibilities that the weapons, armed forces, and strategies developed in peacetime will exert an unintended effect upon international politics and produce unanticipated and uncontrollable effects in war.[5] The novel characteristics of nuclear weapons

5. Sir Solly Zuckerman points to the danger that great technological inputs into complex strategic weapons systems and the vastness and heterogeneity of the defense organization may lead to inflexible, predetermined military responses beyond political

have created a new risk of unintentional war through technical accident and the unauthorized use of weapons. They have created frightening possibilities that any clash of arms between the nuclear powers or their allies may expand into an irrevocable spasm of undiscriminating violence.

On the other hand, the novel dangers latent in nuclear weapons have also produced, most notably in the U.S., an unprecedented systematic effort to manage peacetime military power as a rational instrument of policy short of war and to bring war itself—even nuclear war—under politically directed control and restraint. This effort to restore political control over military power after decades of laissez-faire expansion has been rewarded to a novel extent by the conscious regulation of force through unilateral and reciprocal restraints between the nuclear adversaries. The regulation of force is manifest in three uses of military power—war, deterrence, and other kinds of political and psychological exploitation of force short of war.

Each of these uses manifests a new penetration of military considerations into the regular modes of international politics but each also reflects the greater suffusion of military concerns with political and psychological factors. The reason for this close interaction of military and political matters can be stated generally as follows: Strictly military considerations involve bringing overt or threatened force to bear upon an adversary for some purpose. The purpose is political in so far as it involves the status, interests, commitments, and influence of one state in its relationship to others. In this sense politics, not the imperatives of armed coercion as such, should control and direct the use of force. In the nuclear age the contrived limitation of war by military self-denial requires the deliberate subordination of a surplus of potential military power to limited political objectives. Internal wars are by the very nature of their objectives and methods subject to political limitation.

The political element in the use of force is enhanced to the extent that force is exerted upon the will and intentions of a state through suasion rather than actual physical coercion. As Clausewitz reasoned, the role of politics is likely to be proportionate to the extent the overt use of force is limited. Politics is all the more enhanced when force is used short of war, since then the intangible and subjective aspects of power may be decisive, and the demanding imperatives of violence do not intrude. When peacetime military policies are designed to affect the intentions and actions of states (including allies) through a variety

control. "Judgment and Control in Modern Warfare," *Foreign Affairs*, XL (January, 1962), 196–212. On this point, see pp. 189 and 163.

of psychological effects—awe, respect, and confidence—and not merely through fear of coercion, politics is the very essence of even the most technical military concerns.

In these respects nuclear weapons have accentuated the politicization of force by enhancing its limited and non-violent uses. For this reason they offer novel opportunities as well as incentives to put force under rational political control.

3. *Military Strategy in the United States*

The most novel characteristics of military power in the nuclear age lie in the uses of force by the nuclear superpowers and their allies in the East-West conflict. The development of military strategy provides an important insight into these uses because strategy has rationalized them, governed their practice to some extent, and also served as an instrument of policy. The broad meaning and extensive influence of military strategy is another manifestation of the fusion of military and political affairs.[6]

By the time of Mahan and Douhet, military strategy had become far more than a concept of how to win battles or wars. Mahan elevated strategy to an over-all plan for using force as a continuing instrument of national policy. As military deterrence assumed a central role in the use of force, Douhet's writings, although they were concerned primarily with the effects of actual devastation upon national will, provided the basis of a new realm of strategic thought preoccupied with the psychological effects of the prospect of devastation. Yet Mahan's and Douhet's strategies embraced only a single weapon, and neither led to refined concepts of interacting national capabilities and intentions.

In the nuclear age military strategy has become a still more prominent and integral element of foreign policy. It encompasses deterrence, confrontations short of war, and relations among allies, as well as the support of national interests in open conflict. The political basis of military strategy is implicit in systematic speculation about the likelihood of nations resorting to war and the nature of interacting military responses

6. We have noted that in the nineteenth century strategy became the plan for utilizing all the nation's resources and instruments of war most effectively in order to exert force advantageously in future military contingencies and that with respect to airpower after World War I strategic doctrine became more directly concerned with policy short of war. It was only after World War II, however, that the concept of strategy—sometimes called "national strategy"—as a plan for utilizing military power in relation to a nation's total resources and instruments of power in order to support policy in peacetime as well as war was explicitly developed by American war colleges and military analysts.

and reciprocal restraints in hypothetical contingencies. The calculus of deterrence and the limitation of war compel scrupulous attention to the interaction of military capabilities with national interests and intentions in likely political circumstances.

The subjective, intangible element in military planning is all the greater because planners have no wartime experience with the key weapons and must therefore rely heavily on the analytical techniques of economists and other civilian strategists.[7] Furthermore, in nuclear arms competition the managers of military power must be more than ever aware that strategies and plans may themselves fundamentally affect an adversary's strategies, plans, and forces, through its perception of underlying interests and intentions. For this reason strategy is a primary tool of statecraft.

The many subjective, psychological, and essentially political elements of military planning, in conjunction with the profusion of military technology and the diversity of conditions and restraints under which force might be used, greatly complicate rational choices among weapons systems and their employment. Strategic concepts play a central role in determining these choices. It is no wonder, therefore, that technological changes and changes in political climate, divergent geopolitical circumstances and military resources, differences of perspective among and within armed services and other agencies of government, domestic political influences, and factors of individual temperament and outlook have produced some rich strategic differences and controversies. Nevertheless, one can discern rough consensuses and trends in strategic thinking which have exerted a great impact upon the uses of military power and international politics.

Military deterrence has been in the forefront of strategic thought and controversy because effective deterrence is the prerequisite for the rational use of military power both in war and short of war. It is the most crucial element in the balance of power. Yet because deterrence

---

7. On the role of civilian strategists, see Bernard Brodie, "The Scientific Strategists," in *Scientists and National Policy-Making*, ed. Robert Gilpin and Christopher Wright (New York: Columbia University Press, 1964). Charles Hitch and other RAND civilian strategists set forth the basic approach to military planning as the efficient allocation and use of resources according to systematic choices among alternative means and ends, which became dominant in Secretary McNamara's administration of the Department of Defense, in Charles J. Hitch and Roland N. McKean, *The Economics of Defense in the Nuclear Age* (Cambridge: Harvard University Press, 1960). Albert Wohlstetter deals with "conflict systems analysis," as distinguished from game theory and operations research, in "Strategy and the Natural Scientists," in Gilpin and Wright, *op. cit.*, and "Analysis and Design of Conflict Systems," in *Analysis for Military Decisions*, ed. E. S. Quade (RAND Corporation Report R-387-PR, November, 1964).

depends on the mental processes of individuals assuming risks of war in behalf of governments, even its past and present, let alone its future, success or failure can be divined only by inference and intuition; for the motives of decision-makers are varied and often obscure, and their anticipation of war under hypothetical conditions is but one consideration among many.

Deterrence strategy cannot be understood in isolation from the strategies of fighting a war and using force short of war. Indeed, a central strategic question is the relationship of deterrence to these other two uses of force. For the requirements of an effective military posture for each of the three uses do not necessarily coincide, and from the standpoint of international order as well as national security it would be dangerous to neglect one in favor of another. As Glenn Snyder has observed, the most striking difference between nuclear and prenuclear strategy is the "possibility that deterrence may now be accomplished by weapons which might have no rational use for defense should deterrence fail."[8] Most of the public controversy in the U.S. and Europe—a running controversy with great political import—has revolved around attempts, on the one hand, to overcome this seeming anomaly and, on the other, hand, to capitalize on it as a basis of national security and international order.

In the U.S., which has been the primary generator of strategic ideas, the dominant strategy before the Korean War was to prevent a Soviet attack against Europe or against the U.S. with the threat of nuclear retaliation.[9] It was generally assumed that the Soviet Union would not attack Europe without striking first at the U.S. But in 1949 retaliation was regarded as more than a punitive strike. It was widely conceived as an attack on the Soviet Union's warmaking capacity, which, in conjunction with massive naval and land operations, would win the war essentially the way World War II had been won.

The outbreak of the Korean War in June, 1950, provoked the U.S. and its European allies to make the first and last serious effort to support their stated objective of ground defense, since the North Korean invasion seemed to refute the prevailing assumption that the Soviet Union was deterred by American nuclear power from supporting overt military aggressions. The resulting fears of aggression in Europe led to the creation in 1951 of a NATO force under an American Supreme Commander, to formal adoption in 1952 of large allied force goals intended to be

8. *Deterrence and Defense* (Princeton: Princeton University Press, 1961), p. 9.
9. The author has traced the development of American strategy with respect to Europe in *NATO: The Entangling Alliance* (Chicago: University of Chicago Press, 1962).

adequate for defense, and to the membership of West Germany in NATO in 1954.

But the Korean shock soon passed, and so did the momentarily feverish military preparations for a defense of Europe. The result was a new emphasis on the punitive aspect of nuclear deterrence. For the British and American governments proclaimed their future reliance on a strategy of deterrence purporting to substitute nuclear retaliatory firepower for conventional manpower in order to gain more security at less expense. This strategy of "massive retaliation" promised to reduce dependence on local defense power by relying on the deterrent power of "a great capacity to retaliate, instantly, by means and at places of our choosing," on the theory that "the only effective way to stop prospective aggressors is to convince them in advance that if they commit aggression, they will be subjected to retaliatory blows so costly that their aggression will not be a profitable operation."[10]

The new emphasis on nuclear deterrence was marked by NATO's official adoption in December, 1954, of a strategy that envisaged a virtually automatic use of tactical nuclear weapons against any kind of conventional attack in Europe. Ground forces in Europe were, in effect, reduced to the role of a trip-wire on an all-out nuclear response. But an all-out nuclear response could now be met by a rapidly growing Soviet nuclear capacity to devastate Europe and even, it was thought, the U.S. Therefore NATO strategy was more than ever dominated by a deterrent threat that would be of questionable value to carry out.

In the peripheral areas outside Europe, too, the West became more dependent on a deterrent strategy of nuclear response to conventional aggression. Indeed, it was primarily in order to avoid another Korean-type war, and the expense and alleged military disadvantage of trying to counter local conventional aggressions locally at places of the enemy's choosing, that the Eisenhower-Dulles administration explicitly proclaimed the strategy of massive retaliation and extended it to these new areas of military containment.

The dilemma posed by increasing dependence on nuclear deterrence in a period of growing Soviet nuclear retaliatory strength was accentuated by the American and Soviet thermonuclear explosions in 1952 and 1953, which foretold weapons thousands of times more devastating than the atomic bombs dropped on Japan. In the U.S. and Britain this dilemma caused a strategic reaction, as the tendency to extract the maximum deterrent effect from nuclear weapons began in the late 1950s to confront

10. From Secretary of State Dulles' address of January 12, 1954, *U.S. Department of State Bulletin*, XXX (January 25, 1954), 107–10.

a countervailing tendency to guard against a too-heavy dependence upon a threat that would be catastrophic to carry out. The resulting movement for strategic revision emphasized the need to build up the West's capacity for limited war. The rationale was threefold: to enhance deterrence, on the supposition that massive retaliation would not be sufficiently credible in the face of rising Soviet retaliatory power; to provide for a rational and effective way of fighting local aggressions, including internal wars, that could not be deterred; and to relieve the Western powers of the psychological and political burden of having to contemplate choosing between a thermonuclear holocaust and ineffective resistance in crises short of war.

One strategy of limited war, which gained some intellectual support briefly in 1957 and 1958 (notably from Henry Kissinger and Admiral Sir Anthony Buzzard), envisaged a limited tactical nuclear war.[11] But this strategy never gained official acceptance for a number of reasons that are still pertinent. In the first place, there is the inherent difficulty of limiting a bilateral use of even short-range, low-yield nuclear weapons, considering the immense firepower involved and the lack of mutually clear distinctions among targets and weapons. Secondly, the military advantage of fighting a tactical nuclear war, even if it could be limited, is doubtful. Finally, military planners have been unable to agree upon a concept and method of limitation. Other strategies of limited tactical nuclear war—for example, those involving nuclear land mines or selective nuclear reprisals—have been suggested,[12] but the uncertainties surrounding any use of such weapons seem overwhelming.

Strategies of non-nuclear limited war (both regular and counterinsurgent), however, have attracted significant support. They became official doctrine and led to the enlargement of conventional and unconventional forces under the Kennedy-McNamara administration as part of the concept of "controlled and flexible response" or "graduated response."[13] This concept stressed the need for preparing a broad range of military responses to meet a variety of possible contingencies by means proportionate to the dimensions of aggression, appropriate to the political circumstances, and susceptible to political control.

11. Morton H. Halperin reviews the public literature on the use of nuclear weapons in local war in "Nuclear Weapons and Limited War," *Journal of Conflict Resolution*, V (June, 1961), 146–66.

12. Malcolm W. Hoag, "Rationalizing NATO Strategy," *World Politics*, XVII (October, 1964), 121–42. Thomas C. Schelling, *Arms and Influence* (New Haven: Yale University Press, 1966), pp. 109–16, 181–84.

13. William W. Kaufmann fully presents the meaning, rationale, application, and development of this doctrine in *The McNamara Strategy* (New York: Harper & Row, 1964).

The prevailing view in the Kennedy-McNamara administration was that the use of any nuclear weapons would cross the most critical threshold between wars that were susceptible to limitation and those that probably were not. However artificial and conjectural any threshold or "firebreak" might be, the administration was inclined to emphasize rather than try to de-emphasize it, because limited war, it thought, requires some readily verifiable and obviously compelling standard of mutual restraint, since the standard of maximum military efficiency can so easily lead to irrational violence. The distinction between nuclear and non-nuclear war seemed to be the most conspicuous, widely recognized, and deeply felt standard.[14]

Yet the U.S. did not scrap tactical nuclear weapons or abandon either the threat or the operational plans to use them against a conventional attack. The Kennedy-McNamara revision sought to raise the threshold of nuclear war, not to abandon the prospect of crossing it. It left the location of that threshold deliberately uncertain. The deployment of an increasingly diversified arsenal of tactical nuclear weapons in Europe continued apace, although there was no detailed consensus in the U.S. government, let alone among allied governments, on just how to use them. Far from opposing this deployment, most of the European allies, being less impressed by the feasibility or utility of non-nuclear options, regarded it as essential to deterrence.

In NATO strategy the *deterrent* function of the modest build-up of conventional capabilities under the Kennedy administration was essentially to convince the Soviet Union that it could not quickly occupy territory in a *fait accompli* and to enable Western forces to sustain a limited war long enough and at a sufficient level of conflict to make the initiation of nuclear war more credible. The *defensive* function of conventional forces was not to withstand a determined Soviet assault but to provide sufficient conventional holding power in a military encounter resulting from a local crisis to give the enemy time to appreciate the risks of nuclear war and draw back from the brink. The prospect remained that any military action that was interpreted as an attempt to change the political-territorial status quo would lead to the use of tactical nuclear weapons. Since there might be considerable pressure on the West—at least from West Germany—to use tactical nuclear weapons before the adversary could occupy territory, the nuclear threshold gave the appearance of remaining quite low in Europe.

Those who opposed the emphasis on limited, non-nuclear alternatives

14. Bernard Brodie makes a critique of this view and emphasizes the deterrent value of a tactical nuclear threat in *Escalation and the Nuclear Option* (Princeton: Princeton University Press, 1966).

in Europe argued, plausibly, that such an emphasis was unnecessary because deterrence was virtually guaranteed by the high risk that any war in this vital area would become nuclear and by the inordinate penalties of miscalculating the risk and so precipitating a nuclear war. It followed, as the Eisenhower administration contended, that the strategy and forces capable of deterring a big war will deter a small one (except for unconventional or internal war). Less plausibly, the critics of limited-war doctrine argued that explicit concentration upon limited war options would weaken deterrence by undermining the credibility of a nuclear response. Even if this second argument were correct, however, it did not necessarily satisfy the two purposes other than deterrence that the strategy of flexible and controlled response was intended to serve: (1) to enable the U.S. and its allies to contain a limited conflict on a politically rational basis if for any reason such a conflict should occur and (2) to strengthen the will and bargaining position of the U.S. and its allies in crises by providing them with choices, in the familiar phrase, between a thermonuclear holocaust and passive acquiescence. The growing emphasis upon these two purposes in the 1960s was part of a significant movement in the U.S. to reduce the discrepancy between threatened and usable force—or, putting it another way, between deterrence and defense.

One aspect of this movement was the official de-emphasis upon strategies involving the initial use of tactical or strategic nuclear weapons outside Europe—particularly against Communist China, even though China did not yet possess a nuclear capability and seemed less and less likely to receive Soviet nuclear backing. Presumably the chief reasons for this de-emphasis were, first, the prospect of an adverse psychological and political reaction to the use of nuclear weapons against a nonwhite, non-nuclear state; secondly, the belief that there was insufficient military advantage to be gained from a nuclear attack against China to warrant the political costs elsewhere; and, finally, recognition that Asian "national liberation wars," in the absence of direct Chinese intervention, were simply not suitable objects of a deterrent threat.

Then, while the U.S. was de-emphasizing the first use of nuclear weapons, dramatic evidence of the rapid development of intercontinental ballistic missiles (ICBMs) challenged the adequacy of its strategic nuclear forces and the stability of the balance of terror itself. By 1956 the Soviet Union was already setting up squadrons of intermediate-range ballistic missiles (IRBMs) which would soon make all Europe a "hostage." But more dramatic than this, the Soviets announced in August, 1957, the successful test of a "super long-distance intercontinental ballistic rocket" and in October launched the first two space satellites. Amid reports that intelligence estimates credited the Soviet Union with the ability to produce three times as many ICBMs as the U.S. by 1963, many concluded that before the late 1960s, when the U.S. expected to have quantities of operational solid-fuel missiles capable of reaching the Soviet Union from protected land bases (the Minuteman) and submarines (the Polaris), the Soviets would have the capacity to deliver an attack that would knock out enough of America's retaliatory power to spare the Russian homeland from intolerable damage.

Momentarily, these developments aroused an intense controversy in the U.S. over the danger of a forthcoming "missile gap." But fear of a missile gap proved to have no more substantial grounds than had the fear of a bomber gap in 1955. After the Kennedy administration came into office it discovered not only that the Soviet Union had failed to achieve a missile advantage but that actually U.S. missile and bomber strength was so superior as to give it greater striking power after absorbing a Soviet first strike than the Soviet Union would have in delivering a first strike. The end of the missile-gap controversy, however, did not lessen the strategic and political significance of the bilateral development of bombers and missiles that could reach the adversary's homeland with sudden and devastating force. Rather, it sharpened the strategic dispute underlying the controversy over capabilities.

Advocates of "minimum" or "finite" deterrence concluded that the only feasible strategic force needed was one that could inflict unacceptable civilian damage on a retaliatory strike. Others maintained that in order to "prevail" on a second strike as well as to maintain a credible first-strike capability the U.S. should be able to destroy both Soviet civil society and its strategic forces. A third school of thought stressed the moral and practical necessity of avoiding reliance upon a strategy that would in effect amount to an unrestricted nuclear spasm and advocated the measured use of a strategic counterforce capability—that is, an ability to blunt or destroy the enemy's long-range striking force—as part of a strategy for controlled and limited nuclear exchanges.

Some advocates of the so-called counterforce strategy were motivated partly by a desire to maintain the credibility of an American nuclear first strike against non-nuclear Soviet aggression, but Secretary of Defense McNamara publicly avoided the sensitive question of a credible first strike and concentrated upon the requirements of a rational retaliatory or second-strike counterforce response. In opposing both the minimum and total-response strategies, he stressed the need for a nuclear capability that could limit damage by withholding the destruction of Soviet cities in return for reciprocal restraint while reducing Soviet striking power. The basic rationale for this "counterforce strategy" and capability was the same as that for limited war strategies and capabilities —the practical and moral necessity of having recourse to a rational, politically controlled, and therefore necessarily limited military option if war should occur. This extension of the doctrine of flexible and controlled response to strategic nuclear war marked the ultimate effort to base deterrence on force that would be rational to use. It was also the first explicit official statement extending deterrence beyond the prevention, to the limitation, of nuclear war.

In subsequent statements McNamara and other administration spokesmen emphasized that the counterforce strategy, in conjunction with civil defense against fall-out, was intended chiefly to limit civilian damage by blunting Soviet striking power if nuclear war should for any reason occur. He denied that it would make the deliberate resort to nuclear war more attractive for either side. He explained that the damage-limiting function of a counterforce capability would depend largely upon deterring the Soviet Union from concentrating an offensive strike against American cities by the threat of retaliating with a withheld counter-city force, but that such deterrence would be doubtful as long as Soviet ICBMs remained relatively scarce and vulnerable. Yet he also acknowledged that as Soviet missiles became less vulnerable, the prospects of confining damage from them to tolerable levels would decrease.

American spokesmen made it clear that at best nuclear war would be terribly devastating. Testifying early in 1964, McNamara said, "It will become increasingly difficult . . . to destroy a sufficiently large proportion of the Soviet's strategic nuclear forces to preclude major damage to the United States including fatalities in the tens of millions." He saw no way of escaping this predicament, even by doubling or tripling American strategic forces. In an all-out nuclear exchange, he said, the U.S. would destroy a greater percentage of Soviet industry and population than the Soviet Union could destroy in the U.S., but the amount of destruction in the U.S. and Western Europe would exceed destruction in the Soviet Union. "My personal opinion," he concluded, "is . . . we cannot win . . . a strategic nuclear war, in the normal meaning of the word 'win.' "[15]

Thus the chief purpose of the revision of nuclear strategy was not to enhance the credibility of nuclear deterrence, and certainly not to give nuclear weapons the traditional status of conventional forces designed to win a war by prevailing over the enemy's fighting forces, but rather to make nuclear weapons less likely to be self-defeating and more likely to serve a useful political purpose if for any reason they should have to be used. At the same time, the government took elaborate and expen-

15. Kaufmann, *op. cit.*, pp. 94–95.

sive precautions against nuclear weapons being used inadvertently or on the basis of a technical misinterpretation of enemy actions.

In the middle 1960s reinforced confidence in the U.S. that the Soviet Union would not strike first (considering American strategic nuclear superiority) and almost complete lack of confidence in the utility of an American first strike against the Soviet Union (considering the increasing invulnerability of Russia's strategic force) changed the focus of strategic thought toward the management of military power in crises short of war, in limited military confrontations that might grow out of such crises, and in insurgent guerrilla wars supported by communist states. In all three areas a key objective was the control of escalation (or the graduated increase of force) for maximum political advantage at minimum risk.[16] Whether or not the focus on this concept would generate new strategic ideas and controversies, it seemed bound to give further impetus to a tendency underlying American strategic thought since the Korean War and the development of thermonuclear weapons: the growing disposition to view war and the threat of war as indispensable but potentially catastrophic power to be controlled with utmost discrimination and caution for limited political ends by the scrupulous, calculated management of conflict within reciprocal restraints. This basic orientation toward military power was as significant as any of the refinements of strategic concepts that were derived from it.

4. Military Strategy Outside the United States

The practical significance of the American approach to deterrence and defense depends to a considerable degree upon the extent to which other major states share it. The feasibility of a strategy of controlled and flexible response, for example, is affected by its compatibility with the operating strategies of the Soviet Union and Communist China and with the strategies of the NATO allies.

The European allies, by virtue of their different resources, geographical position, density of population, war experience, and level of military responsibility, were disinclined to adopt American military strategy in some respects.[17] Consequently, the U.S. had to accept a compromise in

16. Herman Kahn, one of the most influential civilian strategists, reflected and assisted this shift in strategic thought in *On Escalation* (New York: Frederick A. Praeger, 1965). His first book, *On Thermonuclear War* (Princeton: Princeton University Press, 1960), was principally concerned with strategies of deterrence and emphasized the value of a credible nuclear first-strike strategy.

17. On the differences of strategy between the U.S. and its European allies, see Raymond Aron, *The Great Debate* (Garden City, N.Y.: Doubleday, 1964), chap. iii, and Henry A. Kissinger, *The Troubled Partnership* (New York: McGraw-Hill, 1965), chap. iv.

its European strategy. The effect of this compromise was to keep the nuclear threshold from being raised more than slightly and to leave the threat of escalation the primary deterrent to non-nuclear aggression.

The opposition or indifference of the European allies to the full logic of the American strategy of limited war on the Continent sprang from a number of sources: their view that the Soviet military threat is minimal; confidence in nuclear deterrence; unwillingness to make the requisite sacrifices of money and conscripted men to build forces capable of sustained local war; doubt that limited war in Europe is sufficiently probable to be worth preparing for; belief that even a local conventional war would be significantly limited only from the standpoint of the U.S. and the Soviet Union; fear that raising the threshold of nuclear response would destroy the credibility of America's first-strike strategy.

Nevertheless, the British and German governments endorsed the general rationale of the strategy of graduated response in Europe, differing with the U.S. chiefly on the timing and automaticity of a nuclear response to conventional aggressions below the level of an all-out attack. Only France, partly because it was intent upon justifying its reliance upon a small counter-city nuclear force, offered total and vehement opposition to a limited-war strategy in Europe and advocated instead a concept of immediate strategic retaliation based on a concept of nuclear deterrence purporting to minimize power differentials.[18]

The European reaction to the U.S. counterforce and no-cities strategy was principally one of acquiescence, mixed with bewilderment, apathy, and some suspicion. The French, who with some reason interpreted the strategy as an attack upon their independent nuclear program, were outspoken in their opposition. Others shared their suspicion that it was another manifestation of U.S. unwillingness to risk its cities to deter an attack upon Europe. Nevertheless, if deterrence should fail and the use of nuclear weapons become a reality or an imminent prospect, it is hard to believe that any of the allies would prefer an automatic, undiscriminating nuclear exchange to a limited use of tactical or strategic nuclear weapons and an attempt to negotiate a cease-fire.

More important than the convergence or divergence of allied and

18. According to this concept, the minimal nuclear force of a small state capable only of destroying a city or two of a major nuclear power can exert a deterrent effect equal to that of a major state's large nuclear force because the threat value of its lesser destructive capacity is enhanced by the proportionately lower value of a small state to the adversary. The retired French Air Force General Pierre Gallois carried this concept to its farthest reach in *The Balance of Terror* (Boston: Houghton Mifflin, 1961), a modified translation of *Stratégie de l'Âge Nucléaire* (Paris: 1960), and earlier articles in *Politique Étrangère*. For a criticism of Gallois's views and other strategic justifications of a small nuclear force, see Aron, *op. cit.*, chap. iv.

U.S. strategy is the extent to which Russia's management of great nuclear power may lead to a correspondence of Soviet and American strategic concepts.[19] Like Western allied strategic thought, Soviet strategy depreciates the feasibility of limiting a nuclear war or, indeed, any war arising in Europe. Yet the development of Soviet strategic thought has moved broadly, though less markedly than in the U.S., toward narrowing the gap between threatened and usable force. As in the U.S., Soviet strategic thought after World War II began with the assimilation of nuclear weapons to traditional military doctrine, next underwent a radical revision emphasizing the catastrophic nature of nuclear war and the unique potency of nuclear weapons as a deterrent and an instrument of diplomacy, and then was gradually refined and elaborated to envisage a wider variety of limited warfare and a closer correspondence between deterrent and fighting strategy. Explicit Soviet strategy stopped short of American strategic concepts in rationalizing the controlled and flexible use of war as an instrument of policy. Nevertheless, the fundamental Soviet approach to force is more congenial to controlled and flexible responses than the traditional American approach, and important elements of convergence between explicit Soviet and American strategies suggest the emergence of a partial but important consensus on the uses of military power in the nuclear age.

Under Stalin, Soviet doctrine held that nuclear weapons did not invalidate the Marxist-Leninist principle that the final triumph of communism must result from an inevitable total war with the capitalist-imperialist camp. Eventually, a hard-pressed and desperate capitalist camp would initiate a total war against the socialist camp and meet its ultimate defeat. In total war victory would depend not upon a devastating surprise attack but upon the defeat of enemy forces and the occupation of territory in a protracted war in which superiority in the "permanently operating factors" that determine the fighting strength of armies would prove decisive.[20]

19. Raymond L. Garthoff, *Soviet Strategy in the Nuclear Age* (New York: Frederick A. Praeger, 1958), and *Soviet Military Policy* (New York: Frederick A. Praeger, 1966); Herbert S. Dinerstein, *War and the Soviet Union* (New York: Frederick A. Praeger, 1959); Thomas W. Wolfe, *Soviet Strategy at the Crossroads* (Cambridge: Harvard University Press, 1964); Marshall V. D. Sokolovskii et al., *Soviet Military Strategy* (Englewood Cliffs, N.J.: Prentice-Hall, 1963).

20. The permanently operating factors were "the stability of the rear, the morale of the army, the quantity and quality of divisions, the armament of the army, the organizational ability of the army commanders." The significance of the emphasis on these factors is that they were based on the experience of two world wars and were not related to the peculiar problems posed by nuclear weapons. Thus they were interpreted as indicating that transitory factors, such as a surprise attack, could not determine the outcome of war.

After the death of Stalin and the achievement of thermonuclear explosions, however, Soviet leaders announced that nuclear weapons negated the Marxist-Leninist axiom. The triumph of communism no longer depended on the "fatal inevitability" of an apocalyptic clash of arms. Under Khrushchev, Soviet doctrine qualified this view: A general war between the socialist and capitalist coalitions would result in the "annihilation of almost all life" in both camps, but the communist camp would somehow prevail. In a total war nuclear exchanges might quickly decide the outcome; hence the need for nuclear superiority. But such a war could be indefinitely forestalled, because Soviet retaliatory power would deter the capitalist camp from launching it. Thus in Soviet doctrine nuclear war in effect ceased to be an instrument of policy; but nuclear deterrence—especially deterrence of a Western military response against Soviet measures to alter the political status quo—was regarded as a powerful new force. Under the cover of deterrence, nuclear superiority or at least the conveyed impression of superiority was regarded as a powerful new lever of policy short of war.

In the late 1950s Khrushchev tried to extract the maximum political leverage from Soviet missile advances by claiming nuclear superiority over the U.S. After the Kennedy administration revealed the great nuclear superiority of the U.S., however, he shifted from claims of superiority to claims of virtual parity and contended that even an inferior nuclear force could deter a nuclear first strike with a capacity to inflict unacceptable retaliatory damage. Nevertheless, he continued to hail strategic nuclear striking power as the principal element of Soviet military strength, which rendered many types of traditional armed force obsolete and made possible the reduction of conventional forces without loss of combat capability. He depreciated the possibility of "local war" —that is, limited war between states, as opposed to wars fought within the boundary of a state—except between nonbloc states outside Europe. He identified internal or "national liberation wars" as the form of violence by means of which the Marxist-Leninist prophecy would inevitably be fulfilled, although it turned out that he was far cooler toward the support of such wars than Mao Tse-tung.

Yet in the Soviet Union, as in the United States, a more conservative school of strategists feared that nuclear deterrence would be emphasized too much at the expense of fighting a war if deterrence should fail. This school gained considerable influence after the Cuban missile crisis and the deposition of Khrushchev. Thereafter Soviet strategic thought made more explicit allowance for the limited and flexible use of force. It partially restored the traditional role of ground forces, even for a protracted war in Europe. It stressed the risk of escalation rather than the development of limited-war capabilities as the deterrent to lesser conflicts, but recognized the need to raise the nuclear threshold. It continued to reject the concept of a limited tactical nuclear war and deny the feasibility of a limited war involving the nuclear powers, but it took a more flexible position on the likelihood of local wars, implying that limited wars not involving the forces of the nuclear powers were possible even in Central Europe.

Soviet nuclear strategy still denies the possibility of a controlled nuclear war and continues to envisage a simultaneous strike at cities and military targets, despite Soviet recognition of the unconscionable damage that both sides would incur in an unlimited nuclear exchange. Yet there has been open dissent from the view that nuclear war ceases to be an instrument of policy and open assertion that the Soviet Union, if only for political and psychological reasons, ought not to reject the possibility that a nuclear war could be controlled and won.[21] Considering the deep historic and ideological roots in the Soviet Union of the view that war must be a flexible and controlled instrument of policy, it is not unlikely that Soviet strategists and statesmen will adopt some explicit doctrine of limited nuclear war as they gain a less vulnerable striking force and continue to ponder the anomaly of planning to conduct a total war with weapons that could so readily nullify the utility of victory.

Communist China's strategic thought is far less refined than that of the superpowers.[22] Its divergence from Soviet views is a major source of the Sino-Soviet rift. Yet it is as far as Soviet strategy from the French emphasis on nuclear deterrence at the expense of the flexible and controlled use of war. Russia's propagandist criticism notwithstanding, the Chinese share the Soviet view that the catastrophic nature of nuclear war negates the Marxist-Leninist dictum about the inevitable triumph of communism in a total war. Despite their depreciation of the decisiveness of nuclear war, they are no less impressed than the Russians by the mutual devastation it would cause. Although they hold, like the Russians, that only capitalism would be completely destroyed in a nuclear war, they neither want nor expect one.

Chinese strategists and statesmen differ from the Russians chiefly in their greater confidence that the U.S. can be deterred from initiating

21. See, for example, the development of this view by Lt.-Col. E. Rybkin in *Survival*, VIII (January, 1966), 12–16.
22. Alice L. Hsieh, *Communist China's Strategy in the Nuclear Era* (Englewood Cliffs, N.J.: Prentice-Hall, 1962); Donald S. Zagoria, *The Sino-Soviet Conflict, 1956–1961* (Princeton: Princeton University Press, 1962); William E. Griffith, *The Sino-Soviet Rift* (Cambridge: M.I.T. Press, 1964); Morton H. Halperin, *China and the Bomb* (New York: Frederick A. Praeger, 1965); Garthoff, *Soviet Military Policy*, chaps. ix–xi.

a nuclear war and in their lower estimate of the risk that local and national liberation wars will escalate across the nuclear threshold. In emphasizing the great dividends to be extracted from revolutionary wars, they argue that the best way to prevent the imperialists from launching a world war is to accept the risks in lesser wars, by which imperialism will eventually be defeated. They emphasize the need for violent revolutions conducted by foreign communist parties in the underdeveloped areas in order to disperse and exhaust American military strength, whereas the Soviets, while granting an important role to national liberation wars in these areas, stress the advantages of revolution in industrialized areas like Algeria and point to the opportunities for the peaceful acquisition of political control by communist parties. The greater resources of the Soviet Union give it greater confidence in "peaceful coexistence" as a framework for the vigorous expansion of influence and power by means short of war. But although Sino-Soviet polemics have accentuated important differences of emphasis in Russian and Chinese strategy, these countries share a common approach to force as a flexible instrument of policy to be controlled and limited by scrupulous political direction.

5. *Stability of the Principal Balance of Power*

The significance of strategic thought lies in the conceptual foundation it provides for the actual uses of force. The relationship between concept and reality is quite indirect. Yet in the nuclear age the actual uses of force as a deterrent in war and short of war confirm the great mutual restraint that is rationalized in American strategic thought. Let us examine the uses of force as they affect and are affected by the dominant feature of international politics since World War II: the cold war contest and balance between the U.S. and the Soviet Union. Even if this contest were to be so substantially moderated, in response to developments in international politics—the Sino-Soviet split, polycentrism in Eastern Europe, France's independent course—and in Soviet domestic life, that the underlying bipolar military balance would cease to be a decisive factor in international politics, the history of this balance would still be relevant to other contests and subsequent balances of power. It tells us much about the role of force in the nuclear age.

Experience as well as doctrine points to the critical importance of the balance of terror between the nuclear superpowers and their allies. One cannot know what the cold war would have been like if there had been no nuclear weapons, but it is hard to believe that such an intense contest between such powerful states, involving political stakes as important as Western Europe, would have been so readily contained beneath the threshold of general war had it not been for the prospect of nuclear devastation. Nevertheless, if the distribution of nuclear power had favored the Soviet Union or if the Soviets had not had to contemplate intolerable costs from overt aggression, war might well have occurred in spite of nuclear fears, either as a preventive knockout blow or as a result of some local encounter. Of course it is possible that the Soviet Union simply had no ambitions in Western Europe that she would have pursued at the slightest risk of war under any circumstances, but the opposite supposition—held by most students of Soviet foreign policy—seems more prudent: that the prerequisite of the Soviet Union's great caution in eschewing direct conquest and avoiding a direct military clash has been the American commitment and capability to oppose Soviet aggression with overwhelming force, if necessary.

If the great caution of the principal adversaries in taking risks of war has been due to the balance of terror—or, more specifically, to the mutual deterrent effect of countervailing nuclear capabilities—one of the principal instruments of this balance has been the North Atlantic Treaty. The North Atlantic alliance was created, essentially, to convince the Soviet Union and Western Europe that the U.S. would counter aggression in Europe from the outset and thereby deter an aggressor from precipitating general war. Through a succession of unforeseen events the alliance expanded into a political-military institution, an overseas American-led international command, and the semipermanent stationing of American forces on the Continent; but the original guarantees of the North Atlantic Treaty, intended to convince the Soviet Union that aggression against one ally would be tantamount to aggression against all, remain the essence of its deterrent function. And apparently it has been effective in this respect.

NATO represents the most far-reaching example of a development foreshadowed before World War I—the tendency of the new imperatives of peacetime military power to increase the stability of military commitments, while the arms race replaces shifts of alignment as the chief dynamic element in the competition for power. The Warsaw Pact exemplifies this tendency in a different form. Together, these alliances have enhanced deterrence by clarifying the question of who will defend whom. At the same time, they have avoided one of the destabilizing effects of rigid formal commitments, which was exhibited in the German blank check to Austria before World War I—the danger that such commitments may enable one state to gain the military support of its ally for special national interests and so encourage it to take actions that will involve all its allies in war. They have avoided this danger primarily because of the dominant influence of the East-West containment issue over all special national interests and the preponderance of the two superpowers in controlling the military balance. We shall consider later whether this situation is changing and what difference a change might make, but it is clear that so far the concentration of power within the superpowers' alliances has simplified deterrence by making it essentially a balance between two states.

The bipolar balance is actually a set of countervailing imbalances. From the beginning of the cold war, U.S. ability to inflict nuclear damage on the Soviet Union, even in a retaliatory strike, has been far superior to Soviet ability to inflict nuclear damage on the U.S. But although the Soviet Union lacked an impressive second-strike capability against the U.S. before the 1960s, by the late 1950s it could devastate Western Europe with MRBMs and bombers in retaliation against an American nuclear strike. Thus Stalin's successors in effect held Europe hostage with nuclear striking power, as Stalin had done with the Russian capacity to occupy Europe. At the same time, the Soviet Union's superior capacity to sustain a non-nuclear war and to occupy territory in central Europe has been offset by the threat of American nuclear retaliation, enhanced by local tactical nuclear strength.

In this balance of imbalances the U.S. probably deterred the Soviet Union from pursuing its ambitions more adventurously in Berlin, Cuba, and elsewhere largely by threatening a military response that would almost surely have been disadvantageous to carry out. By the same token, the U.S. was probably deterred from taking greater risks of war in withstanding Soviet pressure by the threat of a counter-response that the Soviet Union would have found disadvantageous to carry out. Necessarily, this situation created great uncertainties about the exact circumstances in which one side or the other might be willing to resort to war. Consequently, although military alignments in the nuclear age have been relatively clear and inflexible, the willingness to go to war under various contingencies has been quite conjectural, whereas in the eighteenth century, when the willingness to go to war was hardly in question, the formation and continuity of alliances were very much in doubt. At the same time, uncertainty about the consequences of prospective warfare has increased immensely because of the expanded spectrum of potential violence and the greater possibilities of escalation, as well as the complete absence of wartime experience with the most powerful weapons. Thus, the difficulty of calculating which actions of adversaries might lead to war and the chance of miscalculating the magnitude and consequences of war are much greater than before the nuclear age.

The danger of war by miscalculation, however, is counterbalanced by greater caution, which springs from the fact that the cost of political miscalculation, added to the cost of military miscalculation, is known to be enormously greater than at any time before the nuclear age. Awareness of the unconscionable cost of political miscalculation has inhibited the superpowers from deliberately taking risks of war on the basis of uncertainties about the adversary's intentions and responses that would have been quite acceptable to statesmen contemplating war in earlier periods of history. Uncertainties about relative military strength that might have led to war through military miscalculation before the nuclear age do not now upset the novel caution imposed by the certainty that any major war would quickly become utterly disastrous.[23]

On the other hand, lower risk-taking propensities have not dissuaded the nuclear states from boldly confronting each other in crises short of war. Quite the contrary, for the threshold of provocation below which the nuclear powers will confidently compete by threats of war has been raised by their knowledge of each other's great reluctance to fight. The Soviet Union has been emboldened to instigate offensive maneuvers in Korea, around Berlin, and in Cuba by its confidence that the U.S. would be deterred from opposing it with armed force by the prospect of nuclear war. The U.S. has been emboldened to oppose such maneuvers by its confidence that nuclear prospects also inhibit the Soviet Union from engaging American forces in war.

So far, the main protagonists of the cold war have kept well within the bounds of the expanded range of forceful political maneuver short of war, although the Cuban missile crisis seemed at the time to come perilously close to exceeding these bounds. But clearly there is an unavoidable degree of danger of war in maneuvers supported by the threat of war. How does one assess this danger? Let us look first at the stability of the military balance, which underlies the restraints on maneuver, and then at the relation of the military balance to other factors of mutual restraint.

The maintenance of the present bipolar nuclear balance is no more automatically assured than any previous military balance. Yet it seems very unlikely that one side or the other will gain a sufficient technical

23. Raymond Aron expresses this contrast between the nuclear and prenuclear periods well when he notes that before nuclear weapons "a simple dilemma blocked the way to lasting peace in systems founded on power politics: either the balance seemed perfect, in which case each belligerent hoped for possible victory, or else one side seemed manifestly superior and thus constituted a threat to the other." Now, however, "uncertainty may no longer hold the same psychological attraction as it did in the past. When no one was able to gauge the precise ratio of strength ahead of time, an adventure seemed tempting by virtue of its very unpredictability; now that this unpredictability involves fatalities on the order of tens of millions, even the most adventuresome of leaders might conceivably be inclined to caution." *The Great Debate*, pp. 211–12.

military advantage to tempt or provoke either to launch a nuclear attack. This seems unlikely for three general reasons: (1) The great number and diversity of strategic weapons, supported by active military research and development programs, mean that a quantitative or qualitative advance by one side will almost surely be offset by a quantitative or qualitative improvement by the other before the first side gains a useful first-strike capability. (2) The intolerably high level of prospective damage that even an inferior strategic force might inflict in retaliation against a nuclear first strike, together with the redundancy of civil-destruction capabilities possessed by both sides, means that additional increments of offensive capacity are unlikely to change the military balance enough to reduce the deterrent effect of the prospect of un-acceptable retaliatory damage. (3) The impossibility of knowing whether a nuclear exchange could be limited or of predicting the outcome of such an exchange with certainty, combined with the virtual certainty that an unrestricted nuclear war would soon be disastrous, means that neither government is likely to have enough confidence in its strategic superiority rationally to launch a nuclear attack.

A dramatic unilateral technological break-through, a major unilateral reduction of effort in the arms race, or a radical bilateral advancement of defensive systems against strategic offensive weapons could negate at least the first two conditions.[24] A drastic reduction of nuclear weapons through a disarmament agreement could negate all three. These de-velopments are not impossible, but they are very improbable. Thus the

24. The most consequential technological break-throughs would be those that greatly reduced the invulnerability of strategic retaliatory weapons or greatly reduced the vulnerability of civilian life to nuclear destruction. In the foreseeable future the technological development with the most significant effect on the U.S.–U.S.S.R. strategic balance would be the extensive deployment of antiballistic missiles (ABMs) and other antimissile systems to protect cities. The U.S., however, can readily offset any Soviet deployment by virtue of its superior financial resources and strategic offensive capabilities, which include many measures and devices to counteract ABMs. Furthermore, it is cheaper to offset ABMs by offensive improvements than to offset offensive weapons by deploying ABMs. American deployment of ABMs might enable the U.S. to reduce damage in a nuclear exchange if the Soviet Union failed to counter them with sufficient increases in offensive missiles and penetration devices, but there is very little prospect that ABMs will be so numerous and effective as to give the U.S. assurance that it could strike first without receiving unacceptable retaliatory damage, including tens of millions of fatalities. Whether the deployment of ABMs would enhance the invulnerability of ICBMs or give some protection against the prospective nuclear force of China in the 1970s were different questions. See Secretary of Defense McNamara's "posture statement" of March 8, 1966, *op. cit.*, pp. 53–58, and his expanded analysis of the ABM question in the corresponding statement for FY 1968 (January 23, 1967), pp. 46–55; also, Charles M. Herzfeld, "BMD and National Security," *Survival*, III (March, 1966), 70–76. Of course, unilateral or bilateral deployment of ABMs might have political and psychological effects of a significance far disproportionate to its effect on the technical balance.

U.S.-Soviet arms race seems likely to follow the pattern of previous races: the establishment of an equilibrium based on one adversary's superiority (which, in this case, may amount to parity), maintained until the political cause of the competition erodes.

The stability of the bipolar military balance, however, must not be judged only by the prospect of a deliberate nuclear attack out of the blue. Much more plausible is the prospect that a military imbalance might change the risk-taking propensities of one side sufficiently to lead to non-nuclear war.

As for direct armed clashes between the superpowers and their allies (as opposed to proxy internal wars in underdeveloped states), it seems that the risk that the smallest encounter might become a nuclear war has extended the deterrent effect of the latter prospect throughout the whole spectrum of warfare, so that the apothegm of the Eisenhower-Dulles period—that whatever will deter a big war will also deter a small one—may have turned out to be true. Nevertheless, it does not follow that the critics of that strategy were wrong. The strategic revisionists charged that the growth of Soviet nuclear striking power would dangerously undermine the credibility of nuclear deterrence against local aggressions unless the West built up its conventional resistance capabilities. But by the time the Soviet Union embraced *détente* in the aftermath of the Cuban missile crisis in 1962, it had not yet acquired the kind of parity in second-strike capability that the revisionists posited; and, furthermore, the American government had partially carried out the revisionists' recommendations by explicitly adopting a strategy of local resistance and improving the U.S. capacity to support it. Therefore the great question of the late 1950s remained unanswered: If both nuclear antagonists should have the capacity to inflict unacceptable damage on each other in retaliation against a nuclear strike, and if both knew it, what effect would this have on the efficacy of deterrence? Would it so diminish the credibility of either side initiating the use of nuclear weapons as to induce the offensive state to take greater risks of war in pursuing local gains and induce the defensive state to take greater risks of war in withstanding them? Might second-strike parity even make the nuclear threshold seem so stable and predictable as to convince the superpowers they could fight each other in limited wars at a tolerable risk of escalation? Or would the residual uncertainty about an adversary's willingness to resort to war and about the feasibility of keeping war below the nuclear threshold, combined with the exorbitant penalties of miscalculation, maintain mutual deterrence as effectively as before?

In favor of the last hypothesis one might cite the lack of a clear correlation between the Soviet Union's relative nuclear power and its instigation of crises and the persistent great caution of the U.S. and the Soviet Union in avoiding a direct clash of arms during crises regardless of actual and apparent changes in the strategic balance. One can infer from this evidence and the evidence of official statements that the curve of deterrence, so to speak, has become very inelastic in response to changes in relative nuclear power—so inelastic, perhaps, that only a sudden and spectacular unilateral advance in defensive or offensive capabilities could significantly increase the beneficiary's propensity to take greater risks of local war with its nuclear competitor. Putting it another way, at the level of possible mutual devastation already inherent in the nuclear balance for a number of years, the psychology of second-strike parity, which induces both governments to act as if war were unacceptable, may prevail even though the physical disparities of striking power are great.

This supposition gains credence from the fact that the President and other American spokesmen were describing nuclear war in the apocalyptic rhetoric of mutual suicide even when the U.S. had overwhelming superiority in nuclear striking power in the early 1950s. Soviet leaders have reiterated the same rhetoric despite its negation of a major Marxist-Leninist tenet. Of course the rhetoric is a metaphorical, not a literal, expression of careful assessments of prospective nuclear damage. Moreover, it does not prove that the Soviet Union would view the risks of war with the psychology of parity if it actually enjoyed parity, let alone the kind of nuclear superiority the U.S. has held. Yet all the evidence we have of the Soviet approach to the risks of war indicates that as long as Soviet leaders believe that the U.S. can inflict terrible damage upon the Soviet Union in a nuclear exchange, they will remain as reluctant as ever to risk war with the U.S.

It follows that the mutual restraint of the superpowers in avoiding war or coming perilously close to the brink of war depends less on the military balance than on their estimation of each other's comparative resolve to use force in a clash of interests. This comparative resolve is affected by the military balance but less directly affected than deterrence.

Under conditions in which neither side can be sure of avoiding terrible devastation in a nuclear war, the comparative resolve or relative risk-taking propensities of the U.S. and the Soviet Union may depend more on disparities of local conventional strength than on disparities of nuclear power, but they will depend far more on relative intensities of interest—one might call it the balance of interests—than on either the conventional or the nuclear military balance.[25] It was above all the

25. Since the relative intensity of interests is made manifest in the competition of risk-taking by the relative determination of the adversaries to resort to war in

manifest American interest in withstanding Khrushchev's semi-ulti-matum concerning Berlin in 1958 and in stopping his emplacement of Soviet missiles in Cuba in 1962 that dissuaded the Soviet Union from altering the military and political status quo at the risk of war.

If the improvement of American conventional capabilities has en-hanced deterrence in areas of primary interest like Europe and the Caribbean, where the prospect of escalation to nuclear war is great, it has probably done so indirectly, simply by strengthening the American will to assert convincingly the great interest of the U.S. in preventing forceful changes in the status quo. Significantly, one of the principal arguments for improving conventional capabilities was, from the outset, that this would strengthen American resolve in situations where the government would otherwise have to choose between acquiescence and nuclear war.

The balance of interests between the superpowers is necessarily quite subjective and, one might suppose, highly susceptible to miscalculation. Therefore, even assuming the great caution of American and Soviet lead-ers, it would be a fragile basis of deterrence were it not for the clarifica-tion of interests that has emerged from the sporadic clashes of national power and will. In the give and take of the cold war certain more or less reciprocal conventions or rules of the game between the nuclear superpowers have become established. One of these is that neither side shall suddenly change the territorial-political status quo or the military balance by direct offensive action outside its recognized sphere of in-fluence—a rule, of course, that must be continually reinforced, as in the Cuban missile crisis, to be effective.

From the Soviet standpoint, however, this rule does not preclude subversion, internal war, and the kind of harassment practiced against Berlin. One reason is that these indirect offensives are sufficiently ambiguous to evade a deterrent threat. The West protests the illegiti-macy of this behavior. Yet in practice the risks of war and the wide-spread popular preference for internal over external war compel the status quo powers to try to legitimize direct intervention as a counter to subversion.

In trying to clarify and emphasize its interest in protecting potential victims of communist attack or subversion by direct action if necessary, the U.S. has capitalized on the tendency of the bipolar contest to ac-centuate the value of local stakes that do not significantly affect the

---

behalf of their interests, one might also call the balance of interests the balance of resolve. Interests, however, are more nearly analogous to military strength as the chief constituent element of a balance, whereas resolve is chiefly a function of these constituent elements.

material or strategic balance. This accentuation is partly due to the fact
that bipolarity has the aspect of a zero-sum game in which one adversary's gain is the other's loss, together with the feeling that a small
loss may lead to further losses, and it is partly due to the enhanced
importance of demonstrating resolve when so much depends on deterrence and intimidation.

Of course there is still an irreducible element of risk that the U.S.
or the Soviet Union might miscalculate each other's military intentions
and responses so badly as to put one or the other in a position in which
it cannot avoid an overt clash of arms without sacrificing compelling
interests. The seeming stability of mutual deterrence might make one
or both governments so confident of their freedom of maneuver below
the threshold of provocation to war that they would abandon the caution
necessary to avoid war. So far, however, the crises that have involved
some prospect of war between the nuclear superpowers seem not to have
increased risk-taking propensities. Rather, they have strengthened their
precautions against crossing that nebulous threshold dividing military
from nonmilitary conflicts with each other.

6. *Superpower Crises*

The competition of the superpowers within the expanded area of
maneuver under the threat of war takes many forms, ranging from words
of warning and intimidation, to hostile military deployments and demonstrations, to interference with communication and traffic. What is
historically new about these tactics, apart from the greater technical
resources of communication and demonstration with which they are
conducted, is that they take place in the shadow of far more terrible
violence than ever before, so that the psychological and political impact
of any maneuver is accentuated by the latent prospect of catastrophe.

The primary manifestation of this phenomenon is the local crisis; that
is, a clash of national objectives and interests over the status of a particular place, leading to an increase in international tensions and in
the apparent risk of war. Such crises became a characteristic mode of
international politics in the nineteenth century, but in the nuclear age
the expansion of the range of conflict short of war has multiplied the
number of steps toward the brink of war and refined the competition
for superior position along these steps. Yet this competition is so cautious, the steps so ambiguous, and the location of the brink so uncertain
that neither of the superpowers can be sure just how close it is to war
during a crisis. Threats of war are studiously implied rather than ex-

plicitly defined. Demands and ultimatums are sufficiently indefinite to permit compliance or revocation without humiliation.[26]

The great caution of the nuclear powers in avoiding a direct military encounter with each other and the consequent step-by-step mode of controlling force short of war extend to their involvement in military demonstrations (as in Lebanon and Berlin) and wars (as in Korea and Vietnam). Accordingly, as we shall see in our examination of limited war and escalation, the characteristics of a crisis may now pervade war itself, at least up to a certain indefinable level of violence. So far, however, the superpowers have carefully avoided actions that would lead to a local military encounter between both of their forces. The Soviet Union seems to have regarded each forward step toward its objectives in a crisis as contingent upon the adversary's response and has always been ready to back down rather than fight. To avoid a clash with Soviet forces the U.S. refrained from running a land convoy to Berlin in 1949 and from attacking Cuba in 1962, although perhaps neither act entailed a serious risk of war.[27]

The relative military power of the superpowers affects the outcome of their crises even though it is not tested. But there is a greater disproportion than before the nuclear age between objective disparities of military capabilities and the political leverage or bargaining power of antagonists. In crises the impression of relative military strength in the minds of the adversaries is surely a factor in the outcome; but the relation of these impressions to actual military ratios is not precise, and their correlation with relative bargaining power is obscure. The Soviet Union has been as cautious in avoiding war and as willing to retreat from an offensive maneuver in Berlin, where it had great local conventional superiority and held Western Europe a nuclear hostage, as in Cuban waters. The U.S.

26. William Welch examines the studied equivocality, cautiousness, and ambiguity of Khrushchev's manipulation of threats during five crises in *The Nature of Khrushchevian Threats Against the West* ("University of Colorado Studies: Series in Political Science," No. 3; Boulder, Colorado: University of Colorado Press, 1965). Of particular interest on the dynamics of crises involving indirect Soviet and American confrontations are W. Phillips Davison, *The Berlin Blockade* (Princeton: Princeton University Press, 1958); Hans Speier, *The Soviet Threat to Berlin* (Santa Monica: The RAND Corporation, 1960); Jack M. Schick, "The Berlin Crisis, 1958–1962: A Study of Comparative Miscalculation" (unpublished manuscript, 1966); Arthur J. Dommen, *Conflict in Laos: The Politics of Neutralization* (New York: Frederick A. Praeger, 1965); and Tang Tsou and Morton H. Halperin, *Communist China and the Offshore Islands* (Chicago: University of Chicago Press, 1967).

27. Bernard Brodie makes this point in the context of an analysis of escalation that argues its susceptibility to control and stresses the effective caution of the superpowers in avoiding nuclear war in crises. *Escalation and the Nuclear Option*, pp. 45ff.

was neither more nor less inclined to take risks of war in opposing Soviet moves in Cuba, where it had great local conventional superiority in addition to over-all strategic nuclear superiority, than in Berlin.

Like the efficacy of deterrence, the competitive advantage in crises turns largely on the balance of interests as manifested in the relative capacity of the opponents to convince each other that they will support their positions with war if necessary. But the fact that both of the superpowers have such frightening destructive capabilities, while neither can escape the high but uncertain risk that any clash of arms may get out of control, makes the translation of relative military strength into bargaining power depend on many subjective factors interacting in unpredictable ways with objective military capabilities.

When a crisis reaches the point at which the prospect of war must be taken seriously, relative bargaining power may be affected more than deterrence by a disparity of military capabilities, since a military advantage that is too small to determine the choice between war and peace may still be sufficient to encourage lesser moves in the competition below the threshold of war. As before the nuclear age, the political environment and circumstances of the crisis are apt to be as decisive as military capabilities in determining the relative advantage in brinkmanship. The difference is simply that when war was regarded as less dangerous, the prospect of war was usually more credible and imminent at a lower level of provocation. Accordingly the contest of wills depended more than now on estimates of relative fighting strength and less on complicated estimates of intentions, political determination, and risk-taking propensities, tested step by step in a war of nerves.

Not only was the resort to war more credible before the nuclear age; partly for this reason, crises were customarily terminated by some sort of political settlement, whereas now they tend to erode, ending in the tacit acceptance of a state of affairs that no one wants to change by force. Before, crises that were not resolved by diplomatic realignments and accommodation tended to progress relatively directly and swiftly from political maneuvering to more explicit threats of war and often to war itself. Now the maneuvering and the contest of wills may last for weeks or months without ever reaching the stage of imminent warfare. Yet during this time the multiplicity and the urgency of decisions required may impose sustained pressure in the management of force and threats of war, comparable to the pressure of war itself.

Although the margins of quantitative superiority or inferiority are now less directly related to political leverage and bargaining power in confrontations short of war, they are far from irrelevant. For example, a numerical advantage in bombers and missiles, even if superfluous from the standpoint of a sophisticated calculus of deterrence, may be an important instrument of political and psychological warfare. Whether because of the remnants of traditional military thinking or because of the practical need for some relatively simple measure of military power, governments tend to attribute to simple numerical disparities—especially in the most powerful weapons—a significance that is not always warranted by the fine analyses of experts in military strategy. Even though they might not be willing to base their own maneuvers on these numerical disparities as such, governments are inclined to regard them as an instrument of psychological warfare capable of affecting the will of the adversary to take risks of war. Therefore if one state thinks it is disadvantaged by a strategic inferiority, its opponent may try to capitalize on an apparent psychological advantage. In this way American fears of an approaching missile gap may have encouraged Khrushchev's campaign to convey an impression of Soviet strategic superiority and use it as a political lever against Berlin in 1958–61. The deception worked for a while, but it failed to change the status of Berlin—perhaps partly because Soviet leaders knew the real basis of strategic inferiority from which they were operating.

It is not only nuclear weapons that serve as instruments of political and psychological warfare. As in the case of deterrence, the conventional forces that can be brought to bear upon a local point of conflict are also an important lever in the superpowers' crises in spite of, and in a way because of, the tremendous nuclear force available to both sides. As the risk of escalation to nuclear war is the immediate deterrent to local non-nuclear war, it is also the immediate lever to be manipulated for advantages short of war. Local conventional forces may be critically important in controlling this threat of escalation advantageously.

For this purpose the U.S. does not necessarily need local conventional superiority; it needs enough of the right kind of conventional force to withstand offensive moves in such a way as to put the onus for initiating war on the adversary. The ability to compel the Soviet Union to engage allied forces instead of achieving a painless *fait accompli* may be essential for withstanding maneuvers and demands intended to upset the status quo. Conventional forces can enable the U.S. to assert a favorable balance of interests at a tolerable risk.

A strategy of meeting the first hostile Soviet move with an automatic tactical nuclear response might be the most effective deterrent to Soviet-inspired crises *if* the U.S. were obviously determined to carry it out. In the evident absence of such bravado, however, American determination must be based on a more prudent response.

The short-of-war role of nuclear and conventional forces was illustrated in all its significance and ambiguity in the Cuban missile crisis of 1962.[28] Of all the cold war crises, this one seems to have come closest to an overt clash of arms between the superpowers. Yet no one is sure just how likely war became or exactly what effect the local or strategic military balance had on the outcome. The evidence consists chiefly of the subjective impressions of these crucial questions in the minds of some of the participants.

The prelude to the Soviet emplacement of missiles in Cuba was a studied effort by the Soviet government to foster and translate into political gains the unwarranted U.S. fears of strategic inferiority at the time of the sputniks and the missile-gap controversy, perhaps with the intention of weakening American resistance to Soviet moves against Berlin. When the U.S. discovery and announcement of its real strategic superiority ruined this effort, Khrushchev evidently sought to regain the initiative in the quickest and cheapest way by establishing missiles in Cuba, again as a general political lever rather than as preparation for an anticipated war.

To the American government, at the time, this seemed like an act so rash as to border on the irrational. Equally to Soviet surprise, the U.S. reaction to the first firm evidence that "offensive" missiles were being installed was quick and vigorous. It established a "quarantine"—actually a selective blockade—against missile-carrying ships. After several days of intense crisis, the Soviet Union stopped the shipment of missiles and removed the missiles already in Cuba in return for a face-saving American pledge not to invade the island.

Like the Soviet emplacement of missiles, the American response was motivated chiefly by concern about the general political significance of the action. Even the actual effect on the military balance seemed less important than the appearance of an effect; for, as President Kennedy remarked, appearances are very important when matters of national will and leadership are involved. The American government interpreted the chief significance of the Soviet Union's apparent revision of the nuclear balance as a daring political gambit designed to shore up a local communist regime at America's doorstep, demonstrate American impotence, and above all support Soviet pressure against Berlin. It considered this

28. Arnold L. Horelick, "The Cuban Missile Crisis: An Analysis of Soviet Calculations and Behavior," *World Politics*, Vol. XVI (April, 1964). Albert and Roberta Wohlstetter, *Controlling the Risks in Cuba*, Adelphi Papers, No. 17 (London: Institute for Strategic Studies, 1965). Elie Abel, *The Missile Crisis* (New York: J. B. Lippincott, 1966). Arnold L. Horelick and Myron Rush, *Strategic Power and Soviet Foreign Policy* (Chicago: University of Chicago Press, 1966), examines the crisis in the context of the Soviet effort to gain and exploit an impression of a favorable strategic balance.

"peaceful" deployment of weapons no less provocative than mobilization for war would have been in an earlier period. In announcing the quarantine, President Kennedy did not charge the Soviet Union with any military designs; he condemned it for a sudden and secret alteration of the military status quo. "We no longer live in a world," he declared, "where only the actual firing of weapons represents a sufficient challenge to a nation's security to constitute maximum peril. Nuclear weapons are so destructive, and ballistic missiles are so swift, that any substantially increased possibility of their use or any sudden change in their deployment may well be regarded as a definite threat to peace."[29]

In retrospect one can reconstruct an explanation of the Soviet action as the product of a rational anticipation of American acquiescence to a *fait accompli*, based on a reasonable interpretation of a succession of American actions (for example, the abortive Bay of Pigs operation) and American responses to Soviet actions. The disturbing fact, however, is that the Soviet Union miscalculated American reactions as badly as the U.S. miscalculated Soviet intentions. Having fallen into this reciprocal miscalculation, both sides were all the more uncertain about the risks of war that might follow from their opposing moves in the deepening crisis.

Yet the effect of this uncertainty was to reinforce caution, not to provoke rashness. From the U.S. standpoint Cuba might well have been the ideal place to fight and contain a local war rather than to permit the Soviet Union to carry out its design, considering U.S. local conventional superiority, its strategic nuclear superiority, and Cuba's position as an isolated island near the U.S. and very far from Russia. Yet the group of Americans involved in managing the crisis took the course of resistance least likely to lead to local war, because they saw a serious prospect that any clash of Soviet and American forces might lead to nuclear war.

Because of the great caution of both sides in avoiding a military encounter, the role of the military balance on the outcome of the Cuban missile crisis is bound to be obscure. Clearly the physical ability of the U.S. to dominate the local situation was advantageous. Yet this advantage was to an important extent offset by the conviction that any overt military encounter with Soviet personnel might quickly expand out of control and by the fear that too conspicuous a success in applying pressure locally might be countered by Soviet pressure around Berlin or against American missiles in Turkey. One might reasonably suppose that

29. "The Soviet Threat to the Americas," address delivered on October 22, 1962. U.S. *Department of State Bulletin*, November 12, 1962, p. 716.

the nuclear balance had something to do with the relative bargaining power of the antagonists, since it was partly on that assumption that the Soviets undertook the missile emplacement in the first place. Yet although the U.S. had a sizable nuclear superiority and both sides knew it, it could scarcely have taken greater precautions to avoid any clash of arms, and it could no more have afforded to acquiesce in the Soviet gambit if its nuclear force had been inferior. Perhaps American nuclear superiority deterred the Soviet Union from playing its Berlin card or from challenging the blockade and keeping its missiles in Cuba. But considering the low risk-taking propensities the Soviets displayed, one must doubt both that their restraint was governed by a fine calculation of the particular nuclear balance and that they would have been any more willing to run the risk of local war under a favorable strategic balance.

In the end, the clearest advantage of the U.S. was its distinctly favorable balance of interests. In the intense clash of interests the U.S. soon made it evident that the prevention of a Soviet missile base in Cuba was more important to it than the establishment of a missile base was to the Soviet Union. The critical measure of this interest was its greater willingness to use force in pursuing its objective. Undoubtedly this willingness reflected to some extent the favorable balance in local conventional and strategic nuclear force, but not in any direct or simple way.

When so much depended upon subjective impressions about the intensity of opposing interests and the relative willingness of governments to take risks of war in their behalf, there must have been some danger of war by political and psychological miscalculation. Yet, although the level of provocation was high, the risks of war were scrupulously controlled. In the U.S. every decision was taken only after carefully anticipating the consequences that might follow from Soviet reactions and weighing these consequences against those of alternative courses of action. As in the Berlin crisis of 1958–61, the operating strategy of crisis management, like the U.S. strategy of limited war, was governed by the concept of a measured application of force under political control, designed to influence the adversary's will advantageously at the least risk and cost. With Soviet leaders exercising equal caution, escalation was at no time automatic. At no time did the dynamics of reciprocal pressure impel events inexorably toward war.

Yet the control and restraint of this crisis provide no cause for complacency about future crises. After all, the Cuban crisis grew out of grossly erroneous estimates of national interests and behavior between states with years of hard experience in confronting each other. During the crisis even a slight miscalculation of one antagonist's reaction to the other's moves, or a single lapse of prudence, might have led beyond the point of no return. We do not know by what margins of mutual restraint the crisis was kept below the threshold of war. Therefore we cannot be sure that the margins will be safe another time.

The important role of crises and their uncertain margins of safe restraint raise the question: Are crises becoming more dangerous? Does each crisis build up frustrations that are more likely to erupt in war the next time? Does the conduct of one crisis without war create unwarranted confidence in the avoidance of war in a subsequent crisis? Might the superpowers become so confident of each other's determination to avoid the first use of arms that one or the other would become too bold during a crisis and convince its opponent that the resort to local war would be less objectionable than acquiescence? Might the very fears of nuclear war that have so far imposed great caution, eventually, in the prolonged absence of actual war, seem so hypothetical and unreal as to cease to grip the imagination?

An affirmative answer to all these questions is quite plausible in the abstract. Yet so far the evidence does not support it. Actually, successive crises seem to have kept alive the sobering prospect of war in both nations while reinforcing American vigilance and teaching the Soviet Union the narrow limits of safe maneuver.

7. *The United States–China Balance*

On the whole, the Soviet-American competition looks remarkably restrained and safe, and the underlying balance of military power quite stable. But what about the competition and balance elsewhere? The uses of force by the superpowers in direct competition with each other are bound to be different from the uses of force between the superpowers and other states or between states not allied with the superpowers. Where the uses of military power are different, one would expect the political consequences and the prospects of order also to differ.

To what extent do the generalizations about the central bipolar balance apply to the conflict between the U.S. and China? The role of military power in this conflict shows the limits of nuclear deterrence outside the confrontation of the superpowers.

Between the U.S. and China the balance of terror operates only to the extent that the Soviet Union seems willing to use nuclear force in behalf of China as it would for itself. The Sino-Soviet split makes this condition quite unlikely. Until China can devastate the U.S. with its own nuclear weapons, the U.S. will have an undisputed first-strike capability against it. China undoubtedly respects and fears American nuclear power and is cautious not to give the U.S. a pretext for using it.

Yet the credibility of the U.S. using nuclear weapons in a local war supported by China certainly cannot be taken for granted. After all, in two large, though limited, wars—one with China in Korea and the other with China's ally in Vietnam—the U.S. refrained from using or threatening to use even tactical nuclear weapons against military targets. In the retreat from the Yalu the U.S. refrained while sustaining one of its worst defeats in history. Presumably there are compelling considerations that account for nuclear abstention in these wars and in other, prospective conflicts in Asia.

In the first place, under the relatively primitive conditions of warfare in Asia there is not likely to be a suitable opportunity to use tactical nuclear weapons for anything but a dubious marginal military advantage.

In the second place, the adverse reaction of world opinion to an American nuclear first strike would be accentuated in Asia by the special opprobrium attached to the use of nuclear weapons against nonwhite nations. Furthermore, unlike in Europe, no major states are likely to support even a first-strike *threat*, although this could change if China's capacity for direct military action looks more menacing and if Japan or India should develop nuclear forces to counter China.

In the third place, perhaps a notion of fairness adds inhibitions to the use of nuclear weapons against those who lack them—a psychological advantage that China may steadily be losing.

Finally, U.S. interest in containing Communist expansion in Asia is not as compelling as in Europe. Therefore, the political costs of using nuclear weapons are likely to seem disproportionate to the political stakes, even if the use of tactical nuclear weapons were militarily advantageous.

These considerations, combined with the de-emphasis on nuclear retaliation as a substitute for local conventional resistance, and the worldwide spread and intensification of nuclear inhibitions, have eroded the credibility of American nuclear power as a deterrent against local incursions outside Europe. Yet one should not conclude that American military power, either nuclear or non-nuclear, is an unimportant restraint on China. No other nation attaches as much importance in doctrine and practice to the uses of military power, yet China is as cautious as the Soviet Union in minimizing the risks of war. China's respect for American power is reflected in its great caution in avoiding a direct military encounter with the U.S. except during the American drive to the Yalu, when it probably believed its own territory was endangered. Its maneuvers against Quemoy and Matsu were more circumspect than the Soviet Union's maneuvers in the Cuban missile crisis. If deterrence seems less efficacious against China than against Russia, it is because China has been too weak to challenge American interests as directly, yet has had much more promising opportunities for indirect aggression.

If China retains opportunities for proxy aggression and insurgent warfare in Asia, there will remain a wide range of warfare in which the risk of nuclear escalation will be quite small compared to that risk in any clash of arms between the U.S. and the Soviet Union. China's eventual achievement of a significant capability for nuclear retaliation against the U.S. will further call into question the credibility of an American nuclear response to non-nuclear aggression in Asia and will probably increase Peking's confidence in its ability to keep local wars below the nuclear threshold. Therefore, military deterrence in Asia must depend far more than in Europe on local non-nuclear fighting capabilities. Yet no military deterrent can prevent wars that capitalize on the vulnerability of the Third World to insurgency, except by the demonstration through military resistance that such wars will fail or involve too great a risk of disadvantageous escalation.

8. *The Third World*

Ever since the victory of the Communist revolution in China, the Third World—that is, the areas, chiefly in the southern hemisphere, inhabited by new, weak, and poor states—has become an increasingly active and violent area of international politics with growing repercussions upon the politics of the advanced states. Even if the Third World could be isolated from the advanced states, its pervasive disorder would be lamentable. But it cannot be isolated. Therefore, as in the periods of imperial expansion, events in the "backward" areas threaten to disrupt the balance among the advanced states.

The activation and disruption of the Third World springs largely from indigenous upheavals—the rise of nationalism, the end of colonialism, the political instability and inexperience of new states, the friction between traditional societies and the forces of modernization, the disparity between high economic expectations and little economic progress, and the crystallization of national antagonisms. But the disturbing impact of developments in the Third World has also sprung from their involvement in the contest between the major contenders in the cold war.

In this vast and turbulent area the Soviet Union, checked in Europe and anxious to recapture Marxist-Leninist dynamism, and Communist China, convinced that Mao's revolutionary strategy holds the key to victories beyond its borders, discovered the most fruitful opportunities for advancing their control and influence at the expense of the great capitalist states. The U.S., committed from the beginning of the cold war to a general strategy of containment which makes even intrinsically unimportant targets of communist expansion major points of contention, has responded to Soviet and Chinese offensives by a progressive extension of its military commitments far beyond its original expectations. Neither Russia nor China has succeeded in extending its hegemony into countries its armed forces cannot occupy—Cuba and South Vietnam, the closest to being exceptions, are doubtful satellites. Both have been deterred from undertaking direct military adventures, partly by the prospect of encountering superior American forces. Nevertheless, the Third World is the most volatile arena of competition.

There the two major Communist states seek aggrandizement that is antithetical to American interests even though they follow different tactics and compete with one another. Yet no major power has much control over the field of competition, for the field is no longer populated by passive colonial holdings. Moreover, the advanced states are constrained from direct punitive and policing expeditions, except at the invitation of a local state, against threats posed by a major adversary. They are constrained by their fear that counterintervention will lead to a major war and by self-imposed inhibitions, which reflect the opprobrium attached to the use of force against small powers and spring from their competition for the allegiance of the nationalists in former colonial areas. At the same time, among the new states of the Third World there are virtually none of the political or military conditions that facilitated a stable balance of power in Europe.

In these circumstances of deep change and conflict, military power has played an active role, overtly as well as tacitly. Its critical importance is not negated by the facts that significant nonmilitary forms of power are also shaping the international politics of the new and poor states or that force, as always, can affect politics only in special ways. Every major change in the territorial and political status of states in the Third World has depended on armed force, except for the instances in which colonial powers conferred independence peacefully—and even then the achievement of independence was closely associated with the effects of World War II and the decline of the European states as global military powers. Since World War II the Third World has been agitated by a succession of local wars, some of them protracted and intense.[30] Many of them have

---

30. There have been more than fifty limited wars—that is, local non-nuclear wars—of various kinds in the twenty years since World War II. Of these, only the Greek civil war (1946–49) and the Hungarian rebellion (1956) were fought in Europe, although the Cyprus civil conflict (1955–60) involved two NATO allies, Greece and Turkey. About a dozen wars were conventional interstate wars, the

involved major states on one or both sides. The largest and most violent have been the Chinese and Algerian civil wars, two Chinese-supported "national liberation wars" in Indochina, the Korean War, and the part revolutionary, part interstate war in Vietnam. The Vietnam war involved Americans directly and on a large scale, the Soviets indirectly in a very limited way. The Korean War brought the U.S. into direct, large-scale combat with the Chinese. American forces were employed in Lebanon (1958) and in the Dominican Republic (1965), although against little or no opposition. The U.S. Navy was a decisive element in the Quemoy-Matsu encounter in 1958, even though it did not directly engage Communist Chinese forces. American troop deployments in Southeast Asia may have played an important role in stabilizing the Laotian crisis of 1961. There is no reason to think that the frequency and scope of local wars in the Third World will decline. They may increase. Some are likely to impinge upon the vital interests of the U.S., Russia, and China, and therefore pose some prospect of expanding into a direct military confrontation between major nuclear powers.

In the face of these realities it seems strange to maintain that war, let alone force, is obsolete. In some cases the use of armed force may have been ineffective, unnecessary, or counterproductive. In other cases it was surely indispensable. In each instance one must judge the utility of force by comparing the outcome with the hypothetical situation that might have existed in the absence of force. The fact that war does not always serve the interests of a particular state may only indicate its utility for another. If the principal status quo powers lack an effective military response to revolutionary war—a proposition that is certainly not verified as a universal truth—that only emphasizes the utility of war from the standpoint of those states exploiting revolutions.

The general utility of military power short of war in the Third World is equally evident. Surely the world would be quite different if the U.S. had not projected its immense mobile power to the remotest parts of the globe. This power evidently deterred both the Soviet Union and China

---

politically most significant being fought in Korea (1950–3), Quemoy-Matsu (1954–58), and Suez (1956), and on the Sino-Indian border (1959–62). There were a few interstate wars fought at a low level by unconventional means but a large number of internal wars fought mainly within the boundaries of a single state. Many of these internal wars were important international, as opposed to purely local, events because they involved a major power from outside the region or involved local communist parties seeking power with the active support of the Soviet Union, China, or one of their proxy states. Most notable among these were the wars in French Indochina (1947–54), Burma (1948–54), Philippines (1948–54), Malaya (1948–58), Guatemala (1954), Cuba (1957–59), the Congo (1960–3), and Vietnam (1959– —), which began as an internal war supported by North Vietnam and became a war involving the U.S. in both North and South Vietnam.

from taking actions that would have brought them into direct combat with American forces. It also bolstered the resistance of weak states to political penetration and subversion. But for the presence or proximity of American forces, Chinese penetration of Asia and Soviet penetration of Latin America and the Middle East would almost surely have been more extensive.

The U.S. alliances in Asia and the Pacific are essentially deterrent devices to establish the credibility of American determination to use armed force in behalf of containment in areas of minor intrinsic value. If the U.S. had not conveyed its resolve to use force by these and other means, there would have been no effective military counterpoise to communist military adventures in the whole area. Conceivably, that would have made no difference, but the views of Asian statesmen and the Chinese complaints against "eneirclement" suggest otherwise.

The Korean War can be regarded as a failure of deterrence which nevertheless reinforced deterrence by demonstrating that American forces were indispensable for effective resistance against conventional military aggression in Asia and would be used to that end. Throughout the peripheries of Asia, wherever sea- and airpower can reach, the preponderance of American military power is even more marked than in Europe. Remove that preponderance and the resulting expansion of Chinese power by direct or indirect means would make it obvious that the distribution of military power is just as important in what we now call the Third World as it was in the formerly colonial world. Thus by authoritative local testimony, the ability of the nonaligned states of Burma and Cambodia to retain their independence has depended critically on the protective shadows that are cast by America's military presence in the area.

Although the principal advanced states operate under substantial inhibitions against taking forceful punitive and police actions in the Third World, we should not exaggerate the contrast with earlier periods. Long before the nuclear age and the rise of nationalism in the less developed areas, small or weak states often enjoyed a freedom of action in defiance of large states by virtue of their protected position in a balance of power for which they were not responsible and by virtue of the intensity of their interests in a local conflict compared to the broader stakes of great powers. Moreover, now the military weakness of the new states imposes limits upon their capacity to protect or advance their interests which are no less substantial than the limits facing weak states before. Even nonalignment among the new states, although deriving much of its popularity as a policy of independence from great-power politics, has reflected the dominance of the chief military powers insofar as it has been a strategy for capitalizing on Soviet-American competition. The moderation and complication of that competition, together with the growing concern of small states with local conflicts, now tends to diminish the appeal and relevance of nonalignment and to reveal more clearly the continuing importance of military power and power differentials.

But although military power is as important in the Third World as elsewhere, it takes different forms and has different consequences there. Unlike in Europe, the deterrent effect of even the most powerful armed forces does not extend to the full range of feasible force. This is not so much because deterrence is ineffective as because it is inapplicable to the primary forms of war in the area—internal war[31] and local interstate war. It is likely to be inapplicable even when the Soviet Union or China supports such wars as an instrument of state policy, because the local origins of these wars and their covert external support cannot readily be made the object of an appropriate threat of military response from outside.

Revolutionary and insurgent warfare is as old as civilization, but since World War II its practitioners—most notably but not exclusively the communists—have developed a systematic doctrine, a disciplined organization and managerial technique, and sophisticated operational strategy and tactics that distinguish the "militarized mass insurrection" from earlier revolutionary wars.[32] Combining mass mobilization with highly professional direction, nationalistic and Marxist messianism with calcu-

31. "Internal war" covers a wide range of insurrections waged for the control of a government within the boundaries of a state, from *coups d'état* to revolutionary wars. The revolutionary wars since World War II have been based principally upon struggles for national independence and for a solution to grievances arising from the processes of modernization and westernization. Unlike the urban-centered revolutions of the nineteenth and early twentieth centuries, they have involved the total society, usually focusing at the outset on gaining control of the countryside. The principal revolutionary wars have been the Chinese civil war, the Viet Minh war in Indochina, the insurrection in Greece, the Hukbalahap rebellion in the Philippines, the guerrilla war in Malaya, the Algerian insurrection, Castro's revolution in Cuba, and the Vietnamese war. All of these, except the Algerian and Cuban insurrections, were waged by communist organizations. Castro brought the Cuban revolution into the communist camp after it had succeeded largely under non-communist auspices. Harry Eckstein, "On the Etiology of Internal War," *History and Theory*, IV (1965), 133–63; Lawrence Stone, "Theories of Revolution," *World Politics*, XVIII (January, 1966), 159–76; Samuel P. Huntington, "Patterns of Violence in World Politics," in *Changing Patterns of Military Politics*, ed. Huntington (Glencoe, Ill.: The Free Press, 1962); George Modelski, "The International Relations of Internal War," in *International Aspects of Civil Strife*, ed. James N. Rosenau (Princeton: Princeton University Press, 1964).

32. Chalmers Johnson, *Revolution and the Social System* (Hoover Institution Studies, No. 3; Stanford, Calif.: Stanford University Press, 1964), pp. 56–57.

lated control, modern insurrections have attained a new dimension of force. They mark the ultimate popularization, professionalization, and (in terms of techniques, if not technology) modernization of revolutionary warfare. In effect, they aim to organize and discipline under central control a clash of societies like the *grand mêlée* of the seventeenth century.

Revolutionary war, fomented and sustained by an outside power, not only evades the forms of military deterrence that have established a balance in Europe; it nullifies much of the quantitative superiority of the most modern armed forces. Its success turns on the morale and loyalties of the population and the efficacy of local government more than on the occupation of territory and the clash of organized armies. Military operations are an integral part of political action in modern revolutionary war, but the revolutionary forces are supposed to come into direct confrontation with massed organized armies only in the final stage, when the political contest has been substantially won.

As a method of overcoming the technological superiority of the West, revolutionary warfare is especially attractive to China, which sees itself as the champion of the poor, rural areas against the outposts of modern capitalist power and which lacks the Soviet capacity to secure its sphere of control by military parity or to advance its status by space ventures and other nonmilitary means. Following the strategy developed by Mao Tse-tung and other revolutionary leaders against the Kuomintang, the Chinese regard national liberation wars as total wars fought by limited means, which must prove as successful outside China as within.[33]

The greatly diminished number of colonies susceptible to nationalist uprisings curtails one major source of revolutionary war, but other revolutionary conditions—xenophobic nationalism, social and political disorder, the uprooting of people from traditional societies in the wake of modernization, and the disparity between material expectations and reality—seem likely to persist for decades. A large part of the Third World will remain fertile soil for Marxist-nationalist radicalism, the distinctive source of twentieth-century revolutions. New sources of revolution are latent in the tribal, communal, racial, and national conflicts in Africa. Indeed, one can expect the potential for revolution, as opposed to ordinary coups and lesser insurrections, to increase with the extension of mass participation, political organization, and communication that accompanies modernization.

On the other hand, revolutions may not lead to communist expan-

33. Tang Tsou and Morton H. Halperin, "Mao Tse-Tung's Revolutionary Strategy and Peking's International Behavior," *American Political Science Review*, LIX (March, 1956), 80–99.

sion. Even ideologically radical revolutions will not necessarily come under communist control or, if communist, under Chinese or Soviet control. Communist exploitation of revolutionary war may turn out to be unfeasible except in areas near or adjacent to China where there is a strong proxy state with a well-organized army and a basic nationalist appeal in a target country, and Vietnam may be unique in this respect. But we have too little experience with too many variables to predict this. It remains to be seen whether the diversification of communist parties, as they respond to the Sino-Soviet split and adapt to local nationalism, will be a source of strength or weakness for them and whether it will make them more or less adventurous. Eventually one can expect ideological division and weariness among communists and the growing familiarity of underdeveloped countries with communist aims and operations to drain communism of its revolutionary potential in the Third World, as has happened elsewhere. The explosive nationalism and radicalism of frustrated elites might continue to keep the Third World in chronic disorder. Yet, detached from a common organizational structure and from powerful national bases of material support and tactical direction, revolutions could more readily be confined to the environment from which they sprang.

In any event, whatever the prospects of revolutionary war and whatever the communist capacity to foment and control such war as an instrument of state policy, the next decade or so may well experience a growing number of local interstate wars in the Third World. Most of these—particularly in Africa—will resemble guerrilla war more than the well-organized encounters of disciplined armies in the eighteenth or nineteenth centuries; but they will be fought by national armies over national issues, ranging from border and other territorial disputes in the immediate future to the larger issues of status and ideology at a hypothetical later stage of internal development and nationalism.

The conditions for such wars lie not only in older national grievances, like those between India and Pakistan, but also in the emergence of new territorial and political ambitions and new national rivalries and hostilities as the old colonial and neocolonial issues give way to local issues of power, wealth, and security among fledgling nations fractured by strong subnational and transnational loyalties and separated by politically tenuous borders inherited from their colonial past. The underdeveloped states will have little capacity for territorial aggrandizement for a long time, but the very weakness and fragility of their ruling regimes may foster lesser forms of military intervention and adventure as distractions from internal troubles and as levers of national cohesion.

Probably most of the interstate wars in the Third World will remain local affairs with little relevance to the politics of the advanced states. Many may serve a constructive purpose in the sense that war may be the only way of resolving national conflicts that would otherwise continually fester and impede the development of more stable relations in a period of international system-building as well as nation-building. Yet despite their origin in purely local rivalries and ambitions, some of these wars are bound to impinge on the interests of the superpowers and other advanced states; and some will threaten to involve these antagonists directly or indirectly in armed conflict. Soviet and Chinese leaders may even come to view local national wars as more rewarding to foment and support than internal wars.

On the other hand, the Soviet Union at least may view local national conflict as even more difficult to control and more risky to support than internal wars and may therefore pursue its interests only through carefully limited forms of nonmilitary intervention, including mediation and pacification. As with other forms of Soviet-American competition in the Third World, both sides have an interest in confining their competition to dimensions that are compatible with a modicum of control, a limited investment of energy, and a tolerable risk of military and political entanglement. Again, there are no grounds for confident prediction. One can only conclude that the interaction of the Third World and the advanced states seems destined to determine much of the quality of international order in the next few decades.

The prospects of order in the Third World would be brighter if the states in these areas, as they become more concerned with the traditional tasks of organizing power for security and order, were to develop relatively stable and autonomous structures of countervailing power. But in the next decade or two the Third World seems more likely to be an unstructured, unsteady congeries of shifting local animosities and alignments in which the weak states will become no less dependent on the advanced states. If stable local or regional patterns of countervailing power are to develop, they will probably be based on the establishment of hegemonies or spheres of influence by ascendant indigenous states or possibly, in Africa, by confederations. But the necessary political and military conditions for such centers of power scarcely exist. If Africa, for example, were an isolated group of developing states, run by legitimate monarchs and aristocracies, one might expect an international system like that of sixteenth-century Italy or eighteenth-century Europe to emerge. But in reality Africa is not isolated from the dominant system of the advanced states, and it generally lacks the material and political ingredients of a fully developed state system.

Consequently a great part of the underdeveloped areas of the world seems destined to enter a period of international as well as internal transition that is full of prospects of local conflicts and wider warfare. Earlier expectations that the new states, once freed from colonial bondage, would fulfill the old liberal dream of a harmonious community of states, unsullied by national animosities and power politics, seem increasingly utopian. The fact is that among the states of the Third World there are more incentives for and far fewer inhibitions against war than among the advanced states. That warfare among these states has not been more severe must be attributed not to the inherent peacefulness and stability of their international politics but rather to their material and political weakness, which has limited their capacity to project military power beyond their borders, and to their dependence on the advanced states, which has channeled their political energies toward seeking advantageous relations with the great powers and has absorbed local conflicts within extraregional politics.

The prospects of order in the Third World are especially dim if a protracted period of international and internal change should be complicated by local acquisition of cheap but powerful weapons, since the political and technological restraints against the use of force are as underdeveloped as the indigenous economies and politics. The prospective spread of nuclear weapons seems particularly disturbing. In the short run, few if any states in the poor areas of the world are likely to acquire nuclear weapons, but it will be remarkable if some do not acquire them in the next twenty years. Since a number of states will gain the economic and technological ability to produce their own nuclear weapons in this period, only the lack of convincing security incentives may dissuade them from doing so.[34] The consequences of nuclear proliferation will depend

34. In 1966 there were still only five nuclear powers. Several states could have been nuclear powers at least as advanced as China if they had chosen to produce their own weapons: Canada, West Germany, Japan, Italy, India, Sweden. In the future the rapid spread of nuclear reactors for civilian energy will make the spread of nuclear weapons even more dependent on political decisions rather than capabilities. In the next decade India, Israel, and Japan seem the most likely nuclear-potential states to make such political decisions, although there are strong disincentives in each case. Within two decades at least eight more states in addition to these three could build nuclear weapons if they chose, making a total of sixteen nuclear powers. Leonard Beaton, *Must the Bomb Spread?* (Baltimore: Penguin Books, 1966), chap. iv. For an earlier but more detailed estimate of present and prospective capabilities to produce nuclear weapons, see Leonard Beaton and John Maddox, *The Spread of Nuclear Weapons* (New York: Frederick A. Praeger, 1962). *The Dispersion of Nuclear Weapons*, ed. Richard N. Rosecrance (New York: Columbia University Press, 1964), examines principally the existing and prospective spread of nuclear forces among advanced states, but its discussion of the motives and implications of nuclear acquisition are of general relevance. Rosecrance presents a later and comprehensive, though brief, analysis in *Problems of Nuclear Proliferation* (Security Studies, No. 7; Los Angeles: University of California, 1966). Robert

on the particular states that acquire nuclear weapons, the kind of nuclear forces they acquire, the rate and sequence of acquisition, and, above all, the environment of conflict and alignment. Hence, the likely effects of proliferation are quite varied and unpredictable. Nevertheless it is difficult to view with equanimity the prospect of a half-dozen states injecting nuclear (and possibly chemical and biological) weapons into the agitated crosscurrents of the Third World.

Alarming predictions that nuclear proliferation will make the weakest and most irresponsible states as powerful as the strongest and most prudent, that it will lead to anonymous attacks against the cities of the rich nations, or that nuclear weapons will get into the hands of madmen may be no more realistic than were earlier predictions about trigger-happy statesmen and surprise attacks between the most modern nuclear powers.[35] But there are other dangers to worry about. The nature of the nuclear forces and the political context within which they would probably be acquired indicate that their most disturbing effect in the Third World would be the aggravation of existing rivalries and hostilities. The uneven rate of nuclear acquisition and growth among lesser states and the physical vulnerability of the weapons might encourage offensive actions and invite preventive or pre-emptive attacks. Local crises would probably be more tense and volatile. The fears of their escalating to nuclear blows might be intense. The superpowers would be more immediately concerned. Therefore they would be more apt to become involved in one way or another in local struggles. Their military involvement might rapidly expand into large local wars and even general war.

On the other hand, all these disturbing prospects might also create antidotes, just as the fear of nuclear war inspires deterrence and restraint between the superpowers. Major nuclear powers themselves might— through guarantees, sanctions, mediation, endorsement of U.N. peace-keeping operations, and other methods—play a major part in creating such antidotes.

As in the case of all prognostications about the future of international politics in the nuclear age, there is equal justification for reaching optimistic and pessimistic conclusions. The most general conclusion that may safely be made is that the peace and order of the whole world

---

L. Rothstein examines the prospects and implications of nuclear acquisition by small states in "On Nuclear Proliferation" (Occasional Papers, School of International Affairs, Columbia University, 1966). For a rich, pessimistic analysis of the political consequences of nuclear proliferation, see Stanley Hoffmann, "Nuclear Proliferation and World Politics," in *A World of Nuclear Powers*, ed. Alastair Buchan (Englewood Cliffs, N.J.: Prentice-Hall, Inc., 1966).

35. Rothstein, *op. cit.*, pp. 20ff.

will depend heavily upon the interaction of two quite different modes of international politics in which the roles of military power are also quite different—that of the old and advanced states and that of the new and poor states.

On the one hand, large parts of the Third World could become areas of chronic chaos and predatory struggle between the major world powers. At worst, this course might lead to competitive interventions that could expand into major—possibly even nuclear—wars. At best, it would compel the major powers, by tacit agreement, either to condemn the disturbed areas to isolation or to subject them to preventive intervention. On the other hand, given a modicum of political prudence and internal order among the new states and given constructive initiatives toward regional and local systems under the leadership of indigenous centers of power, the foundation for more stable regional balances of power could develop. The very enormity of potential disorder could induce the major world powers to limit their contest for power and influence in the Third World to relatively benign forms of competition while they provided a stabilizing framework for local competition through the selective use of economic and military assistance, informal political guarantees, mutual abstention from intervention, the insulation and mediation of conflicts, and other forms of international pacification. They would provide this framework, not because of their abstract interest in order but because of their mutual recognition that restricted competition is safer than intense competition in such a volatile and violent field of politics. If the super-powers follow the latter course and China is induced to adjust to it, the cautious practice of reciprocal restraint that has limited the critical con-frontations of the present nuclear powers might gradually extend to the Third World.

9. Beyond Bipolarity

If one measures order principally by the avoidance of a major war be-tween advanced states, disorder among these states would be a much more serious menace than the kind of disorder that seems likely to afflict the underdeveloped states. So far we have examined the elements of order and disorder in a world in which essentially two powers—the U.S. and the Soviet Union—have controlled the most advanced armed forces and in which the dominant political conflict has been the cold war between them. We must now ask what the implications for international order would be if this condition ceased to prevail. How would the erosion of bipolarity and the emergence of multipolarity affect the stability of the Soviet-American balance? What would be the prospects of a new balance serving international order equally well? The answers to these questions are obscured in countless unpredictable variables interacting in unknown patterns. Extrapolations from our limited experience under the special conditions of bipolarity are highly intuitive and probably misleading. Nevertheless the loosening of alliances in Europe, tripolarity and perhaps the beginnings of multipolarity in Asia, and the prospect of nuclear proliferation compel speculation.

The polarity of power refers here to the number of centers of military power (whether individual states or coalitions) which are capable of substantially affecting the balance of power in an extensive area of the world, which are independently committed to the support of vital interests distinct from the interests of other centers, and which therefore might go to war independently of other centers. In a bipolar system of international politics, two opposing states or coalitions manage the balance of military power. In a multipolar system, more than two states or coalitions account for the dominant pattern of countervailing power. In a bipolar system, typically, a single set of issues or conflicting interests dominates international competition. In a multipolar system, there are several primary conflicts. But the latter situation can prevail despite military bipolarity. Indeed, Europe is already experiencing the onset of a kind of political multipolarity within a bipolar military balance.

So far the analysis suggests that a world in which two nuclear superpowers dominate the management of the military balance may well be a world of unprecedented order, insofar as order is measured by the maintenance of the territorial and administrative integrity of the principal antagonists and their allies without a major war. By making the avoidance of war among the superpowers and their allies an intense and universal interest, the expansion of military power since World War II has brought about a far closer, because simpler and more compelling, correspondence between the essential requirements of international order and the immediate interests of the most powerful military states than existed before the nuclear age, especially when the measure of order was less the avoidance of war than the limitation or equitable sharing of territorial and commercial gains. Yet this correspondence may be due as much to bipolarity as to nuclear weapons. By clarifying and simplifying the question of who is committed to defend whom, bipolarity has greatly facilitated the maintenance of an international order based on mutual deterrence.

It is true that bipolarity accentuates international conflicts by tending to make every gain by one of the antagonists a loss for the other, by magnifying intrinsically unimportant conflicts into critical tests of power, and by extending the two-power competition to a wide range of international conflicts that originate outside this competition. Moreover, polarized competition lacks the mediating and moderating influence that "third" parties in a multipolar system have sometimes exerted. On the other hand, the intensity and pervasiveness of the competition between the superpowers have strengthened deterrence and extended it to cover a wide range of potentially explosive conflicts. By absorbing international conflicts into the two-power competition, the preponderant Soviet-American rivalry has minimized the danger that local conflicts will get out of hand and expand into a major war because of the indifference or shortsightedness of the superpowers. The very intensity of their competition has fostered the extreme vigilance that has always been the prerequisite of a working balance of power.[36]

Of special importance in light of the experience between the two world wars, bipolarity has fostered an active concern on the part of the status quo powers to oppose piecemeal aggrandizement with united opposition. There is no exact comparison between Fascist aggression before World War II and communist strategy in the cold war. Nevertheless the Munich analogy has served as a vital "myth" that has greatly strengthened the management of deterrence in the name of containment. But the myth depends upon a single overwhelming threat of expansion on the one hand and a group of status quo powers galvanized into united resistance by their common interest in opposing that threat, on the other. In a multipolar world, because the configurations of interests and commitments would be more complex, the Munich myth would be less compelling.

Finally, the very dangers of bipolarity in a nuclear age have engendered a pacifying conservatism, and even an expanding area of mutual interest, in the superpowers' pursuit of their competing ends. Their common interest is rooted not in common political objectives or converging political systems but simply in their mutual recognition of an overriding advantage in keeping their antagonism within safe limits and subject to their own control. Although both superpowers try to stimulate centrifugal forces among each other's allies, neither wishes to see the emergence of new centers of military power—least of all nuclear power—that might endanger its own management of power. To this extent each has an interest in the other's preponderance within its coalition. Both

---

36. Kenneth N. Waltz argues for the superior stability of a bipolar system on these and other grounds in "The Stability of a Bipolar World," *Daedalus*, XCIII (Summer, 1964), 881–909. For analyses stressing the stabilizing effect of multi-polarity in the nuclear age, see George Liska, *Nations in Alliance* (Baltimore: The Johns Hopkins Press, 1962), pp. 269ff., and Roger Masters, *The Nation Is Burdened* (New York: Alfred A. Knopf, 1967), chap. iii.

are eager to avoid catalytic or triggering actions by other states which might involve them in a direct clash of arms with each other. The military preponderance of the Soviet Union and the U.S. in their European alliances and the homogeneity of vital interests in these alliances have minimized the danger of an ally precipitating general war, as in the Austro-Serbian war of 1914. Bipolarity promises to maximize the control of the superpowers over their own destinies in a field of international competition that might otherwise be more dangerous and unpredictable.

Nevertheless we should not take for granted the correctness of the instinctive feeling of these two powers—and in fact of many other states, including most of their allies—that bipolarity is safer than multipolarity. There are many factors besides the structure of power and commitments which bear upon the quality of international order. The effects of multipolarity on a world in which nuclear inhibitions prevail may be quite different from the effects of multipolarity in previous periods. Much depends upon which states or coalitions of states become new poles of power and in what political context.

Military multipolarity is not inevitable in any part of the world, but it is likely to develop sooner in Asia than in Europe and sooner in Western than in Eastern Europe. In Europe bipolarity has been a product of two opposing multilateral alliances, the North Atlantic Treaty and the Warsaw Pact, and of the military preponderance of the U.S. and the Soviet Union within them. The consolidation of bipolar nuclear parity, the onset of *détente*, the reassertion of separate national interests, and dissatisfaction with political dependence on the superpowers have diminished the cohesion of both alliances and encouraged what one might call "political polycentrism."[37] But they have not destroyed the superpowers' management of the military balance, and this seems unlikely to happen as long as the superpowers remain physically engaged in forward positions and credibly committed to the defense of their spheres of interest. The essential condition for disengagement is probably a European settlement based on a unified, multilaterally constrained Germany; but this development is not in sight.

In Eastern Europe one can discern some trends toward the transformation of the Warsaw Treaty Organization from an instrument of Soviet rule to an alliance more like NATO, in which active bargaining

37. Stanley Hoffmann relates this polycentrism, or "muted bipolarity," to a disproportion between material and usable power in the nuclear age: "Thus, muted bipolarity reduces the superpowers to the rank of prominent centers because their rivalry and the nature of their arsenal inhibit their effectiveness as powers, and it also elevates to the rank of 'centers' units with the ambition to play a world role on the stage despite their lack of the traditional ingredients of power." "Nuclear Proliferation and World Politics," *op. cit.*, p. 94.

with the superpower takes place within a freer contractual relationship.[38] Centrifugal forces might get out of hand and create a radical and possibly violent upheaval, leading either to a reassertion of Soviet dominance or else to a fragmentation of Eastern Europe under Soviet sufferance. But even in the event of a re-Balkanization of Eastern Europe, national separatism would be unlikely to lead to new centers of independent military power and commitments. Soviet military power would probably still be preponderant, Eastern Europe would still find Soviet protection the most satisfactory guarantee of its security, the risks of militant nationalism would threaten domestic as well as security goals, and the distaste for the pre-World War I pattern of international politics would impede a reversion to military pluralism.

The emergence of a new pole of power in Western Europe is less unlikely, for in this more homogeneous area there are some solid political, material, and cultural bases for a coalition capable of providing its own conventional and nuclear protection with only marginal dependence on the U.S. In reality, however, there are many factors militating against such a coalition: the differences in foreign and military policies, which in spite of a widespread European feeling are becoming more marked; the preoccupation of nations with domestic issues and immediate conditions of living rather than with the tasks of international political construction; the lack of a sufficient security incentive for coalition-building in a period of protracted *détente*; the freedom of political maneuver which allies enjoy within a polarized military balance that seems to assure them protection; the cost of building and maintaining even a limited second-strike counter-city nuclear force; the awesome responsibility that goes with managing a force of terror—a responsibility that only France among the allies has actively coveted in the last decade;[39] and the prohibitive difficulty of any group of roughly equal states agreeing on a mutually satisfactory basis for sharing the control of nuclear weapons.[40]

38. Thomas W. Wolfe, *The Evolving Nature of the Warsaw Pact* (Santa Monica: Memorandum RM-4835-PR, RAND Corporation, December, 1965).

39. The British have simply declined to relinquish independent control of a force that they created before the full demands of an effective and safe nuclear force were known. They regarded their force as a natural concomitant of their being a great state that had been a powerful wartime partner of the U.S. and had participated in the development of the atomic bomb.

40. Although the allies have willingly or reluctantly accepted the U.S. as their principal nuclear agent by virtue of its material preponderance and its concomitant position as the principal deterrer, none would be willing to let one of its other allies act in this capacity. The only kind of European nuclear force capable of giving Western European states real independence from American nuclear preponderance would have to be jointly controlled, if only because none of its participants,

Considering these obstacles to coalition, only extreme frustration with the preponderance of the superpowers or a strong drive for prestige and power seems likely to provide the motivation necessary to create new poles of military power in Europe as long as the East-West conflict remains dominant and Soviet and American forces remain engaged. Yet these traditional kinds of inducements to military realignments and competition seem now to have lost their appeal in Europe. So far, European nations seek other outlets for fulfilling goals of status and influence.[41] Territorial grievances remain; in Eastern Europe they may grow in intensity. Yet it is unlikely that military power will again become the instrument for rectifying them.

One might attribute this partial disappearance of traditional power politics in Europe to the impact of World War II, the loss of colonial power, the decline of first-rank powers to second-class status, the experience of allied politics, the extension of economic ties, the growth of a satisfied middle class, and the domestic satisfactions of thriving economies and expanding welfare. But nuclear weapons are equally important, for they have sapped the old incentives for playing the game of independent military maneuvers on the international chessboard. They seem to have ruined the game—for these particular states, at least—by raising the risks and possible costs so far beyond the value of the stakes. The dread of war has aroused a deep distaste for the "war system" itself.

Additional European states may eventually seek to enhance their political influence by acquiring nuclear weapons; but even this would not necessarily lead to multipolarity—any more than the British and French nuclear forces have led to multipolarity. On the other hand, with or without independent nuclear forces, allies are likely to gain greater room for political maneuver if the sense of military insecurity in Europe remains quiescent. Within the bipolar balance there is a wide realm of political objectives, of alignments and realignments, for the pursuit of which military power and nuclear weapons in particular are largely irrelevant.

Seen in the light of the many constraints on multipolar power politics as it was practiced in the eighteenth and nineteenth centuries, the super-

including Germany, would want Germany to participate as an independent nuclear power. Yet in a jointly controlled force neither France, Britain, nor Germany would be willing to commit itself to a nuclear war by majority vote against its will, and neither would give another state a veto over the use of nuclear weapons in its behalf. For these reasons the very attempt to establish a common European nuclear force would be divisive.

41. Britain's and France's nuclear forces are intended to serve goals of status and influence; but only France's is intended to buttress a distinctly separate foreign policy, and it is not clear that De Gaulle looks forward to a military realignment in Europe.

powers' alliances in Europe can be regarded as organizations for perpetuating bipolarity on acceptable terms among states that might otherwise form several competing military coalitions or else a congeries of nonaligned states. In this respect the two alliances are extensions of a phenomenon that was foreshadowed in a different form in Bismarck's alliance system—the tendency of military alliances to become increasingly concerned with adjusting the relations of allies among themselves. The tendency is a natural concomitant of efforts to stabilize military commitments and make the field of international power more calculable and reliable as the necessities of peacetime military development and the disadvantages of shifting commitments have become more apparent.[42] It would be extrapolating this tendency too far to suppose that the American and Soviet alliances could, by virtue of the vitality of their internal functions, survive the disappearance of their external necessity; but within a consolidated *détente* based on stabilized mutual deterrence, the internal political functions of the two military alliances are bound to be a dominant concern.

Yet in spite of the elements of continuity in bipolarity, it would be astonishing if, in the longer run, as the major political and ideological conflicts in the world change and the economic and technological

---

42. Thus military strategy and policies became a primary medium of allied politics in NATO while fear of a Soviet military threat declined. The agitated issue of nuclear control, with all its involved technical and strategic ramifications, was concerned only tangentially with external security but quite directly with the relations of the U.S. to its allies and with their relations to each other. The plan for a multilateral nuclear force (MLF) arose partly as a method of meeting SACEUR's stated military requirement for a European-based missile system to counter Soviet MRBMs without deploying missiles in Germany, which was thought to be contrary to the principle of integrating strategic weapons on an over-all basis. The American government, however, was not principally concerned about meeting the military requirement (except to conciliate the allies who believed in it) and, in any case, could have met it with missiles under exclusive American control just as well, if not better. The most important consideration behind the MLF proposal was the desire to give Germany a responsible share in the management of strategic nuclear weapons by means that would not entail an independent German finger on the trigger and that would integrate jointly controlled weapons with U.S. weapons. When the plan came to a head in the final year of the Kennedy administration, it touched upon the most sensitive issues of interallied politics and greatly aggravated the conflict between the grand designs of the U.S. and of President De Gaulle. Robert E. Osgood, *NATO: The Entangling Alliance*, chap. ix; Alastair Buchan, *The Multilateral Force: An Historical Perspective* (Adelphi Papers, No. 13; London: Institute for Strategic Studies, October, 1964); Henry A. Kissinger, *The Troubled Partnership* (New York: McGraw-Hill, 1965), chap. v. During President Johnson's administration the issue of nuclear control was de-emphasized, and military issues became somewhat less politically sensitive; nevertheless technological and strategic changes could readily reactivate military policies as a sphere of allied policies.

capacity to acquire nuclear forces comes ever more easily into the reach of a number of states, there did not arise at least one new center of nuclear power and commitments in Europe. Eventually, one must anticipate, the cold war will fade away or become subordinate to other issues. Eventually there will probably be a European settlement entailing either the reunification of Germany in some form and the disengagement of American and Soviet forces or else a German reconciliation to the division of Germany. If new conflicts of vital interests then replace the East-West conflict, new poles of military power and commitments would almost surely arise. Then we should see whether the present demilitarized political maneuvers in Europe are the result of lasting or only transitional factors.

In Asia, where bipolarity has not been reinforced by highly organized multilateral alliances and where the configurations of interest are more fluid and the commitments of the superpowers less firm and extensive, an incipient tripolarity based on the emergence of China as an independent military power already exists. In Asia, too, the Gaullist-like drive for national power and status may turn out to be more attractive to the politically active elites than in Europe, because a positive national self-assertion may seem both a safer and a more compelling instrument of security. China's production of advanced nuclear weapons, coupled with its pursuit of independent policies intended to revise the territorial and political status quo, is bound to stimulate this drive. The likely recrudescence of Japan and the possible emergence of India as states actively engaging in power politics would create a full-scale multipolar international system.

It is pertinent, therefore, to speculate about the effects of multipolarity on international order. With more than two independent nuclear poles of power and commitment pursuing divergent policies in the mainstream of international politics, there would be more opportunities for adversaries to miscalculate military intentions and responses, not only because there would be a greater number of active players in the contest but also because a more complicated pattern of alignments would tend to make commitments more uncertain and ambiguous. The greater complexity of international competition would probably generate more crises, which would compound the present risks of testing national resolve and nerve under the threat of war. The kinds of restraints on brinkmanship and intervention in third-party disputes which the American and Soviet governments have arrived at in the course of years of competition would be less likely to control the rivalries of new nuclear powers. The military balances between such powers would at the outset almost surely lack the technical obstacles to the rational first use of nuclear weapons that dominate the Soviet-American balance. An increase in the nuclear poles of power, especially if accompanied by new guarantees and commitments, might multiply the occasions on which nuclear powers could be dragged into war by aligned states. This would foster new tensions among allies, which might lead them to qualify their commitments and thereby increase uncertainties about who would defend whom in which contingencies.

On the other hand, the emergence of a nuclear multipolar international system, like the spread of nuclear weapons to the weaker and smaller states, might create new antidotes to new dangers. Perhaps greater uncertainty about commitments would reinforce mutual deterrence and caution so as to offset the increased danger of miscalculation.[43] If more complicated patterns of conflict and alignment would multiply the chances of adversaries miscalculating each other's political and military intentions, they should also increase the reluctance of adversaries to resort to war on the basis of their calculations. Thus analogies to the fluid system of alignments in the eighteenth or early nineteenth centuries are inappropriate.

Among advanced states, nuclear proliferation should accentuate defensive security goals and the methods of using power short of war, as in the bipolar contest. There is no reason to think that several more nuclear states would be less preoccupied with deterrence than two or five. By the very nature of deterrence, the deterrent alignments that developed in a multipolar international system would be far less transitory and uncertain than offensive alliances in the multipolar systems of the eighteenth or nineteenth centuries; for defensive interests are usually more stable, and even offensive goals tend to become frozen when states are inhibited from attaining them by war. Moreover, when deterrence is the primary goal, other nuclear states, like the U.S. and the Soviet Union, must try to enhance the credibility of defense commitments by basing them on a solid, enduring identity of security interests and, perhaps, on institutional and visible demonstrations of this identity rather than on shifting convergencies of acquisitive goals.

It is doubtful that deterrent alignments would be institutionalized in multilateral alliances like NATO, which reflects in large measure the strategy, logistics, and command structure for a large ground war that prevailed immediately after World War II. The marginal role of non-nuclear forces in the balances among advanced states and the growing

43. General André Beaufre makes a subtle case for the superior stability of multipolar deterrence as a result of this greater uncertainty in *Deterrence and Strategy* (New York: Frederick A. Praeger, 1966), chap. iii.

capacity of advanced technology to move weapons, men, and supplies over long distances quickly by air will reduce the need for the kind of peacetime military co-ordination that originated in the prelude to World War I and culminated in NATO. But there will be no less need for advance mutual planning and for mutual reinforcement of intentions between vulnerable states and their protectors. The absence of a strictly military reason for institutionalized co-ordination may only mean that states will either have to find nonmilitary reasons (such as military and political sharing) for maintaining these deterrent devices or else invent alternative ways of demonstrating military solidarity (such as military exercises, exchange of military personnel, and the like). In any case, a tendency toward bilateral alignments and even military autarchy need not negate the stabilizing effects of deterrence upon military alignments.

Perhaps any single nuclear balance in a multipolar pattern of international politics is apt to be less stable in terms of invulnerable retaliatory forces and flexible responses than the Soviet-American balance has become. On the other hand, one balance would probably be entangled with others in such a way that inequalities of power between any particular antagonists would be offset by the prospect that pre-emptive attacks or other hostile actions would involve other states capable of redressing the imbalance. A pattern of close interaction in which several states might resort to nuclear war independently would be safer than an eroding bipolar system in which the willingness of allies to unite against an external threat to one of them and the willingness of the superpowers to use force in behalf of their allies were in doubt. A bipolar system makes it easier to convince an aggressor of an existing will to use force, but it also makes it easier for the aggressor to calculate what it can get away with when that will is in doubt.

In the final analysis, the particular (and largely unpredictable) circumstances of nuclear multipolarity will be more decisive than the multiplicity of plausible, though somewhat conflicting, tendencies that emerge from abstract speculation. The stability and safety of multipolar deterrence will depend as much on the prudence of the particular governments involved and on their particular relationship of conflict or alignment with other states as on any structural feature of the international system. So the most pertinent questions about the effects of proliferation on international order may be those like whether the governments of India, Israel, Japan, Sweden, or West Germany would be more or less cautious and responsible in the uses of force than the present nuclear powers and whether a nuclear India or Japan participating in an Asian balance with China, the Soviet Union, the U.S., and perhaps other nuclear powers would create a more or less stable equilibrium than one based largely on American and Soviet nuclear counter-poises to China in a period of growing Chinese nuclear strength.[44]

Yet whatever the particulars of nuclear proliferation may turn out to be, the fact remains that the present bipolar system has fostered a re-markably stable military balance and that, therefore, any change in the structure of world power may create a more dangerous international contest than the one with which we have become familiar. However stable a more complicated nuclear balance based on several poles of power might be, any increase in the number of potential sources of a nuclear war is ominous when only one nuclear war could produce such terrible devastation.

10. Arms Control

This survey of the role of military power in the nuclear age is full of conjecture about a bewildering variety of unpredictable developments. Nevertheless, one central conclusion stands out with relative clarity: Force is as pervasive an element of international politics as before the nuclear age. Indeed, in its uses short of war between the nuclear powers and their allies it is more highly developed and more thoroughly fused with politics than ever before. At the same time, local wars not initially involving a direct engagement between the superpowers have been common and seem destined to remain so.

Implicit in the pervasiveness of force, both short of war and in local war, there is the ineradicable possibility that a major war exceeding the bounds of rational restraint will occur. Given the requisite prudence and vigilance on the part of the major states managing the nuclear balance, whether they are few or many, such a war *might* be avoided indefinitely. But this is a far from comforting thought.

Therefore, radical solutions to the radically new problem of avoiding the unprecedented disaster that a single major war would cause have a semblance of reasonableness they seemed to lack before the nuclear age. Among the more reasonable solutions that come to mind is the tradi-tional one of disarmament. But we have concluded that any disarma-ment agreement that requires the transformation of the international system is unworkable. Therefore we must ask whether disarmament can *regulate*, rather than centralize or eliminate, force so as to mitigate the hazards of the nuclear age.

44. For balanced assessments of the cases for and against Indian and Japanese nuclear forces, see the chapters by Sisir Gupta and Kei Wakaizumi in Buchan, *A World of Nuclear Powers*.

In the aftermath of World War I the remedy for the excesses of modern war that caught the popular fancy was getting rid of arms and, hence, the arms race and the whole balance of power system. The concept of regulating or moderating military competition lacked popular appeal or intellectual development. In practice, governments were concerned with regulation of arms (when they viewed the interwar disarmament discussions as anything more than a contest for military advantage and propaganda), but they felt compelled to justify their proposals as popular panaceas. This pretense did not make arms agreements more feasible or useful, but it did weaken the will of the status quo powers to maintain a safe military balance; for, having popularized disarmament as an alternative to armaments, they were in a poor position to organize countervailing power against the revisionist states.

After World War II there were remnants of the outwardly utopian approach to disarmament, especially in the period from the presentation of the Baruch Plan in 1946 to the turn toward limited arms agreements after 1954.[45] General and complete disarmament, revived by Khrushchev in 1959 and endorsed by the U.S. in political self-defense, lingers as an increasingly irrelevant and ineffectual propaganda position in the background of disarmament discussions. Elements of the peace movement, buttressing old arguments with nuclear alarms, continue to argue that the only way to escape the hazards of power politics is to get rid of arms.

Yet these echoes of the prenuclear approach to disarmament are much less significant than the emergence of the concept of arms control to a dominant position in private and official circles in the West. This con-

45. Unlike the League, the United Nations, as originally constituted, did not envisage world-wide disarmament. Recalling the sad experience of the League, its founders emphasized instead a concert of great powers to prevent renewed aggression. It was America's atomic explosions that turned diplomatic attention toward disarmament. The Baruch Plan, which dominated disarmament discussions for five years, was essentially a scheme to establish a limited form of international government in order to eliminate nuclear weapons and prevent war. Not only would peaceful nuclear facilities be internationally owned. There would be international punishment without any national veto in order to enforce the agreement. This was consistent with the official view that the prospects of a nuclear arms race were too dangerous to be dealt with "in the framework of old ideas" of national sovereignty, as President Truman put it in his message to Congress on October 3, 1945. Even after the demise of the Baruch Plan and the full onset of the cold war, the official U.S. position on disarmament explicitly rejected the concept of regulating arms. Thus its proposal submitted to the Disarmament Commission in 1952 stated, "The goal of disarmament is not to regulate but to prevent war by relaxing the tensions and fears created by armaments and by making war inherently, as it is constitutionally under the Charter, impossible as a means of settling disputes between nations." Bernhard G. Bechhoefer, *Postwar Negotiations for Arms Control* (Washington: The Brookings Institution, 1961), Parts I–IV, pp. 30, 179.

cept views arms agreements not as a means of transforming international politics nor merely as a guise for gaining a military or propaganda advantage but rather as a means of restraining and controlling military competition.[46] It marks the explicit recognition that disarmament and military strategy are two sides of the same coin in the currency of international politics.

Arms control is a palliative, not a radical solution to contemporary military dangers. The novel and most serious danger in the nuclear age is sudden, catastrophic war. Perhaps the only sure way of getting rid of this danger would be to get rid of the weapons that could cause it. But even if that were practicable, it would destroy the present basis of military equilibrium and security, which lies in the capacity of the principal adversaries to inflict intolerable retaliatory damage upon each other. To be sure, with major adjustments of non-nuclear power, another military equilibrium might be reached, but only at the price of reverting to a prenuclear military balance in which the inhibitions against going to war would be much weaker. Reducing the sudden destructive potential of forces-in-being might be worth the price of increasing the likelihood of a major war except for the virtual certainty that once the advanced technological powers became engaged in such a war, if not during the preceding tension, they would quickly rearm to regain the most destructive weapons. Possibly the fear of counter-rearmament would either deter these states from engaging in war or restrain them from using the catastrophic weapons during war, but it is much more probable that, in the absence of a high-level balance of destructive power-in-being, the rearming belligerents would be virtually compelled to use their most powerful weapons before their adversary could threaten proportionate destruction.

Faced with these realities, arms control, unlike complete nuclear disarmament, relies primarily on a balance of power to mitigate the dangers of the nuclear age. The rationale of arms control—as in the case of deterrence, the exploitation of force short of war, and the limitation of war—lies in the imperatives of reciprocal restraint among ad-

46. The concept of arms control is expounded in a copious literature. Often it is defined to include a wide range of arms limitations beyond formal agreements. Thus Schelling and Halperin define arms control "to include all the forms of military cooperation between potential enemies in the interest of reducing the likelihood of war, its scope and violence if it occurs, and the political and economic costs of being prepared for it." It embraces measures leading to "induced or reciprocated 'self-control,' whether the inducements include negotiated treaties or just informal understandings and reciprocated restraints." Thomas C. Schelling and Morton H. Halperin, *Strategy and Arms Control* (New York: The Twentieth Century Fund, 1961), pp. 2, 5.

versaries that have a common interest in avoiding catastrophic war. Thus it, too, falls within the regulatory, as opposed to the laissez-faire or systemic, approach to international order. The principal objective of arms control is not to save money but to make military competition safer, not to eliminate the balance of power but to stabilize deterrence.

But what is the actual utility and feasibility of arms control? As in the case of prenuclear disarmament, states often seem to be less interested in the ostensible purposes of arms control than in scoring a propaganda victory, embarrassing the adversary, or gaining a military advantage.[47] Consequently, it is difficult to tell whether arms control is an important instrument of international order or primarily a lever of political warfare. Yet we have by now expended enough thought and energy on arms control and accumulated enough experience with arms control proposals, discussions, and treaties to hazard some generalizations about its utility.

In some respects there would seem to be a greater need for arms control now than before the nuclear age. The proliferation of technology and the great increase in military energy which spring from qualitative and quantitative innovations give arms races a new impetus, which can drive states into expensive and possibly provocative efforts that fail to improve their security in the end. This impetus enhances the need for mutual limitations on the types and quantities of weapons, particularly nuclear weapons. The peculiar destructiveness of nuclear weapons and the distinctive fears they arouse make the regulation of nuclear ownership, control, and deployment a major concern of international politics. Agreed regulation might, for example, be a necessary condition of political settlement (as in the case of the nuclear prohibitions that would probably have to accompany the unification of Germany) or a key preventive measure against the spread of nuclear dangers (as in the case of nuclear nonproliferation agreements). The increased prospect of inadvertent war inherent in the great range, destructiveness, and quick response time of nuclear missiles argues for international safeguards against inadvertent war. The unprecedented danger that the very testing of weapons may damage civilian life has already led to the atmospheric nuclear test ban and may be applicable to other weapons in the future.

Yet the hypothetical need for arms control does not establish its

47. John W. Spanier and Joseph L. Nogee, *The Politics of Disarmament: A Study in Soviet-American Gamesmanship* (New York: Frederick A. Praeger, 1962), in interpreting the entire postwar disarmament dialogue as a competition for political and military advantage, provides a useful antidote to taking arms proposals and negotiations at face value. But it exaggerates the tactical element, underestimates the genuine conviction along with some self-deception in the West, and overdepreciates the potential utility of some kinds of arms control.

technical and political feasibility. The political obstacles to states formally committing themselves to military restrictions are no less than before. Indeed, they are increased by the greater psychological and political significance attributed to conveying the appearance of nuclear parity or superiority.[48] The emergence of new poles of military power and new, pluralistic patterns of countervailing force would compound this and other kinds of political obstacles to formal arms restrictions. Moreover, the unprecedented complexity and diversity of the arms competition, the accelerated rate of technological innovation and obsolescence, the complete absence of wartime experience with the most advanced weapons, and the increased fusion of civilian and military technology complicate the technical as well as political problem of qualitative and quantitative arms restrictions. In addition, the physical characteristics of nuclear weapons—particularly their ease of concealment and their concentration of destructive energy—make the verification of arms restrictions a major obstacle to agreement for the first time in history.[49] Furthermore, the discovery that the arms race carries its own limitations, that states can go far in regulating it and mitigating its dangers unilaterally, and that it is not incompatible with *détente* diminishes the incentives for trying to control it through treaties.

For these reasons arms freezes and reductions and other kinds of formal arms restrictions that directly affect the distribution of military power among states seem generally unpromising. Thus a nuclear nonproliferation treaty encounters the formidable political obstacle of freezing a conspicuous inequality between nuclear haves and have-nots, an inequality that may not be acceptable to real and potential nuclear aspirants except at the price of political compensations (for example, security guarantees or nuclear reductions) that the haves are unwilling to grant.

In some respects, however, the feasibility, if not necessarily the utility, of arms control agreements is enhanced in the nuclear age. The fact that the superpowers enjoy such a surplus of nuclear retaliatory power

48. Horelick and Rush, in *Strategic Power and Soviet Foreign Policy*, illustrate Soviet sensitivity to the psychological and political implications of the military balance. The Soviet Union's strategic inferiority and its eagerness to convey an impression of a more favorable balance must have reinforced Soviet opposition to arms restrictions.

49. The importance of this obstacle springs from more than the special political distaste for inspection in the Soviet Union and other totalitarian states, and it is not negated by the fact that both the U.S. and the Soviet Union have used the inspection issue as a pretext for supporting or opposing agreements. For a complete but brief discussion of the problem of verification by inspection, see Lawrence S. Finklestein, "Arms Inspection," *International Conciliation*, No. 540 (November, 1962).

as to greatly diminish the security returns that either could gain from additional increments of strategic nuclear strength facilitates some kinds of readily verifiable restrictions on nuclear striking power, like restrictions on nuclear testing and prohibitions against orbiting missiles or deployments of land-based missiles, because both sides have an interest in avoiding an extension or intensification of the arms competition that would impose costs and dangers unwarranted by prospective gains. Moreover, there are now a variety of functions that arms control measures might perform—such as reducing the danger of war by technical accident, misapprehension, or faulty communication—which do not significantly affect the distribution of power, yet advance the security of the competitors. The so-called hot line between Washington and Moscow is an example. The hot line and the atmospheric test ban, following the Cuban missile crisis, also demonstrate that, even more than before the nuclear age, arms agreements carry an aura of accommodation that gives them value as diplomatic gestures. Therefore in a period of *détente* agreements that do not alter the military balance may play a political role more important than their explicit purposes.

Nevertheless, these functions are of only marginal utility. Formal arms agreements seem ill adapted to reducing the destructiveness of war, freezing or reducing the quantity of arms, or attenuating the arms race directly and comprehensively. The most important restraints on the kind, quantity, ownership, deployment, and use of nuclear weapons must come primarily from unilateral measures, such as abstention from superfluous or provocative arms production, deployment, and dissemination; guarantees and declarations of strategic intent, safeguards against inadvertent war, and advanced methods of surveillance. Some unilateral restraints may be contingent upon reciprocal restraints by adversaries. Then they are, in effect, tacit or informal arms-control agreements. Such agreements have qualities of flexibility and discreetness that are generally more appropriate than formal treaties for controlling a diversified, readily concealed, and rapidly changing technology mightily involved in the pursuit of status and influence.

Fundamentally, therefore, arms control must gain its impetus and efficacy from the most powerful states' habitual practice of the deliberate, contrived regulation of force within a system of international politics that is altogether too near anarchy to afford much scope for formal and institutional pacification. Basic changes in the structure of international power and the patterns of international conflict and alignment would further limit the scope of useful arms agreements until new equilibriums and stalemates were established. Yet in a multipolar world the regulatory approach to force that underlies the concept of arms control would be more pertinent than ever. One must hope, therefore, that the precedents for controlled competition which the superpowers have established in an essentially bipolar conflict will flourish in a more pluralistic order among states.

11. The Limitation of War

An international order that is based on countervailing force but that neglects the problem of extending reciprocal restraints to war itself will be gravely deficient in two respects: (1) If wars involving major states should occur because of the failure of deterrence, the escalation of crises, or the actions of smaller states, governments may have forfeited the opportunity to fight them effectively and keep them within bounds as a rational instrument of policy. (2) In the long run, nuclear powers will find it difficult to maintain the deterrent effect of their available force or the will to use it when they have forfeited the prospect of limiting it.

The second point is more debatable than the first. Yet in the U.S. the psychological need to retain the will to use force overtly when the risk of catastrophe is unavoidable has been a more important incentive for strategies of limited war than the expectation of having to fight the Soviet Union. The same psychology would probably apply to other defensive nuclear powers with independent military responsibility.

The need for the deliberate, calculated limitation of war is proportionate to the magnitude of force available to the belligerents and to the value of their interests at stake in a war. Most of the local wars since World War II have been intrinsically limited by virtue of the limited force available to the states involved, even when one state may have sought the total defeat and occupation of the adversary (for example, Indonesia's abortive war for West Irian or Egypt's futile campaign against Yemen). Some revolutionary wars have been virtually unlimited from the standpoint of the belligerents in that they were fought for control of a state and determination of its political system and involved virtually all segments of a nation's life, yet limited from the standpoint of external powers because they were confined to the boundaries of a single state, and even limited from the standpoint of the belligerents because they were based on unconventional war and political action as opposed to massive civil destruction and the direct clash of regular armies.

Other wars, however, have been artificially limited; that is, limited by unilateral self-denial, contingent upon the adversary's self-denial. In these wars whether or not one or both of the belligerents imposed restrictions on the geographical scope, targets, and weapons and upon the military and political objectives of war was dictated not solely by military necessity or capability but also by the imperatives of reciprocal restraint. This was most conspicuously the case in the U.S. conduct of the wars in Korea and Vietnam.

In Vietnam the limits on the expanded war in which American forces became directly involved were even more notable than the sanctuaries of the Korean War. The American government, as though consciously carrying out a concept of tacit bargaining that gained currency in the early 1960s, systematically sought to communicate its restraint as well as its resolve by means of politically discriminating military demonstrations and graduated applications of force while listening carefully (if in vain) for responsive "signals" from Hanoi, Peking, and Moscow.[50] Repeatedly, the government announced specifically limited objectives (confined to the approximate *de facto* status quo before intervention); continually, in private as well as in public, it sought formal and informal agreements that might de-escalate or terminate the war on the basis of these objectives. A remarkable feature of America's studied restraint was the tight executive control over military operations, which extended to the authorization of specific targets for air strikes.[51] But more significant than any particular restraints was the fact that the artificial limitation of warfare under central political control, which was deeply controversial in the Korean War, became a generally accepted

50. The most influential public exponent of this general approach to war was Thomas C. Schelling. In his view the conduct of limited war is part of a general "strategy of conflict." Such a strategy looks upon conflict situations as bargaining situations in which the ability of one participant to gain his ends is largely dependent on the choices the other participant makes and both know it. Typically, the bargaining is by tacit maneuvers, through which both threats and restraints are communicated so as to achieve a favorable *modus vivendi* with the adversary. Schelling presented the basic theoretical structure of this approach in *The Strategy of Conflict* (Cambridge: Harvard University Press, 1960). He expanded it conceptually and illustratively in *Arms and Influence*, examining its application to the Vietnam war on pp. 141ff. and 170ff.

51. In contrast to the use of airpower in the Korean War, the bombing of North Vietnam was intended not only to impede the enemy's military operations but also, by precise attacks on carefully selected military targets out of an extensive list (short of intentional civilian damage), to induce the North Vietnamese government to end the war. On this kind of coercive strategy, which Schelling calls "compellence," see *Arms and Influence*, pp. 170ff. By 1966, however, escalation of bombing in North Vietnam seemed to have reached a point of diminishing, nonexistent, or even negative returns from the standpoint of its psychopolitical effects on the Vietminh government as opposed to its military effects on the war in South Vietnam. Moreover, in response to widespread domestic and foreign criticism of the bombing, the U.S. government felt compelled to insist on its purely military nature and even to deny escalation was involved. This suggests the limited value of punitive military action today, especially against an economically backward country seeking unconditional victory.

doctrine and practice in Vietnam. Reasoning critics of America's conduct of the war generally called for more, not less, limitation, despite remnants of the quick-victory-or-withdrawal attitude. This change of attitude toward limited war was due partly to the unpopularity of the Vietnam war, but it also reflected a long-developing appreciation of the need, the strategy, and the requirements of the contrived limitation of war, which the Kennedy administration had popularized.

By doctrine and experience the Soviet Union and China were inclined at the outset of the cold war not only to avoid direct military confrontations (except in defense of their homeland and buffer territories) but also, despite the Soviet depreciation of the feasibility of a limited war in Europe, to use force in measured proportion to political objectives, with careful attention to the psychological and political dimensions of war. The U.S., on the other hand, did not enter the cold war with a doctrine or tradition of limited war. Quite the contrary. Yet it developed both a doctrine and the means of limited war in response to the conditions of global commitment and the prospects of nuclear war.

The particular reasons for the U.S. limitation of war, however, have been varied. One can point, in various instances, to such motives as the fear of diverting armed forces from areas of higher priority, reluctance to frighten allies and offend world opinion, and consciousness of competing domestic goals and domestic political inhibitions. A more basic source of limitation has been the fact that the value of resisting aggression locally lies less in the intrinsic economic or strategic importance of the area in contention than in the larger political effects to be derived from successful containment. Therefore the prospective gains and costs of the war have to be measured in terms of general interests in the main arena of international politics, not just in terms of local victory. This situation inflates the significance and increases the intensity of local wars, but it also facilitates the conduct and resolution of such wars on a limited basis, since the larger political objectives can be sustained short of complete victory (generally by agreement on the *status quo ante*), and the immediate military objectives are not worth the cost of extending the war.

The principal motive for the U.S. limitation of both the Korean and Vietnam wars, however, was the fear of their escalation to a major war, with the heightened risk of a nuclear confrontation such a war would entail. This kind of restraint is bound to weigh heavily in any nuclear power's conduct of war. One would expect fears of escalation to be even more compelling in a nuclear multipolar world.

Fears of escalation combined with the necessity of using force under contrived limitation lead naturally to the concept of controlled escalation.[52] Escalation, or the step-by-step expansion of the scope and intensity of war, was originally regarded as an uncontrollable danger. In the 1960s, however, it came to be regarded as a controllable and reversible process, a complicated game of many possible ascending steps, each one of which would follow the calculated decisions of governments weighing a variety of considerations affecting their relative bargaining positions in an effort to bend the adversary's will. Controlled escalation reaches its ultimate refinement when each side, although capable of inflicting unacceptable damage on the other, studiously refrains from doing so while trying to coerce its adversary with limited expansions of the war that carry the threat of going further. Under the most stringent and exacting control, even a war of escalating limited nuclear reprisals is conceivable.

It would be dangerous to overestimate the efficacy of control. Untempered by a sense of the role of chance and unpredictable interactions or of the agonistic and impetuous elements in any clash of arms, the concept of controlled escalation may lead its exponents to exaggerate the feasibility of calculated mutual restraint and conscious bargaining in war.[53] Nevertheless, as a paradigm for approaching war with the

52. The most detailed and striking analysis of escalation is Herman Kahn, *On Escalation*. Kahn defines escalation as a competition in risk-taking or resolve in a limited conflict. In this competition increase of efforts, characterized by an interaction of the issues in conflict with the level of violence and provocation, is restrained chiefly by fears of an adverse overreaction by the opponent.

53. Herman Kahn not only believes that the most reasonable approach to war in the nuclear age is the "Byzantine attitude of professionalization without heroics"; he also thinks that the American public has abandoned its quixotic approach to war and endorsed a cool, calculating rationality on the part of its leaders in crises and wars. One can appreciate the essential validity of these two overstated propositions yet profoundly doubt Kahn's view that World War III would be "relatively technical, run by government authorities and technicians, with little or no attention paid to the immediate problems of support from, or the morale of, the civilian population" or that "it would probably be fought relatively coolly and be guided by considerations of national interest little affected by propaganda or popular emotion." It is extremely unlikely that a war on the scale of a world war would end quickly unless it were because of mass revulsion against the horrible level of destruction. In that case, however, there would be little scope for cool bargaining and demonstration by the government authorities and technicians. On the other hand, if World War III were an extended competition of national resolve and risk-taking in which the adversaries deliberately refrained from exerting their maximum destructive power and consciously bargained about the political terms of a cessation of hostilities, the experience of the Korean and Vietnamese wars indicates that popular emotions and preferences and national propaganda would play a major role in the conduct of the war. One can scarcely predict what effects public involvement would have in the conduct of a much broader and more intensive war with a principal adversary. But experience indicates that every public emotion and preference would be represented in the conflicting and none too dispassionate views of the authorities and technicians. *Ibid.*, pp. 22, 201, 221.

professional coolness of a poker player rather than with Von Schlieffen's single-minded devotion to military efficiency or Foch's romantic exaltation of the total offensive, its emergence in the field of strategic thought is an important sign of the changing role of force in international politics and seems bound to affect the actions of governments as well as the ideas of analysts.

Significantly, the concept of controlled escalation has already been put into practice in crises short of war, even between states capable of obliterating each other's major cities. If the Cuban missile crisis had resulted in an actual clash of arms between Soviet and American forces, both sides might well have continued to play the game out within carefully circumscribed limits of violence. Almost surely, neither would have dared act on the assumption that an all-out war was inevitable. Therefore it is not utopian to suppose that, so far as nuclear powers are concerned, calculated restraints induced by fear of escalation will serve something of the same function in limiting war as the agonistic and inherent physical restraints of earlier eras. Fear of nuclear war provides the compelling incentive to extend to warfare itself the concept and practice of mutual deterrence that has prevented major war.

The ultimate extension of the concept of controlled escalation is the strategy of limited nuclear war in which cities would be deliberately spared from attack. It is difficult to know whether this concept corresponds to real possibilities or whether it is merely a fantasy, which may console those with the awful responsibility of managing deterrence but which could not be put into practice if deterrence should fail. It would be dangerous to underestimate the contingent, unpredictable nature of any war. Wars have an impetus that drives men to violence beyond their original intentions. The development of nuclear power has greatly increased the latent energy of armed forces and hence the volatility and unpredictability of war. Fortunately, in response to the growing complexity, speed, and range of arms, the U.S. and, less conspicuously, the Soviet Union have systematically injected into peacetime military planning and into research and development programs measures to maximize wartime flexibility and political control. But although such measures facilitate improvisation by allowing for a diversity of responses, the scope and complexity of planning and of the organization for executing plans tend to make war—especially nuclear war—more subject to preplanned or merely preconditioned responses, and to that extent less subject to political choice. The great destructiveness of a few nuclear weapons and the complete lack of experience with nuclear war compel skepticism about the feasibility of controlling the impetus of nuclear exchanges.

On the other hand, our ignorance of nuclear war and the irrationality of fighting such a war without limits should warn us against assuming that any use of nuclear weapons must inevitably and automatically lead to unrestricted devastation. If the superpowers should become involved in a nuclear exchange as the result of the enlargement of a local war—perhaps in a clash of arms growing out of a miscalculation of intentions or out of the actions of a third party in a crisis—they would be intensely aware of the fearful risk of annihilating each other. It does not seem unreasonable, therefore, to suppose that they will be progressively less willing to deny themselves, through lack of foresight and preparation, the opportunity to avoid mutual annihilation in a nuclear war. Possibly other nuclear states would be less prudent. But any state that must rely principally on its own nuclear power for support of its political ends will probably find it intolerable in the long run to gamble everything on a deterrent bet that would be catastrophic to lose. Nuclear states may bluff their determination to use their weapons *à outrance*, but they will probably hedge against having to carry out the bluff; and we dare not assume that their hedging must fail. In any event, it would be worse than silly to assume that any nuclear war must necessarily become a general nuclear war.

A spreading realization of the folly of unlimited war and of the necessity of artificially limiting war promises to restore the concept, and hopefully the reality, of the political control of violence among states—a concept that was almost lost in modern man's fascination with the expansion of military power. As deterrence is based on the calculated management of military power in relation to political factors of will and intent, so the contrived limitation of war depends on scrupulous attention to the interaction of the political and military elements of war. The deliberate limitation of the specific political objectives for which a war is fought and on the basis of which it might be terminated becomes an indispensable condition and rationale for limiting warfare when virtually unlimited means of destruction are available. Recognition of the political element in revolutionary and other internal wars supported by external powers is compelling simply from the standpoint of success. Such wars are by their very nature heavily suffused with politics, since they are waged for internal political control. Although typically they are fought for total objectives within a country, they cannot be effectively waged unless the military contest is scrupulously limited by internal political imperatives, especially on the part of an intervening state with a surplus of destructive power.

Thus in the middle of the twentieth century the overt uses of force, like the uses of force short of war, tend to become more and more fused with politics. After a period of history punctuated by two world wars—a period in which the modernization of force carried war beyond the control of politics—the most powerful states have subordinated war to political limitations in a more systematic and calculated way than in the eighteenth century. It is as though they sought to restore the utility of war as an instrument of policy, not because they take war for granted as a normal extension of politics, but precisely because they are terribly aware that war could be a disastrous "thing in itself."

12. A Changed Attitude Toward Force?

We must acknowledge that the conscious limitation of force in all its forms presupposes a change of attitude as fundamental as the changes that led to the unrestrained expansion of force. It presupposes an attitude that neither takes force for granted, nor glorifies it, nor purports to supranationalize or abolish it, but that systematically cultivates the limitation and regulation of force in order to make it a rational instrument of policy.

The crucial importance of man's attitude toward force is not diminished by the many objective things with which he must come to terms. Like the widespread weariness with war and longing for peace in other periods of history, the determination to bring force under systematic control could have a greater effect on international politics than the distribution and organization of power or even the particular characteristics of weapons. Given this determination, all the developments that have tended to expand force beyond the control of states—the centralization, popularization, professionalization, and modernization of force—might bring force back under control: centralization, because the modern state has the indispensable institutions for organizing and managing force as a disciplined instrument of policy; popularization, because the widespread concern with nuclear dangers places novel inhibitions on the overt use of force and creates novel opportunities for developing its tacit use; professionalization, because the complexity and dangers of the new technology have fostered the establishment of a new civil-military group of planners and managers who are dedicated to the scrupulous regulation of force for political ends; modernization, because the proliferation of technology has finally created such a fearful weaponry and yet one so suited to stable deterrence as to make feasible an international order based largely on the goal of avoiding major war.

The prospect of regulating force seems realistic and in some quarters even reactionary compared to the vision of abolishing or transforming the war system. Yet to place much hope for international order on a fundamentally changed attitude toward force is to propound a realism that is akin to the most pervasive form of utopianism: the belief that man, through a transforming effort of will and intelligence, can master his social and political environment as he has mastered his physical environment; that he can overcome the scourges of international life just as he has largely overcome the adversities of his life as a citizen in the modern state. Considering the disturbing history of international politics and the modern expansion of military power, all advocates of the restraint of force—whether committed to laissez-faire, systemic, or regulatory concepts—must confess a degree of utopianism.

The reader must judge for himself whether technological and political developments in the nuclear age put the particular utopia of a world of tolerably regulated force within the realm of likelihood. But utopianism that looks toward a transformation of attitudes rather than an automatic progression of impersonal forces has a peculiar obligation to probe the deepest roots of man's approach to war and politics. In light of the tenacious psychological and political roots of man's international behavior before the invention of nuclear weapons, it must critically assess the claims and the evidence that nuclear weapons have so altered these roots of behavior or so transformed the international environment as to sustain a new international order based on the mastery of force.

PART II
THE RATIONALE OF FORCE

1

THE NEED TO JUSTIFY FORCE

1

Has a change occurred in men's attitude toward war? To most observers the answer no longer admits of doubt. If the view that war itself has become obsolescent continues to provoke controversy, the view that men's attitude toward war has changed, and drastically so, is now a commonplace. Nor is the latter view without apparently persuasive support. At the beginning of the present century it was not uncommon for men to speak and to write of the allegedly beneficent effects of war or, at least, of certain wars. Thus the wars for empire of the period preceding World War I were widely represented as marking a great advance for humanity. "It is indeed a warped, perverse and silly morality," a future American President wrote of these wars, "which would forbid a course of conquest that has turned whole continents into the seats of mighty and flourishing civilized nations."[1] After World War I the theme that war represented an instrument of progress, particularly when employed to spread the civilization of superior peoples, ceased to be fashionable or even acceptable. When it was briefly revived in the 1930s by the apologists of fascism, it bore not only a sinister but a curiously archaic ring. In subsequent years the attempt to rehabilitate this most ancient of institutions has not been repeated. War may not yet be obsolescent, but convention no longer permits men to find any saving virtue in war. To appeal today to the ennobling influence of war on the character of men and nations would seem at best eccentric. To write today of the beneficent effects of war on civilization would mark the author as perverse. Within the course of the past half-century the

1. Theodore Roosevelt, *Winning of the West* (1896). Quoted in Howard K. Beale, *Theodore Roosevelt and the Rise of America to World Power* (Baltimore: The Johns Hopkins Press, 1956), p. 160.

historic strain of thought glorifying war or finding in war a constructive force in humanity's development has all but disappeared.[2]

The change in men's attitude toward war finds a still more striking reflection in the unwearying insistence with which governments today condemn war as a means of settling international differences and profess their devotion to peace. What is striking is not the mere disavowal of aggressive intentions, something governments have always disavowed, but the persistence of the efforts made to develop a peace-loving image. These efforts, it seems plausible to assume, would not be made if they did not reflect the ever-increasing importance of public opinion, both domestic and foreign, and the requirements normally imposed by opinion. Accordingly, when force is threatened or employed, the justification attending its threat or use is a matter of no small importance.

Indeed, it is in the need to justify force, or rather in the intensity of this need, that we may perhaps find the most significant indication of a change in men's attitude toward war. To be sure, the justification of force, and the apparent need to justify, are not in themselves novel. Apart from purely expediential considerations, the need to justify force arises wherever there is an awareness of a moral order independent of, and in potential opposition to, the order of the collective. It is only when men identify themselves completely with the collective to which they belong, when they consequently believe that the "health and strength" of the collective is not only the highest but the only moral imperative, that the need to justify force does not and cannot arise. In the modern state system, at least, these circumstances have rarely, if ever, been entirely satisfied. Even so, there may be considerable variation in the degree or intensity of the need to justify force, just as there may be significant variation in the ends considered to justify the threat or use of force. If some ends of state action have justified the use of force

---

2. It is common among observers to except the Chinese from this change in men's attitude toward war. To what extent the Chinese do form an exception, however, is not entirely clear. In the statements of Chinese leaders the theme of the moral and educative virtues of war is regularly attended not only by the condemnation of all wars other than "people's wars" but also by an emphasis on the intrinsic evils of war generally and the necessity of emancipating men once and for all from this institution. Thus in a bellicose statement that attracted widespread attention, the Chinese defense minister, Marshal Lin Piao, described war as a "great school for the people" and castigated the "Khrushchev revisionists" who take a "gloomy view of war." At the same time, Lin Piao recalled the prophecy of the master, Mao Tse-tung, that the day was not far off when "this monster [war] will be finally eliminated by the progress of human society." Text in *The New York Times*, September 4, 1965, p. 2. If the present Chinese attitude toward war is indeed reminiscent of the past glorification of war in some respects, in other respects it nevertheless reflects the changed attitude discussed in these pages.

in all periods, and continue to justify force today, other ends that were once generally accepted are no longer invoked, and can no longer be invoked, as a justification of force. What must be emphasized here, however, is the intensity of the need to justify force even in circumstances where the legitimacy of its threat or use is, in principle, generally acknowledged.

2

The theme need not be labored. It is apparent that a change has occurred in men's attitude toward war. It is equally apparent that this change has been prompted in large measure by the increasing destructiveness of war. What is not apparent is the significance of this change for men's behavior. Is it the harbinger of moral progress? There is a certain plausibility in the view that it is. On this view, the change in men's attitude toward war, particularly as manifested by the need to justify force when it is resorted to, testifies to a growing sense of obligation that is potentially universal in scope. The wellspring of this sense of obligation is man's capacity for sympathy, and the force that gives this sense a potentially universal scope is man's capacity for reason, which enables him to comprehend mankind in its entirety and to act consistently with that comprehension.[3] Despite the development of these faculties, men may of course still resort to force in their collective relations. In doing so, however, they find it increasingly difficult to remain indifferent to the effects of their behavior on others—even when the others are the adversary in war. The unease thereby experienced must somehow be appeased. At root, then, the need for justification is found in the desire to still this unease. It does not seem unreasonable to assume that the intensity of the need to justify force reflects the depth of this unease and, in consequence, must operate to impose progressive restraints on the measures men will be prepared to take against their fellows.

3. The view that man's capacity for sympathy when joined to an ever-developing reason must eventuate in a universal sense of obligation also forms the basis of most contemporary discussions of "universalism." In his essay *Utilitarianism*, written in 1861, John Stuart Mill articulated the essential premises that continue to nourish the optimistic expectations of present-day advocates of universalism. "The same superiority of intelligence (which broadens the range of interests), joined to the power of sympathising with human beings generally, enables him to attach himself to the collective idea of his tribe, his country, or mankind, in such a manner that any act hurtful to them, raises his instinct of sympathy, and urges him to resistance." (Everyman's Library ed., 1951), p. 63. To these considerations, many contemporary universalists will of course hasten to add the "oneness" of the world as a fact and not simply, or even primarily, as a norm. It is this alleged factual oneness of mankind today from which the universalist frequently deduces mankind's moral unity.

Nevertheless, this need for justification is in itself no guarantee of moral progress. If it were, the present age would surely far surpass all preceding ages in moral achievement. Yet we are confronted with the fact that the increasing need to justify force has gone hand in hand with the increasing destructiveness of war itself. Moreover, the change in men's attitude toward war, and the consequent intensification of the need to justify force, have not prevented men from threatening the physical extermination of a collective adversary, a threat the novelty of which in the modern era is still frequently overlooked. It may be true that an obsession with justification reflects an uneasy conscience, that the principal source of this unease is the sympathy aroused by the suffering of others, and that the need for justification is ultimately always a need for self-justification. But an uneasy conscience provides no assurance of an improvement in behavior. At least it provides no assurance that men's behavior will be marked by greater restraint. The actions men take in war or the actions they contemplate taking once in war may well give rise to an uneasy conscience. This unease need not have a restraining effect on action; it may only prompt men to give greater significance to the purposes for which force is threatened or employed. If the justification of force requires that the values preserved through war be proportionate to the values sacrificed in war, and the principle of proportionality necessarily forms a part of every justification of force,[4] men have but to persuade themselves that the purposes for which a war is fought have an absolute significance. Once persuaded of this, the conscience may accommodate itself to increasingly destructive measures. An uneasy conscience may therefore turn out to be a mixed blessing when judged by its effects in restraining men's actions. Rather than restrain men, it may provoke behavior that is less restrained than the behavior provoking the initial unease.

Whatever the ultimate sources of the need for justification, and however intense the manifestations of this need, it must largely be satisfied—if it is to be satisfied at all—by man's reason. There is nothing to prevent the rational faculty from satisfying this need by demonstrating that the purposes men entertain in employing force represent the ultimate purposes, the deepest aspirations, of all humanity. These demonstrations, it is true, are always partially rooted in the unease man experiences at the suffering he inflicts on others. However spurious in character, they still reflect his sympathy for and sense of obligation to his fellows. The very fact that he is not satisfied with a relative and contingent justification for action is itself eloquent testimony to this sense of obligation. By

4. Cf. pp. 233–35, 299–301.

his insistence upon an absolute justification for action he acknowledges, however unconsciously, that his behavior ought to serve not only his own interests but the interests of his fellow man. And this it may do only if the purposes or interests served by action have universal and unconditional validity. At the same time, in devising an absolute justification for action the rational faculty may still the unease men otherwise experience at the suffering they inflict on others and may provide the basis for behavior that is free of any meaningful restraint.[5]

It may prove hazardous, then, to take much comfort from the argument that the intensity of men's need to justify force and the difficulty of satisfying this need are roughly proportionate to the sheer destructiveness of war. Even if true this may only mean that as the destructiveness of war increases so will the insistence upon setting an ever-higher value on the purposes for which men believe they are fighting. Experience suggests that once at war the temptation is great for the participants to assume that there is a meaningful, even a necessary, relation between the measures they take and the purposes they entertain. As the destructiveness of a conflict increases, the purposes for which it is presumably fought also take on an increasing significance for the adversaries. But the purposes that are eventually entertained need not precede the conflict or mark its initiation; they may instead emerge in the course of the war and then largely as a result of the war's very destructiveness.

In retrospect, this sequence appears to the dispassionate observer a tragedy that might have been readily avoided. Yet once nations are involved in a conflict that requires great sacrifice and imposes an ever-increasing measure of destruction, a repetition of this sequence is difficult to avoid. The participants will come to believe, as apparently they must believe if they are to continue the struggle, that the interests at stake somehow bear a meaningful relation to the suffering and destruction. And in one sense, at least, this conviction is always ultimately true. Once men abandon themselves to unrestrained violence the interests they thereby jeopardize must also become unlimited.

5. The belief that growing rationality must result in moral progress is of course largely rooted in the assumption that reason not only enables man to comprehend the interests and claims of others but compels him to apply the same criteria to the claims of others that he applies to his own. To this extent justice is the result—in Reinhold Niebuhr's phrase—of reason's insistence upon consistency. But if it is reason that bids man to treat equals equally, it is not reason—or, at least, it is not reason alone—that tells him who are, or ought to be, equals. Moreover, the same reason that bids man to act consistently also enables him to demonstrate that apparently similar actions are nonetheless dissimilar in their significance and, in consequence, must be judged differently. Thus the ingenuity with which governments demonstrate that an apparently similar action constitutes legitimate self-defense when taken by themselves and aggression when taken by an adversary.

The judgments men make in the course of war may of course be altered and even reversed in the aftermath of conflict. In the years following World War I, the victors found it increasingly difficult to believe that there had been a meaningful relation between the costs of the war and the interests at stake. A reappraisal of these interests led to the widespread conviction that the war represented an unjustified sacrifice. The experience following World War II proved quite different. Despite controversy over and critical reappraisal of some significant features of this later conflict—notably strategic bombing—there has been a consensus that on the whole a meaningful relation did obtain between the costs of the war and the purposes for which the war was fought. Thus the principal criticism of the more excessive practices that marked strategic bombing has simply been that these practices were unnecessary for achieving victory and that they even represented a wasteful diversion of resources. The great majority of critics, though by no means unmindful of the moral issues raised, have been prepared to concede that had victory been clearly impossible without these practices—including so-called terror bombing—the purposes for which the war was fought would have sanctioned them. Even in World War II, however, the interpretation finally given the conflict by the victors neither entirely preceded nor clearly marked the initiation of hostilities; the purposes eventually entertained were in some measure at least a result of the war's very destructiveness.

Nor does an awareness of the destructive power of nuclear weapons afford any assurance that the relation men commonly establish between the measures they take in war and the purposes they entertain will lose its compelling character. An appreciation of the brief duration and possible consequences of nuclear conflict only insures that what could formerly occur during the course of war must now occur prior to its initiation. The need to justify an increasingly destructive application of force once in war is accordingly replaced by the need to justify the threat of force. But the conviction that a meaningful and necessary relation exists between the measures threatened and the interests for which a threat is made may remain unchanged. If anything, this belief may appear more compelling than ever, given the possibility that any overt resort to force may eventually lead to the introduction of nuclear weapons and that once nuclear weapons are employed it may prove difficult to limit their use. In these circumstances even the threat of non-nuclear force will hardly seem justified if the interests at stake are not made to appear somehow commensurate to the consequences that might follow a failure of the threat. When failure may eventuate in general nuclear conflict it is not surprising that the temptation constantly arises to interpret almost every conflict of interest over which force is threatened as posing a critical issue of security, if not the bare issue of survival.[6]

This temptation is due to other factors as well. In some degree, it is nearly always the result of the very pervasiveness and seeming intractability that come to characterize a great conflict. Where survival itself is the issue that is seen either on one or on both sides to be at stake, specific conflicts of interest will be invested with a significance they would not otherwise have, for each confrontation is looked upon as a test of the will to resist and ultimately therefore to survive. "Let none of you think," Pericles says in urging his fellow Athenians to reject Sparta's ultimatum, "that we should be going to war for a trifle if we refuse to revoke the Megarian decree. It is a point they make much of, and say that war need not take place if we revoke this decree; but, if we do go to war, let there be no kind of suspicion in your hearts that the war was over a small matter. For you this trifle is both the assurance and the proof of your determination. If you give in, you will immediately be confronted with some greater demand, since they will think that you only gave way on this point through fear."[7] Substitute the surrender of West Berlin for revoking the Megarian decree and Pericles' words seem entirely analogous to the words of President Kennedy in the summer of 1961. "West Berlin," the President declared, "is more than a showcase of liberty, a symbol, an isle of freedom in a communist sea . . . above all it has now become, as never before, the great testing place of Western courage and will, a focal point where our solemn commitments . . . and Soviet ambitions now meet in basic confrontation. . . . If we do not meet our commitments to Berlin, where will we later stand? If we are not true to our word there, all that we have achieved will mean nothing."[8] Essentially the same interpretation was given in the fall of 1962 to the Soviet-American confrontation that resulted from the clandestine Soviet installation of missiles in Cuba. This "deliberately provocative and unjustified change in the status quo," the President declared in announcing the imposition of a blockade on all offensive military equipment under shipment to Cuba and in demanding the withdrawal of all offensive weapons from the island, "cannot be accepted by this country if our courage and our commitments are ever to be trusted again by

6. The possible consequences of employing nuclear weapons may of course have the opposite effect as well. Rather than cause men to exaggerate their interests the prospect that nuclear war might result from any conflict in which force is threatened may cause them to depreciate these interests, if not to deny them altogether.

7. Thucydides, *History of the Peloponnesian War*, trans. Rex Warner (London: Penguin Books, 1954), p. 92.

8. Address to the Nation, July 25, 1961, *Department of State Bulletin*, XLV, 268, 273.

either friend or foe."[9] Again, the American effort to contain the Communist insurgency in South Vietnam has been widely characterized as a "test case" for the Communist strategy of "national liberation," a test case which if allowed to succeed would imperil the security, and perhaps ultimately the survival, of the U.S. Even so, it is clear that the possibility of general nuclear war growing out of any resort to armed force, however limited initially, must strongly reinforce the temptation to link specific conflicts of interest with the issue of survival itself or to see in such conflicts a vital symbol of this ultimate issue.

To these considerations must be added the peculiar moral arithmetic that men habitually employ in calculating the costs of war. The same bias that prompts them to inflate the significance of their interests when employing or threatening to employ force also prompts them to assess the costs of war primarily in terms of the destruction their particular nation is likely to suffer. Experience does not indicate that in this respect democratic governments may be expected to behave with less partiality than others. They may behave with even greater partiality, if only for the reason that the governors are accountable to electorates that insist that in war the observance of humanitarian requirements begin at home. Moralists may protest that the partiality with which nations calculate the costs of war is a perversion of the principle of proportionality, the true meaning of which must be found in its generality. But nations have regularly found the significance of this principle to rest, at least in the first instance, in its particularity. To the former, the destruction in war that is to be justified, if at all, by the principle of proportionality can only mean destruction wherever it occurs. Human lives are human lives, wherever they are taken. To the latter, the principle of proportionality applies above all else to those injuries the particular nation is likely to receive in war. Human lives may be human lives, but some human lives are still more important than others. Not infrequently, the manifestations of this partiality may be quite unconscious. In his study of thermonuclear war, Herman Kahn relates asking a large number of Americans "how high a price" they would be willing to pay in order to punish the Soviets for a major aggression against Western Europe. Kahn reports that "estimates of an acceptable price generally fall between 10 and 60 million, clustering toward the upper number."[10] Neither the questioner nor the questioned considered it necessary to specify in any greater detail

9. Address to the Nation, October 22, 1962, *Department of State Bulletin*, XLVII, 716.
10. Herman Kahn, *On Thermonuclear War* (Princeton: Princeton University Press, 1960), p. 30.

which human lives were relevant in setting a "price." The reference was presumably regarded as self-evident.[11]

It is quite true that a need to justify force may, and will, arise from either of these interpretations. Still, the significance of this need for men's actions will obviously depend very largely upon which interpretation is given the principle of proportionality. Given the one interpretation, the need to justify force arises from a calculation that does not differentiate markedly between the collective self and others in determining the costs of war. Given the other interpretation, the need to justify force stems principally from a calculation of the costs of war to the particular nation. In either case, these costs may appear excessive and give rise to an uneasy conscience. But it makes a difference whether this unease is prompted by the one form of calculation or by the other.

Thus in the conduct of war the moralist may insist that the principle of proportionality is perverted when it is used to justify measures that take a multitude of the enemy's lives in order to save a few of one's own. Nevertheless, instances abound in which belligerents have interpreted this principle as a sanction for measures designed to save the lives of some, however exorbitant the cost in the lives of others. Should the resulting disparity give rise to moral embarrassment, belligerents may always plead military necessity as a justification for their action. Save in isolated instances of wanton behavior which evidently serve no military purpose, this plea can readily be given a semblance of plausibility. That it is normally possible to determine objectively what degree of military necessity justifies what amount of human suffering has frequently been asserted but has never been satisfactorily demonstrated.[12]

11. The same unconscious partiality may appear in otherwise sensitive and critical discussions of the moral issues raised by force. Thus Arnold Wolfers writes that "the controversy between exponents of nationalistic and non-nationalistic ethical standards in our culture is not over the moral right to pay the price of survival. None but perfectionists or absolute pacifists deny a nation which is engaged in a life and death struggle the right to make and demand every sacrifice necessary for self-preservation." *Discord and Collaboration*, p. 60. Every sacrifice of whom?

12. It is quite true, as the jurist will remind us, that the restraints imposed by the law of war may, and frequently do, restrict the operation of military necessity. Not every action a belligerent may consider necessary is permitted by the law of war. Thus in one of the major war crimes trials held after World War II, an American military tribunal declared that "the rules of international law must be followed even if it results in the loss of a battle or even a war." *Trial of Wilhelm Lest and Others* (The Hostages Case), *Law Reports of Trials of War Criminals*, 8 (London: United Nations War Crimes Commission, His Majesty's Stationery Office, 1949), p. 67. But this stricture, even if taken seriously, is clearly relevant only to weapons and methods already regulated by specific rules. It is hardly relevant at all to novel weapons and methods. The latter are regulated—to the extent they are regulated at all—only by the so-called general principles of the law of war.

Then, too, the broader meaning that is commonly given to military necessity—or necessity in war—is itself largely dependent upon the purposes of war; what may prove to be militarily necessary is not determined simply by the immediate requirements of military operations and the means available to belligerents for effectively carrying out these operations. Still more important in the determination of military necessity are the ends for which a war is fought. The partiality belligerents regularly betray in the conduct of war therefore finds its ultimate sanction in the purposes for which a war is presumably waged; partiality in the conduct of war is accordingly transformed into impartiality when judged by the higher purposes of war. The same need for justification that prompts men to endow these purposes with an absolute significance may in turn make of military necessity a principle that justifies almost any behavior in war, however one-sided its consequences. For this reason alone the profession of humanitarian aspirations may provide little indication of the concrete measures men will nevertheless be willing to take in war. The appeal to humanity may have a moderating effect when its expression does not run athwart what are conceived to be the requirements of military necessity. But how men conceive of these requirements will in turn largely depend upon the nature of the interests for which they fight, or, at any rate, believe they fight. In practice, therefore, if not in principle, humanity in war is largely a function of military necessity; an expansion of the latter will have as its consequence a contraction of the former.[13]

Nor is the expansion of military necessity at the expense of humanitarian considerations avoided merely by limiting the purpose for which force is avowedly employed to the defense of "territorial integrity" and "political independence." The scope afforded to military necessity must still depend upon the scope afforded by self or collective defense; mili-

13. These considerations must also qualify the sometimes too confident assertion that the primacy of politics will reduce the scope and intensity of violence. It will do so only if politics have a certain character. Raymond Aron may be right when he declares that the primacy of politics *permits* the evasion of the extremes of violence. *Paix et Guerre entre les Nations* (Paris: Calmann-Lévy, 1962). But it clearly does not *insure* this result. Whether the primacy of politics will have this result depends not only upon other factors (e.g., technology) but upon the character of politics. Aron writes that the more the statesman calculates in terms of cost and profit the less he is inclined to abandon the pen for the sword. But this will surely depend upon the values that go into the calculus. Aron simply assumes these values in declaring: "The reasonable conduct of politics is only rational if one postulates as the end of state relations the survival of all, common prosperity and the least bloodshed of peoples." (p. 57.) If one makes this assumption about the end of politics (and of war), it evidently follows that the primacy of politics will reduce the scope and intensity of violence. Unfortunately, this assumption has no necessary relationship to the principle of the primacy of politics.

tary necessity will still be limited only to the extent that the objects for which defense is undertaken are themselves clear and limited. In fact, however, the residual vagueness of self-defense is the result of the residual vagueness of the objects to be defended, particularly "political independence."[14] Moreover, what is militarily necessary depends not only upon the purposes for which a war is fought but the actual circumstances in which a war is fought—above all upon the weapons available to and used by the belligerents. If defense is a limited purpose, in a war fought with nuclear weapons that purpose may still sanction measures which—in the name of military necessity—result in the adversary's annihilation.

It is equally clear that revolutionary changes in the means of destruction will normally result in a weakening of the restraining effects of sympathy, if only by aggravating men's fears of what others are capable of doing. In a still broader sense, technological innovation will weaken the sense of sympathy to the degree that it suddenly and radically alters both the conditions and possible consequences of conflict. The corrosive effects of these changes demonstrate the danger of exaggerating the intellectual basis of moral restraints on men's actions at the expense of their emotional roots.[15] It is understandable that moralists are on the whole disposed to emphasize the intellectual basis of these restraints and, consequently, to find in the mitigation of war, as well as in the eventual disappearance of war, primarily a consequence of the belief that all men form a greater community and that the elementary duties they owe one another derive from their common membership in this greater community. Whereas the effective radius of the emotional faculty of sympathy is limited, the scope of the conviction that forms the intellectual counterpart of this emotional faculty is at least potentially universal.

14. Cf. pp. 271–75, 279–99.
15. In the years prior to World War I, this danger was given prophetic utterance by John Westlake. Surveying the marked improvement in the conduct of war that had occurred in the course of the nineteenth century, Westlake noted: "the cause of this rapid . . . improvement must be something more than the renewed belief in a commonwealth of mankind which has been mentioned above as marking our time. If that belief had stood alone, it might have done no more for the mitigation of war than was done by it when it was first introduced by the Stoic philosophy. But along with the renewal of that belief there has come a remarkable development of the sentiment of pity, of an enthusiasm of humanity which has caused a wider and keener sympathy with suffering than has perhaps ever before been known. . . . No doubt the enthusiasm of humanity and the recognition of a human brotherhood are closely allied. They are indeed the emotional and intellectual aspects of the same psychological attitude, but history proves that . . . the latter is of course the weaker of the two for any operative purposes." *The Collected Papers of John Westlake* (Cambridge: Cambridge University Press, 1914), pp. 278–79. Writing in the high noon of Victorian optimism, Westlake concluded that there were "ominous signs that pity, as an operative force in the mitigation of war, has nearly reached its limit."

Yet experience has shown that of the two it is the emotional roots that
are ultimately the more significant as a restraint on men's behavior in
war and, at the same time, the more vulnerable to changes in technology.
The impact of weapons that enable men to kill at a distance has long
been recognized and is by now a commonplace in the literature. Clausewitz described this impact when he wrote that "weapons with which the
enemy can be attacked while he is at a distance . . . allow the feelings,
the 'instinct for fighting' properly called, to remain at rest, and this so
much the more according as the range of their effect is greater. With a
sling we can imagine to ourselves a certain degree of anger accompanying
the throw, there is less of this feeling in discharging a musket, and still
less in firing a cannon shot."[16] While allowing the "instinct for fighting"
to remain at rest, weapons which enable men to kill at ever-increasing
distances may also allow the faculty of sympathy to remain at rest.

Technology not only permits men to kill at ever-increasing distances
but in ever-increasing quantities. If sympathy is affected by distance, it
is perhaps even more profoundly affected by quantity. While the ability
to kill at a distance enables men to kill without "seeing" their victims,
the ability to kill in quantity enables men to kill without "recognizing"
their victims. Although men may no longer literally "see" their victims,
they may still have a clear image of them as men and one that evokes
sympathy for their suffering. In these circumstances, we may still speak
of men "recognizing" their victims. On the other hand, men may see
their victims though no longer recognize or know them as men and, in
consequence, feel little if any sympathy for their suffering. The history
of warfare provides numerous examples of seeing the enemy though not
recognizing him. In such wars, the dehumanization of an adversary is
largely expressive of what Hans Speier has termed the "premoral emotions of horror and disgust."[17] But the significance of weapons that
measure their victims in millions is that although the slayer may no
longer recognize the slain, the failure to do so need no longer express
the premoral emotions of horror and disgust. Instead, the absence of
recognition and of sympathy may result simply from a leap in the
destructive power of weapons of sufficient magnitude to transform the
act of killing into an abstraction, an act increasingly difficult for men
to give concrete meaning to in terms of the emotional categories that
make up their daily lives and experiences. What, after all, is 100 million

16. Karl von Clausewitz, *On War*, trans. F. N. Maude (1911), III, 250. Quoted
in John U. Nef, *War and Human Progress* (Cambridge: Harvard University Press,
1950), p. 372.
17. Hans Speier, *Social Order and the Risks of War* (New York: G. W. Stewart,
1952), p. 271.

lives, or, for that matter, even 5 million? By what appears to be a curious psychological inversion, a radical increase in the number of victims serves to dull rather than to sharpen men's sense of sympathy—or of guilt.[18] When judged by the actor's awareness of the enormity of his act, the terrible question arises whether "killing in the abstract" is killing at all.

These considerations afford a partial answer at least to one moralist's plaintive question: "How can a nation live with its conscience and know that it is preparing to kill twenty million children in another nation if the worst should come to the worst."[19] Must we conclude that technology has made men worse? The answer will evidently depend upon what we mean by "worse." If we mean a conscious and deliberate rejection of sympathy, it may be argued that men are not worse. Thus Raymond Aron declares that a thermonuclear war "would be more terrible than any previous war, not because men are worse, but because they know more."[20] In a similar vein, Hans Speier has written that "cultural differences in the technique of fighting cannot be imputed to differences in the morality of the fighters. The modern pilot who bombs a munitions factory kills more persons in a few seconds than the mercenary soldier of the 16th century did in all his life. This indicates different technological levels of violence rather than different personal inclinations to kill."[21] On the other hand, if moral judgment is based on the objective consequences of behavior rather than on the conscious rejection of sympathy—or a personal inclination to kill—there is reason to insist that technology has made men worse. Contrary to Aron, men are worse—or may be worse—precisely because they do "know more."

The impact of technology on men's behavior is nonetheless a theme that readily lends itself to exaggeration. It is after all comforting to assume that if men support policies that may one day eventuate in the destruction of millions, this is due to their inability to comprehend the enormity of the strategies to which they are committed. If technology has blinded them to the meaning of their action, the burden of guilt may thereby be lightened even if it cannot be wholly removed. For the same reason it is comforting to believe that the breakdown and aban-

---

18. This inversion appears curious, however, only because we take for granted that the intensity of men's sense of sympathy must prove roughly proportionate to the scope and quantity of human suffering. Unfortunately, experience does not warrant the faith that is commonly placed in this comforting assumption.

19. John C. Bennett, "Moral Urgencies in the Nuclear Context," *Nuclear Weapons and the Conflict of Conscience*, ed. John C. Bennett (New York: Scribner, 1962), p. 101.

20. Raymond Aron, *Paix et Guerre entre les Nations*, p. 767.

21. Hans Speier, *op. cit.*, p. 254.

donment of restraints once observed in the conduct of war have resulted from the constraints generally imposed by the changing technology of war. This belief may prove especially congenial to a society that extols the principle of individual responsibility in its domestic life and professes to see in aggression an act for which only a ruling group should be held responsible. How else can it justify to itself the prospect of taking measures in war that in effect, if not in principle, may hold millions responsible for acts they have neither participated in nor perhaps approved nor possessed the power to prevent? It is a mark of the profound disparity between the possible consequences of deterrent strategies and the principles nations may otherwise continue to profess that, in the 1949 Geneva Convention on the protection of civilian populations in time of war, all forms of collective penalties against an occupied population are prohibited. So far-reaching a prohibition may well create serious difficulties for an occupant power. The prohibition was inserted, however, not only as a reaction to the extreme reprisal measures taken in occupied territories by Germany during World War II, but as a measure of the general repugnance at the practice of holding a group collectively responsible for the actions of a few. Nevertheless, nations that have been insistent upon condemning the principle of collective responsibility when applied to victims of war have been equally insistent upon retaining complete freedom in war to take measures that may hold entire populations responsible for the behavior of their governments.

Nor may it prove possible in a nuclear conflict to effect even a tenuous reconciliation between the act of attacking civilian populations and the profession of continued adherence to the principle of noncombatant immunity by resort to an argument frequently employed in the earlier conflicts of this century. To the close of World War II it was still possible for men to salve an uneasy conscience by the claim that in modern industrial war the efforts of the great part of the population are invariably harnessed to the war effort. It was this novel relationship that was alleged to render traditional restraints inoperable rather than deliberate intent to abandon these restraints. The argument both exaggerated the degree of co-operation of the civilian population in the nation's war effort and conveniently neglected the fact that belligerents have always drawn upon resources provided by the noncombatant population. Its logic finally led belligerents to the assertion that the terrorization of civilian populations was itself a legitimate military purpose, given the extent to which the entire population co-operated in and supported the nation's war effort. In fact, the steady abandonment in both world wars of the principle of civilian immunity cannot be attributed primarily to the reason most emphasized—the novel relationship of civilian populations to combatant forces. Technology, which permitted belligerents to strike effectively at the sources of a nation's military power, and a willingness to use the new weapons in order to achieve the ever-expanding purposes of war were far more significant in contributing to the decline of the combatant-noncombatant distinction. The relationship of the civilian populations to combatant forces had indeed changed, but the change was due far less to the objective character of modern industrial war than to men's insistence upon redefining this relationship in a manner that largely deprived it of its former meaning. At any rate, the argument that the character of modern industrial war made observance of the combatant-noncombatant distinction increasingly difficult, whatever the intentions of belligerents, appears largely irrelevant to the conduct of nuclear war. In their numerical size and relative isolation from society, the forces required for general nuclear war bear a striking resemblance to eighteenth-century warfare. At the same time, these forces are perhaps even less dependent, upon war's outbreak, on the efforts and co-operation of the noncombatant population than were the forces of the eighteenth-century monarch. By one of those curious ironies of history, nuclear technology has rendered absurd the principal justification relied upon in breaking down the distinction between combatants and noncombatants. The nature of that justification is perhaps illuminated by the ease with which men abandoned it, though by no means abandoning a willingness to threaten measures far in excess of those that initially elicited it.

We are therefore reminded that it is in the very nature of war as a collective enterprise that the innocent must suffer along with the guilty. Measures in war injurious to the innocent, as Adam Smith remarked two centuries ago, "can by no means be founded upon justice and equity, properly so called . . . [they] must be founded upon necessity which, indeed, in this instance is a part of justice. . . . In war there must always be the greatest injustice, but it is inevitable."[22] To this extent, then, it is

---

22. Adam Smith, *Lectures on Justice, Police, Revenue and Arms*, ed. Edwin Cannon (1896). Quoted in Arnold Wolfers and Laurence W. Martin, *The Anglo-American Tradition in Foreign Affairs* (New Haven: Yale University Press, 1956), pp. 84–85. It is significant, however, that Smith explains the measures in war which fall upon the innocent, not only on the grounds of necessity but on the grounds of reciprocity as well. "We have suffered unjustly on account of our connexions," he declares, "let them also suffer unjustly on account of theirs." That the innocent are made to suffer at all is unjust; but if the innocent on one side are made to suffer, one cannot complain that the innocent on the other side are also made to suffer. Although this appeal to an "equality of suffering" on the part of the innocent appears to strengthen the appeal to necessity, in view of its partly normative character it also illustrates the limits to the satisfaction men are able to draw from the appeal to necessity.

not a matter of making the innocent responsible for the actions of a ruling group but of doing what must be done if war is to be waged at all. Modern technology has simply expanded the scope of this tragic necessity inherent in all war.

Here as elsewhere, however, the appeal to necessity is seldom undertaken with consistency. Though men may decry the practice that makes many responsible for the acts of a few, it is unreasonable to suppose that the measures they have taken and are yet prepared to take in war can be sanctioned without also endorsing the practice of collective responsibility. An unwillingness to acknowledge the evident meaning of these measures fosters the curious illusion that the principle on which they are based has been exorcised. In fact, the disavowal of collective responsibility commonly goes hand in hand not only with actions but with statements that are tantamount to its affirmation.

Thus during World War II we found little difficulty in asserting that although we had no intention of making the German people responsible for the crimes of their leaders, "Germany must learn her lesson." The strategic bombing of Germany was widely interpreted as part of that lesson and as just retribution for the injury and suffering Germany had caused others. How "Germany" could be distinguished from the German people was never made apparent. In announcing the destruction of Hiroshima, President Truman declared that we had used the atomic bomb against "those who had attacked us without warning at Pearl Harbor, against those who had starved and beaten American prisoners of war, against those who had abandoned all pretense of obeying international laws of warfare." But "those" who were the victims of the bomb obviously had not performed the acts President Truman ascribed to them. Endemic in the course of the cold war are statements to the effect that the Russian people ought not to be made responsible for the acts of their leaders. Yet these statements are readily coupled with expressions of determination to "punish the adversary," including, if necessary, "his cities" should he once resort to armed aggression. How the adversary's cities can be punished but the Russian people not be held in effect collectively responsible for the acts of their leaders remains unclear.

These expressions reflect not only men's insistence on personifying their collective relationships; they also reflect the persistence of the conviction that the "innocent" among the adversary are not entirely innocent. Even though many of those who comprise the enemy nation do not directly contribute to or actively participate in the actions of the ruling group, they are nevertheless considered to contribute indirectly to making possible the actions of the ruling group, if only by virtue of the relationship they bear to the rulers through common membership in the nation. In consequence, they must bear at least a measure of the responsibility for the actions of the ruling group.[23]

The intensity with which this conviction may be held and the consequences to which it may lead have varied considerably. In some degree, however, it appears to mark all group conflict. In its purest manifestations the belief that forms the basis for the practice of collective responsibility scarcely rises to the level of conscious justification. Where the personality of the individual is not yet differentiated from the group of which he is a member, there is no need to justify measures in war that fall indiscriminately upon the members of the opposing group. These measures are no more than an application to intergroup relations of a principle sanctioned in the domestic life of the group. It is simply accepted as self-evident that, in war, membership in the group should form the necessary and sufficient basis of responsibility.[24] Where the personality of the individual is clearly distinguished from the group and individual responsibility prevails in the domestic life of the group, a need will arise to justify measures, even though taken in war, that appear to depart in radical manner from a principle otherwise professed and practiced. It does not follow, however, that the substance of the justification now given for measures that may prove indiscriminate in their effects will differ essentially from the belief that has always been at the root of the practice of collective responsibility. If in taking such measures men must now consciously persuade themselves that the innocent are not entirely innocent, the means for doing so remain substantially unchanged and consist in the relationship the innocent bear to the guilty by virtue of their common membership in the group.

Efforts to avoid this conclusion, however ingenious, only serve to confirm it. Thus Paul Tillich has written: "It is never the nation which is directly guilty for what is done by the nation. It is always the ruling

23. It is true that the immunity traditionally accorded in war to noncombatants was never based on their innocence, in the sense of requiring noncombatants to refrain from giving even moral approval to wars undertaken by the state. Nevertheless, the growth of the combatant-noncombatant distinction did occur in a period when the civil population had relatively little emotional identification with the state. Psychologically at least, the innocence of noncombatants was largely identified with their apathy toward the state and the conflicts in which it engaged.

24. "In such cases," Westermarck writes of primitive group conflicts, "the whole group takes upon themselves the deed of the perpetrator, and any of his fellows, because standing up for him, becomes a proper object of revenge. The guilt extends itself, as it were, in the eyes of the offended party." Edward Westermarck, *The Origin and Development of Moral Ideas* (London: Macmillan, 1906), I, 33.

group. But all individuals are responsible for the existence of the ruling group. Not many individuals in Germany are directly guilty of Nazi atrocities. But all of them are responsible for the acceptance of a government which was willing and able to do such things."[25] But not all individuals "accept" a government and, in this sense, are responsible for its acts. Moreover, the initial act of accepting a government need not be construed to imply the acceptance, let alone the support, of all of its subsequent acts. If responsibility is to depend upon consent or acceptance and if these terms are to be given their customary meaning, it is clear that many who comprise a nation cannot be held responsible for the acts of a ruling group save on the basis of their relationship to the rulers. On the other hand, if Tillich's insistence upon the nation's collective responsibility is once accepted, it is difficult to see why moral guilt cannot also be imputed to the collective. Moral guilt—or, to use Tillich's term, "direct guilt"—is not imputed only to those who have directly participated in or actively contributed to acts deemed immoral; it is also extended to those who have accepted the actors and presumably have consented—if only passively—to their acts.

The simple truth is that despite the unease to which its application gives rise, the principle whereby the collective is identified with the actions of its rulers will persist so long as man's membership in the state —and in the nation—forms his most important relationships. The age-old pattern of collective responsibility necessarily follows from these relationships. At the same time, the significance men attach to these relationships must in large part explain how they may condemn the practice of collective responsibility yet condone the taking of measures in war the effects of which are indistinguishable from the practice that is condemned.[26] The unease men may indeed experience in the presence

25. Paul Tillich, *Love, Power, and Justice* (New York: Oxford University Press, 1954), pp. 93–94.
26. The significance of the practice of collective responsibility may therefore be missed if it is seen to arise simply from the habit of personifying social relationships. Louis Halle writes: "Moral responsibility belongs to persons, whether individual or corporate persons. If we maintain . . . that only individual persons really exist, then we must hold that a nation cannot be responsible for good or evil, even for the good or evil done in its name, that it cannot be subject to reward or punishment. On the other hand, to the extent that we think of nations as corporate persons which really exist as such, it will seem right that they should be held accountable to them." *Men and Nations* (Princeton: Princeton University Press, 1962), p. 52. It is quite true that the attribution of responsibility to nations has always been facilitated by their personification. Nevertheless, we may believe that only individuals "really exist" and still hold a nation collectively responsible for the actions of its government. Since the practice of collective responsibility ultimately depends upon the importance men give to certain relationships, it may be expected to persist even though these relationships are no longer personified.

of such measures can no more be relied upon to limit their actions than the need to justify force in general can be relied upon to restrain the measures men are still prepared to take against their fellows.

3

These considerations do not warrant the conclusion that the unease men may experience over the effects of their actions or prospective actions is without significance for their behavior. They do warrant the conclusion that when considered in isolation, the significance of this unease is indeterminate. Whether or not it leads to greater restraint in men's behavior, and particularly in men's collective behavior, depends very largely upon other circumstances, some of which have been noted in preceding pages. These other circumstances may be such as to promote less rather than more restraint, and this despite an unease that is admittedly novel if only in its intensity. Moreover, experience indicates that in such circumstances an intensification of the need for justification, and consequently an intensification of the unease this need presumably reflects, may serve only to loosen further the restraints men were otherwise prepared to observe. Given these circumstances, the reliance on men's capacity for sympathy to restrain their behavior may not only prove futile but, to the extent this reliance leads to the neglect of other and more effective sources of restraint, even dangerous.

Technological and organizational restraints apart, there is no difficulty in identifying the most significant sources of restraint in war. The evidence is overwhelming that such restraint as men have been able to impose upon the conduct of war has stemmed far more from considerations of expediency and utility than from a sense of sympathy for the suffering—or even the "unnecessary" suffering—of others. Probably the greatest single step ever taken to mitigate the conduct of war occurred when men began to enslave the defeated rather than to torture and to kill him. There is good reason to believe that considerations of utility rather than of pity prompted this change. Yet the advent of slavery marked a signal advance in the humanization of war. Moralists are frequently, and understandably, loathe to recognize the significance of this and similar examples that may be drawn from the history of warfare, but their reluctance to do so does not make these examples any the less relevant. Indeed, if purely moral restraints are equated with the faculty of sympathy, with the sentiment of benevolence which Hume considered to be an "original principle of human nature," it would appear that most of the restraints men have observed in war have had a nonmoral origin.[27]

Restraints that have their origin largely in considerations of expediency or utility may nevertheless acquire in time a normative character. If they do, the prospect for their continued observance is thereby strengthened, though seldom if ever to the point that their observance is no longer dependent upon the considerations that originally prompted them. The history of warfare affords numerous illustrations of the evolution of behavior originally undertaken for expediential reasons and in time undertaken, at least in part, because it is felt to be obligatory and right. Perhaps the most important illustration of this evolution may be seen in the distinction between combatants and noncombatants. There are writers who have found in the principle according immunity from direct attack to the civilian population of belligerents something so apparently compelling to man's moral and rational faculties as to form a kind of "natural law" of warfare.[28] If this is so, then we can only conclude that the history of warfare has been, on the whole, a very "unnatural" one. In fact, the distinction between combatants and noncombatants became meaningful in terms of the actual practices of belligerents only in the period following the Thirty Years' War.[29] Despite

27. There is of course no compelling reason why moral restraints must be so identified. If they are so identified, we must still acknowledge other restraints men have often observed in war, restraints that have had the quality of norms but that cannot be attributed to the faculty of sympathy, as for example the restraints that formed a part of what Hans Speier has termed "agonistic war." In the latter, war is interpreted as a game or a play that may confer glory on the victor and reveal his side as just, only if he complies with the rules that form an integral part of the contest. Violations of the rules governing war not only deprive victory of its meaning, or worth, but dishonor the victor. Chivalry in war may be seen, at least in part, as a major variation on this basic theme, requiring as it did a fairness even in war and a certain mutual respect for the adversary. Beginning in the eighteenth century the principle of chivalry in war, and its closely related concept of honor, were increasingly regarded as archaic. It is characteristic of the nineteenth century to find practically all the normative restraints in war in the principle of humanity. The consequences of placing too great a reliance on the sense of humanity to restrain the conduct of warfare became manifest only in the twentieth century.

28. Thus one writer declares that the "natural right of noncombatants to immunity from direct attack is at one and the same time an analysis of the natural law of warfare itself." Paul Ramsey, *War and the Christian Conscience* (Durham, N.C.: Duke University Press, 1961), p. 135.

29. A historian of early state practice writes of the warfare of the fifteenth and sixteenth centuries: "A single sentence, in fine describes the character of the war-practice of the age: the distinction between combatants and non-combatants remained to be drawn. When Marshal de Bressac negotiated in 1552 with the Spanish opposing generals for the exemption of peasants from the scourge of hostile operations he could only appeal for a precedent to the conduct of Xenophon's ideal Cyrus." T. A. Walker, *A History of the Law of Nations* (Cambridge: Cambridge University Press, 1899), p. 192.

the cruel excesses that marked this conflict and the widespread desire to prevent their recurrence, the early development of the combatant-noncombatant distinction cannot be attributed primarily to humanitarian motives.[30] It is only in the nineteenth century that the restraints placed on the conduct of warfare are attributed primarily, if not almost exclusively, to the desire to prevent or mitigate suffering. The early growth of the combatant-noncombatant distinction must instead be attributed very largely to the realization that if war was to prove at all compatible with an order whose principal units are sovereign states, belligerents would have to accept certain limitations upon their behavior. It was less the desire to prevent or mitigate suffering than it was the desire to insure that some semblance of order would be preserved even in war that this restraint, and still other restraints, began to influence the behavior of belligerents.[31] Even then, the modest success attending the development of the combatant-noncombatant distinction was greatly facilitated by the limited power resources—social and material—at the disposal of the state. Ironically, it was at the very time the state's war-making capacity was being suddenly increased that the restraints attendant upon the distinction between the armed forces and the civilian populations of belligerents finally acquired the quality of a norm in the public consciousness.

The decline of the combatant-noncombatant distinction in this century illustrates the essentially fragile character of the restraints on the conduct of war—even of restraints developed only after a long period and finally endowed with an obligatory character—when the factors originally prompting them and conditioning their further development have either disappeared or been substantially impaired. It is true that military historians and jurists have occasionally attributed to the combatant-non-combatant distinction a clarity it never possessed and a degree of effectiveness it never attained.[32] And moralists have occasionally seen in

30. Still less, perhaps, can the emergence of this distinction in practice be attributed to the promptings of the Christian doctrine of *bellum justum*. The period marking the development of the combatant-noncombatant distinction, and of the mitigation of warfare generally, is also the period marking the decline of the theory of the just war. Cf. pp. 302ff.

31. If the importance of this consideration is often neglected by contemporary writers, it is largely for the reason that they find the restraints on the conduct of war almost entirely humanitarian in purpose—that is, to prevent or mitigate suffering. It is only in very recent years that the idea has once again appeared that the primary purpose of these restraints is the regulation and direction of hostilities—that is, the preservation of some semblance of order even in war. This idea is not inimical to humanitarian purposes. On the contrary, it has been the only practical way of realizing, however imperfectly, these purposes.

32. The conduct of war in the seventeenth and eighteenth centuries was by no means as idyllic as a later and rather envious age is often prone to imagine. Thus by

the application formerly given this distinction little save the spontaneous workings of a more virtuous age.[33] But these misconceptions are no greater than those reflected by the apologists of twentieth-century warfare, who concluded that the distinction was never relevant to the conduct of war. Despite its imperfections and lapses in practice, the principle according immunity from direct attack to the civilian populations of belligerents formed the core of the restraints traditionally imposed upon the conduct of war. On its observance the not inconsiderable achievement of "civilized warfare" essentially rested.[34] The extent to which belligerents in the two world wars eroded this once vital principle is scarcely more impressive than the brevity of the period in which the erosion occurred. Only thirty years separate the modest "reprisal" measures at sea taken by Great Britain and Germany and the destruction of Hiroshima and Nagasaki with atomic weapons. The former measures tentatively initiated a change that the latter measures appeared to consummate.[35] Still more instructive, perhaps, is the fact

---

almost any standards, save perhaps those of the present age, the Seven Years' War was very destructive and marked throughout by immoderation, particularly in the measures taken against civilian populations. The great historian of the French Revolution, Albert Sorel, has written that the excesses of the revolutionary wars were no greater than the excesses of the wars of the old regime. *L'Europe et la Révolution Française* (Paris: Librairie Plon, 1885), I, 81–88. Sorel's harsh judgment of eighteenth-century warfare is exaggerated, but no more so than the almost idyllic picture suggested by some contemporary writers—e.g., B. H. Liddell-Hart, *The Revolution in Warfare* (New Haven: Yale University Press, 1947), and J. F. C. Fuller, *The Conduct of War* (New Brunswick, N.J.: Rutgers University Press, 1961).

33. Their attitude prompts Hans Speier to observe: "Moralists often attribute to scruples what has been due to prudence, and observers whose passions exceed their knowledge do not accurately distinguish between the impossible and the immoral; like children and fanatics they are unable to tell the unattainable from the forbidden." *Social Order and the Risks of War*, p. 269.

34. This achievement, however, was always limited to the European state system. Colonial conflicts continued to be characterized by the practices of an earlier age. The lack of restraint which marked the latter conflicts was due in part to the nature of these conflicts and in part to a disparity in strength which frequently seemed to make prudence unnecessary. Europeans sought to explain, and thereby to justify, their conduct of colonial warfare on the grounds that colonial peoples either refused to reciprocate or were congenitally incapable of reciprocating those practices comprising "civilized" warfare. The argument was not without substance, though it conveniently neglected other considerations.

35. An extraordinary commentary on the decline of the combatant-noncombatant distinction is afforded by a noted historian of World War II, who writes: "It may be contended with assurance supported by history that no justification for the use of the bomb [on Hiroshima] is needed, since the accepted and ruling attitude sanctions the use of any and all weapons in war except any banned by implicit international agreement. . . . Our right, legal, and historical, to use the bomb may thus be well defended." Herbert Feis, *Japan Subdued* (Princeton: Princeton University Press, 1961), p. 179.

that only six years prior to Hiroshima, an American President could characterize the act of attacking population centers from the air as "inhuman barbarism which has profoundly shocked the conscience of humanity." Yet a period of scarcely fifteen years separates this statement by President Roosevelt from the official adoption of a strategy dependent for its success upon threatening potential aggressors—and, implicitly, the population centers of aggressors—with nuclear annihilation. It is not surprising that so sudden and so radical a change should have given rise to unease. What is important to recognize, however, is that this unease has been less significant than the fear of retaliation in kind in occasioning recent consideration on the possibility of preserving the combatant-noncombatant distinction even in a nuclear conflict.

It is necessary to emphasize these commonplaces if only in order to disabuse ourselves of the sanguine views taken by many moralists. Of these views, none is more unfounded, and perhaps none is more dangerous, than the view that there are "inherent" restraints on the conduct of war. If inherent has a historical reference, it is patently false. Yet it is no less false when given a moral reference, unless we are to take the validity of this reference as somehow self-evident. And this we are in no position to do if we wish to learn anything from history.[36]

36. It is of interest in this respect to note the very few restraints that do appear as somehow inherent, in the sense that men have regularly drawn back from their use. Perhaps the most instructive example is afforded by the deep-rooted aversion to employing weapons that have a toxic effect (poison, gases, biological weapons). Many observers have commented on the extent to which this aversion to toxic weapons remains seemingly impervious to rational considerations. None of the explanations given to account for this remarkably persistent attitude is very satisfactory. In some measure, it is probably attributable simply to the fear of retaliation in kind. But the fear of retaliation by an enemy attends the use of any weapon and is scarcely unique to toxic weapons. In part, it is apparently attributable to the closely allied expectation that toxic weapons might escape control and thereby injure the user as well as the intended victim. W. H. Oldendorf argues that there is at present little basis for the "widely held belief that toxic gases and infectious agents are unsuitable because they are uncontrollable and might backfire." ("On the Acceptability of a Device as a Weapon," *Bulletin of Atomic Scientists* [January, 1962].) This may be true, but the belief may persist nonetheless. The view is occasionally taken that the special reluctance to endorse the use of biological weapons in war may be traced to the "twentieth-century cleanliness campaign" and to the universal concern for promoting the goals of public health and sanitation. But this view, if it is to be taken seriously, would have to account for the aversion to toxic weapons in earlier periods; men have only seldom looked with favor on the use of poison or the spread of plague. Perhaps the most satisfactory explanation is that toxic weapons arouse an aversion bordering on the instinctive, partly because their use is connected with the origins of life (and is considered to threaten the origins of life) and partly because their use seems necessarily treacherous. Objection may be raised, and not without good reason, to this suggestion of an inherent notion of treachery in view of the disparate views men have entertained in the history of war-

fare over what acts constitute permitted ruses and what acts constitute treachery. Even so, there is a marked persistence in identifying the treacherous act with the clandestine act. The special category in which biological weapons, for example, are placed probably is the result in part of the belief that such weapons are by their very nature clandestine and that their use therefore amounts to treachery. This belief might also account for the interesting hypothesis of Oldendorf's to the effect that men seem congenitally disposed to accept more readily those weapons which can be applied as physical violence. "It would seem that an acceptable weapon, regardless of the level of culture and technological achievement used in delivering the device, shall finally be applied to the victim as physical violence. The more closely this approaches the basic effects of the fang and claw, the more readily it is accepted. . . . It is especially interesting that when these devices are individually spotlighted, scrutinized, and dissected, and their merits are weighed, the explosive weapons seem so *right* and the quietly lethal weapons so wrong." (p. 36.) Whatever the correct explanation, the frequent attempt to find the age-old abhorrence of toxic weapons in man's sense of pity—in his reluctance to impose unnecessary suffering— appears artificial. The reluctance to employ weapons that have a toxic effect has commonly been attended by the willingness to use other weapons and methods that have resulted in greater suffering and destruction than the weapons proscribed.

2

THE MORAL ECONOMY
OF FORCE

1

If the need to justify force is in itself no guarantee of moral progress, it is at least clear that this need may be traced primarily to the destructiveness of war in this century. The change in men's attitude toward war is of course due to other factors as well. In significant degree, it is a result of the growing disparity since the nineteenth century between the conditions of domestic life and the conditions of international life. Until the last century this disparity was not pronounced, even for the then more advanced Western societies. It is only with the marked amelioration of the conditions of domestic life that the contrast between domestic and international life has become increasingly apparent and morally oppressive. The conditions that continue to characterize international society represent a radical discontinuity with the conditions that increasingly characterize domestic societies. In part, the condemnation of war evidently follows from an awareness of this discontinuity. Moreover, it must be acknowledged that when men refer to the destructiveness of war, that reference is itself often ambiguous. If war is condemned for the reason that it has become "too destructive," this may imply only that men's standards of judgment have changed, not that war has in fact become relatively more destructive in quantitative terms. Even a small war—i.e., small in terms of the quantitative destruction—may appear too destructive if men are no longer willing to tolerate war at all. Despite these considerations, it remains true that if a change has occurred in men's attitude toward war, the change cannot be understood save against the background of a particular experience with war in this century. It is this experience and the common expectation formed from it that above all else have given to arguments condemning force as an

219

instrument of statecraft the character of seemingly compelling truths. Take away the expectation of war's destructiveness, and many of these arguments appear either trivial, inconclusive, or simply false.

Thus the argument that force is an "undesirable instrument" is saved from being the merest triviality only because of the assumption men have formed of war's destructiveness. "The assumption that underlies this policy," an international jurist declares in urging that change occur only through procedures of peaceful persuasion, "is that coercion and violence, necessarily entailing the destruction of values, are not suitable instruments for asserting and prosecuting claims for change."[1] Considered in the abstract, the point is as true and as trivial as it is irrelevant to the substantive issues force raises. Few would care to deny that force is an undesirable—or unsuitable—instrument of policy, provided only that other means are at hand and prove reasonably effective in achieving men's purposes. On this point at least, the bellicose and the pacific are as one. "The entire foreign policy of the Soviet Union is aimed at strengthening peace," Premier Khrushchev repeatedly insisted, "since peace is the loyal ally of socialism." If the oppressed throughout the world could only liberate themselves from their oppressors by peaceful means of persuasion the threat or use of force would clearly be unnecessary and undesirable. "We love peace," President Sukarno exclaimed in announcing the determination of the Indonesian government to wrest the western part of New Guinea from the Netherlands, by force if necessary. In giving the order to Indian armed forces to march against the Portuguese enclaves of Goa, Damao, and Dui, Prime Minister Nehru declared that the decision gave him "no pleasure" and added that if the Portuguese had only been amenable to peaceful means of persuasion force would have been unnecessary. There is no reason to question the sincerity of these assertions. With rare exception, peaceful means of persuasion are preferable to forcible means. Force is not only destructive of human values but introduces an undesirable element of uncertainty in statecraft. To achieve one's purposes by peaceful means of persuasion rather than by force, where this is at all possible, is mere prudence.

So, too, it is nearly always desirable—and prudent—to achieve one's purposes by the threat rather than the overt use of force where this is at all possible. That the threat of force is a more peaceful means of persuasion than the use of force is a truism, though one bordering on levity. Those who insist upon considering the threat of force as a "peace-

1. Myres S. McDougal and Associates, *Studies in World Public Order* (New Haven: Yale University Press, 1960), p. 298.

ful means" of persuasion are at liberty to do so, though the argument will always ring rather hollow. It is another matter to argue that if change is inevitable it is generally desirable that it occur by means other than the use of force. But it does not follow that there is some virtue inherent in the nature of change effected by the threat of force that does not inhere in change effected by the actual use of force. If a moral distinction of sorts is nevertheless drawn between the kinds of change resulting from these two methods, it rests on the belief that once force is resorted to the possibility of resolving a conflict of interests on any basis other than one of relative power advantage is severely diminished. So long as force is not overtly employed, there remains a greater possibility that the resolution of a conflict of interests will at least be moderated by considerations other than those of relative power. Being thus moderated, the prospects of a more lasting reconciliation of the parties may thereby be enhanced. There is much to be said for this view, though all too frequently it has given rise to the temptation to equate peace—conceived simply as the absence of the overt use of force—with justice.

Nor is there any clear way in which peace may be defined other than as the absence of force. The recurring attempts to define peace not only as the absence of force but as the presence of certain substantive conditions of order necessarily lead to the identification or equation of peace with justice. Once this identification is accepted, it follows that in the absence of agreement on the essential attributes of a just order there can be no peace. Yet it would require a very curious interpretation of history to exclude this alleged contradiction in terms—an "unjust peace." It is another matter to insist that justice is a necessary ingredient of peace in the sense that men's dissatisfaction with their lot and an inability to improve their position by peaceful means will heighten the prospect of force. But this is to define justice largely in terms of the absence of a serious threat to the status quo. The absence of such a threat need not result from men's satisfaction with the status quo; it may instead be the result of inertia, habit, or fear. In any event, the result is an empty definition of justice, empty because it is evidently compatible with very different social orders. Nothing substantive is said about the nature of the justice which presumably forms the indispensable concomitant of peace. All we are told is that peace is secure when there is no serious disposition to resort to force, and this we already know.

The relevant question, of course, is not whether statesmen and their publics increasingly regard force as an undesirable instrument of policy, but whether they are consistently prepared to abstain in practice from the threat or use of force where peaceful means of persuasion prove ineffective. They have never been prepared to do so in the past and there is little evidence that they are at last prepared to do so today, despite the change that has occurred in men's attitude toward war. Peace may be the loyal ally of socialism, as Soviet leaders have insisted, but if the oppressed peoples cannot be liberated by peaceful means, the use of force to help them obtain their freedom is considered just. Whether or not force is threatened or employed on behalf of peoples fighting for liberation must depend, then, upon prudential calculation.[2]

The Soviet view of the just war, the war of national liberation, may be unique in some respects, but it is surely not unique in its refusal to place peace above all other interests. In this respect it does not differ substantially from the position taken by those innocents of the contemporary state system, the new states. The new states may look upon great power rivalry as both unnecessary and undesirable, but they do not view the conflict "between the old established and the new emerging forces" in the same light. If Soviet-American rivalry has been interpreted as a mere struggle for power, the conflict between the old established and the new emerging forces has been interpreted as a struggle for justice. The great powers have therefore been incessantly reminded of their responsibility for eliminating military force as an instrument of state policy and of their duty to settle all cold war issues by the give and take of negotiation. But the principal duty of the emerging nationalist forces is to fight for the radical elimination of colonialism-imperialism and neocolonialism in all their manifestations. And if these manifestations cannot be eliminated by peaceful means of persuasion, they may—indeed, they must—be eliminated by force.

Thus in defending the Indian seizure of Portuguese possessions before the United Nations Security Council, the Indian representative merely applied this general view of the new states. "This is a colonial question," Mr. C. S. Jha pointed out, and therefore simply one "of getting rid of the last vestiges of colonialism from India. This is a matter of faith for us,

2. On the level of doctrine, at least, it remains difficult to distinguish between Soviet and Chinese views on the justification of war. It is quite true that the Sino-Soviet conflict is marked by varying assessments of the potentialities of employing military power on behalf of wars of national liberation. Even so, the significance of these varying assessments in explaining the Sino-Soviet conflict is easily exaggerated. If the Soviets presently place markedly less emphasis than the Chinese on the utility and need of military power in order to achieve revolutionary goals, this is due in part to the fact that the Soviets increasingly possess "peaceful means of persuasion" whereas the Chinese are still almost entirely lacking in these means. In part, however, the disparity of emphasis is simply due to the disparity of interest in supporting "people's wars," even when this support is seen on both sides to entail no more than a minor risk of large-scale military conflict with the U.S.

Charter or no Charter, Council or no Council."[3] Not surprisingly, the Western powers did not share the Indian view that in colonial questions the use of force is just if peaceful means of persuasion prove ineffective. The U.S., in particular, once again insisted that in a dispute or conflict of interests between states, the failure of peaceful means of persuasion could not serve to justify the initiation of force. "Let us be perfectly clear what is at stake here," Ambassador Adlai Stevenson explained to the Security Council. "It is the use of force by one state against another and against its will, an act clearly forbidden by the Charter. We have opposed such action in the past by our closest friends as well as by others."[4]

In fact, American devotion to peaceful means of persuasion has been less consistent than Mr. Stevenson implied. It is a matter of recent record that where this nation's security interests are concerned, its devotion to peaceful means is also not without limits. Only seven months prior to the Security Council debate on Goa, in April, 1961, the American government had organized and supported armed intervention against the government of Cuba. Although in explaining the abortive action President Kennedy asserted that "any unilateral American intervention in the absence of an external attack upon ourselves or an ally" would be contrary to our traditions, he went on to warn that: "If the nations of this Hemisphere should fail to meet their commitments against outside Communist penetration, then I want it clearly understood that this

3. *The New York Times*, December 19, 1961, p. 1.
4. *Ibid.*, p. 14. In this regard it is both instructive and enlightening to compare the indignation with which the U.S. government reacted to India's seizure of Goa and the remarkable restraint shown during the same period toward the Indonesian insistence upon "liberating" Netherlands New Guinea, if necessary by force. Whereas the Portuguese government refused throughout to accept the principle of self-determination as a basis for settlement, the Netherlands government insisted that any settlement must be guided by the desires of the population of the contested area. Given the circumstances in which the Netherlands government finally came to champion the principle of self-determination, its position was not without the taint of hypocrisy. Even so, the contrast remains between the Indian position over Goa and the initial Indonesian rejection of—in the memorable words of the Indo-nesian ambassador in Washington—"the farce of self-determination." Throughout the stages of negotiating a final settlement the Indonesian government repeatedly reaffirmed its intention of using force to wrest the disputed area from the Nether-lands if the terms of the settlement did not afford assurance that the area would eventually become Indonesian—and, in fact, did resort to force sporadically in order to demonstrate its intent. The final product of the negotiations, largely a U.S. inspiration, granted the substance of the Indonesian demands while preserving in form—though in all probability only in form—the sanctity of the principle of self-determination. Nevertheless, the U.S. government welcomed the settlement as a vic-tory for the principle that disputes should be resolved by peaceful means of per-suasion.

Government will not hesitate in meeting its primary obligations, which are the security of our nation."[5] A rather more guarded though essentially similar declaration of intent to take unilateral forcible measures, if necessary, "to prevent the establishment of another Cuba in this hemisphere," was made in May, 1965, by President Kennedy's successor in explaining the American intervention in the Dominican Republic. Understandably, the American government considers the prevention of Communist penetration in this hemisphere as providing a greater justification for the use of force than the elimination of the vestiges of colonialism and neocolonialism. But it cannot prove surprising if others do not share this conviction.

This continued unwillingness of statesmen and their publics to place peace above all other interests does not resolve the moral issue of whether and for what purposes force ought to be threatened or employed in circumstances where peaceful means of persuasion prove ineffective. But it is surely misleading to insist that this issue must now be formulated in other terms, on the assumption that the interests of states are no longer effectively served by force. Granted this assumption, no meaningful moral issue need even arise. If force has lost its utility, its condemnation on moral grounds is superfluous. If in the pursuit of their interests states need no longer choose between peaceful methods of persuasion and force, what remains is not a moral issue at all but a task of adjusting to an environment in which certain behavior is no longer a rational or expedient means for achieving a nation's ends. In such an environment the argument persistently urged for three centuries by the great liberal critics of foreign policy appears at last vindicated. Force must be rejected as an instrument of statecraft because its use has become self-defeating. "War has lost its utility as a human institution," one writer declares in equating this environment with the realities of contemporary world politics, and "military strength is no longer an effective measure of national power."[6] "What we have seen develop in our time," another concludes, is not only a "complex of well-nigh decisive inhibitions against the use of force by a great power, whether against another great power or against a weak state," but even more generally "the radical obsolescence of war as an accepted means of conducting international relations."[7]

5. Address to American Society of Newspaper Editors, Washington, D.C., April 20, 1961. *Department of State Bulletin*, XLV, 659.

6. Walter Millis, *Permanent Peace* (Santa Barbara: Center for the Study of Democratic Institutions, 1961), pp. 10–11. Also Walter Millis and James Real, *The Abolition of War* (New York: Macmillan, 1963).

7. Louis J. Halle, "Is War Obsolete?" *The New Republic* (April 2, 1962), p. 16.

These conclusions are as unfounded as is the common assumption from which they proceed. Although the significance traditionally attached to territorial conquest has clearly diminished for many states, the experience of the past fifteen years has not invalidated the venerable rule that territorial change in international society when it does occur rarely occurs save through the threat or use of force. Nor has this experience demonstrated that nations need no longer rely on force in order to preserve rights or interests they deem vital. Where change has occurred in this period it has almost invariably been attended by the threat, if not the actual use, of force. Where force has been neither employed nor seriously threatened on behalf of interests challenged by others, such interests have been preserved, if at all, only with great difficulty. Which of these effects should be viewed more seriously is a question that continues to provoke divergent answers when it is not simply considered in the abstract.[8] In the light of this experience, however, it scarcely seems warranted to conclude that force has lost its utility as an instrument of statecraft. If anything, it is clear that the erosion of conditions which in the nineteenth century often permitted force to play a modest and unobtrusive role has instead given rise to a world in which force has assumed a role and significance it seldom before possessed.

Even where the argument that force has lost its utility appears the most persuasive, in the immediate relations of the great powers, it cannot be accepted without serious qualification. If the use of force has lost its utility and has in fact become obsolescent, the threat of force may be expected to share a similar fate. Yet it is apparent that the threat of force continues to play a vital role in the relations of the great powers. Indeed, there have been few periods when the threat of force has seemed

8. Thus a former American Secretary of State has plaintively declared: "The British, despoiled in Egypt, as we have been in Cuba, were pilloried for attempting to defend their rights under international law. . . . we can expect that an enforcement of our rights, in the only way they can be enforced in this dual world, by arms, will find many of our own citizens joining in the Soviet inspired clamor before the United Nations for a cease fire. In other words, we shall be urged in the name of law to cease enforcing our rights which cannot otherwise be rights. No wonder that this doctrine has led to the general breakdown of whatever respect for international law survived the nineteenth century." Dean Acheson, "Fifty Years After," *The Yale Review* (Autumn, 1961), pp. 5–6. The skepticism, and hostility, with which many of the new states view this argument cannot prove surprising. Nevertheless, to the extent that these nations succeed in removing the "vestiges of colonialism and neocolonialism," they, too, can be expected to speak increasingly of legal rights. In defending India's seizure of Goa, Indian representatives made much of the "tide of history and public opinion" and decried legalistic considerations which were "part of the atmosphere of colonialism." But this is not the kind of argument the Indian government has employed in its territorial disputes with Pakistan and China.

more determinative of these relations. No doubt the continued absence of direct military conflict between the great powers must be largely attributed to the expectation of the destruction likely to attend a general nuclear war and to the fear that any use of force immediately involving the great powers might eventuate in such a conflict. It would be rash to conclude from this, however, that a conviction presently exists that the initiation of force—any force—against a major adversary must be avoided in all circumstances, presumably because it will prove self-defeating on any reasonable calculation of interest. The assurance of this conviction remains wanting, else the threat to employ force in any circumstances other than in response to a direct attack would be deprived of further significance. Even so, the conviction that it is no longer rational for a great power to initiate force against another great power does not mean that in great power relations military power is losing its utility, let alone that it has become obsolete. That force is no longer overtly used among the great powers does not necessitate the conclusion that it is therefore useless. The deterrent or intimidatory threat of force may retain its utility and continue to dominate great power relations. In some respects it may even dominate great power relations more effectively than the use of force dominated these relations in the past.[9]

Moreover, the calculations that inhibit the great powers in their mutual relations need not inhibit them in their relations with the smaller nations. If force has lost its utility here as well, the change cannot be attributed simply to the fear that any overt use of force might escalate into a nuclear conflict between the mighty. Nor can this change be attributed to the universality of nationalism and the consequent difficulty of pacifying a conquered population. To the extent that great powers are no longer interested in military conquest and territorial annexation but in the control of governments, the difficulty of pacification may even be expected to become increasingly irrelevant as a deterrent

9. It is the besetting sin of the argument which is dealt with in these pages that it insists upon evaluating the significance of military power largely in terms of its potentially uncontrolled use. The conclusion—that force is no longer a useful or rational instrument of national policy—therefore appears foreordained. Military power no longer confers security upon its holder; instead, in the words of John Herz, "utmost power coincides with utmost impotence." "International Politics and the Security Dilemma," *Nuclear Weapons and the Conflict of Conscience*, John C. Bennett, ed., p. 21. Whereas force was once the indispensable instrument of whatever degree of order the international society possessed, today it promises only to lead to the complete breakdown of order. If force could once serve the ends of justice, at present its use can lead only to the greatest injustice. But alter the assumption on which this argument proceeds—consider the functions served by military power so long as it is not overtly employed or employed only with restraint—and very different conclusions may be drawn.

to the use of force. Self-imposed restraints apart, the primary deterrent, then, must presumably be found in the hostile reaction to be expected of popular opinion throughout the world, including opinion within the great power itself. With increasing frequency it is argued that in a world where governments are everywhere dependent upon the support of popular opinion and where international conflict is largely directed to winning over the allegiance of peoples, what a great power may initially acquire through force either cannot be secured in the face of hostile world opinion or can be secured only at a prohibitive price. "Opinion . . . at home and abroad," one writer has recently observed, "has become, in a world of contending ideologies, the ultimate deterrent."[10]

What is the evidence offered in support of this view? In part, it consists of little more than speculation on the might-have-beens of contemporary history, on the frequency with which force might have been employed had it not been for the expected reaction of world opinion. In part, however, it consists in the endeavor to establish that the several occasions within recent years in which strong powers did openly employ force against weak states are no more than exceptions serving to confirm the general rule. Thus it is argued that the Soviet suppression of the Hungarian uprising in 1956 was undertaken only with great reluctance and as a measure of last resort and that this reluctance was due primarily to the anticipated hostility of world opinion. But even if this interpretation is accepted, it hardly vindicates the view of world opinion as the ultimate deterrent to force. Still less does it appear to support the argument that force has lost its utility as a means of statecraft. It is always possible to argue that in the long run Soviet intervention in Hungary will be seen as a failure and even perhaps as the great turning point in the Soviet bid for world leadership. Against this conjecture over future possibilities must be set the virtual certainty that from the Soviet point of view vital interests would have been sacrificed by the failure to intervene.

Perhaps the favorite illustration cited in support of the deterrent effect of popular opinion is the abortive military adventure by Great Britain and France in Egypt in the fall of 1956. The hostility with which world

10. Evan Luard, *Peace and Opinion* (New York: Oxford University Press, 1962), p. 167. Elsewhere Luard states: "The social pressures which international opinion can exert on the behavior of individual nations perform a function similar to those exerted on the behavior of individuals within societies." (p. 164.) It is this assumption that invariably gives rise to extravagant estimates of the restraining effects of world public opinion. If it were true, international society would no longer be distinguished from domestic society; the same cohesiveness and consensus that normally mark the latter would equally mark the former.

opinion—including opinion within Britain itself—reacted to the Suez intervention was indeed impressive in many ways. Still, it is useful to recall that the intervening powers violated the first and fundamental rule governing successful intervention by failing to present the world with a *fait accompli*.[11] At the same time, they were resolutely opposed by their principal ally and threatened by their principal adversary. In these circumstances, to insist that the failure at Suez must be found in the power of world public opinion is to push a door that is already open. Public opinion apart, given the same circumstances the intervention would in all likelihood have failed in the nineteenth century as well.[12]

Did the pressure of public opinion abroad—certainly not at home— compel the abandonment of the American-supported intervention in Cuba in April, 1961? There is little reason to believe that it did. It may of course be argued, and many have so argued, that had the American government followed through with the intervention the result would have been to alienate the Latin-American nations as well as many of the Afro-Asian nations. Whatever the immediate benefits that might have been derived from a successful intervention, these benefits would have been more than offset by the hostility incurred in Latin America and elsewhere. But a very different argument, and one that must appear in retrospect attractive, may be just as plausibly entertained. The removal of the Castro government, followed by an ameliorative policy toward its successor, might have led to an increase in American influence and prestige in Latin America. It would be foolish to argue that, in the relations of nations, consent is ever achieved by force alone. Yet it is even more foolish to argue that, in a society that remains as rudimentary and divided as the international society, consent may be achieved—indeed, can only be achieved—by the disavowal of force. Whatever the lessons of Cuba, it is far from clear that one lesson is the self-defeating character of force when employed today by a great power against a small state.

Finally, is it reasonable to find this lesson in the American bombing of North Vietnam? It would hardly seem so. What is instead striking in this latest "exception" to the general rule under consideration is how little deterrent effect public opinion appears to have had. Moreover,

11. In his survey of the history of "peaceful change" in Europe, C. R. M. F. Cruttwell writes that experience demonstrates it is "always wisest to face Europe with a *fait accompli*." *A History of Peaceful Change in the Modern World* (New York: Oxford University Press, 1937), p. 3. Given the conditions attending intervention today, the wisdom of the *fait accompli* is even more apparent.

12. Five years after Suez, in July, 1961, the French demonstrated at Bizerte the action that might still be taken against a small state by a stronger power determined to act swiftly and resolutely and without regard to the immediate reaction of world public opinion.

it is far from clear that the long-run consequences of the American action must be to alienate opinion in Asia. Whether or not opinion is alienated will depend upon a number of factors, not the least of which being the military outcome of the American action and, if successful, the measures of rehabilitation and development subsequently taken. The successful application of military power against North Vietnam and, for that matter, within South Vietnam evidently cannot insure that American interests will eventually be furthered; it can only secure the necessary conditions for advancing those interests. To acknowledge this is not in the least to deprecate the utility of force. That force cannot accomplish everything does not mean that it can accomplish nothing. If the application of military power against North Vietnam demonstrates the limits of military power, it also demonstrates—and strikingly so—the continued utility of military power.

These remarks ought not to be interpreted as a denial of the increased importance of popular opinion as a deterrent to the use of force by a great power against a small state. It is apparent that in this respect a significant change has occurred. The only issue of relevance here is how significant is this development. Those who take the view considered above cannot be content merely to argue that popular opinion is a deterrent of sorts to the use of force, or that on occasion it may even represent a very serious liability, for no one would care to deny these commonplaces. Instead, they must be prepared to demonstrate that adverse public opinion, whether at home or abroad, must now make the resort to force a self-defeating venture, and this they clearly have not been able to do. It is significant that the attempt to demonstrate the deterrent effect of public opinion is limited to situations involving the overt use of force and not extended to the more covert and indirect methods of employing force. Indeed, the marked ineffectiveness and confusion of public opinion when reacting to cases of so-called indirect aggression are generally acknowledged. Thus the same writer who asserts that public opinion has become the "ultimate deterrent" to overt aggression also writes: "Precisely because aggression in its crudest form is now so universally condemned, many of the assaults that are made will be dressed up in some more respectable garb . . . because public opinion is itself so confused, aggression may secure its fruits without paying the deserved penalty in international goodwill. The most formidable of all the sanctions will have been nullified. . . . The sanction of opinion therefore remains powerful only against those forms of flagrant and undisguised assault which are, in the modern world, least likely to occur."[13]

13. Evan Luard, *Peace and Opinion*, pp. 53–55.

Luard believes, as do many others, that this confusion of public opinion results primarily from the absence of "recognized principles to help maintain objective standards" and that "where no clear principles are recognized assessment [of aggression] will tend to be swayed by ideological or national predilections." Yet it is precisely these disparate and conflicting ideological or national predilections that must account for the absence of clear and recognized principles to help maintain objective standards. Without these predilections, which reflect the deep divisions marking world public opinion, there would be little difficulty either in achieving reasonably clear principles or in maintaining objective standards of judgment. No doubt, there are instances of alleged aggression sufficiently ambiguous to confuse, and to divide, even an otherwise united public opinion. But the real difficulty is obscured by putting the matter in this way, since it implies a latent consensus on "aggression" that stands only in need of the proper instruments in order to express itself. Experience indicates that this consensus simply does not exist.

It is another matter to insist that even if force has not lost its utility as an instrument of statecraft its threat or initiation ought nevertheless to be condemned. But apart from the expectation of war's destructiveness the moral argument would remain—save for the pacifist—as inconclusive as ever. Force has always been subject to abuse, given the circumstances in which it is employed in international society. These circumstances, as critics have never tired of pointing out, insure only the triumph of the stronger over the weaker; they do not insure that force will be employed as an instrument of order, let alone of justice. The condemnation of force proceeds from an awareness of these perennial moral hazards. At the same time, the moral argument remains inconclusive in the absence of the further demonstration that these hazards must of necessity prove greater than the moral risks incurred by a policy of consistent abstention from the threat or initiation of force. A persuasive demonstration to this effect has yet to be made. Force may be an increasingly undesirable instrument, but to condemn its threat or initiation, irrespective of purpose and of consequence, is evidently not to express a compelling moral truth even in the nuclear age. This unqualified condemnation of force has never been possible, and is not possible today, except at a price that very few have been willing to pay. To the extent that this willingness has increased, however, we may find its principal source in the common expectation of war's destructiveness.

It is the same expectation that presently gives to the distinction between international and internal war a moral significance it would not otherwise possess. Many of the objections urged against traditional methods of interstate violence may be equally urged against the various forms of internal war. Nevertheless, the condemnation of war as an instrument of state policy is frequently juxtaposed with the approval—or at least the tolerance—of force when confined within a state's frontiers and employed to effect domestic political and social change, even though one or both sides to the internal struggle receive the support of outside powers.[14] The distinction thus drawn between international and internal war is parallel to the distinction traditionally drawn by liberal thought between war and revolution, the latter distinction being largely rooted in the conviction that—defensive wars apart—war merely decides "issues of power" whereas revolution decides—or, at any rate, may decide—"issues of justice" as well. But this conviction, which persists today, expresses no more than a limited historical experience, and even then it is at best a partial truth. In this century the significance of war clearly cannot be limited to the boundaries war has altered or to the changes war has effected in the relative power status of the belligerents (assuming for the sake of argument, though the assumption is surely a tenuous one, that these traditional stakes of war do only represent mere issues of power).[15] If the degree to which war decides issues of justice in addition to mere issues of power is to be gauged by the political and social transformation within states consequent upon war, the moral preference given to revolution over war cannot but appear as arbitrary.[16]

No less unfounded is the related argument that war can never really

14. This moral distinction has its obvious counterpart in the legal distinction increasingly drawn by many international jurists between force used directly and overtly by one state against other states and force used indirectly and covertly in support of domestic insurrection. Although acts of indirect aggression and subversion are forbidden by international law, it is argued that the right to employ force in self-defense may be exercised only in response to the direct and overt use of force. Cf. pp. 291–99.

15. The general distinction between conflicts that represent mere contests for power and conflicts that represent contests for justice has never been very clear. Presumably, however, the distinction is between "who should rule" and "how men should be ruled." Thus Bertrand Russell has written: "Most of the disagreements that occur in practice are, not as to what things have intrinsic value, but as to who shall enjoy them. The holders of power naturally demand for themselves the lion's share. Disagreements of this sort tend to become mere contests for power." *Human Society in Ethics and Politics* (New York: Simon & Schuster, 1955), p. 110. War is a mere struggle for power, then, when it simply determines who should rule (or dominate, or be *the* great power). On the other hand, revolution—and, exceptionally, war—is a struggle for justice when it determines how men should be ruled. The tenuous character of the distinction becomes apparent when we apply it to the most commonplace of circumstances—i.e., the independence, or freedom, of states.

16. Indeed, it is clear that in this century international war has itself been the principal agent of revolutionary change within states. Where war has not directly effected such change, it has been the essential prelude to revolution. On the other hand, it is a matter of historic record that no totalitarian regime has been overthrown in this century save through defeat in war.

settle the ideological conflicts that may divide men but can only decide who controls what territory, or, perhaps in the great international conflicts, who is going to organize the world and in the name of what. In one sense the argument is quite true, though banal. Victory in war does not thereby demonstrate the superior justice of the victor's cause. War decides which side is stronger and the more determined, not which side is the more just. In another sense, however, the argument is evidently false. War can and commonly does settle ideological conflicts in that a defeat of the human carriers of ideas will normally also represent a defeat of the ideas propagated. Indeed, it is the plainest of historical lessons that international war has been by far the most common, and certainly the most effective, method by which these conflicts are resolved. Does anyone doubt that the defeat of the Fascist nations in World War II also represented a defeat of the ideas these nations represented? Does anyone doubt that if force could have been successfully employed in the period following World War II to liberate Central and Eastern Europe from the Soviet hold that such action would have represented a defeat of the ideas the Soviet regime proclaimed to the world? And if war cannot really settle ideological issues, how then does it follow that revolution may nevertheless accomplish what war must fail to do?

A more persuasive argument for giving moral preference to domestic violence over interstate war emphasizes the dependence of the former, if it is to prove successful, upon the support of the population. In this view, guerrilla warfare and related forms of insurrection represent a tolerable approximation to trial by ballot, even though one or both sides receive the support of outside powers. "Guerrilla wars," one advocate of this view declares, "ultimately rest for their success upon the support of the population. . . . this makes them probably as true an expression of the underlying 'general will' of those concerned as any form of political expression. . . . there seems to be a kind of general acceptance of their outcome as representing a closer approach to the goals of freedom and justice than do the outcomes of the great international wars."[17] Yet in guerrilla warfare no less than in the great international wars, victory is ultimately determined by relative military strength, and coercion remains the primary instrument for obtaining consent. To equate the outcome of such contests with justice may therefore prove no less objectionable than to equate the outcome of traditional interstate violence with justice.

These considerations must be set apart from the contention that in the present period almost any form of domestic violence is likely to prove

17. Walter Millis, *A World Without War* (Santa Barbara: Center for the Study of Democratic Institutions, 1961), pp. 42–43.

less destructive than war and that the support of domestic insurrection is therefore a less hazardous means of statecraft than war. If change is inevitable and is always in part coercive, it is at least desirable that it come through methods that are less destabilizing and less destructive than traditional interstate violence threatens to be in the nuclear age. But if for this reason war is condemned as an instrument of national policy, while the support of domestic violence is increasingly condoned, the justification for the distinction cannot simply rest either on the purposes or the procedures that presumably mark domestic violence alone. Instead, it must rest in large measure on the greater destructiveness expected to result from war.

2

There is little to support the view that force is no longer a useful means of policy and that, in consequence, military power is no longer an effective measure of national power. At the same time, it is true that some of the ends men are prepared to accept today as a justification of force have changed. Purposes deemed sufficient to sanction force as recently as the beginning of this century are no longer so considered. In one sense, however, the justifications men invoke when employing force necessarily remain unchanged. Whatever the purposes held to justify force, the justification of force on behalf of these purposes is in turn expressed in terms of the principle of proportionality. Invariably, the values that can be preserved only through force are favorably balanced against the values sacrificed, or likely to be sacrificed, by force.[18] The particular justifications of force men have found compatible with this general principle have of course been very disparate. Nor is this disparity due primarily to the varied and complex circumstances in which the principle of proportionality has been applied. Instead, it is a consequence of the principle itself. What it will yield in practice necessarily depends upon what is put into it, and men have put very different things into it. Devoid of substantive content, the principle of proportionality prescribes that the good

18. A recent expression of the principle of proportionality, in the context of an almost ecstatic affirmation of the inevitability and justice of "people's wars," is provided by the Chinese Communist defense minister, Marshal Lin Piao. "We know that war brings destruction, sacrifice and suffering on the people. But the destruction, sacrifice and suffering will be much greater if no resistance is offered to imperialist armed aggression and the people become willing slaves. The sacrifice of a small number of people in revolutionary wars is repaid by security for whole nations, whole countries and even the whole of mankind; temporary suffering is repaid by lasting or even perpetual peace and happiness." *The New York Times*, September 4, 1965, p. 2.

resulting from the use of force ought to outweigh, or to be proportionate to, the evil attending force (or that the evil resulting from the use of force ought to be less than the evil resulting from a failure to use force). This is merely an elaborate way of saying not only what is evidently implicit in the very task of justifying force but what all men can readily agree upon.

Implicit in the very task of justifying force, the principle of proportionality therefore expresses what may be termed the "logic of justification" and is compatible with almost every substantive justification—or condemnation—of force men have ever given. It is difficult to imagine what a meaningful denial of this principle would even be like.[19] The pacifist surely does not deny it; he simply applies it in such a manner as to arrive at the substantive result that war is never justified. But if war is never justified, it is because the values sacrificed by war necessarily outweigh—in the pacifist's view—those values war may preserve. So, too, if it is held that the commission of certain acts in war may never be justified—e.g., the direct and intentional killing of noncombatants—the meaning of this argument is that the evil such acts entail by their very commission must prove disproportionate to whatever good they are intended to serve and might in fact serve. To declare that certain acts are absolutely forbidden is to insist that the value sacrificed in committing such acts is equally absolute and, by definition, disproportionate to any value their commission may conserve or promote. There is, without doubt, a very great difference between a view that places absolute restraints on the means men may employ even in war and a view that does not insist upon the imposition of such restraints. Even so, this difference does not consist in the fact that the former view goes beyond the principle of proportionality whereas the latter view does not. Both are readily encompassed by the principle of proportionality, though the disparate manner in which this principle is interpreted leads to profoundly different positions over the substantive meaning to be given to justice in war. The same reasoning informs the view that condemns preventive war, whatever the circumstances in which preventive war is contemplated or the ends for which it may be undertaken. The absolute condemnation of preventive war necessarily presupposes that the evil entailed by the very act of resorting to preventive war is disproportionate to any good this act is intended to serve and might in fact serve.

19. The nihilist apart, who will contend that force ought to be so employed as to result in a maximum destruction of value? Again, who will assert that force is justified only if the evil resulting from its use proves greater than the evil resulting from the decision not to employ force? Nevertheless, we are frequently reminded that the converse of these propositions expresses a significant and instructive truth.

Nevertheless, it is at least clear that the difficulty of justifying force is dependent upon the destruction resulting from its use.[20] Whatever the significance men may attach to the purposes for which force is employed, and however partial they may be in calculating the costs of war, a favorable balance becomes increasingly difficult to sustain as war becomes increasingly destructive. It is equally clear that the primary and, indeed, the one reliable measure of this destructiveness is quantitative. The most tangible value destroyed in war is human life and human lives may always be counted. To be sure, life itself is not the only nor is it necessarily the highest value at stake in war. Evidently, how men live has frequently been considered more important a value than whether some continue to live at all, else human history might long since have been free of war. But how men live will ultimately depend upon how many live and in what circumstances they live. Whether a society can remain a viable entity and preserve its distinctive ways will also depend upon many qualitative and even intangible considerations. It seems pointless, though, to deny the critical importance in this respect of the sheer destruction, both human and material, sustained in war. To the extent such destruction can be determined at all prior to the event, it must be determined largely—if not primarily—in quantitative terms.

To emphasize the importance for moral judgment of the destruction resulting, or likely to result, from the employment of force is not to deny the importance of the purposes for which force may be undertaken. It is merely to insist that whatever the purposes sought through force, and whatever the significance men may attach to these purposes, they cannot be divorced from the level of destruction attending the use of force. Whether or not these purposes can be realized through force will ultimately depend upon the level of destruction war entails. At some point, however uncertain and controverted that point may be, numbers will have a vital bearing upon purpose and quantitative considerations will have a critical influence upon political and moral judgment. Nor is it necessary to locate this point in order to insist that the need to justify force and the difficulty of satisfying this need are roughly proportionate to the sheer destructiveness of war.[21]

In part, the neglect of the significance of quantity in considering the justification of force stems from the conviction that the way men live, and consequently the purposes for which they fight, are matters of pure quality. The sheer destructiveness of war may ultimately determine whether a way of life can be preserved at all, but quantitative considera-

20. It is wearisome to add "save for the nihilist" to each and every generalization. This qualification may therefore be assumed.
21. For an exception to these remarks, however, see p. 244.

tions presumably cannot enter—or, at least, ought not to enter—into the manner in which men define the way of life they seek to preserve. Yet the way men live is not simply a matter of pure quality, devoid of quantitative considerations. It is quite true that freedom and tyranny are readily distinguishable qualitative states. It is not true, however, that freedom is an indivisible whole, a quality or way of life that one either has or does not have. Despite the penchant for posing the extreme alternatives of freedom or tyranny (and, consequently, of liberty or death), freedom is itself in large measure a matter of quantity, a matter of "more or less." To say this is not to suggest that the extreme case never arises or that the possibility of its arising is so remote that men need not trouble themselves with it. Still less is it to suggest that the limiting situation may be adequately met by a so-called incrementalist philosophy of decision-making. On the contrary, the extreme case does arise in history and does require men to choose—indeed, to make radical choices—between values they may otherwise find equally compelling. Even so, it constitutes—by definition—the exception and not the rule. To insist that freedom is an indivisible whole that one either has or does not have, to find in any sacrifice of freedom the entering wedge that must result in the loss of all freedom, to view each and every aspect of men's freedom as a symbol of the whole, can only result in turning every decision that raises the prospect of some sacrifice of freedom into the extreme case. Save in the extreme case, however, the issue confronting men is likely to be one of determining how much freedom they may be willing to sacrifice, and perhaps for how long a period, rather than to accept the sacrifice of other values and, above all, those values sacrificed in war. What is relevant here is not the answer men may give or ought to give to this question, but rather that they cannot in practice consider the question at all without a heavy reliance upon quantitative considerations. The way in which men live is not only dependent upon quantitative considerations; it is only through quantitative considerations that the choices men must make which affect their way of life normally become at all meaningful to them.

Then, too, it hardly seems necessary to deny the importance men may attach to the way they live to affirm that life itself is a value. And if life itself is a value, the sheer destructiveness of war must provide a critical standard for the moral judgments men make of war. The objection that an emphasis on mere numbers in considering the justification for employing force must issue in the betrayal of strictly moral values conveys little meaning therefore unless it is assumed either that numbers can have no effect on the way men live or that life itself cannot be regarded a strictly moral value. If the former assumption is evidently false, the latter assumption seems almost as evidently perverse. It may appear foolish—or, at any rate, excessively literal—to argue that it is one million times more evil to take one million lives in war than to take one life.[22] But it does not seem foolish to insist that the taking of one million lives is a much greater evil, and this quite apart from the purposes for which force may be employed. Instead, to argue otherwise seems not only foolish but perverse. We should judge Hitler an evil man if he had been responsible for the deaths of six rather than six million Jews. It does not occasion surprise, though, that men's judgment of Hitler is commonly influenced by the fact that he was responsible for the deaths of six million Jews. Nor does it appear either foolish or perverse that in this instance numbers—quantities—influence, and considerably so, the moral judgments men make. Here again it is the disregard of quantity that appears both foolish and perverse.

Of course, although life itself may not be considered a value, "mere numbers" may still prove an important consideration in the moral evaluation of force, if only for the reason that numbers must ultimately affect the way men live. It follows, however, that the sheer destructiveness of war cannot be regarded as an independent consideration in the moral evaluation of force; it is simply a function of the moral values the defense of which does justify force. There are very few who would accept this position. But if it is once rejected, then it is clear that "mere numbers" do become very significant, and this quite apart from the reasons why life itself is considered a value. In this respect John Courtney Murray, elaborating the thought of Pius XII, writes of the principle of proportionality: ". . . comparison must be between realities of the moral order and not sheerly between two sets of material damage and loss. The standard is not a 'eudaemonism and utilitarianism of materialist origin,' which would avoid war merely because it is uncomfortable, or connive at injustice simply because its repression would be costly. The question of proportion must be evaluated in more tough-minded fashion, from the viewpoint of the hierarchy of strictly moral values. . . . There are greater evils than the physical death and destruction wrought in war. And there are human goods of so high an order that immense sacrifices may have to be borne in their defense."[23] It is difficult to disagree with the admonition that moral evaluation must be made on the basis of a comparison between moral gains and losses or that the question of a

22. Thus Bertrand Russell writes: "If it is wicked to kill one man, it is two hundred million times as wicked to kill two hundred million people." *Has Man a Future* (London: Allen & Unwin, 1961), p. 103.
23. John Courtney Murray, *Morality and Modern War* (New York: Church Peace Union, 1959), p. 12.

proportion—as a strictly moral question—must be evaluated from the viewpoint of strictly moral values. Obviously, moral issues must finally be resolved in terms of moral categories. But from this tautology nothing of significance can be deduced. Nor does Father Murray really suggest that "mere numbers"—sheer destruction—are not of vital significance in determining the question of proportion. He simply insists that these are not the only factors to be considered.

Must we interpret the Sixth Commandment to exclude quantitative considerations? Several years ago, in deploring the assurance of scientists that "not many deaths" would result from nuclear testing, George Kennan wrote: "I recall no quantitative stipulation in the Sixth Commandment. Whoever gave us the right, as Christians, to take even one innocent life? I fail to see how any of this can be reconciled with Christian conscience."[24] It is a small step from Kennan's view to the view expressed by Kenneth W. Thompson that "there is some sophism in the claim that taking many lives is morally more offensive than killing one man. War in terms of any ultimate moral judgment is evil; by any absolute standard it is as wrong to bomb a city with cannons as it is with atomic bombs."[25] Neither of these statements necessarily follows the commandment "Thou shalt not kill." They do so only if it is assumed that no significant moral distinction can be drawn on the basis of this commandment between the taking of one life, the taking of ten lives, or, for that matter, the taking of ten million lives. But this latter assumption is hardly self-evident. Whereas Kennan's Christian conscience would in the final analysis make the waging of war—and, indeed, the conduct of statecraft itself—impossible, Thompson's reluctance to distinguish between the taking of many lives and the taking of one life would lead to moral judgments on war that appear both foolish and perverse. To be sure, both of these writers might—and presumably would —say that although in terms of an ultimate moral judgment the taking of one life must be deemed as evil as the taking of many lives, in terms of the relative moral judgments men must make in history there is still a significant moral distinction to be drawn. But if this is true, then we must conclude that quantitative considerations do afford a basis for making significant moral distinctions, that differences in quantity do permit us to conclude that some actions are "more evil" than others.

The purely quantitative effects of war also provide us with perhaps the clearest insight we possess into the manner in which men employ

24. George F. Kennan, "Foreign Policy and Christian Conscience," *Atlantic Monthly* (May, 1959), p. 48.
25. Kenneth W. Thompson, *Christianity and Crisis* (November 13, 1961), p. 202.

force. The view is frequently urged that even more than the sheer destructiveness of war in this century it is the pattern this destruction has taken, and threatens to take in a nuclear conflict, which ought to offend men's consciences. In this view, the moral enormity of modern war must above all be found in the means men have been willing to employ to obtain their ends, in the abandonment of the immunity once accorded to noncombatants, in the marked decline of humanity in war, and in the general lack of restraint that has characterized the conduct of war. But these features cannot easily be separated from the sheer destructiveness of war. Whatever the moral significance that is attached to the means men employ, in practice both the manner—or quality—of war and the intent of the belligerents must be determined very largely by examining the quantitative effects of belligerent actions.

Nor need a preoccupation with quantitative considerations neglect, let alone deny, the significance of the means men employ in war. There is no necessary incompatibility between an emphasis on the quantitative consequences of men's actions and an insistence that the means men employ to achieve their ends are of equal—and perhaps of even greater— significance for moral judgment. It is quite true that an emphasis on the consequences of action may result in subordinating the vital issue of means. It need not do so, however. Whether it does so or not, we cannot avoid relying upon the purely quantitative effects of men's actions in evaluating the moral quality of their behavior.

Thus if we wish to determine the extent to which men have abandoned the principle distinguishing between combatants and noncombatants, we must begin by examining the quantitative effects of those measures they have taken in war as well as the probable effects of measures they plan to take in future conflicts. Belligerents may of course deny an intent to make the noncombatant population of an adversary the deliberate object of attack. But the subjective meaning of a belligerent's actions cannot be determined simply from the avowed intent of the actors. If it could be so determined, and if the moral quality of men's behavior were to depend upon the avowed intent of the actors, there would be neither evil actors nor evil actions. Instead, however, intent is and must be determined in the first instance by inquiry into actual behavior and the consequences that might reasonably have been expected to result from the behavior in question. Such inquiry is above all dependent upon quantitative considerations. And even if the intent of men were as far as possible to avoid making the civilian population of an adversary the deliberate object of attack, this intent could not alter the objective consequences of their actions. Nor would it alter the moral judgment commonly made of those actions when their quantitative effects pass beyond a certain level of destruction. In this respect, at least, there is no material difference between the traditional Christian view on the just means of war and secular views that are equally insistent upon preserving the distinction between combatants and noncombatants. For both, whether the injury inflicted on the noncombatant population is considered merely incidental to the destruction of a military target, and therefore deemed justified, is in the last analysis not a matter of intent at all but one of quantity.[26]

The issues force may always raise for men must be distinguished, then, from the issues that are raised once force takes or threatens to take a particularly destructive character. It does not follow, however, that these issues are ever seen simply in quantitative terms of destruction. Nor does it follow that they can ever be resolved by quantitative considerations alone. At what point the actual or expected level of destruction may be judged to deprive force of any further justification, whatever the other circumstances marking its use, obviously cannot also be determined by quantitative considerations. One cannot deduce from a moral outlook that emphasizes the quantitative effects of employing force what effects ought to provide the basis for moral judgment.[27] Thus a so-called ethic of calculation when applied to war does not tell us what it is that we are to calculate. If it is asserted that moral choice requires that men calculate the probable consequences of their actions and then act on the basis of their calculations, the question remains: What are they to calculate? The call to calculate is but another version of the call to be prudent; but the ends of calculation are no more given, and no more apparent, than the ends of prudence. In either case they may vary, and have varied, greatly in content. That there is a level of destruction beyond which force must lose all justification does not tell us what this level is or, for that matter, to whom it should apply. In this sense the argument that "at its heart, ethics counts not in quantities"[28] is not only true when applied to war, it is self-evidently true. Yet it is only in this sense that the argument is self-evident. It is by no means self-

26. For a discussion of this point, and related issues, see pp. 302–19.

27. It is equally true, however, that one cannot deduce from a moral outlook stressing the quality of an action what qualities ought to form the basis for moral judgment. Moral controversy has frequently proceeded on the assumption that the content of each view is simply given. This is not true. Thus it may be argued that one ought never to make the noncombatant population of an adversary the deliberate object of attack. But this restraint does not follow of necessity from the view that stresses the qualitative character of action; it is a possible, not a necessary, application of that view.

28. Paul Ramsey, *War and the Christian Conscience*, p. 213.

evident in the sense that a resolution of the political and moral issues attending the use of force cannot be made vitally dependent upon the sheer destructiveness of war. Clearly, they can be and commonly are made so dependent.

Indeed, the importance of quantity for the moral judgments men commonly make on statecraft is apparent from nearly every page of history. It is an old story that America's westward expansion was not really imperialism because there were so few Indians. Imperialism, according to this ever-popular national interpretation, begins with the millions not with the thousands. Bismarck's assertion that he effected Germany's unification at the cost of only 80,000 German lives was not intended merely as a statement of fact but as a partial justification of his statecraft. There is nothing unusual in Bismarck's claim, save perhaps its candor. American historians have long made a similar appraisal of the Mexican War. "The war," a standard text on American diplomacy dryly observes, "added a vast domain to the United States, at a total cost of $118,250,000—in addition to the several thousands of lives on both sides. . . ."[29] Perhaps the principal justification given for using the atomic bomb against Hiroshima and Nagasaki has been that the shock administered by the bombs compelled the Japanese government to surrender, thereby saving many times the number of lives—American and Japanese —taken by the bomb. Critics of the decision to use the bomb have questioned whether its use was in fact necessary as a measure to compel an early Japanese surrender. But critics and supporters of the decision are in agreement that the justification for the decision turns on the issue of necessity.

What shocks the moralist in these examples is the evident acknowledgment of the principle that the happiness and well-being of some justify the suffering of others. That principle, he will insist, necessarily implies the rejection of the principle that each individual must be considered a moral finality in himself, never to be used as a means for the purposes of others, however numerous. In fact, acceptance of the principle that each individual must be considered a moral finality in himself would require not a modification of but an end to statecraft. War is only the most flagrant affirmation of the contrary principle, though the latter is indeed inherent in all political action. Unless all statecraft is to be condemned, then, moral judgment—and moral distinctions—cannot literally rest on the impossible demand that the happiness and well-being

29. Samuel F. Bemis, *A Diplomatic History of the United States* (3d ed.; New York: Henry Holt, 1950), p. 244.

of some may never be secured by the imposition of suffering on others.[30] What is implicit in this demand is rather that limits must be placed on the means permitted to the political actor, however noble his professed ends, and that it is of vital importance to determine what these limits are.

3

In the light of these considerations, the moral novelty of thermonuclear war is apparent. If the prospect of thermonuclear war raises novel moral issues, it is not because the arguments that may be employed to justify the use of nuclear force differ essentially from the arguments that have been employed to justify force in the past but because these traditional arguments can no longer be employed with any degree of assurance. And they can no longer be employed with any degree of assurance primarily because of the sheer destructiveness a thermonuclear war is expected to entail. The view, therefore, that the justification of nuclear force does not and cannot differ in substance from the justification of conventional forms of violence, that the normative standards applied to judge the one must be equally applicable in judging the other, and that nuclear force simply represents a new quantitative dimension in the application of these perennial standards is as true as it is irrelevant to the claim that nuclear conflict does raise novel moral issues. For the novelty of these issues and the difficulty of justifying the use of nuclear weapons do not derive from the criteria that afford a basis for moral judgment. They derive instead from the disparity between the criteria affording a basis for moral judgment and the consequences expected to attend the employment of nuclear weapons. Nor would this disparity even arise were it not for the fact that these criteria are at some point vitally dependent upon, and made meaningful by, quantitative considerations. The essential novelty of the issues posed by thermonuclear war is as simple then as it is profound. In introducing a new quantitative dimension into the conduct of war, nuclear weapons take the issues that force has always raised and threaten to carry them to an extreme.

Thus Paul Tillich does not invoke any novel moral principle in concluding that "a war fought with atomic weapons cannot be justified

30. In truth, this impossible demand is seldom made without saving qualification, as in the Kantian injunction that the individual ought never to be used *solely* as a means.

ethically."[31] Tillich's insistence that war must serve the principle of "creative justice"—"a justice whose final aim is the preservation or restitution of a community of social groups, subnational, national or supranational"—does not differ materially from one of the requirements traditionally imposed on war by scholastic moral doctrine. The latter is equally insistent that war is never justified once it ceases, in Tillich's words, to hold out "the possibility of a creative new beginning," when "it annihilates what it is supposed to defend." Whether the disparity between the principle of creative justice and the consequences of nuclear war must prove to be of the order Tillich simply assumes is of course a question the answer to which cannot be regarded as somehow self-evident. Nor is the meaning to be given the principle of creative justice itself free from ambiguity when applied to the contingencies that invariably mark historical conflicts. What is clear, however, is the dependence of this principle—if it is to have any significance at all as a guide to conduct—upon quantitative considerations. It is equally clear that if the moral issues posed by thermonuclear war are novel, their novelty consists in the expectation that the quantitative consequences of such a war will no longer permit its reconciliation with the principle of creative justice.

Whereas Tillich's principle of creative justice places limits—however vague—upon the injury that may be inflicted on the adversary, and not only upon the injury suffered in turn by the self, the same dependence on quantity must hold for those who appeal to the statesman's traditional calculus of success and condemn thermonuclear war in terms of an apparently more restrictive calculation of its costs. "I would say without qualification," Hans Morgenthau declares, "that a thermonuclear war, however begun, cannot be justified on moral grounds. The moral evil inherent in any act of violence is mitigated by the end the act serves. . . . Nuclear war destroys the saving impact that good ends exert upon evil means. For nuclear war is not only irrational, in that it destroys the very end for which it is waged, but, by dint of that irra-

---

31. "The Nuclear Dilemma—A Discussion," *Christianity and Crisis* (November 13, 1961), p. 204. Nevertheless, Tillich declares that a deterrent strategy is justified "because it shows the potential enemy that radical destruction would take place on his side as much as on the other side if he attacks first with atomic weapons." In effect, then, Tillich's solution to the nuclear dilemma is no first use of atomic weapons. Characteristically, the apparent contradiction between condemning a war—any war—fought with nuclear weapons and supporting nuclear armament is largely overcome by a faith in the effectiveness of deterrence. "Practically," Tillich writes, "the very existence of atomic weapons on both sides is probably a sufficient deterrent."

tionality, it is also immoral in that the destruction of the end for which it is waged renders its moral justification impossible."[32]

If the ends sought through force may encompass in this view many and disparate values, the justification of force must presuppose at the very least that whatever the ends sought there is a substantial prospect these ends will not themselves be destroyed by force. To be sure, there is one end that cannot be affected by the means men employ in war, one end the pursuit of which is unaffected by the statesman's calculus of success, and therefore one end that remains independent of quantitative considerations. Whatever the consequences of employing force, men might still elect to destroy themselves—and, if need be, the world— rather than to forego their independence and to capitulate to the adversary. Not for the end of preserving their freedom, but for the end of preserving their freedom to choose not to surrender their freedom (though this choice once made may result in the loss of both life and freedom), men may justify the use of force whatever the consequences attending its employment. Among the few who are willing to contemplate this end without reservations, Karl Jaspers writes: "Man is born to be free, and the free life that he tries to save by all possible means is more than mere life. Hence life in the sense of existence—individual life as well as all life—can be staked and sacrificed for the sake of the life that is worth living."[33]

32. *Christianity and Crisis* (December 11, 1961), p. 223. It is the assumption of the "utterly suicidal character" of thermonuclear war that prompts these conclusions. A decade earlier, in discussing whether this nation should develop thermonuclear weapons, Professor Morgenthau wrote: "The question of moral justification cannot fail to be answered in the affirmative." "The H-Bomb and After," *Bulletin of the Atomic Scientists* (March, 1950), p. 76. The moral dilemma implicit in nuclear weapons was then found to be "no different from that of all instruments of destruction."

33. Karl Jaspers, *The Future of Mankind* (Chicago: University of Chicago Press, 1959), p. 169. Jaspers does not of course deny the relevance of quantitative considerations. He does deny that in the extreme case quantitative considerations necessarily represent a limiting condition for moral judgment. Sidney Hook comes very close to the same argument, though his position is tempered in practice by a faith in the effectiveness of deterrence—when directed against an opponent for whom survival is presumably the highest good. See, for example, Hook's remarks in the round-table discussion on "Western Values and Total War," *Commentary* (October, 1961), pp. 277ff. "Survival . . . is the *summum bonum* for Communism, whereas the West, buttressed in part by belief in immortality, whether as a myth or fact, has always maintained that there are certain values which are more important than life itself. To the Communist world there is nothing worse than defeat. . . . That is why the Communists will never start a war which they have reason to fear they will not survive." (p. 282.) The effectiveness of deterrence, then, is to be found in the superior courage and determination of the West, and this superiority is in turn traced to the superiority that a religious or transcendental belief in immortality has over a purely secular version. Whereas for the latter the meaning and purpose of

Apart from this end, however, there is no end that remains unaffected by the means employed on its behalf and, accordingly, by the quantitative consequences those means entail. The view that the immorality of thermonuclear war stems from its irrationality, that thermonuclear war must destroy the ends for which it is waged, evidently rests upon the assumption that the costs of such a conflict will necessarily outweigh the gains. At best, a thermonuclear war will do irreparable damage to those values in defense of which force is presumably undertaken. At worst, it will result in the common suicide of the contestants. This assumption about the character and results of a thermonuclear war, any thermonuclear war, may or may not be true; once again, it is not self-evident. Whether true or not, it is apparent that the negative moral

---

life—and consequently of death—must be found entirely in life itself, for the former physical survival must remain subordinate to values more important than life—even the life of mankind. Others have concluded, however, that if the effectiveness of deterrence is to rest upon this foundation it will prove to be a very shaky one indeed and for the reason that the distinctly religious sense of immortality no longer carries real conviction. For the West as well it is contended that physical survival has become the *summum bonum* and a secular version of immortality has effectively replaced a transcendental one. Thus a theologian writes that the advent of nuclear weapons can only bring a deep despair because "Modern man has regarded as self-evident the fact that the life of the individual will always be outlasted by the life of the group. He has made this assumption the unexamined presupposition of both his theory of value and his philosophy of history. . . . Death as an individual extinction, as the radical end of the earthly expression of a creative personality, may be mitigated by recognizing the relation of the individual to the group." Edward Leroy Long, Jr., *The Christian Response to the Atomic Crisis* (Philadelphia: Westminster Press, 1950), p. 95. A similar view is expressed by Hans J. Morgenthau, who writes: "If our age had not replaced the belief in the immortality of the individual person with the immortality of humanity and its civilization, we could take the prospect of nuclear death in our stride. . . . Yet a nuclear age, which has lost faith in individual immortality in another world and is aware of the impending doom of the world through which it tries to perpetuate itself here and now, is left without a remedy. Once it has become aware of its condition it must despair." "Death In The Nuclear Age," *Commentary* (September, 1961), p. 234.

Nevertheless, the moral issues raised by the prospect of thermonuclear war cannot be decided one way or the other by these considerations. They may tell us something about men's willingness—or reluctance—to undertake thermonuclear war. They cannot tell us anything about whether men ought to be willing to undertake such a war, whatever the consequences. Nor in fact do those who take the view that in the extreme case quantitative considerations do not represent a limiting condition for moral judgment contend otherwise. When Sidney Hook asserts that men ought to be willing to risk whatever consequences nuclear war may entail in order to preserve their freedom, he does not intend the moral argument to rest simply on the proposition that if men are so willing they will never have to face these consequences. This proposition obviously adds a very considerable support to the moral argument, but the root of that argument—if it is not to be taken merely as another manifestation of a faith in deterrence—must remain independent of any estimate of the efficacy of a deterrent strategy.

judgment made is largely dependent upon an estimate of the quantitative consequences of employing nuclear force.

Then, too, it is the expectation of the sheer destructiveness of a thermonuclear war that must pose in its most severe form the question of the means men are prepared to sanction in the conduct of war. For a moral outlook that takes at all seriously the question of means, the justification of force cannot be found simply in the ends for which force is employed. This is true however beneficent the alleged ends of action and however substantial the prospect of their achievement, if only the actor is not hindered with respect to means. Nor is it sufficient to declare that the means employed in war should be adequate to the ends sought and that no more force should be employed than is necessary for achieving these ends. Other than to forbid wanton and purposeless—and inefficient—violence, these prescriptions do not place any clear and meaningful limits on men's actions; indeed, it is difficult to find anything in them that need ever prove incompatible with the statesmen's calculus of success and the adoption of whatever means are required to secure success. To so consider the issue of means as applied to the conduct of war is, if not to dissolve this issue altogether, then at least to make a caricature of it.[34]

If the statesman's calculus of success is not accepted as a sufficient justification for the means men employ in war, the reason must evidently be found in the virtually unlimited sanction thereby afforded for the conduct of war. But what is the character of the limits that would not in practice permit substantially the same result, though perhaps in a different guise? Surely they cannot be found in the demand that in employing force the statesman must positively intend only the good effects of his action and merely tolerate the concomitant evil effects— for example, that in employing thermonuclear weapons the actor intend only to destroy military targets and merely tolerate the incidental, though unavoidable, destruction of noncombatants. At any rate, the

34. For a recent—and rather pretentious—example of this, see Joseph Cropsey, "The Moral Basis of International Action," *America Armed*, ed. Robert A. Goldwin (Chicago: Rand McNally, 1962), pp. 71–91. Although Cropsey begins by asserting that the "essential notion" of morality is self-restraint, through an unusual exercise in rhetoric he manages to demonstrate that "the teaching of morality may be reduced to this: we must do everything that needs to be done to insure the survival of ourselves, our friends and our free principles . . ." (p. 83) and to conclude that the "dictate of morality coincides with the interests of men and nations whose purposes are compatible with freedom and high-mindedness" (p. 87). If this is true, how then can moral dilemmas over the means employed in statecraft even arise? Or are these apparent dilemmas merely the result of men's failure to appreciate their interests and, consequently, the means necessary for the effective realization of their interests?

limits imposed on the conduct of war cannot be found primarily in the intention of the actor if they are to retain practical significance.[35] Nor is this all. Whatever the other differences between the conduct of war in the past and the possible conduct of a thermonuclear war, these differences may not—at least they need not—extend to men's intent. Their intent may well remain the same in both. It may even be the case that the intensity of the statesman's intent to avoid attacking the noncombatant population will be far greater in a thermonuclear war than in past conflicts. If a moral distinction is nonetheless drawn between the two with respect to the critical issues of means, it is because of the assumption that there is a point at which the objective consequences—the purely quantitative results—of men's actions, rather than the subjective intention of the actor, must prove determinative for moral judgment. If the issue of means when applied to the conduct of war is to be taken seriously, men have no choice but at some point to define these means primarily in quantitative terms and either to disregard intent altogether or to deduce the actor's intent from the consequences of his act. Thus a Catholic moralist, decrying attempts to reconcile the conduct of a thermonuclear war that would encompass the destruction of cities with the norm forbidding the direct and intentional killing of noncombatants, writes: "There comes a point where the immediate evil effect of a given action is so overwhelmingly large in its physical extent, in its mere bulk, by comparison with the immediate good effect, that it no longer makes sense to say that it is merely incidental, not directly intended, but reluctantly permitted. It is not a question of the physical inevitability of the evil effect. It is a question of its incidentality."[36] The expectation that thermonuclear war must push the critical issue of means to a breaking point may or may not be true. It is clear, however, that this expectation ultimately rests upon an estimate of the quantitative results of employing nuclear weapons. Once again, the significance of quantity for moral judgment is apparent.

---

35. "In deciding to use this bomb [i.e., the atomic bomb on Hiroshima] I wanted to make sure that it would be used as a weapon of war in the manner prescribed by the laws of war. That meant that I wanted it dropped on a military target. I had told Stimson that the bomb should be dropped as nearly as possible upon a war production center of prime military importance." Harry Truman, *Year of Decisions* (Garden City, N.Y.: Doubleday, 1955), p. 420. Mr. Truman's declared intent in so using the bomb was "to avoid, in so far as possible, the killing of civilians."

36. John C. Ford, S.J., "The Hydrogen Bombing of Cities," *Morality and Modern Warfare*, ed. William J. Nagle (Baltimore: Helicon Press, 1960), p. 101.

3

THE RATIONALE OF FORCE

1

If the prospect of thermonuclear war raises novel moral issues, it does not follow that men's response to these issues will prove equally novel. The justifications that have been invoked in threatening force, including nuclear force, bear an essential similarity, when stripped of their purely verbal innovations, to the principal justification men have invoked in the past in threatening or employing force. It is the state's security, independence, and survival—and, of course, those values the state serves to protect—that continue to provide the principal justification of force.[1] This continuity with the past is often obscured by the one response that does deserve the mark of novelty. But the novelty of that response must be found precisely in the degree to which the possibility of thermonuclear war is denied, if not explicitly then at least by implication.

Although the idea of deterrence is as old as the history of human conflict, the functions that strategies of nuclear deterrence are expected to serve and the consequent expectations these strategies have elicited are as novel as the weapons on which nuclear deterrence rests. If deterrence in the nuclear age is in truth something new under the sun, it is because of the scope and intensity of the expectations deterrent strategies have generally called forth. Given these expectations, what would otherwise appear to be a series of almost inexplicably inconsistent convictions instead takes on the appearance of a simple and compelling consistency. A willingness to endorse a deterrent strategy but a profound reluctance even to consider—let alone to make serious preparation for— the possible consequences of a thermonuclear war; a readiness to employ

1. The argument is not essentially altered if we substitute "alliance" for "state." However, the substitution would be unwarranted since it is clear that the transformation of values thereby implied has not—or not yet—occurred.

248

the threat of thermonuclear violence to preserve interests deemed vital but an insistence that thermonuclear war must destroy the ends for which it is presumably waged; a belief in the moral rectitude of a deterrent strategy but a pervading skepticism that the use of thermonuclear weapons could ever be justified; these and still other convictions are resolved into a consistent pattern if only the expectations placed in a deterrent strategy are sufficiently strong. With sufficient faith in the efficacy of deterrence there is no need then for men to torture themselves over the possible justification for ever employing nuclear weapons; the issues arising from the use of nuclear weapons deal with a contingency that for all practical purposes has been excluded from their view of the future.[2]

It is this faith in the effectiveness of deterrence that must, in substantial measure, explain the ease with which the policy of deterring aggression by the threat of massive retaliation was accepted in an earlier period of the cold war. If one obvious moral objection to the policy of massive retaliation was the marked disparity between the evil to be prevented and the retaliatory measures threatened, this objection could be overcome by the assurance that the Draconian measures threatened would never have to be carried out. If it was charged that massive retaliation implied a strategy that harbored aggressive aspirations beneath its apparently defensive overtones, that it was in effect tantamount to a strategy of preventive war in everything but form, the answer was that it would never have to be acted upon. It is quite true that the acceptance of massive retaliation was facilitated by the belief that the adversary could not carry out an effective nuclear strike against this nation. It is also true that however disproportionate the measures threatened by massive retaliation, these measures were still to be taken only in response to an aggressive act; that they thus appeared to be purely defensive in character provided a balm for sensitive consciences. Even so, without faith in the effectiveness of deterrence it would be impossible to account for the relative moral euphoria attending the policy of massive retaliation.

It is this same faith in the effectiveness of deterrence that frequently serves to reconcile the "mutual suicide" view of thermonuclear war with a willingness to support deterrent strategies. The conviction that a

2. The persuasiveness of this faith has been recently acknowledged by one of its most persistent and acute critics. "Some years ago, I said, with a certain degree of contempt, that 'some . . . seem to view the deterrence of a rational enemy as almost a simple philosophical consequence of the existence of thermonuclear bombs.' I recognize today that these people may have been much closer to the truth than I then thought reasonable." Herman Kahn, *On Escalation* (New York: Frederick A. Praeger, 1965), p. 246.

thermonuclear war—any thermonuclear war—between the great powers must result in their mutual suicide may of course lead to pacifism. It is far more likely, however, to prompt the belief that thermonuclear war will never occur, particularly if men remain determined to risk thermonuclear war in defense of their vital interests.[3] This vision of thermonuclear war provides not only the basis for the belief that such a catastrophe will never occur; the tenacity with which it is held also provides an accurate reflection of the profound emotional need to believe that it will never occur. It is a commonplace that men experience extreme difficulty in conceiving of their own death. It is all the more difficult for them to conceive of the death of the collective to which they belong and the continued existence of which gives meaning to their lives—and, in war, to their deaths. The propensity to believe that thermonuclear war must of necessity result in the common annihilation of the participants therefore affords, paradoxically, a source of comfort and assurance, since it is implicitly assumed that if the results of an act are

3. At the very least, the mutual suicide view of thermonuclear war must prompt the belief that such a war will never occur through the deliberative action of men. Thus Walter Lippmann writes: "Only a moral idiot with a suicidal mania would press the button for a nuclear war. Yet we have learned that, while a nuclear war would be lunacy, it is an ever-present possibility. Why? Because, however lunatic it might be to commit suicide, a nation can be provoked and exasperated to the point of lunacy where its nervous system cannot endure inaction, where only violence can relieve its feelings." "The Nuclear Age," *Atlantic Monthly* (May, 1962), p. 46. But Lippmann evidently does not believe that it is lunacy to threaten nuclear war. Writing of the crisis brought on by the Soviet placement of strategic weapons in Cuba, he declares: "Washington did not forget that while nuclear war would be suicidal lunacy, it is an ever present possibility. Nuclear war will not be prevented by fear of nuclear war. For, however lunatic it might be to commit suicide, a great power, if it is cornered, if all the exits are barred, if it is forced to choose between suicide and unconditional surrender, is quite likely to go to war." "Cuba and the Nuclear Risk," *Atlantic Monthly* (February, 1963), p. 57. Presumably, then, the lesson of Cuba, and the paramount rule of policy in this age, is that "as between the nuclear powers, there can be no important change in the status quo brought about by the threat of force or by the use of force. Nuclear war cannot be used, as wars have been used in the past, as an instrument of national policy." (*Ibid.*, p. 56.) There is surely a difference, however, between a willingness to threaten thermonuclear war to avoid "unconditional surrender" and a willingness to do so in order to prevent "important changes in the status quo." Moreover, even if the view is accepted that any nuclear war is necessarily "suicidal lunacy," it clearly does not follow that no important change in the status quo can be brought about by the threat of force. On the contrary, it seems just as plausible to contend that important changes in the status quo may be effected by the threat of force precisely because "nuclear war means mutual suicide." The issue of lunacy apart, Lippmann's position evidently implies two contradictory assertions about deterrence. On the one hand, deterrence is held effective because there are no interests over which states are willing to use nuclear force. On the other hand, deterrence is held effective precisely because there are interests over which states are willing—if necessary—to use nuclear force.

inconceivable the act itself must be equally inconceivable.[4] And if the act itself is inconceivable, what need is there for men—at any rate, for practical men—to trouble their consciences over threatening to resort to thermonuclear war? In an imperfect world it is enough if men are able to prevent the inconceivable from ever occurring simply by threatening to take the inconceivable act and, of course, by remaining outwardly quite determined to act upon that threat. The requirements of a deterrent strategy that prompts this faith may still trouble some moralists, but there is little reason to believe that collectives experience moral unease in accepting these requirements.

Nor is it apparent that men should experience unease in threatening the inconceivable. If the threat—however horrendous—that provides the basis for a deterrent strategy will never have to be carried out, the only clear objection the moralist is entitled to raise is that one is never justified in threatening measures which, if taken, could have no justification. He cannot condemn a deterrent strategy by pointing to the debilitating effects of the threat to annihilate an adversary, for he cannot know whether the threat will have such effects. Indeed, to the extent that we are in a position today to examine these effects, they do not appear debilitating. And even if the effects of threatening to do the inconceivable were eventually to prove morally corrosive for those who make or endorse the threat, there remains the task of weighing the evil resulting from the threat against the evil that might be expected to result if the threat were not to be made at all. At the very least, the moralist is on uncertain ground here, though of course he is not alone in his uncertainty. Given sufficient faith in the effectiveness of deterrence, then, we are left with the argument that an act which would be unjust to commit ought never to be threatened, however remote the contingency that the act will ever be committed and whatever the consequences that may follow if the threat is not made. When reduced to this rather pure form, however, the argument seems singularly unpersuasive. One may even question whether the moralist is himself consistently prepared to accept it.[5]

It is only if this faith in the effectiveness of deterrence is seriously

---

4. A striking expression of this assumption may be seen in the following statement: "In a matter of moments you can wipe out from 50 to 100 million of our adversaries or they can, in the same amount of time, wipe out 50 or 100 million of our people, taking half of our land, half of our population in a matter of an hour. So general war is impossible and some alternatives are essential." Address of President Johnson to National Legislative Conference of the Building and Construction Trades Department of the A.F.L.-C.I.O., Washington, D.C. *The New York Times*, March 25, 1964, p. 4.

5. Cf. pp. 313–19.

questioned that issues men thought they had successfully exorcized reappear, and in acute form. It is only if thermonuclear war is once acknowledged as a not too finite possibility that the commonplaces of a deterrent psychology do indeed become a series of almost inexplicable inconsistencies. If a deterrent strategy may fail, it is absurd to refuse even to consider seriously the possible consequences of failure, let alone to make any preparations for them. If a deterrent strategy may fail, it is absurd to insist upon using the threat of thermonuclear war as an instrument of policy but to deny that any meaningful purpose could be served by such a war. If a deterrent strategy may fail, it is absurd—and devious as well—to argue that although deterrence is justified there can be no justification for ever using nuclear weapons.

But what is the alternative to these absurdities? Once thermonuclear war is consciously acknowledged as a historical possibility, we are compelled to ask those questions, political and moral, that force has always raised. If the questions themselves hardly seem relevant when applied to the prospect of thermonuclear war, it is not surprising that men's responses to those questions have also been found wanting. Nevertheless, the hope persists that man's scientific and technical achievements will somehow be matched by his political and moral achievements, that a technical break-through in the means of destruction will call forth a political and moral break-through in the means of conflict resolution. A great scientist reflects this persistent hope in complaining that "no ethical discourse of any nobility or weight has been addressed to the problem of the atomic weapons."[6] The complaint ignores the rather obvious possibility that only a very limited number of responses can be made to the problem of nuclear weapons, or for that matter to the problem of force in general. The difficulty may be not that in addressing themselves to the issues raised by nuclear weapons men's efforts lack "nobility or weight," or that in elaborating methods of conflict resolution their efforts lack ingenuity, but simply that there is no satisfactory solution to these issues—at least none that appears to avoid in practice what most men would still regard as an intolerable sacrifice of value. Nor is this failure to achieve a tolerable solution to the moral issues posed by nuclear weapons necessarily a mark of their complexity, any more than the successful resolution of scientific problems is necessarily a mark of their simplicity. However congenial the assumption that equates the apparently insoluble with the complex, it rests on a confusion of understanding and will. The failure to resolve satisfactorily

6. J. Robert Oppenheimer, "In the Keeping of Unreason," *Bulletin of the Atomic Scientists* (January, 1960), p. 22.

political and moral issues may indicate only that these issues, though perhaps quite simple to encompass by the understanding, are nonetheless impossible to resolve by the will.[7]

2

It is significant that perhaps the most pervasive justification of nuclear strategies appears—at least in principle—as no justification at all. The view that nuclear deterrence, and the possibility of nuclear conflict, are necessities imposed upon men does not ostensibly seek to justify but rather to explain. The moral dilemmas nuclear force may be thought to raise are not resolved; they are simply dissolved by denying the presuppositions without which they are no longer meaningful. If the struggle for security, independence, and survival itself is a necessity that men may decry but one from which they cannot escape, so must be the *ultima ratio* of this struggle. In threatening force to deter a potential aggressor, the statesman merely acts as he is compelled to act; in employing force to preserve the nation's independence and survival, the statesman only does what he cannot help but do. To insist, however, that these actions raise moral dilemmas and form the proper object of moral judgment is to misapprehend their nature and significance. They may of course be seen as tragic in much the same way that death is seen as tragic. Still, we do not ask whether death as such poses moral dilemmas for men, much less whether death is moral or immoral, just or unjust. It is as meaningless to pass moral judgment on death as it is to pass

7. It is in this sense that Einstein's much quoted remark—"politics is harder than physics"—may readily be accepted as true, though it is doubtful Einstein intended it to convey this meaning. More significant, perhaps, is his equally well-known remark: "We shall require a substantially new manner of thinking, if mankind is to survive." It is this latter remark that in numerous paraphrases has become one of the banalities of the age. The demand for a "new manner of thinking," for a "leap in our thinking," for a more serious and sustained effort to break through the "thought barrier," is made by natural and social scientists alike. One of the latter has recently written: "There exists . . . a gap between what we think about our social, political, and philosophical problems and the objective conditions which the nuclear age has created. It is the peculiar quality of this gap that it exists in spite of our rational awareness of the unprecedented novelty of nuclear power and in spite of our anxiety to account for the novelty in our thoughts and action. Thus it is not that we do not know what nuclear power portends and that we are not willing to do something about it. Rather we do not know what we ought to do, and what we are doing does not meet the issues at stake. For we are capable of thinking about nuclear power only in terms that are obsolete." Hans J. Morgenthau, Introduction to Harold L. Nieburg, *Nuclear Secrecy and Foreign Policy* (Washington: Public Affairs Press, 1964), p. xiii. It is misleading to say that we do not know what we ought to do because we are capable of thinking about nuclear power only in terms that are obsolete. Our reason encompasses the "new fact."

moral judgment on an earthquake or a flood or on any natural catastrophe. Very nearly the same may be said for the attempt to pass moral judgment on the catastrophe that despite men's intentions might some day attend the failure of a deterrent strategy.

Although the propensity to endorse this view is considerably increased by the prospects entertained of thermonuclear war, experience suggests that its attractiveness has always been roughly proportionate to the size of the entities involved in conflict. Beyond a certain size the disposition readily arises to assimilate the behavior of men to the great forces of nature. A view that is ordinarily denied when applied to mere individuals and to small groups is nevertheless commonly accepted as the counsel of wisdom when applied to the great conflicts of history. Nor is it difficult to see why this view, despite an apparent intent only to explain, must also serve to justify. We do not normally attach moral opprobrium to those who have only acted as they were compelled to act, and it would seem pointless as well as perverse to do so. We may not praise men and nations for having failed to do the impossible or at any rate for what we regard as having been the impossible, but we do not as a rule condemn them either. "What we cannot alter or can alter less than we had supposed," Isaiah Berlin writes, "can hardly be used for or against us as free moral agents . . . our tendency to indignation is curbed, we desist from passing moral judgment."[8] Nor is this all, given the ubiquity and the intensity of men's need for justification. When explanation takes the form of necessity what is evidently a *non sequitur* from the point of view of logic becomes a truism from the point of view of psychology, and to explain is in effect to justify. It may be true that by placing men's behavior beyond meaningful choice—and presumably beyond the moral or immoral, the just or unjust—the appeal to necessity can provide only a negative justification of behavior; in terms of satisfying the obsession for justification, it is no more than half a loaf. Even so, half a loaf is better than none; a negative justification is still preferable to no justification at all.

There are many versions of this ancient, yet very contemporary, theme of necessity in statecraft. In some, the actions men take, whether in resorting to force or in the manner of employing force, are the outcome of vast and impersonal forces—fate, the dynamics of power, the logic of history, and—the most recent addition—technology. In others, war is above all the consequence of an enduring human nature. Since the essential quality of man's will never changes, the mainsprings of human

8. Isaiah Berlin, *Historical Inevitability* (London: Oxford University Press, 1953), pp. 35–36.

behavior are always and everywhere the same. Accordingly, the roots of war are found in man's selfishness and particularly the radical selfishness he manifests in his collective behavior, in his vanity, in his desire for power and for dominion over others, in his perpetually dissatisfied soul, in the fear he entertains of others and of the possible harm others may do him, or in his very ignorance of and congenital incapacity to discern both the actual intentions of others and the unwanted consequences of his own actions. Which trait, or combination of traits, is emphasized has varied. The more pessimistic versions stress man's vanity, his selfishness, and his desire to dominate, though they need not deny—and generally have not denied—the importance of fear and the desire for security. They merely deny that fear and the urge for self-preservation afford an adequate explanation of the roots or ultimate origins of man's collective conflicts. In the more optimistic—or, at any rate, the more benign—versions, war is essentially the consequence of fear and the instinct for survival. The obvious corollary of the latter is that aggrandizement is prompted above all by the urge for self-preservation, that men are driven to aggression through a sense of insecurity. In either version, however, armed conflict appears as a necessity imposed upon men and nations.[9] In both, the world is seen as "irrational" because men are driven—whether by their nature or by a defect in their nature—to frustrate and to defeat the very ends they seek to attain. They want to rid themselves of fear; yet by their behavior they create situations that accentuate their fears. They desire security; yet their actions give rise to an ever greater insecurity. They strive after order; yet their shortsightedness drives them to promote disorder. They yearn to create a world in their own image; yet their inordinate ambition impels them to go beyond the limits of their power. The history of statecraft, therefore, is not only—and not even primarily—a record of the unintended con-

---

9. In the latter version, however, conflict does not so much result from the ends men pursue, security and survival, as it does from the manner in which they pursue these ends. In the former version, conflict results quite as much from the ends pursued since these ends, prestige and dominion, are by their very nature exclusive. As Hobbes put it: ". . . glory is like honor, if all men have it, no man hath it, for they consist in comparison and precellence." Sir William Molesworth (ed.), *The English Works of Thomas Hobbes* (Aalen, Germany: Scientia, 1962), Vol. II, *De Cive*, chap. i, sec. ii, p. 5. In fact, both views are one-sided and must prove difficult to maintain consistently. The reason for this is that while security and survival on the one hand and prestige (glory) and dominion on the other hand are seemingly quite disparate motives, experience shows that they are closely related. This is particularly so in the case of nations where security is seldom, if ever, limited to physical security and survival seldom equated with the preservation of the nation's "physical self." Particularly in the case of great nations, the self is conceived to go far beyond these attributes and to encompass prestige and dominion. Cf. pp. 270–84.

sequences of men's actions but of the positively unwanted consequences of these actions.[10]

In still other versions, conflict is seen to arise as much from the historical situation—the political, social, and technological environment—in which men find themselves and in which they must act as from any universal and unchanging human nature. By far the most common version of necessity in statecraft, the appeal both to human nature and to historical situation is persuasive if only because of its all-encompassing character. If the variety of behavior history records cannot be satisfactorily explained simply by reference to a universal and unchanging human nature, it may still be accounted for by the interaction of human nature and historical situation. Besides, the attempt to explain the necessity of international conflict—whether in general or in a particular instance—by ignoring the political and social environment in which conflict occurs would evidently prove as absurd as the attempt to explain the necessity of conflict without assuming any laws of human behavior—however crude and elementary and even trivial these laws may appear.[11]

10. It is this view of statecraft that is reflected in A. J. P. Taylor's remark: "The greatest masters of statecraft are those who do not know what they are doing." *The Origins of The Second World War* (New York: Atheneum Press, 1961), p. 72.

11. Thus the necessity of war may be found to follow from the so-called security-power dilemma. In turn, the causes of the security-power dilemma may be found to inhere primarily in a given social-political situation (the state system) or in man's nature. But it is hardly possible to contend that this dilemma must be attributed either to the one or to the other set of causes. Among contemporary writers, John Herz finds in the security-power dilemma a "fundamental social constellation, a mutual suspicion and a mutual dilemma: the dilemma of 'kill or perish,' of attacking first or running the risk of being destroyed. There is apparently no escape from this vicious dilemma. Whether man is 'by nature' peaceful or cooperative, or aggressive and domineering, is not the question. The question that concerns us here is not an anthropological or biological, but a social one." *International Politics in the Atomic Age* (New York: Columbia University Press, 1959), pp. 231–32. (Also Herz's *Political Realism and Political Idealism* [Chicago: University of Chicago Press, 1951], pp. 3ff.) It is clear, however, that the question is not and cannot be merely a "social one." The "fundamental social constellation" Herz describes evidently presupposes certain universal and unvarying traits of human nature—e.g., the fear or anxiety man entertains of others and of the harm others may do him as well as man's ignorance of and incapacity to discern both the actual intentions of others and the unwanted consequences of his own actions. The thesis that international conflict arises from the security-power dilemma in which men find themselves cannot avoid postulating a certain "human nature," though it may insist that fear and the urge for survival rather than selfishness and the lust for power are the dominant traits of this nature. True enough, this thesis also insists that the incidence of, and apparent necessity for, conflict cannot be understood apart from the social and political environment in which men find themselves; the characteristics of the historical situation therefore determine in large measure the causal significance of fear in producing conflict. But no one has ever seriously maintained the contrary and sought to establish the causes of international conflict—whether in general or in specific instances—directly and exclusively in man's nature.

In each and in all of those versions, however, one central theme dominates: the limitations that invariably condition and inexorably determine the conduct of statecraft. It is equally clear that whatever version is considered the emphasis and hard core of the argument is always centered on the issue of force. It is in the threat of force, the actual resort to force, or the manner of employing force once in war that the necessities of statecraft—and, above all, the necessity reflecting the instinct for security and self-preservation—are the most strikingly revealed and the most apparently compelling. Only when the issues confronting the statesman do not affect—or at least do not vitally affect—a state's security and independence does it become possible to speak in a meaningful way of freedom to choose among alternative courses of action. To be sure, even when a state's security and independence are vitally affected the appearance of choice may result from uncertainty over the path necessity dictates.[12] But choice in such instances is itself the result of one of those limitations that invariably determine the conduct of statecraft. What appears as choice therefore turns out, on closer analysis, to be little more than the limitation imposed by men's ignorance. The more the statesman knows the more he will appreciate the necessities that govern his actions and the less he will believe in the illusion of choice.

3

Despite its evident attractions, the appeal to necessity in statecraft has almost invariably been selectively applied, the nature of the selec-

---

Even those who have been most insistent upon man's radical selfishness and will to power have nevertheless acknowledged—as they have had to acknowledge—that in certain circumstances these traits will prove and have proven more productive of conflict than in other circumstances. What can this admission mean save that the historical situation in which men act is always a factor that must be taken into consideration? Even in theory, then, the difference is largely one of emphasis, and in practice this is all the more clearly the case—though differences in emphasis are of course significant. Finally, it should be stressed that the view of necessity in statecraft does not depend upon the nature of the forces that are assumed to determine men's behavior but upon the degree to which these forces are considered to foreclose the possibility of choosing, in any meaningful sense, among alternative courses of action. It makes little difference if we are told that international conflict arises primarily from a given environment rather than from man's inherent selfishness or aggressiveness, so long as the one remains as apparently resistant to change as does the other. At least, it makes little difference in the short run and that is all statesmen can ever take into realistic consideration.

12. "Only so long as the statesman is uncertain which is the true *raison d'état* is it possible for him to choose." Friedrich Meinecke, *Machiavellism: The Doctrine of Raison D'Etat and Its History*, trans. Douglas Scott (New Haven: Yale University Press, 1957), p. 2.

tion reflecting the experience of an age, the disposition of writers, the traditions of nations, or even the transient interests of governments. There have been periods in which men have seen in war a fixed and inescapable feature of history. At the same time, the necessity found to inhere in this institution has not always been attended by the belief that the conduct of war is equally governed by necessity. The acceptance of war as a necessity of international life has nevertheless been juxtaposed on occasion with a markedly voluntaristic attitude toward the manner in which men may employ force. The abolition of war itself might be deemed impossible, but the conduct of war could still be controlled and its effects moderated. Given this outlook, it followed that to the extent men concerned themselves with the justification of force, they did so not only in terms of the ends for which but particularly in terms of the manner in which war was conducted.

There have been other periods, notably our own, in which these beliefs have been very nearly reversed. A markedly voluntaristic attitude toward the occurrence of war has been attended by an almost equally marked determinism toward the conduct of war. War is seen not only as an evil but as an unnecessary evil. Yet the conduct of war—the instruments men will employ once in war and the manner in which these instruments will be employed—is governed by necessity. The necessity found to inhere in the conduct of war also affords perhaps the principal basis for the conviction that war may at last be abolished. The idea that war will disappear once its destructiveness promises to become sufficiently great, that war contains within itself the means for achieving its own disappearance, is of course very old; it has nearly always appeared along with the introduction of novel weapons and methods of warfare.[13] Prior

13. According to John U. Nef the view that advances in the technology of war represent progress toward the eventual disappearance of war appears in the seventeenth century and becomes rather common in the following century. "This new thesis rested mainly on two arguments which are to some extent complementary. The first was put by Gibbon in classic form. The invention of powerful weapons is possible only when the level of civilization is raised, and the more civilized individuals and nations become, the less they are disposed to let force be the final arbiter of their destiny. The second argument is that powerful weapons are capable of such frightful destruction that they will bring a war to a speedy end, or even cause the leaders of the nations to recoil from war altogether." *War and Human Progress*, p. 200. Whenever it arose, the persistence with which advances in the technology of war have been viewed as a blessing to humanity is a remarkable tribute to modern man's ingrained optimism. There have been a number of variations on this recurring theme. One of the more common has been the argument that novel weapons, though increasingly destructive, would make wars "short and sharp" and thereby prevent unnecessary bloodshed. From the introduction of artillery to the advent of the long-range bombing aircraft, this argument has had its attractions. Nuclear-missile weapons have, at long last, made short shrift of it. At the same time, of course, these weapons have given great persuasiveness to the closely related argu-

to this century, however, it never achieved widespread currency. The experience of the two world wars and, above all, the prospects held out by nuclear war have given it an altogether unprecedented persuasiveness. Significantly, the most widely quoted expression of this theme comes not from a visionary but from one of the age's greatest practitioners of statecraft.[14]

Thus the technology that has carried man to the edge of the abyss may yet provide—and in the opinion of many has already provided—the means of his deliverance from danger. "War has to become technologically impossible," one writer declares, "in order to be stopped."[15] The statement is not to be taken literally, since it is scarcely possible for war to become "technologically impossible." But war may become politically, psychologically, or morally impossible if it holds out the certainty of mutual destruction. Once that point has been reached, if man wishes to survive in this world he must, in the words of the editor of the *Bulletin of Atomic Scientists*, "adjust history to science and not put science in the service of history."[16] Science and technology will thereby compel men to do what their political and moral inventiveness alone have never been able to do. In the absence of universal disarmament and a radical change of the present state system, technology will remain a despot presiding over the destinies of men and nations, but it will be transformed into a benevolent despot. In guarded and in unguarded form, in extravagant as well as in cautious and tentative expression, this hopeful theme is struck. In recent years it has informed much of the speculation

---

ment that advances in the technology of war must ultimately do away with war altogether by making war too costly and destructive. The latter argument has been commonly supported by the conviction that along with technological advance must go parallel improvements in the art of war and that the increasing rationalization of war will eventuate in doing away with the need to fight. As war becomes increasingly predictable, men will be saved from acting out a conflict the outcome of which can be calculated in advance. In his essay on militarism in the eighteenth century, Hans Speier notes that many writers of the period looked forward to the day when military science would result in putting an end to war. *Social Order and the Risks of War*, pp. 240–41.

14. The reference is to Winston Churchill and to his remark: ". . . it may well be that we shall, by a process of sublime irony, have reached a stage in this story where safety will be the sturdy child of terror, and survival the twin brother of annihilation." At the beginning of the present century, the *Manchester Guardian* (Nov. 11, 1902), in strikingly similar manner, expressed the faith that: ". . . mechanical progress is one of the strongest of our allies in the cause of peace; this evil god of war may some day be devoured by his own children." Quoted in Arthur J. Marder, *The Anatomy of British Sea Power* (New York: Alfred A. Knopf, 1940), p. 17.

15. Oskar Morgenstern, *The Question of National Defense* (New York: Random House, 1959), p. 295.

16. Eugene Rabinowitch, *The Bulletin of Atomic Scientists*, XII (April, 1956), 98.

over the prospects of achieving lasting military stability through a balance of terror and has frequently reflected a curious combination of both voluntarism and determinism. If between adversaries stability does not automatically follow simply from the mutual possession of nuclear weapons, it may still be achieved through conscious choice and effort. Once achieved, the specter of nuclear war will be exorcised by those very instruments and arrangements man's ingenuity has devised. In what appears as a paradox of classic proportion, men choose to create a situation that once created will presumably deprive them of future choice.[17]

The conviction that military stability—and peace—will ultimately be imposed upon men by technology is only infrequently pushed to its logical and extreme limit. Even for the more unguarded of optimists, allowance may be made for the danger of a nuclear war arising inadvertently as a result of either technical or human failure. Stability is not simply a technological contrivance; it is a political and social arrangement as well. Technical contrivances may fail and political arrangements may break down. But this allowance of the possibility of an inadvertent war or a war of miscalculation need not qualify the deterministic view men may have of technology. On the contrary, it may afford still another manifestation of this view. The war that results from technical accident or human miscalculation, or—more likely—from a combination of the two, is not seen as a war that men choose in any meaningful sense. It, too, is somehow determined; it, too, represents a kind of "residual necessity" that must qualify in however small a degree the necessity represented by stability. In any case, an inadvertent war is not the product of policy, it is not the result of conscious choice. Nor do the qualifications introduced by the possibility of inadvertent war detract from the idea of technology as a despot; they simply detract from the idea that technology will necessarily prove a benevolent despot.

The conviction that technology will ultimately prove a benevolent despot is of course outwardly derided by those who insist that all attempts to achieve and to safeguard a balance of nuclear terror must end in a common catastrophe. Yet this apparently radical disagreement may reflect, and often does reflect, a deeper identity of view. If men can only be persuaded that a continuance of their present ways must inevitably issue in catastrophe, they may not unreasonably be expected to change these ways. If men can only be persuaded that technology is a nemesis, they may yet deliver themselves from their present peril.

17. Not literally, of course, though for all practical purposes. Even in a world that possessed Doomsday Machines men would still not literally be deprived of the possibility of choice. They might still elect to destroy themselves—and the world— in order to prove they retained their freedom.

If men can only be persuaded that the danger of inadvertent war does not represent a mere "residual necessity" but a significant possibility they may yet be reformed. Despair over the current prospects of avoiding thermonuclear war may therefore mask a deeper optimism—an optimism that is also rooted in the belief that technology will ultimately prove a benevolent despot.

There may still remain differences of opinion, however, over what is required to persuade men that they must alter their ways, and these differences may be taken to reflect varying degrees of "optimism." Some years ago the novelist and scientist C. P. Snow wrote: "Within, at the most, ten years, some of those bombs are going off. . . . *That* is the certainty. On the one side, therefore, we have a finite risk [in arms control]. On the other side [the arms race] we have a certainty of disaster. Between a risk and a certainty, a sane man does not hesitate."[18] Many strategists took strong exception to Snow's forecast. Herman Kahn, for example, labeled it as inaccurate and irresponsible. Nevertheless, Kahn himself subsequently made very nearly the same argument, except that he removed it to a later stage. Kahn pictured a relatively "benign" thermonuclear war between the U.S. and the Soviet Union and declared: ". . . one could confidently predict that the morning after the war there would be utter conviction among all nations, and particularly the two antagonists, that alert forces were intolerable and that the world simply could not go back to the old balance of terror and once again assume the same risks then shown unmistakably to be real."[19]

Whether technology is seen as a benevolent or a malevolent despot, the conviction that it is a despot that increasingly presides over the destinies of men and nations has become a commonplace. Given the experience of the age, this is hardly surprising. Nor is the appeal to the necessity imposed by technology easily dismissed. Technology may give rise, and in certain circumstances will invariably give rise, to acute fear and insecurity; it may create a situation sufficiently novel to make prudent behavior extremely difficult; it may leave men with less time to make any kind of reasoned decisions and with almost no time to remedy the effects of unreasoned decisions; and it may commit them in a way that is for all practical purposes irrevocable. It may prove comforting to believe that man can always and at every stage choose the purposes for which and control the manner in which he will use the technology he

18. C. P. Snow, "The Moral Un-neutrality of Science," *Science* (January 27, 1961).

19. Herman Kahn, *Thinking About the Unthinkable* (New York: Horizon Press, 1962), p. 25.

has created.[20] Unfortunately, this belief finds little support in our experience. Instead, much of contemporary history is a record not only of the unanticipated but of the clearly unwanted effects of technological innovation. In a period of armed conflict, these unanticipated and unwanted effects are particularly compelling, if only because the pace of events is quickened and men must act under extreme pressures. War has always provided the greatest exception to the rule that what men intend, plan, and prepare for is what they shall get.

No doubt, a partial corrective to the technological surprise in war may be found in an awareness of its probability—or certainty—and in the endeavor to provide accordingly. But the success that can reasonably be expected to attend such efforts will still be limited in the first instance by the sheer novelty of the situation with which men must contend. In retrospect, it does not seem unreasonable for the belligerents in 1914 to have anticipated the consequences of employing the technology of the period. Nor, for that matter, does it seem unreasonable for the belligerents in 1939 to have anticipated with greater accuracy the consequences of employing airpower. In fact, in both conflicts the disparity between the anticipated consequences of technological innovation—however modest—and the actual effects when once employed were very considerable.[21] Given this record, is it reasonable to expect that men will be able to anticipate the range of consequences and control the conduct of nuclear war, despite the considerable efforts that have been and are presently being directed to this end? The problems of controlling modern weapons, difficult as they are when confined solely to the purposes of deterrence, still appear very modest when compared with the task of effectively controlling the conduct of almost any kind of nuclear war. The elegance and sophistication with which pure deterrence theory has been elaborated continues to form a striking contrast to speculation

20. And, of course, the science on which his technology is based. It is interesting that as a group scientists are among the most insistent upon man's complete freedom to choose the ways in which he will use the science, and the technology, he has created. "Science by itself is neither good nor evil," one of them declares, "and the effect of science upon humanity depends wholly on the way in which we make use of the power given to us." Bart J. Bok, "Freedom of Science and the Universal Declaration of Human Rights," *The Bulletin of Atomic Scientists*, V (August, 1949), 213. This view begs the question whether man, given his limitations, can control the use of the science and technology he has created. If he cannot, the advancement of science may not be quite the moral imperative that scientists are generally so ready to assume. It is quite another matter to argue that scientific advance is in any event inevitable.

21. The unfounded expectations of airstaffs on the outbreak of World War II have been the subject of numerous studies. One of the most impressive is the work of Charles Webster and Noble Frankland, *The Strategic Air Offensive Against Germany, 1939–1945* (London: Her Majesty's Stationery Office, 1961), I, 125ff.

over the conduct of nuclear war and the consequences of employing nuclear weapons.

It does not follow that attempts to plan for the possible ways in which a nuclear war might be fought and to anticipate the consequences of waging a nuclear conflict must prove futile. Nor does it follow that men will prove unable to exert any real control over the manner in which nuclear weapons are employed. What does seem clear is that the attempt to plan for and to control nuclear conflict must be made—if it is to be made at all—prior to the outbreak of hostilities, despite the severe limitations this procedure evidently imposes. "The technological panoply of set-piece warfare is the panoply of deterrence," one observer writes of tactical nuclear war.[22] This judgment appears no less true when applied to a strategic nuclear war. In its initial though perhaps decisive stages, the course of the conflict is almost certain to follow one of several predetermined patterns. At the critical moment of decision men may still be able to choose among several fixed strategies for conducting war. But it seems very unlikely they will also have the opportunity to alter these fixed strategies and to improvise as the situation may require. They may be able to choose target pattern B rather than target pattern A. But they will not easily be able to improvise a novel target pattern. They may be able to choose not to employ a weapons system at all. But they will not readily be able to adapt a weapons system to a new and unexpected situation. Whatever the prospects for a "controlled nuclear response"—and it would be rash to rate such prospects highly—a controlled nuclear response is still a set response. A nuclear war to which substantive and meaningful limits are set is still set piece warfare; if it is to prove at all possible, it must be planned for and its consequences anticipated, difficult though this must be. To this extent, it is misleading to compare the limited warfare of the past with the inflexibility that can be expected to characterize limited—or controlled—nuclear war. Nor is the "necessity" that appears to inhere in the conduct of nuclear war simply a function of time—or rather the lack of time—and the rate at which destruction will occur, though these are the decisive elements. It also results from the rigidity of weapons systems that are restricted in their possible uses and dependent for their effective control on a vast, complex, and unwieldy organization.[23]

Although technology provides today the most persuasive and dramatic version of necessity in statecraft, it does not exclude other and older

---

22. Sir Solly Zuckerman, "Judgment and Control in Modern Warfare," *Foreign Affairs* (January, 1962), pp. 190–200.

23. Zuckerman terms the latter characteristic "an ultimate limitation on the practical uses of good judgment" (*op. cit.*, p. 198).

versions. If anything, it must give the latter a new persuasiveness. Why, after all, does the new technology appear so constricting and so oppressive? Why does it appear to frustrate and to defeat the ends men seek to attain? Men want to rid themselves of fear; yet the technology they create to achieve this purpose only serves to accentuate their fears. They desire security; yet their technology gives rise to an ever-increasing sense of insecurity. They strive after order; yet their technology threatens to bring the greatest disorder. They yearn to create a world in their own image; yet their newly found power often seems to leave them strangely powerless to do so. If men were gods their technology would not so limit them. If there is a necessity imposed by technology, this is so only because there is a necessity imposed by man's nature and by the historical situation in which man finds himself and yet must somehow act. In the end, we seem to be driven back to versions of necessity that are as old as speculation on statecraft itself. The limitations technology imposes on statecraft must ultimately be found, then, in those limitations that form a commonplace of traditional political thought.

Nor can one dispose of these "ultimate" limitations by insisting that they are little more than the mere prescriptions of common sense and everyday experience, that they can seldom be articulated save in a vague and imprecise manner, that there are nearly always exceptions to them, and that their usefulness in discerning the more specific requirements of statecraft is often slight. All this is true but does not detract from their significance. What is more evidently a matter of mere common sense than the generalization that the most intractable problems of statecraft often stem simply from the rate at which change occurs? It seems trivial to insist that men's capacity to absorb and to adjust to change—at least to do so without excessive violence and social deterioration—is limited. Yet it is this limitation that alone must account for much of the failure and frustration marking attempts to come to terms with the new technology. Again, what more evidently reflects everyday experience than the generalization that the difficulty of controlling men's behavior and insuring its direction toward the fulfillment of some common purpose increases with the size and complexity of an organization? Yet it is this difficulty that in large measure explains the persistence of the danger of inadvertent war, of war that may be unintended and unwanted on both sides but results from the sheer size and complexity of the forces each side maintains for deterring attack. Finally, is it not apparent that however crude and elementary the limitations on statecraft set by man's nature—his fear of the harm others may do him, his inability to place himself in the position of an adversary, his incapacity to see the unwanted consequences of his own actions, etc.—these limitations nevertheless form the essential presuppositions of any strategic analysis that is not a conscious and deliberate abstraction from reality? Given these presuppositions it is not surprising that the principal result of endless discussions on the psychology of deterrence has been to confirm what we already knew.

The precise relevance of the limitations set by human nature and historical situation, the degree to which they hamper and condition statecraft on any given occasion, may remain an object of uncertainty and a source of controversy. That they do always narrow the alternatives open to man—sometimes severely so—will scarcely be controverted. Without this assumption, which is for all practical purposes identical with the notion of historical causation, history would never rise above the level of a random and chaotic enumeration of apparently meaningless events, while statecraft itself would be impossible.

Nevertheless, these limitations do not establish the argument of necessity in a literal sense. They may, and evidently do, reduce the area within which men may meaningfully choose. They may severely restrict the alternatives open to the statesman. They may push men's freedom to choose farther back in time to a point at which certain developments had not yet begun to unfold. But they do not literally do away with choice and the moral issues choice entails, and the view that they do has seldom if ever been consistently undertaken. The great figures who are commonly identified with this ancient theme—e.g., Thucydides and Machiavelli—did not apply it with consistency and apparently could not do so. Nor do contemporary writers who have pursued the same theme. Thus an eminent historian, Herbert Butterfield, has elaborated the argument of necessity in statecraft in an essay[24] that calls our attention to the progress of historiography as it "gradually disengages the structural features of a conflict which was inherent in the dialectic of events," to the "terrible human predicament that lies at the root of the story of mankind's great conflicts," and to a condition of "absolute predicament or irreducible dilemma [which] lies in the very geometry of human conflict." It is this "absolute predicament" that is held to cause the "race in armaments and even the war that seems to result from it" and that is apparently insoluble given men as they are and have always been. Elsewhere, however, Professor Butterfield denies that in the present situation of "Hobbesian fear" there is no alternative to a balance of nuclear terror with its attendant risks. Instead, he insists that we might still "unplug the whole system . . . if our governments refuse to have

24. "The Tragic Element in Modern International Conflict," *History and Human Relations* (New York: Macmillan, 1952), pp. 9–36.

anything to do with the weapon . . . . [We] cannot say that we will not receive the bomb—we can only say that we will not be responsible for the sin and crime of delivering it."[25] A deterministic view of "mankind's great conflicts" is thus countered by a radically voluntaristic view of the possibilities for resolving our present dilemma. It is true that Professor Butterfield finds in the willingness to use the hydrogen bomb "a symptom of a terrible degeneracy in human relations—degeneracy which the predicament itself has no doubt greatly helped to produce." Even so, he believes that "in the last resort some strong human affirmation . . . may be the only way of stopping the tension and deflecting the course of development to which we are now enslaved."

Then, too, those who have been most insistent in pursuing the theme of necessity in statecraft have regularly marked their effort with the admonition that it is important that men appreciate the inexorable character of the forces determining the behavior of collectives and governing mankind's great conflicts. It has never been clear, however, why this appreciation should make any material difference unless it can have the effect of altering the course events might otherwise take. To this extent, those who admonish us to adjust history to science and to cease our futile attempts to put science in the service of history betray the sense of their own admonition by the very act of making it. Of course, the appreciation of necessity, technological or otherwise, though without effect on the outcome of events, may still be urged on the grounds that it orients men to the realities of this world, that it saves them from illusion, and that it may even give them inner peace and serenity in the midst of tragedy. Instead of torturing themselves over the might-have-beens of history, it may teach them to accept that what has been, has been, and that any other attitude is, in E. H. Carr's words, "purely emotional and unhistorical."[26] It may also teach them to accept that what will be, will be, and that any other attitude is purely emotional. But this is all it can do. We have no persuasive, let alone compelling, reason for accepting this view. Nor do men consistently accept it.

4

It is clear that at the root of the view of necessity in statecraft is not only an explanation but a choice and that the necessity imposed upon the statesman is a "moral necessity."[27] Despite all the effort and inge-

25. *International Conflict in the Twentieth Century, A Christian View* (New York: Harper & Row, 1960), pp. 95–96.

26. *What Is History?* (New York: Alfred A. Knopf, 1962), p. 128.

27. Among contemporary writers, Arnold Wolfers has dealt at length with the themes developed in the following pages. See Wolfers' *Discord and Collaboration*. Also Raymond Aron, *Paix et Guerre*, pp. 563ff.

nuity that have been devoted to this view, in the end it is not necessity as such but a moral imperative that is held to bind the statesman and to direct his actions. If certain behavior—whether it consist in the act of intervention, the threat of nuclear annihilation, the resort to pre-emptive attack—is seen to follow in an iron chain of cause and effect, it is because this behavior is judged indispensable for achieving the ends of foreign policy. However complicated and obscure the guise it has taken, now as in the past the appeal to necessity may be invariably re-duced to this one central theme: the residue of the necessity that justi-fies the threat or use of force—any threat or use of force—is the state's independence and survival.

At the beginning of the modern state system Machiavelli, following Livy, declared: "That war is just which is necessary." Although for Machiavelli, as for Livy, the necessity justifying war extended to causes and motives men no longer consider either necessary or just, the core of this necessity has remained unchanged and is the state's independence and survival. Where the safety of the state is at stake, Machiavelli in-sisted, all other considerations must be set aside and that action taken which will preserve the state's independence and survival.[28] Four cen-turies later, in surveying the growth of reason of state in European diplomacy, Friedrich Meinecke could find little to add to Machiavelli on this vital theme.[29] It is true that Meinecke—as, before him, Machia-velli—frequently insists upon interpreting international conflict as a "natural necessity," beyond meaningful choice and presumably beyond the moral or immoral, the just or unjust. In the end, however, the neces-sity Meinecke found in the conduct of statecraft was a moral necessity—i.e., the moral imperative of the state's independence and survival. It is this "struggle for security and self-preservation at any price and by any means" that he holds to form the "natural basic task of reason of state"—or necessity—and that justifies whatever measures the statesman takes to preserve the state's independence and survival. Another contemporary historian, Gerhard Ritter, in a study that contrasts the Continental tradition of statecraft with the insular tradition, arrives at essentially the same conclusion.[30] Although Ritter, too, is not unsympathetic to the view that professes to find in international conflict a "struggle of op-posing Powers ordained by nature," he nevertheless concludes: ". . . we cannot dismiss self-defense . . . as simply 'natural'—i.e., as being outside

28. The point is most forcibly made in the *Discourses*, Vol. III, chap xli.
29. Friedrich Meinecke, *op. cit.*
30. Gerhard Ritter, *The Corrupting Influence of Power*, trans. F. W. Pick (1952), p. 183.

the world of morality and as just a sign of pure vitality. Neither can it be adjudged morally wrong. Self preservation is a moral duty."

But if the appeal to necessity does not and cannot do away with men's freedom to choose, since this appeal itself ultimately embodies a moral imperative, may it not still limit severely the practical significance of such choice? If the forces conditioning the conduct of foreign policy do not determine behavior in a literal sense, they may still narrowly restrict the kind of action that can be undertaken with any real prospect of success—as measured in terms of a state's independence and survival. Thus it is always possible that men may choose to reject the time-honored method of countering a hostile and expansionist power with power—whether this power consists of stones or of nuclear weapons—if they are only willing to pay the price this rejection entails. It is always possible for them to disavow extreme measures even in retaliation, though the threat to take such retaliatory measures may form the only effective counterbalance to the threat of an adversary. Men are "free" in the sense that it is always possible for them to defy the limits imposed on successful statecraft. But the latter, like the jealous gods whose laws the ancients were also free to defy, will invariably take their revenge upon the transgressor.

While it may be clear, then, that at the root of the argument of necessity is a choice, how meaningful is this choice when it involves the defense of the collective's independence? Even if it is true that in the end the necessity imposed upon the statesman is a moral imperative, what practical significance can this distinction have when the content of that imperative is the equivalent of survival itself? When the issue is that of self-preservation, is there not a point where freedom and necessity, as it were, converge and, in the words Mill used to describe the individual's claim to physical security, *"ought* and *should* grow into *must*, and recognized indispensability becomes a moral necessity, analogous to physical, and often not inferior to it in binding force."[31] At the very least, the scope afforded for choice in these circumstances—if not removed altogether—is considerably narrowed. This being so, the opportunity for exercising moral judgment is equally narrowed. Does it remain a meaningful opportunity at all?

This, in brief, is and has always been the kernel of the argument of necessity. Men have as regularly endorsed it in principle as they have drawn back from acknowledging its possible consequences in practice. Yet its acceptance in principle must afford a justification for any

31. John Stuart Mill, *Utilitarianism* (15th ed.; London: J. M. Dent & Sons, 1907), p. 81.

measures deemed essential to the preservation and continuity of the state.[32] Because, Hobbes wrote, in a state of nature "it is in vain for a man to have a right to the end, if the right to the necessary means be denied him, it follows that since every man hath a right to preserve himself, he must also be allowed a right to use all the means, and do all the actions, without which he cannot preserve himself."[33] What Hobbes considered the right of self-preservation men have in a state of nature, the argument of necessity considers the right of self-preservation states have in the state of nature from which they have never emerged. It is but a further consequence of the state of nature that the occasion for the exercise of this right is left to the judgment of the interested parties. To insist that the "state's right of self-defense or existence is not in question" but only the unfettered freedom states commonly claim to determine the circumstances in which the right may be exercised[34] is to ignore those conditions that necessarily attend the exercise of the right and give it a significance it evidently would not otherwise possess.[35]

The appeal to necessity is not incompatible with the acceptance of restraint on state action, so long as these restraints do not jeopardize independence and survival. In this sense, there is no question—at least there need be no question—of the abstract desirability of imposing restraints on state action. But whether restraints can be observed and the nature of the restraints that can be observed will depend upon circumstances and cannot simply be determined in the abstract. It is dogmatic, however, to insist that certain restraints must always be observed if for no other reason than that they can always be observed without vital sacrifice. Circumstances may of course permit a tolerable resolution of the conflict that is always latent between the imperative of independence

---

32. This need not imply, however, that the state itself represents an absolute value, or that the state is the source of all value. Indeed, the argument of necessity may, and frequently does, consider the state as only a conditional justification for action, the unconditional justification being those values the state—and, presumably, only the state—serves to preserve. The point is dealt with later (pp. 282–84).

33. The English Works of Thomas Hobbes, Vol. IV, *De Corpore Politico*, Art. I, chap. i, sec. vii, p. 83.

34. H. Lauterpacht, "The Grotian Tradition in International Law," *British Year Book of International Law*, XXIII (London: Oxford University Press, 1946), 34–35.

35. At the outset of the Cuban missile crisis in October, 1962, President Kennedy declared: "This nation is prepared to present its case against the Soviet threat to the peace, and our own proposals for a peaceful world, at any time and in any forum . . . without limiting our freedom of action." Address to the Nation, October 22, 1962, *Department of State Bulletin*, XLVII, 717. The desire to obtain international sanction for measures the American government had already decided upon in order to counter the Soviet action did not prevent the assertion of a freedom states have always claimed when allegedly acting in self-preservation.

and survival and the imperative enjoining restraint on state action. However critical the circumstances, a strategy of preventive or pre-emptive attack may still appear inexpedient. So may the threat to employ, or the actual employment of, weapons of mass destruction against the population centers of an adversary. There is no assurance, however, that the ends of independence and survival will always prove compatible with the observance of these and other restraints. When they are not, a choice—if we may still call it that—must be made.[36]

5

It is not difficult to catalogue the many abuses to which the appeal to necessity has in practice led. What measures has it not served on occasion to justify? Thucydides' account of the argument given by the Athenians in destroying Melos provides only the classic illustration of a theme on which many and subtle variations have since been played. This history of recurring abuse is no mere accident; it is not simply extrinsic to the essential nature of the argument. The relative facility with which necessity has been employed to justify the most disparate actions must surely form a commentary on the plea itself.

The appeal to necessity, even when acknowledged to embody a moral imperative, proceeds from the assumption that the vital element of neces-

---

36. It may be urged that the American rejection of preventive war affords at least one clear and important exception in recent years to the operation of necessity. This apparent exception would be more impressive, however, if it implied the rejection of preventive war in circumstances where such rejection was felt to jeopardize the state's independence and survival. But the American position on preventive war has never carried this implication. On the contrary, it has assumed that a strategy of preventive war must prove not only immoral but inexpedient when considered in terms of the state's independence and survival. In this view, then, a serious conflict between the moral imperative enjoining state survival and the moral imperative forbidding recourse to preventive war can scarcely arise. These considerations are particularly relevant in assessing the American rejection of preventive war at a time when this nation enjoyed a monopoly or vast preponderance in nuclear weapons and their means of delivery. In assessing the view that our inaction may be attributed largely to moral inhibition, it is necessary to recall the prevailing outlook that marked this earlier period. That continued American technological superiority was assured, that American economic preponderance and the attractive power of American ideals would insure victory in all contests that fell short of armed force, that the forces of freedom were bound to triumph and the forces of despotism bound to go under, that—in a celebrated phrase of the day—"time is on our side," were articles of faith reasonable men could not question. In the attempt to account for the fact that we did not resort to preventive war when we might have done so without fear of nuclear reprisal the importance of these convictions cannot be doubted. But they testify not so much to the moral quality of our intentions as they do to the character of our expectations. Given these convictions and the expectations they nourished, the endeavor to find our inaction in moral inhibition is easily strained.

sity reflects no more than the will to survive, valid alike for individual and collective. It is only a short step from this assumption to the conclusion that the actions necessity sanctions and for all practical purposes compels are not merely well-defined but indeed almost self-evident. Yet there is little in the history of international conflict that bears out either this assumption or the conclusion it has so regularly prompted.

If in the case of the individual there is a sense in which it is meaningful to speak of a limited instinct of survival or self-preservation, it is because the self that is to be preserved has been clearly delineated and the threat against which the self is expected to react has been narrowly circumscribed. Acts taken by the individual in self-preservation are commonly regarded as instinctive in that they form a momentary and largely unreflecting response to an immediate physical threat against life or person. But what is the "self" that is to be preserved in the case of the nation, and what are the acts in response to which this self must be expected instinctively to react? Despite the many occasions on which these questions have been posed, they have yet to receive a clear answer. We may know where the national self begins; we do not know—or, at any rate, can seldom agree—where it properly ends. What is commonly termed the nation's "physical person" evidently comprises a certain territory and population. The acts against which a nation may therefore be expected instinctively to react with force are those which directly threaten the integrity of its physical person and, in consequence, its independence. Yet it is only seldom asserted that selfhood must be equated simply with the nation's physical person and that acts justified by the appeal to survival must be limited to acts which insure mere physical survival. The nation's physical person may remain intact, and still it is asserted that the nation "itself" may not survive.[37]

The explanation of this apparent paradox may be traced to the con-

37. A striking illustration of this is afforded by the outlook of the Japanese elite in the closing stages of World War II. With the war clearly lost, the immediate object was national survival. But national survival was not equated simply with the physical survival of the collective. Even more important perhaps than the preservation of the nation's "physical person" was the preservation of Japan's distinctive polity, the imperial system. Both moderates and extremists agreed that without the imperial system Japan would no longer be Japan, since the dynasty was considered synonymous with the state. Indeed, so long as the imperial system was retained the nation would survive, even though territory might be lost and political independence temporarily sacrificed. The point is dealt with at length by Robert J. C. Butow, *Japan's Decision To Surrender* (Stanford: Stanford University Press, 1954). The Japanese case is all the more instructive in view of the fact that prior to the war national survival was equated with continued Japanese dominion over the mainland, and particularly over China. Without this dominion, it was argued, Japan would no longer be Japan. Neither in deciding to go to war nor in deciding to surrender was the national self equated with the nation's physical person.

viction—in the case of great nations it may prove an obsession—that the collective's existence has dimensions other than the merely physical dimension, that the nation is something much more than its merely physical attributes. A nation may preserve its body and yet perish through the loss of its soul—or the abandonment of its purpose. Whether or not a nation survives, then, is not a question that can be answered simply in terms of the integrity of the material attributes that make up the nation's physical person; this question must also be answered, it is common to insist, in terms of a self whose identity requires the preservation of certain values and of the political and social institutions that embody these values. The preservation of values and institutions identified with the life of the nation may in turn be seen to require an external environment the characteristics of which extend beyond the requirements of the traditional power balance. Thus the national self may encompass a mission or purpose the pursuit of which is made synonymous with the nation's will to survive and the eventual realization of which is equated with the nation's very prospects of survival. The conviction that the preservation of the institutions of freedom in America is dependent upon their preservation—or eventual realization—elsewhere in the world may or may not be misplaced, but there can be little doubt about the strength with which this conviction is held. The American people can continue to enjoy the blessings of liberty only if other peoples are also afforded the opportunity to enjoy these blessings. To abandon a policy whose objective is both to safeguard and to expand this opportunity is not merely to abandon the American purpose—conceived as an abstract good—but to jeopardize national survival itself, for freedom in America could never survive in an environment hostile to freedom. One writer vividly summarizes this conviction in declaring that if America fails to achieve its purpose "the nations of the world will look elsewhere for models of social organization and political institutions to emulate, and we will be alone in a hostile world. Alone in a hostile world, we would no longer be able to renew our sense of purpose through the experience of territorial expansion and universal emulation. At best, equality in freedom would still have a home in America. Yet, thus mutilated, could the national purpose survive in America itself? And if it should not survive, could America survive without its purpose?"[38]

38. Hans J. Morgenthau, *The Purpose of American Politics* (New York: Vintage Books, 1961), p. 300. This statement is all the more impressive for the reason that a decade earlier Professor Morgenthau declared: "American foreign policy ought not to have the objective of bringing the blessings of some social and political system to all the world or of protecting all the world from the evils of some other system. Its purpose—and its sole purpose—ought to be . . . the security of the nation. . . ."

This progressive extension of the national self forms, it would appear, part of the "natural history" of all great nations. In large measure, it explains the frequent contention that the necessities of a small power are not to be equated with the necessities of a great power. It is particularly with respect to the attribute of independence that this disparity between the necessities of small and great powers is apparent. Of course, to the extent that political independence is identified with, and made dependent on, the integrity of the state's "physical person," this quality has the same meaning for all states. But if control over territory is the indispensable prerequisite for independent status, it is by no means considered to constitute the whole of that status. Although the integrity of a state's territory may remain inviolate and the control of a government over that territory unimpaired, political independence may be jeopardized and even lost through the restriction of the state's external freedom of action by another state. Moreover, the criteria established by law for determining when political independence is thereby lost need not coincide with the criteria established by politics. Here, as elsewhere, the law seeks to generalize and to formalize what politics insists upon individualizing in terms of circumstance and interest. For the jurist, a state normally loses its independence—and, accordingly, its status as a state in the sense of international law—when it no longer retains formal control over the conduct of its foreign affairs—i.e., when these affairs are formally controlled by another state. As a legal status, independence is not as a rule affected by *de facto* relations of dependence, though these *de facto* relations may be quite far-reaching. For the statesman, however, it is not the legal status but the political status, not the *de jure* relations of superiority and subordination but the *de facto* relations of control, that must prove decisive.[39] At the same time, the

---

In Defense of the National Interest (New York: Alfred A. Knopf, 1951), p. 88. Given the character of the conviction sketched out above, the attempt to distinguish between the disinterested and the interested elements in the American purpose, between preserving and extending freedom as an abstract good and as a condition of American survival, is rendered superfluous—if it is not indeed misleading. What we do for others we also do for ourselves, and what we fail to do for others we fail to do for ourselves.

39. It is quite true that for the jurist as well *de facto* relations of control must ultimately prove decisive. In international law a state loses its independence when it no longer possesses effective control over its foreign affairs—i.e., when its foreign affairs are effectively controlled by another state. However, in the absence of a treaty that formalizes this relationship of superiority and subordination, the legal status of independence may be compatible with a very considerable degree of *de facto* dependence. Although the principle of effectiveness is ultimately decisive in law, its application is sufficiently uncertain—and liberal—to create considerable disparity between political and legal judgment. In the post-World War II period, instances of this disparity have been numerous.

political significance given these *de facto* relations in a particular instance, the extent to which they are considered compatible with continued independence, is commonly found to depend on the identity of the parties involved.

Thus the *de facto* control exercised by the Soviet Union over Finland's foreign affairs is not commonly considered to result in the loss of Finland's independence, even when "independence" is judged in terms of relevant political, and not only legal, criteria. Yet if a comparable degree of *de facto* control were instead to be exercised by the Soviet Union over America's foreign affairs, it is very likely that a quite different political judgment would be reached. One of the critical considerations prompting American behavior in the Cuban missile crisis was the conviction that if the Soviet action were left unchallenged the effects of that action would be to restrict substantially America's future freedom of action. The determination to employ any and all means, if necessary, to compel the Soviet government to remove the missiles placed in Cuba was therefore equated with the will to retain a freedom of action regarded as perhaps tantamount to independence itself. Finland's necessities are not to be equated with America's necessities. The same degree of *de facto* control that apparently permits the retention of political independence in the one instance may nevertheless be judged to result in the loss of political independence in the other instance. What is not essential to the national self in the case of a small power may prove quite essential to selfhood in the case of a great power.[40]

40. These uncertainties of politics also find their reflection in law. What is the "self" in defense of which force may, if necessary, be legitimately employed? The customary law of an earlier period was never clear on this question. According to the prevailing interpretation of this law, the right to employ forcible measures of self-defense extended not only to the protection of the state's territorial integrity against direct attack but also to the protection of those interests that collectively comprised the nation's security, and consequently its "existence" in the broader sense of political independence, and that might be endangered by measures other than armed force. Since uncertainty always prevailed with respect to the scope of the rights—the legally protected interests—comprising the state's security and independence, an equal uncertainty always prevailed with respect to the scope of the right of self-defense. Nor is it possible to conclude that the contemporary law satisfactorily resolves what the traditional law left unresolved. Of course, if it is asserted that force may now be employed only in response to force, then the uncertainty that always attended the traditional law is resolved. It is resolved, however, not by defining the "self" but simply by restricting the use of force to the sole circumstance of a prior use of force. On the other hand, if force may be legitimately employed to defend the self against acts that may or may not involve the use of force but that—in any event—imperil the self, then it remains of vital importance to define the self in order to distinguish between the unlawful use of force and its lawful exercise in self-defense. This has not been done. Certainly, the Charter of the United Nations does not do so. On the contrary, the critical provisions of the Charter—particularly

The ambiguity that is inherent in the national self once it is held to comprise these—and perhaps still other—protean qualities cannot but imply an equal ambiguity in defining the threats against which this self must be expected to react. If the meaning given to survival in the case of the nation is both varied and complex, the ways in which a threat to the collective's existence may be perceived are clearly no less varied and complex. These threats must normally prove far more varied and complex, if only for the reason that they need not possess the quality of immediacy in order to justify actions allegedly taken in self-preservation. Although the argument of necessity has always been extended to include the collective's security as well as its survival, security actions by definition must lack the quality of immediacy that characterizes survival actions, else there would be little—if indeed any—reason to distinguish between security and survival. Even where security actions are limited to the protection of the same interests that ultimately impel survival actions, they are nevertheless taken in response to a threat the most important consequences of which extend into the future and, for this reason alone, the significance of which is never entirely apparent. In the case of security, whether for the individual or for the collective, it cannot be instinct alone that prompts—let alone compels—action. Between threat and response there is a gap that must be bridged by means other than instinct. Moreover, how this gap will be bridged—the nature of the response that will be made—can never be simply a function of the objective nature of the threat, for its objective nature—its lack of ambiguity—is largely dependent upon its quality of immediacy in terms of survival. It is this quality of immediacy that makes the problem of calculating an adversary's intent marginal in the case of actions taken in self-preservation. It is the same quality that must also reduce the significance of the task of calculating the consequences of either threat or response. But what is marginal in the case of survival is central in the case of security.

It is not instinct, then, but reason that leads men to project their prospects for survival and by so doing to endeavor to ensure their future.[41] At the same time, even where the object of security actions is

Article 2, paragraph 4—leave the uncertainties marking the self where they found them. Cf. pp. 295–99.

41. Of course, the nature of the projections men make—the security expectations they entertain—is not simply a function of their reason. If security policies point to the future, the standards they erect are largely anchored in the past. It is banal to say that security is a relative, not an absolute, condition, that states are more secure or less secure. But this banality should not be taken to mean that nations appreciate their security requirements in terms of some abstract standard devised by reason. It is history rather than reason that is the decisive influence in the judgments men

limited to physical security, the element of time must attach to security actions an uncertainty that survival actions do not ordinarily possess. Given the circumstances in which nations must endeavor to insure their future, this uncertainty can only be overcome through the identification —or near identification—of security with survival. The propensity to make this identification where security is not effectively collectivized is no more unreasonable than the excesses to which it has so commonly led are surprising. If the state compels men to distinguish sharply between their security and their survival, it also enables them to do so. Between an immediate threat to the self and less than immediate threats stand the protective institutions of the state. Given these protective institutions, the projection of a survival threat beyond the narrow confines marked out by the state and the act of responding forcibly to this threat are not only unlawful but unnecessary. In the absence of the protective institutions afforded by the state, the argument of necessity asserts, quite different conclusions must follow. Where security is not effectively collectivized, the distinction between security and survival remains, at best, tenuous. What appears as an unnecessary, and unreasonable, projection of survival in one environment may appear quite necessary, and reasonable, in another. While it is apparent that there is much to be said for this position, it is equally apparent that once it is accepted the plea of security can be plausibly invoked to justify the most varied of actions.[42]

---

make on their security, or lack of security. In part, these judgments relate to, and are determined by, the security men possessed at a certain point in time; the benchmark for judgments on security nearly always assumes, however unconsciously, a particular historical juncture. In part, these judgments also relate to the larger experience of the nation—i.e., to the experience enjoyed over a prolonged period. This historic experience tends to become the general norm against which security judgments are made. In the case of America, the general norm evidently reflects the experience of the period from the early nineteenth century to the 1930s. The particular historical juncture that continues to serve as a benchmark for most security judgments is the period of the late 1940s.

42. Here again, the dilemmas of politics continue to find their reflection in the uncertainties of law. It has already been noted that the customary or traditional law was never clear on the limits of the "self" in defense of which force could, if necessary, be legitimately employed and that the contemporary law can scarcely be said to resolve the uncertainties that have always marked the self. To these uncertainties marking the self must be added the further uncertainty over the acts in response to which a state could legitimately employ force in self-defense. Need these acts be unlawful to justify forcible measures in self-defense? To the extent that doubt persisted with respect to the answer, as it always did persist, the traditional right of self-defense was never clearly distinguished from the so-called right of self-preservation. In turn, the right of self-preservation was never clearly distinguished from the classic plea of necessity, *salus populi suprema lex*, a plea that has always been distinguished by its metalegal character. The essential characteristic of the so-called right of self-

Nevertheless, the potentiality for abuse inherent in the argument of necessity does not arise primarily from men's propensity to equate their security with their survival where there is no central authority capable of insuring either security or survival. Instead, it is the expansiveness with which men view the collective self which above all prompts expansive notions of security. Nuclear weapons do not appear to have substantially altered this most significant and pervasive characteristic of nations. On the contrary, the new technology of war affords a striking illustration of the persistence of this trait despite radical change in the material conditions of security. This continuity with the past has often been obscured by a preoccupation with the all-too-apparent security-depriving effects of nuclear-missile weapons. When considered from the vantage point of the traditional basis of state security—that is, the state's quality of territoriality—the new weapons assuredly mean, in the words of one observer, "that the decisive change is from 'distinctness' and 'separateness' to 'pervasion,' to the absolute permeability of each unit by each of the others, so that the power of everyone is present everywhere simultaneously. There is, or will be, unlimited might, the capability to inflict absolute destruction, which will go hand in hand with absolute impotence, that is, the impossibility of defense against the same infliction on the part of others; complete lack of 'security' within the most accomplished, the most powerful 'security' systems ever devised; disap-

---

preservation was the virtually unrestricted freedom it gave to a state to take such action as it deemed necessary for its own preservation. "In the last resort," declared the greatest of the English writers on international law of the nineteenth century, "almost the whole of the duties of states are subordinated to the right of self-preservation." (W. E. Hall, *International Law* [8th ed.; Oxford: Clarendon Press, 1924], p. 322.) A state could therefore take, on this view, any action it considered necessary to protect itself against either an actual or a threatened injury to those interests that conditioned its existence as a state. Thus, according to the interpretation commonly given the right of self-preservation, a state could resort to preventive measures of a forcible character, if necessity in self-preservation so required, in order to maintain or restore a balance of power. That the state against which the action was directed had actually violated or directly and immediately threatened to violate a right of the state acting in self-preservation was not required. Although the behavior of the state against which acts of self-preservation were directed might not be forbidden by international law, if this behavior nevertheless jeopardized another state's security, the latter could presumably take such measures as it considered necessary in the given circumstances.

However anomalous and even contradictory the so-called right of self-preservation might appear, when considered from the standpoint of the law's essential function it accurately reflected the difficulties consequent upon the attempt to restrict the use of force where security has not been effectively collectivized. The same difficulties are no less apparent in contemporary notions of self-defense, which, though refusing to limit the legitimate use of force in self-defense to a prior use of force, insist that forcible measures in self-defense are lawful only when taken in response to unlawful conduct. Cf. pp. 293–99.

pearance of the protective function of the state, or the bloc, despite all its might or power."[43] But if nuclear-missile weapons have dealt a decisive blow to the territorial "impermeability" of the modern state, if these weapons have torn away the "hard shell" of the state and rendered it vulnerable to absolute destruction, it does not thereby follow that the security effects of these weapons must prove to be consistently negative. If in one sense the new weapons have made the security problem immeasurably worse for all states, in another sense they have markedly improved the security prospects of the great nuclear powers. If in one sense the new weapons have given an unlimited and all-pervasive character to the security interest, in another sense they narrow and simplify the security problem for the great nuclear powers. At least, they have the effect of narrowing and simplifying—and improving—the security problem to the extent that survival is identified with physical survival, and, in consequence, security is identified with physical security.

The reasons for these apparently contradictory effects of the new weapons are clear enough. The great nuclear powers may be completely permeable with respect to each other in a sense that great powers were never vulnerable in the past. They are so, however, only on the condition that an adversary, possessed of the effective means of destruction, is prepared to risk its own physical annihilation. Short of this extreme situation, and a situation that those who insist on the state's absolute permeability today also insist upon portraying as insane, it is evidently not true to argue that the objective effects of nuclear-missile power must be to give rise to a complete lack of security. Although in the extreme situation the great nuclear power is indeed absolutely permeable vis-à-vis his great adversary, it is no less true that in other than extreme situations these same weapons render a great nuclear power physically secure to a degree that great powers seldom, if ever, enjoyed in the past. For the first time in history the prospect arises of a physical security that need no longer prove dependent on time-honored calculations of a balance of power. The calculations that characterize balance of power policies must appear increasingly irrelevant where no prospective increase by an adversary of the traditional ingredients of power can substantially improve his chances of surviving—let alone winning in any politically meaningful sense—a nuclear conflict. If the hard shell or impermeability of the past has vanished, it has nevertheless been replaced in the case of the great powers by a new kind of shell, a new kind of impermeability. This new shell is no less "real" than the old simply because the old was rooted in the material quality of territoriality whereas the new is rooted in the

43. John H. Herz, *International Politics in the Atomic Age*, pp. 168–69.

psychological quality of deterrence. What is distinctive, and admittedly paradoxical, about the new shell is that it can be broken completely or not at all. If security is identified with physical security, the great nuclear powers are in their mutual relations at once both absolutely insecure and absolutely secure.[44]

The fact remains that political realities do not conform to, and show no real prospect of conforming to, the results suggested by this analysis. If in one sense the objective consequence of the new weapons is to narrow and simplify the security problem for their possessors, it can scarcely be claimed that in their behavior the latter have manifested a clear awareness of that result. Despite the radical changes that have occurred in the material conditions of security, the great powers nevertheless continue to impute much the same security significance that great powers imputed in the past to interests the loss of which today need no longer prove critical if we relate such losses to the enhanced prospects of direct attack. Thus an acute sensitivity to defeat in peripheral territories has been one of the persistent features of Soviet-American rivalry—or, for that matter, of Chinese-American rivalry. In some respects, this sensitivity appears even more pronounced today than the sensitivity shown in the past by great powers when engaged in the struggle for control over peripheral territories. Why is it that South Vietnam is seen as a critical American security interest when it is clear that defeat in

44. This statement is admittedly an exaggeration designed to call attention to what has heretofore been frequently neglected. Even so, it is not much more of an exaggeration than the thesis that emphasizes the impermeability or impenetrability that in an earlier era presumably characterized the state. The effects of territoriality in a former period are also easily exaggerated in terms of the protection from foreign penetration this quality conferred. The hard shell of the state, even of the great state, could be broken and on occasion was broken. To be sure, the price for breaking this shell was often very high. But the price for breaking the nuclear shell would, in all probability, be much higher. It is quite true that nuclear-missile power cannot be defined as power has been conventionally defined in the past—i.e., as a force radiating from one center and diminishing with the distance from that center. It does not follow, however, that "Now that power can destroy power from center to center everything is different." (*Ibid.*, p. 108.) If, in the case of the new weapons, distance is no longer relevant, there is surely no reason to conclude from this that traditional calculations of cost and gain have also become irrelevant. Apart from the utopian situation of the state that literally cannot be attacked by others, the security of states has always depended in the last analysis on the cost-gain calculations of potential aggressors. However radical the break from the past effected by the new weapons, they have not essentially altered the nature of this calculus let alone abolished it. If the ingredients of this calculus have changed, this is no warrant for the conclusion that the calculus itself has somehow become unreal. The argument that if power is no longer measurable and calculable in terms of its traditional ingredients it is no longer measurable and calculable at all is as misplaced as the related argument that if security is no longer primarily a function of territoriality it is no longer security at all.

South Vietnam would not of itself—or even in relation to the whole of Southeast Asia—significantly alter the physical security of the U.S.? Why is it that despite the new weapons the security issue has not in practice been narrowed and simplified for the great nuclear powers but, if anything, has been directly insinuated into situations where it might have been expected to play no more than a modest role?

In part, the answer to these questions must evidently be found in the dynamics of intense hegemonial rivalry. If the new weapons have not had the effects that might have been reasonably anticipated from them, a partial explanation must be found in the nature of the conflicts that have dominated international politics since World War II. Perhaps the most characteristic feature of these conflicts has been the tendency, amounting on occasion to an obsession, to make almost any discrete issue into a symbol of the whole and to relate almost any conflict of interest to the underlying and ultimate conflict of interest. Then, too, the very uncertainty that results from the introduction of a radically new element into the security equation must be expected both to diffuse and to exacerbate the security dilemma. To the extent that nuclear weapons place in question the relation of power to policy, to the extent that new weapons magnify the difficulties of translating power into policy, the result is to expand and to intensify the issues invested with a security interest. In large part, however, the answer to the above questions is simply that nations—and particularly great nations—have never equated their survival with physical survival and show little inclination to do so today. In consequence, they do not equate their security with physical security. If nuclear weapons have not had in practice the effect of narrowing and simplifying the security problem of the great nuclear powers, the reason must be found largely in the expansiveness with which men continue to view the collective self and the "necessities" of this self. In their objective effects, the new weapons must illuminate with a clarity never before possible the difference between the narrow and the broad meaning of survival, between physical and more-than-physical survival. At the same time, they clearly have not changed men's propensity to conceive of their collective survival in terms that far transcend the merely physical dimension of the collective's existence.

It does not follow from these considerations that it is meaningless to speak of the self-preservation or survival of nations. However broadly men may define the national self, it would be absurd to conclude that this self has no reality simply because men are tempted to construe its existence, and what they conceive to be threats to its existence, expansively. But the meaning commonly imputed to the collective's existence bears no close parallel to that of the individual. Nor does the will to survive of the collective bear a close analogy to the will to survive of the individual. Whereas the one is a product of history and society, the other is largely rooted in nature. What may prove instinctive—or very nearly so—in the case of the individual is a complex historical and social construct in the case of the nation. In equating the will to survive of individual and collective the argument of necessity begins by refusing to acknowledge the disparities between the two. In the end, however, a distinction is made, though the significance given this distinction is almost the reverse of that drawn above. What else can be the meaning of the assertion—common to all versions of necessity—that although the individual can sacrifice his existence the state cannot do so? If the meaning of this assertion is a fact and not a norm, it is the collective that is unalterably tied to nature and ultimately always governed by instinct, not the individual. It is only the individual who is on occasion able to transcend the self and the self's instinct to survive, not the nation. Yet the argument of necessity has never been content to rest its case merely on what is put forth as no more than a proposition of fact, devoid of moral significance. Instead, it is argued that the collective can do no other than preserve its existence, at any price and with any means, because it has a duty to do no other. The statesman can do no other because he has a duty as trustee not to surrender an estate that has only been entrusted to his care and that is not his to dispose. A people can do no other because they have a duty to the generations that have gone before and will come after. Beyond this, it is asserted that the nation can do no other than preserve itself because it has a duty to an alliance of nations. Finally, the duty of the nation to preserve itself at whatever cost is vindicated by reference to those values the nation serves to protect and on whose protection the hopes and aspirations of humanity itself perhaps depend. An argument that invariably begins by asserting considerations of a biological order invariably ends by pleading considerations of a moral order, and of the highest moral order at that.[45]

45. Expressions of this theme abound. An eminent contemporary historian writes: "The individual may sacrifice his life: the community must live on. A trustee cannot surrender to threats or violence an estate which is not his own. In other words, the action of a government within certain limits is determined by considerations of what we may call a biological rather than a moral order." G. P. Gooch, *Studies In Diplomacy and Statecraft* (London: Longmans, Green & Co., 1942), p. 323. Elsewhere, the same writer declares that the state "cannot and must not" sacrifice itself, that it has a "duty" to resist when it is threatened. "We could not disavow the possible use of the [atomic] weapon," Reinhold Niebuhr remarked some years ago, "partly because no imperilled nation is morally able to dispense with weapons which might insure its survival. All nations, unlike some individuals, lack the capacity to prefer a noble death to a morally ambiguous survival. But we also could not renounce the

It is quite true that the argument of necessity may not make and, indeed, commonly has not made of the political order the source of all value.[46] If any and all measures may be taken to preserve the state's independence and survival, it does not necessarily follow that the state is itself the ultimate justification for action. A distinction must be drawn between the view that finds in the state the source of all value and the view that finds in the state the condition of value. Although the argument of necessity is compatible with and has always comprised both views, in theory at least there is a considerable difference between them. If the political order is considered as the source of all value, the problem of justifying measures—any measures—taken to preserve or to strengthen the state does not and cannot arise. If the political order is considered as the source of all value, the conduct of statecraft may raise dilemmas of prudence—that is, dilemmas arising from uncertainty over the consequences of alternative courses of action—but it cannot raise true moral dilemmas. For the latter may arise only where there are first-order conflicts of value, and such conflicts of value are excluded where there is no value that does not emanate from and, accordingly, is not subordinate to the state. If the political order is instead considered as the condition of value, the problem of justifying measures taken to preserve or to strengthen the state may arise. The "health and strength" of the state, even its independence and survival, cannot be self-justifying if the state is itself justified only insofar as it protects, and promotes, individual and cultural values. If the state has only a conditional justification, its "necessities" may be denied when it in turn threatens to destroy those values that must ultimately sanction not only its actions but its very existence.[47]

weapon because the freedom or survival of our allies depended upon the threat of its use." *The Irony of American History* (New York: Scribner, 1952), p. 39. A study group in American foreign policy finds that "a nation does not and cannot have the religious self-transcendence, whereas individuals may have a self-transcendent quality by which they face death with the certainty that their souls live on in immortality." W. Y. Elliott (chairman), *United States Foreign Policy, Its Organization and Control* (New York: Columbia University Press, 1952), p. 14. Although the individual can be a witness, a theologian writes, and by his sacrifice testify to the truth, the same cannot be said of the nation. "The lofty ideal of individual martyrdom cannot be transposed into a justification for the voluntary self-immolation of a nation." Robert Gordis, *Politics and Ethics* (Santa Barbara: Center for the Study of Democratic Institutions, 1961), p. 19.

46. Even when the state is openly avowed to be "the highest community existing in exterior human life" and for this reason exempt from "the duty of self-effacement," the proviso is added that "lest it should contradict its own nature the goals it strives after must be moral ones." Heinrich von Treitschke, *Politics*, trans. Blanche Dugdale and Tarben de Bille (New York: Macmillan, 1916), I, 94.

47. Although the distinction drawn above is only seldom made explicit, it is nevertheless implicit in most discussions of necessity in statecraft. It is implicit, for

But if the difference between these two views appears in principle considerable, the practical significance of the distinction will evidently depend upon the assessment men make of the functions the state serves —or is thought to serve—in a given period. The state's independence and survival may be a conditional end, in turn justified as a means to still higher and even unconditional ends. Perhaps no theme has been articulated more often by American statesmen than the theme that the purposes and objectives of American foreign policy may be properly understood only as means to the end of protecting and promoting individual freedom and well-being. No end of foreign policy, even the end of preserving the state's independence and survival, can be morally autonomous, self-justifying, an end in itself. Instead, all the ends of foreign policy must be viewed as means to the ends of society, which are in turn ultimately the ends of individuals. It is clear, however, that the practical significance of this view will still depend upon the impor-

---

example, in the writings of Machiavelli. Moreover, it would seem that the most reasonable interpretation of Machiavelli points to the conclusion that Machiavelli viewed the state as a condition of value and not as a source of all value. Nevertheless, Carl Friedrich, in his interesting study *Constitutional Reason of State* (Providence: Brown University Press, 1957), asserts that the problem of reason of state—that is, the problem of justifying such conduct as may be required to preserve the state's independence and survival—"does not even arise for Machiavelli. For only when there is a clash between the commands of an individual ethic of high normativity and the needs and requirements of organizations whose security and survival is at stake can the issue of reason of state become real." (p. 4.) Elsewhere Friedrich writes: "The state is for Machiavelli the supreme and all-inclusive good and therefore no genuine good can be found outside the state. As a result, Machiavelli sees no need for 'justifying' the means which are required for building and maintaining a state. The state's security and survival are 'hors de discussion.' Consequently, we might say that it is self-justifying as any absolute value is (for that is presumably what absolute means). . . . For Machiavelli . . . the problem of reason of state does not exist in its more pointed and typical form, because the necessity of acting in accordance with the state's requirements needs no justification." (p. 23.) But if the problem of reason of state does not exist for Machiavelli, why does he exhort the ruler in *The Prince* and the citizen in *The Discourses* not to be deterred by ordinary considerations of moral conduct when the state's independence and survival are at stake? If the state is the source of all value, why is Machiavelli at pains to show that acts that are "apparently evil" are "in reality good" when judged in terms of those values which though they do not emanate from the state cannot be enjoyed apart from the security and order provided for by the state and, in Machiavelli's view, only by the state? If the state has for Machiavelli a life of its own, this is still not to say that the state and its necessities are "self-justifying." It is of course another matter to argue that although the problem of reason of state does arise for Machiavelli, the issue of justification is resolved in favor of the state and its "necessities." In this respect, however, Machiavelli surely does not differ from the overwhelming majority of those who have followed, while perhaps condemning, him. If the problem of reason of state exists only for those who have rejected the necessities of the state, or who have remained truly undecided between the imperative of the state's survival and the imperatives of an "individual ethic of high normativity," then we can only conclude that this problem has been, for all practical purposes, nonexistent.

tance attached to the state as a means to the protection and promotion of individual values. If the independence and survival of the state are nevertheless regarded as the indispensable means to the protection and promotion of individual values, how meaningful is it to insist that the state has no more than an instrumental value? If the state is not simply a condition but an indispensable condition of value, what is the practical significance of distinguishing between the state as a source of value and the state as a condition of value? For all practical purposes, a condition of value which is nonetheless indispensable as a condition might just as well be regarded as a source of value.

In practice, it would seem, the principal result of the view that the state is an indispensable condition of value is to permit its holders to enjoy the best of both worlds. In giving to the state and its "necessities" only a conditional justification, they may preserve a good conscience, secure in the conviction that what the state does to preserve its independence and survival is ultimately justified in terms of values that transcend the state. At the same time, in insisting that the state represents an indispensable condition of value, they may reconcile themselves to almost any action necessary to preserve the state's independence and survival, even to actions that threaten to destroy the very values that must presumably provide the state's ultimate justification. The probable consequences of a thermonuclear conflict merely afford a final and compelling proof of the essential circularity that has always characterized the argument of necessity.[48]

6

Despite all criticism and qualification, the central issue raised by the argument of necessity remains and cannot be spirited away: Are there any limits to the actions that ought to be threatened or taken, if necessary, in order to preserve the state's independence and survival? The criticism sketched in preceding pages does not answer this question affirmatively by imposing limits on the action permitted the state, limits

48. In part, of course, this circularity must be attributed to the fact that men do not simply regard the state as a condition of value. However insistent a democratic ethic may be on the purely instrumental value of the state and hence the purely instrumental value of foreign policy, the relative ease with which even a democratic society reconciles itself to almost any action necessary to preserve the state's independence and survival would be impossible to account for were it not for the fact that men evidently do regard the state a value in itself. It is the state that continues to give them, in addition to order and security, a sense of self-respect and of worth, a feeling of confidence and of well-being. Even so, it is important to recognize that the essential circularity of the argument of necessity would remain even if men did regard the state as no more than a condition of value.

that cannot be exceeded whatever the circumstances. Indeed, this criticism does not answer the question at all since it refuses even to pose the central issue. Instead, the attempt is made to do away with this issue, to deny its reality, by showing the abuses to which the argument of necessity has so often led in practice. The criticism is neither difficult to make nor easy to reject. The appeal to necessity has been employed time and again to justify expansion abroad and repression at home. Moreover, it is clear that this abuse is rooted largely in the expansiveness with which men seem almost congenitally disposed to construe the collective's existence and what they conceive to be threats to the collective's existence. When acted upon, the appeal to necessity must constantly risk the sacrifice of the very values it would uphold, values the preservation of which presumably provides the ultimate justification of the state and its "necessities." In this respect, modern weapons make dramatically explicit a risk that has always been at least implicit. Thermonuclear war holds out not only the prospect of destroying in an unprecedented manner the very values the preservation of which must provide the state's ultimate justification; thermonuclear war also holds out the prospect that this indispensable condition of value—the state—will itself be destroyed.

In certain respects, it is true, this criticism is one-sided and misleading even when considered on its own terms. It is, for example, misleading to insist that the appeal to the paramount demands of state security must always prove internally debilitating, that acceptance of the primacy of foreign policy over domestic policy must result either in the erosion of domestic political institutions or, at any rate, in the abandonment of otherwise desirable domestic goals. Whether or not the internal face of reason of state will betray these features depends upon a number of circumstances the significance of which in terms of their domestic effects may vary greatly. During the past fifteen years much has been made of the supposedly adverse effects of the cold war upon American institutions and the quality of American society. In a large literature the central theme of which is always the same, the demands imposed—or, to many, self-imposed—by the cold war have represented a continuing threat to the viability of American institutions and have generally resulted in the marked impoverishment of domestic life. Yet the persuasiveness of this theme does not and cannot rest upon a comparison of the pre-World War II America with the America of the middle 1960s, since the results of such a comparison simply do not support the conclusions intended. Instead, the persuasiveness of this theme must and does largely rest upon juxtaposing what has been done to improve the quality of domestic life with what might have been done if foreign policy and, particularly, a preoccupation with the state's security and position of world leadership had not been paramount.[49] That juxtaposition, however, proves nothing, since in the nature of things we can have no assurance that what might have been done in the absence of the cold war would in fact have been done. If anything, experience suggests the opposite conclusion that what might have been done in the absence of the cold war probably would not have been done. However that may be, what is beyond conjecture is that the nature of the hegemonial competition in which this nation has been engaged has provided much of the impetus for domestic change—e.g., in race relations, in education, in the economy—the desirability of which is generally acknowledged. No doubt, the conclusion that the domestic effects of the cold war have been salutary, on balance, will strike many as perverse. Yet the case for this conclusion appears at least as strong as, if not a good deal stronger than, the contrary argument. That the change which has occurred has been prompted for the "wrong reasons," that it has been undertaken in response to external pressures rather than from the internal conviction of its intrinsic desirability, is a relevant consideration only if it is assumed that the motives from which men initially act must thereafter determine the consequences of their actions. Clearly, however, there is no more warrant for this assumption than for the assumption that the consequences of men's actions will be without effect on the motives from which they may have initially acted.[50]

49. See, for example, the essays on the cold war in David Riesman, *Abundance For What* (Garden City, N.Y.: Doubleday, 1964), pp. 1–103.
50. More recently, the criticism considered in the text has been employed to interpret the domestic effects of the Vietnamese war. Thus it is argued that in relation to civil liberties, race relations generally, and the antipoverty program, the American involvement in Vietnam has had an adverse effect. In at least two of these areas, however, the argument appears singularly unpersuasive. There has been no perceptible erosion of civil liberties as a result of the Vietnamese conflict. If anything, the war has afforded an occasion for the exercise of these liberties. With respect to race relations generally, there is no clear relation between the war in Vietnam and the recent apathy of the white majority toward the continuing social and economic improvement of the Negro. On the contrary, this apathy, and even hostility, appears to result primarily from causes that have little or no relation to Vietnam. A more plausible case can be made for the adverse effects of the nation's involvement in Vietnam on the antipoverty program. The war has been used with some success by opponents of the program who have argued that a choice must be made between increased military expenditures and substantial expenditures on eradicating poverty. The effectiveness of this argument, however, is easily exaggerated in view of the vulnerability of the antipoverty program on grounds that have no relation to the Vietnamese conflict. Perhaps the most persuasive of the arguments dealing with the adverse domestic effects of the Vietnamese conflict emphasizes the less tangible, though no less significant, effects of this conflict. One prominent critic of the involvement in Vietnam writes: ". . . although it may be contended that the United States has the material resources to rebuild its society at home while waging war abroad, it is already being demonstrated that we do not have the mental and spiritual resources for such

It is, of course, another matter to argue that if the alleged necessities of foreign policy have not proven internally debilitating, in time they must be expected to have this effect. Put in its broadest form, this view holds that if the preoccupation with the state's physical security to the subordination of all other goals has not yet eventuated in the "garrison state," it is still the most likely outcome.[51] In its more pointed form, the indefinite retention of present military establishments must eventually result in their pervasive domination of domestic societies, and this despite a possible attenuation and even stabilization of the competitive struggle in weapons development. But if this projection of the future is to prove persuasive it must at least identify progressive tendencies toward this future in the present. What in very recent years we are increasingly aware of, however, are tendencies that appear to have retarded this projected outcome, if not to have operated in quite the opposite direction.[52] In part, this retardation is the result of an economy that easily permits both large military expenditures and an ever-increasing civilian consumption. In part, this retardation results from the nature of the military establishment that is maintained. In marked contrast to the military establishment that characterized the age of industrial mobilization, the military establishment of the nuclear age—at any rate, the military establishment of the great nuclear powers—is less demand-

---

a double effort. . . . The President simply cannot think about implementing the Great Society at home while he is supervising bombing missions over North Vietnam. . . ." J. W. Fulbright, *The Arrogance of Power* (New York: Random House, 1966), p. 133. In some measure, Senator Fulbright's argument is surely well taken. Once again, it is not argued in the text that the internal face of reason of state is necessarily benign; it is only argued that the appeal to the external necessities of the state is not always internally debilitating.

51. Thus Harold Lasswell writes, from the vantage point of 1962, that "the precondition of the garrison-state outcome is likely to be fulfilled." "We conclude, however reluctantly, that the garrison hypothesis provides a probable image of the past and future of our epoch." "The Garrison-State Hypothesis Today," *Changing Patterns of Military Politics*, ed. Samuel P. Huntington (Glencoe, Ill.: Free Press, 1962), pp. 59, 67. In Lasswell's garrison-state hypothesis, world politics is dominated by the "specialists on violence." The fundamental conditions of the garrison system are: "(1) the power elites value power enough to resort to large-scale coercion when they regard such coercive strategies as useful to the maintenance of their ascendancy; and (2) the elites accept the expectation that the retention of power during at least the immediate and middle-range future depends upon capability and willingness to coerce external or internal challengers." (p. 53.) Although Lasswell notes that the garrison state is not by definition nondemocratic, it is clear that the conditions of the system are very probably inimical to democratic institutions and values.

52. "For those societies of the atomic age that are not vulnerable to subversion, the image is no longer that of the garrison state but of bourgeois comfort and of millions of automobiles in the shadow of the apocalypse." Raymond Aron, *Paix et Guerre*, p. 305.

ing not only in terms of the efforts it generally requires of entire societies
but in terms of the military personnel it comprises. Moreover, by comparison with the preceding age this military establishment is relatively
unobtrusive in its physical presence. It is this quality of relative un-
obtrusiveness in the daily life of society which, when coupled with the
seemingly incalculable effects of their employment, confers on the new
weapons an esoteric character. Moralists may decry the tendency to
view the new weapons as somehow unreal and find in this tendency a
principal cause of the persistent apathy and moral indifference attending
the implications of deterrent strategies. Yet it is the same tendency that
must also partially explain the marginal effects deterrent strategies have
had to date on the societies supporting them. If the indefinite retention
of such strategies now appears unlikely to prove morally debilitating in
its effects, if a security that continues to be based in large measure
on the threat of extermination has not proven morally corrosive for the
tenor of domestic life, one reason for this reversal of earlier expectations
is the very reaction that has so frequently distressed the moralist.

These considerations may, and do, qualify the criticism of necessity;
clearly, they do not invalidate that criticism. In fact, there is no satisfactory answer to that criticism. Nor is it likely that there will ever be a
satisfactory answer so long as men continue to live in a world of states
and so long as they continue to regard the state if not as the source of
all value then at least as the indispensable condition of value. But if it is
true that the criticism of necessity is in an ultimate sense unanswerable,
it is no less true that today as in the past the criticism fails to afford a
solution to the dilemmas it lays bare. Granted the abuses to which the
argument of necessity has so regularly been put, abuses that appear inherent in the very structure of the argument. Granted the essential circularity of the appeal to necessity, a circularity that must constantly tend
to deprive the appeal of the very justification that is its foundation.
Granted, finally, that as between nuclear powers extreme measures can
no longer serve as a means for preserving the state's independence and
survival. What conclusions follow from these admissions? Surely the
conclusion does not follow that the state's independence and survival
are never in question, that the appeal to necessity is always fraudulent.
Nor does it follow that when the state's independence and survival are
at stake the statesman may always observe limits—however elementary—
on his actions. Although circumstances may not only permit but require
the observance of restraint, there is no sufficient reason to assume that
observance of even the most elementary restraints will always prove
possible. And even if it is true that as between nuclear powers extreme
measures must prove self-defeating, whether considered in terms of the

values the state presumably protects or in terms of the existence of the state itself, it is not true—at least, it is not yet true—that a willingness to threaten extreme measures must also prove self-defeating. In the one great confrontation that has arisen to date between nuclear powers, it was the manifestation of a will to take extreme measures if necessary which provided a vital ingredient—perhaps *the* vital ingredient—in resolving the confrontation on a relatively satisfactory basis to the U.S. To be sure, the numerous self-congratulatory analyses that followed the Cuban missile crisis have almost invariably placed a central emphasis on the moderate character of the measures actually employed by this nation. But the background of those moderate measures was the avowed policy of the American government to employ any and all means to stop the further shipment of "offensive weapons" to Cuba and to compel the withdrawal of such weapons as were already on the island. If the Cuban missile crisis points to the supreme importance of moderation and prudence in dealing with the conflicts that arise between nuclear powers, it is nevertheless a plain misreading of that crisis to find in it either the disavowal of extreme measures or the self-defeating character of a determination to take such measures in the last resort.

7

There are no limits to the measures that may be taken to preserve the state's independence and continuity. This is, and has always been, the crux of the argument of necessity. On this absurdly simple yet ultimately terrifying conclusion there must be complete clarity. It is not the abuse to which the plea of necessity so readily lends itself that constitutes its profoundly disturbing feature but its refusal to acknowledge any restraints on the measures that may be threatened or taken on behalf of the state. Thus the argument of necessity does not leave the critical issue of means unresolved. On the contrary, it is precisely in the manner by which this issue is in principle resolved that the distinctive character of the argument must be found. The solution thereby afforded the problem of means must not be obscured by general prescriptions which, though they do not essentially alter the argument, may operate to soften its impact. Perhaps the most commonplace of these prescriptions is the insistence upon prudence as the supreme virtue of the statesman. The injunction to be prudent is immanent, however, in the very imperative that forms the core of the argument of necessity. If the highest duty of the statesman is to preserve the state's independence and continuity, it evidently follows that he ought to act prudently in doing so. But whether prudence permits the observance of restraints, and if so what restraints, are dependent upon circumstance and cannot be answered in the abstract.[53]

It is clear, then, that any serious critique of necessity must be directed to the critical issue of means. Any serious critique, that is to say, must seek to impose limits on the acts the statesman may take, limits that are at once clear and meaningful in the actions they proscribe. Is there a critique that does so limit the content of necessity without at the same time renouncing statecraft altogether? Is there a critique that without abandoning the distinctive and heretofore indispensable means of statecraft nevertheless imposes restraints upon this means, restraints the statesman is never justified in exceeding? Is there, in a word, a critique that permits a solution—if only a barely tolerable solution—to the critical issue of means?

In posing these questions it is natural that we should turn to the Christian doctrine of *bellum justum*. It is natural if only for the reason that in all its versions the doctrine of *bellum justum* has been in Western thought the principal alternative to the ancient plea of reason of

53. Thus in a recent discussion of the problem of means in statecraft ("le problème machiavélien"), Raymond Aron insists upon prudence as the supreme virtue of the statesman. To be prudent, he writes, ". . . is to act in accordance with the particular contingency and the concrete givens, not to be enslaved by logic or by passive obedience to a norm or pseudo-norm; it is to prefer the limitation of violence to the punishment of the allegedly guilty or to a supposedly absolute justice; it is to set for oneself concrete and accessible objectives which conform to the secular law of international relations rather than limitless goals which are apt to be devoid of all significance. . . ." *Paix et Guerre*, p. 572. It is clear, however, that the injunction to be prudent is of itself no real solution to "le probleme machiavélien," if for no other reason than that the preservation of the state's independence and continuity—surely the most important of Aron's "concrete and accessible objectives"—may not always permit the limitation of violence. Aron acknowledges this in refusing to condemn any particular means employed in war, irrespective of purpose and consequence. In considering the act of deliberately destroying a city in war he writes: "I do not dissimulate the risks of this means, but there is no ethical judgment possible without taking into account historical circumstances. All acts of war today being destructive, a brutal action which would bring a quick capitulation of an aggressor might conceivably be justified." (p. 599.) Elsewhere, he declares: ". . . *ethical* judgment on diplomatic strategic conduct is inseparable from *historical* judgment on the aims of the actors and the consequences of their success or failure." (p. 592.) In substance, Aron's solution of the problem of means is nothing other than the traditional solution, the acceptance of which affords in principle a justification for any and all measures deemed essential to the preservation and continuity of the state. The appeal to prudence as the supreme virtue of the statesman does not alter this conclusion. Nor does Aron's "la morale de la sagesse" succeed in resolving what prudence fails to resolve. This morality of wisdom ("The only morality superior to the morality of combat and to the morality of law is what I should call the morality of wisdom, which attempts to consider each case on its concrete merits, without ignoring any of the arguments of principle and of opportunity, or forgetting either the relationship of forces or the desires of the peoples." [p. 596]) is little more than a restatement in somewhat different terms of the norm of prudence.

state. If the latter emanates from the state itself, the former has a source that is independent of and presumably superior to the state and its necessities. If the argument of necessity places no inherent restraints on the measures that may be taken to secure the state's independence and survival, the doctrine of *bellum justum* insists that there are such inherent restraints—inherent not in the sense that they may not in fact be exceeded but in the sense that there can be no justification for ever exceeding them. Nevertheless, the observance of these restraints, whatever the circumstances, is not equated with the renunciation of statecraft. Now as in the past, the doctrine of *bellum justum* does not attempt to deal with the critical issue of means simply by abandoning statecraft. In most of its contemporary versions, as in its traditional versions, it seeks instead to square the circle by acknowledging that the state has its necessities and at the same time insisting that the measures by which these necessities may be preserved must remain limited.

In considering contemporary versions of *bellum justum* it must be immediately observed that with respect to the justification for resorting to force there is little to distinguish these versions from contemporary developments elsewhere, notably developments in international law. Both in contemporary international law as well as in the prevailing twentieth-century reconstruction of *bellum justum*, war is no longer a means generally permitted to states for the redress of rights that have been violated. Still less is war considered a legitimate means for changing the status quo. To the extent that armed force remains a means permitted to states, it does so only to protect the state's self—its territorial integrity and political independence—against unjust attack.[54]

This restriction of the right of recourse to war in modern versions of *bellum justum* has been represented as a far-reaching change from the classic doctrine, though as we shall presently see the precise significance of the change is dependent upon the meaning and scope accorded to legitimate self-defense. In the classic doctrine the just war was a war of execution, an act of vindicative justice, taken to punish an offending state for a wrong done and unamended. But the rights in defense of which, or for the vindication of which, the traditional doctrine permitted states to resort to war, when alternative means of self-redress proved unavailing and unsatisfactory, were not restricted to the right of

54. These statements summarize the contemporary *jus ad bellum*. Some of the complexities and persisting ambiguities that attend this development are discussed in succeeding pages. Here it is sufficient simply to note that the formulation given in the text appears to represent the present consensus of Catholic and Protestant thought. The right of self-defense against unjust attack is complemented by the right of collective defense—i.e., the right of third parties to come to the defense of the party acting in legitimate self-defense.

self-defense. Indeed, the "blameless self-defense" of the classic doctrine represented only one cause justifying the resort to war, and a cause the justice of which appeared so self-evident to the expositors of the doctrine as scarcely to warrant discussion. The primary concern was rather with the problem of "aggressive" or offensive war (i.e., aggressive or offensive in the sense of the initiation of force). The broad response of the classic doctrine to this problem was simply that aggressive war was justified when undertaken by constituted authority, with right intention and as a last resort, to restore the order of justice violated by the offending state.

If it is nevertheless said that the classic doctrine of *bellum justum* was, in principle, defensive, it was so in the sense that war was to be undertaken in defense of justice. It clearly was not defensive in any other sense; at least, it was not necessarily defensive. Not only was aggressive war permitted to redress an injury, to enforce one's rights, it was also permitted to forestall injurious action. The *bellum justum* could thus comprise a preventive war. Yet the "order of justice" in the defense of which aggressive or offensive war could be taken was never apparent. The rights in defense of which, or for the vindication of which, states might resort to war remained obscure, even as among the expositors of the doctrine. Comprising both legal and natural rights, the just war in the classic doctrine was a war waged to enforce both positive and natural law. But there was no more assurance in an earlier era than today that law and justice would always coincide, despite the contrary assumptions of the classic doctrine.[55] When they did not, states might choose between the two. If the identification of positive right and its violation has always proven difficult, the identification of natural right in terms of the conflicting claims and aspirations of states has proven far more difficult. Given the circumstances in which they were applied, these features of the classic doctrine could scarcely constitute a serious restraint on state action. The criticism that has always been made with such telling effect against the argument of necessity may be made with equal effect against these features of the classic doctrine of *bellum justum*. As a justification of war the latter clearly must invite as much abuse at the hands of governments—and, it is only fair to add, not only at the hands of governments—as does the former. In this respect, at

55. The classic doctrine assumed not only the harmony of law and justice but the coincidence of peace and justice. In this view, peace is an ordered concord based upon justice. That a choice might have to be made between law and justice on the one hand or between peace and justice on the other hand was excluded by the classic doctrine. This equation of peace, order, and justice remains in contemporary versions of *bellum justum*, although it can scarcely be said to carry the same conviction today.

least, the contrast often drawn between *bellum justum* and reason of state seems unpersuasive; the one appears no less, or no more, subject to abuse than does the other.[56]

There is no need to labor the considerations that have prompted the change in the twentieth-century reconstruction of *bellum justum*. In the main, the restriction of the just war to the war of self-defense rests on the presumption that war can no longer serve as an apt and proportionate means for resolving international conflicts. That presumption, in turn, presumably reflects our contemporary experience with war. There are dissenters from this reconstruction of the classic doctrine.[57] Their objections to restricting the just war to a war of self-defense are not unlike the objections raised by a number of jurists to restricting the legal war to a war of self-defense. In the absence of a society possessed of effective collective procedures for protecting the rights of its members as well as for changing conditions that have become oppressive and inequitable, it is argued that the attempt to deny states this ultimate means of self-redress—save as a measure of self-defense against attack—is bound to fail. Nor is it clear, in the view of some, that the attempt to proscribe "aggressive" war ought even to succeed—and this despite the destructiveness of war in this century—so long as those conditions persist that have always marked international society.[58] Whatever the merits of this view,

56. It is significant that in a vast literature devoted to the problem of war in Christian thought, and particularly to the doctrine of *bellum justum*, there has been so little inquiry into the relation of doctrine to practice. It is only in recent years, and for recent wars, that such inquiry has been increasingly undertaken. For the most part, however, the literature of pure exegesis on *bellum justum* is as abundant as the literature on the practical uses to which the doctrine has been put in statecraft is scarce. That the doctrine has been abused on numerous occasions over the centuries, that it has been invoked time and again to justify policies of aggrandizement, is scarcely open to dispute. It may of course be argued that these abuses are without relevance to the intrinsic merits of the doctrine. But if this argument is employed in the case of *bellum justum* it must also be applied in the case of reason of state. To confront the theory of the one with the practice of the other clearly will not do. We can only assume that the historical fate of *bellum justum* forms a commentary on the doctrine as much as the historical fate of reason of state forms a commentary on the argument of necessity.

57. Thus Paul Ramsey writes: "No sweeping proscription of 'aggressive' war can hope to stand, based as it is on the assumption that history can be frozen where we are, i.e., always in a relatively unjust *pax-ordo* or on the entirely erroneous assumption that any existing international organization is capable of introducing *fundamental* change into this order but in an entirely orderly fashion and by mutual consent. And in any case, aggression has to be defined so as to include within its meaning, not only the first resort to arms, but also any basic challenge to the security of a rival nation, to its *pax-ordo-justitia* and the laws of its peace, against which the only effective defense may be, and is known to be, a resort to armed force." *War and the Christian Conscience*, pp. 89–90.

58. The most persuasive presentation of the above view is the work of Julius Stone, *Aggression and World Order* (Berkeley: University of California Press, 1958).

and it is not to be lightly dismissed, the dominant position today is that armed force is forbidden except as a measure of legitimate self-defense.[59]

Does this change with respect to the justification for resorting to war permit a more persuasive contrast to be drawn today between *bellum*

59. These summary remarks on a critically important—if ultimately insoluble—controversy warrant some further discussion. Quite apart from the central question of the scope and meaning to be given "legitimate self-defense," this proscription of "aggressive" wars in the twentieth-century reconstruction of *bellum justum* must encounter two difficulties. On the one hand, it cannot be understood to imply that defensive wars are necessarily just wars. Clearly, the principle of proportionality (cf. pp. 300–1) applies to wars of "legitimate self-defense" as well, whatever the scope and meaning to be given the latter. Even a defensive war may not be an "apt and proportionate means"; even a defensive war, then, may be an unjust war if the good secured by such a war is outweighed by the evil attendant upon—or expected to attend—the conduct of war. This is precisely the issue raised by the prospect of thermonuclear war; even if defensive in character, a thermonuclear war may nevertheless be an unjust war. On the other hand, if a defensive war may nevertheless be an unjust war, it does not necessarily follow from the principle of proportionality that under present conditions an "aggressive" war must be an unjust war. The presumption is not self-evident that war—any and all war—can no longer serve as an apt and proportionate means for resolving international conflicts. (Nor, for that matter, is it self-evident that war—any and all war—can no longer be waged with "right intent" and the proper means.) To say this is not at all to dismiss our experience with war in this century; it is simply to say that despite this experience, and despite the possible consequences of thermonuclear war, there may still be wars and wars. Neither is our experience so unambiguous nor our future so certain as to warrant making what is in effect an irrebuttable presumption. In his celebrated encyclical *Pacem in terris*, John XXIII spoke of the "cruel destruction and the immense suffering" which the use of modern arms would bring to humanity and for this reason condemned the notion "that war is a fit instrument with which to repair the violation of justice." In taking this position John XXIII followed his predecessor, Pius XII, who also condemned the theory that war could serve today as an apt and proportionate means of state policy. Yet it is clearly quite possible to imagine that war might still serve in certain circumstances as an apt and proportionate means to repair injustice, although technically such a war would be an "aggressive" war. Moreover, as noted above, if the "aggressive" resort to armed force is always to be condemned on the basis of its disproportionality, the justice of defensive wars must also be seriously questioned. It is another matter to argue that while there may still be just "aggressive" wars, to proscribe any and all aggressive wars is nevertheless desirable, given the conditions that have always attended the use of force in international society. On this view, whatever may be the merits of a particular case, the sum of our experience indicates that given these conditions force is more likely to promote injustice than justice, and that this expectation is very considerably strengthened by the novel conditions presently attending the use of force. The parallel argument in law must be that to permit states the right to use force as a measure of self-help to redress violations—or, rather, alleged violations—of their rights is more likely to promote disorder than order. It must be admitted, however, that this particular argument—whether undertaken on the moral or legal level—is inconclusive, even under present conditions. It depends, among other things, upon an interpretation of the history of state relations, past and present, that leaves ample room for uncertainty and disagreement.

justum and reason of state than could be drawn in an earlier era? Does the twentieth-century reconstruction of *bellum justum* thereby limit the "necessities" of the state in a way that the classic doctrine did not? The answer to these questions evidently depends largely upon the manner in which current versions of *bellum justum* circumscribe this one remaining cause justifying war. In fact, however, current versions of *bellum justum* do not appear to have a great deal to say about the meaning and scope of this one remaining justification for war. What they do have to say does not differ substantially from the more extended and detailed juristic analyses of the right of self-defense. In consequence, the same difficulties and ambiguities marking the concept of self-defense in contemporary international law also mark the concept of self-defense in most current versions of *bellum justum*. In the latter no less than in the former uncertainty and controversy persist over the vital issues of the rights on behalf of which, and the acts in response to which, forcible measures of self-defense may be undertaken.

The principal reasons for this persisting uncertainty and controversy are clear enough. What is at best a subordinate principle of order within the state must be something altogether different within a society that does not afford the measure of security normally afforded to individuals within the state. Given the conditions that have always characterized international society, it can hardly be expected that here the scope of the right of self-defense will be as narrowly defined or that the actual exercise of this right will be as severely controlled as within the state. Moreover, to the extent that the circumstances in which states may employ force generally as a measure of self-help are progressively restricted, yet this progressive restriction is not accompanied by parallel change in the basic structural characteristics of international society, the significance attached to the right of self-defense must if anything increase. Force may be in principle forbidden to states, not only as a means for effecting change but as a means for the protection of established rights. At the same time, no viable and effective alternative to the institution of self-help may exist.[60] In these circumstances, the scope of the right of self-defense may largely determine the degree of security states enjoy, since a right of self-redress that nevertheless forbids the threat or use of force may prove insufficient to the task of preserving many of the rights on which the security of the state rests.

---

60. The argument is no doubt true that the persistence of the institution of self-help must impede progress toward an effectively centralized juridical organization of international society. It is no less true, however, that the absence of such juridical organization must account for the persistence of states in retaining the right of self-help. Unfortunately, these truisms do not carry us very far.

These considerations largely explain the controversies that have always attended interpretations of the critical provisions of the United Nations Charter, controversies that find an echo in the disparate interpretations of self-defense in current versions of *bellum justum*. A restrictive view of the Charter's provisions, in limiting the right to exercise force in self-defense to the sole contingency of a prior armed attack, is vulnerable to the criticism that, if adhered to, it might well result in defeating the essential purpose of this right.[61] To require that an armed attack must have actually begun before the right of self-defense may be exercised is to exceed even the requirements for exercising self-defense imposed by most municipal legal systems, which permit acts in self-defense not only against an actual danger but also against one that is imminent. The restrictive view would therefore appear to place more rigid requirements on the right of self-defense precisely in those circumstances where this right must continue to afford the principal basis for security. More generally, however, the objection to the restrictive view is simply that a state may be unable to preserve its vital interests—above all its political independence—if self-defense is only legitimate where the measures taken to endanger the state's interests take the form of an armed attack. The measures that may jeopardize a state's independence need not involve armed force, though they may nevertheless be unlawful. To deny states the right to respond to such measures by employing, if necessary, forcible measures in self-defense may well result in turning the right of political independence into little more than a sham. Nor is it useful here to draw a parallel between the state and international society. Within the state a right of self-defense is denied the individual short of an armed attack or the imminent threat of armed attack precisely because the individual may seek and receive protection against other acts endangering his vital, and legally protected, interests. The same assurance evidently does not obtain for states in international society. To require of states what is required of individuals within the state is to ignore the disparate circumstances that make the employment of armed force a reasonable

61. Even the restrictive view, however, would leave a substantial measure of uncertainty over the permitted scope of self-defense. In limiting the right to exercise force in self-defense to the sole contingency of an armed attack, it is still necessary to determine what constitutes an armed attack. Need an armed attack be "direct" before it may be responded to with forcible measures of self-defense? Those who respond affirmatively cannot rely upon the United Nations Charter, since Article 51 of the Charter does not require that an armed attack be "direct" before it may be responded to with force. It may of course be argued that the consequence of including indirect uses of armed force within the concept of armed attack is to expand this concept to a point where it may well become meaningless as a restraint. This may be true. Yet it is also true that a state's independence may be jeopardized by the indirect employment of armed force.

condition for the exercise of self-defense in the one case and an un-reasonable condition in the other case.

Although this criticism of the restrictive view of the right of self-defense is not without considerable merit, it is much easier to make than to suggest an alternative that is not equally vulnerable to criticism. How-ever paradoxical the restrictive view appears in denying the legitimacy of anticipatory acts of self-defense, the explanation of this apparent paradox must be found in those very conditions that normally attend the exercise of self-defense in international society. The same conditions that do indeed lend support to the argument on behalf of anticipatory acts of self-defense also point to the considerable dangers of granting such a right. Nor does the nature of modern weapons substantially alter this conclusion. If the speed and destructive power of modern weapons may defeat the purpose of self-defense in the absence of a right to take anticipatory measures against an imminent attack, it is these same char-acteristics of modern weapons that must also render a right to take anticipatory measures particularly dangerous and subject to abuse.

Apart from the issue of anticipatory self-defense, if the restrictive view of the right of self-defense is considered inadequate and unacceptable, what is the alternative? The broad response given this question has been to insist that the resort to forcible measures of self-defense is legitimate not only to protect the state's territorial integrity, its "physical person," against armed attack; self-defense is equally legitimate when resorted to for the protection of those interests that collectively comprise the state's "existence" in the broader sense of political independence and that may be endangered by measures other than armed force. But if uncertainty has always prevailed with respect to the scope of the rights—the legally protected interests—that presumably comprise the state's security and independence, an equal uncertainty must prevail with respect to the scope of the right of self-defense. Given the congenital disposition of states to interpret their existence, and threats thereto, expansively, the claim of self-defense, even when limited to the protection of legal rights against delictual conduct, may come very close in practice to the more general claim of a right of self-help.[62]

62. There is the further consideration that a state's independence may be im-paired by acts that do not involve the threat or use of armed force. To the extent that unlawful intervention is held to encompass only those acts of interference in the affairs of another state that take an imperative or dictatorial form and involve the threat or use of force, the duty of nonintervention becomes irrelevant in dealing with behavior that may nevertheless effectively jeopardize political independence. If the right of political independence is held to justify the resort to forcible measures of self-defense, and if the right of independence is only given a sufficiently broad interpretation, the result must be to enlarge the scope of self-defense to a point

The immediately preceding considerations have assumed that how-ever ill-defined in their scope the acts in response to which self-defense is presumably legitimate are at least clearly unlawful. Measures of self-defense are permitted, then, in response to unlawful acts that at the same time endanger another state's territorial integrity or political in-dependence. It is clear, however, that a state's political independence, and the security on which independence rests, may be endangered by acts that are not forbidden—at least, not specifically forbidden—by international law. In recent years, the most dramatic illustration of this possibility resulted from the discovery in October, 1962, that the Soviet Union was secretly establishing missile sites on the island of Cuba. The action of the Soviet government was interpreted by the U.S., as well as by the Organization of American States, to constitute a threat to the peace and security—and, accordingly, the political independence—of the states comprising the Western Hemisphere, thereby justifying the resort to forcible measures designed to prevent the further shipment to Cuba of missiles and aircraft having an offensive capability as well as to compel the withdrawal of such weapons as were already on the island. Yet in sending these weapons the Soviet government acted with the consent and co-operation of the Cuban government. There is no rule of international law that specifically forbids a state from giving arms to another state or from establishing military bases in the territory of an-other state, whether openly or in a clandestine manner, so long as this is done with the latter state's consent. Nor does international law forbid a state from attempting to alter the military balance of power in its favor, so long as this is done through actions that do not in themselves violate the rights of other states. To the extent that the forcible measures taken by the U.S. in response to the action of the Soviet government are nevertheless justified as measures of legitimate self-defense, they afford a striking example of the claim to take measures of self-defense against acts that are not at least *prima facie* unlawful.[63]

It may of course be argued that acts that endanger the security and independence of other states are unlawful even though they are not specifically forbidden by international law. This is, it would appear,

---

where it is difficult to distinguish from the much more general claim of the state to possess the competence to take measures of self-help—including forcible measures of self-help—as a reaction to acts of other states which violate its rights. These con-siderations explain, in part, why the claim of self-defense in the customary law always bordered in practice on the much more general claim of a right to self-help.

63. In undertaking the naval quarantine of Cuba, however, the U.S. did not attempt to justify the action as a legitimate measure of self-defense. Nor did the OAS attempt to characterize the Soviet action as one giving rise to a right of indi-vidual and collective self-defense.

the implication of the claim that a state has the right to take forcible measures of self-defense, if necessary, against any and all acts that endanger its political independence. But once this argument is granted, it is not easy to see wherein it differs from the traditional claim of a right to self-preservation. If the substantive rights in defense of which force may be employed remain both expansive and ill-defined, if all that can be said with assurance is that in some vague manner these rights encompass the security and independence of the state, it is not easy to see wherein the right of self-defense limits the "necessities" of the state.[64]

These uncertainties marking the scope of self-defense in international law are equally apparent in current versions of *bellum justum*. They are scarcely overcome by other restraints placed on the exercise of self-defense. The lawful exercise of force in self-defense presumably requires that the danger giving rise to this right be immediate and of such a nature as to leave no reasonable possibility for recourse to alternative means of protection. Even then, the use of force in self-defense must prove reasonable, and it may prove reasonable only if it is proportionate

64. Thus the authors of a recent study point out that claims of self-defense "are claims to exercise highly intense coercion in response to what is alleged to be unlawfully initiated coercion." Myres S. McDougal and Florentino P. Feliciano, *Law and Minimum World Public Order* (New Haven: Yale University Press, 1961), p. 209. The legally protected interests for the protection of which measures of self-defense may be undertaken are summarized as "territorial integrity and political independence." Political independence is defined as that "freedom of decision-making or self-direction customarily demanded by state officials. Impairment of 'political independence,' as an attack upon the institutional arrangements of authority and control in the target state, thus involves substantial curtailment of the freedom of decision-making through the effective and drastic reduction of the number of alternative policies open at tolerable costs to the officials of that state." (p. 177.) On this view, measures of self-defense are legitimate in response to acts of coercion by another state which impair or threaten to impair this "freedom of decision-making" of the target state, provided only that such measures are necessary in the circumstances and proportionate to the danger (cf. pp. 300–1). Nor is it necessary that the acts in response to which measures of self-defense are undertaken be specifically forbidden by international law. They are unlawful, on this view, even if their effect is only to endanger a state's political independence. It is difficult to see any substantial difference between this view of self-defense and the older—and avowedly political—doctrine of self-preservation (cf. pp. 273ff). Professor McDougal confirms this conclusion, without admitting it, in his remarks on the Cuban quarantine. Cf. Myres S. McDougal, "The Soviet-Cuban Quarantine and Self-Defense," *American Journal of International Law*, LVII (July, 1963), 597ff. For a candid reaffirmation of the right of self-preservation in the context of the Cuban quarantine it is necessary to turn from the international jurists to a former Secretary of State, who declares: "I must conclude that the propriety of the Cuban quarantine is not a legal issue. The power, position and prestige of the United States had been challenged by another state; and law simply does not deal with such questions of ultimate power—power that comes close to the sources of sovereignty. . . . No law can destroy the state creating the law. The survival of states is not a matter of law." Remarks by the Hon. Dean Acheson, *Proceedings, American Society of International Law* (Washington: 1963), p. 14.

to the end of protecting those interests that are endangered. Force in excess of this purpose is forbidden, since action taken in self-defense is held to have a strictly preventive character.

It is clear that these requirements of law still leave largely unaffected the vital issue of the rights on behalf of which, and the acts in response to which, forcible measures of self-defense may be undertaken. Even so, the interpretation to be given these requirements has never been free from substantial uncertainty. Thus it has never been clear whether the requirement of proportionality limits acts taken in self-defense to repelling the immediate danger or permits action directed to removing the danger. The latter interpretation is not unreasonable, given the circumstances attending the exercise of self-defense in international society. Within domestic societies the state assures that a danger once repelled will be removed. Hence the justification for the severe restriction of measures taken in self-defense. In international society this assurance evidently cannot be given to states. Hence an equally severe restriction of measures taken in self-defense may prove unreasonable in that it may defeat the essential purpose for which measures of self-defense are permitted in the first place. The argument is not without merit. Yet if it is once accepted, it must become increasingly difficult to set meaningful limits to the exercise of self-defense.[65]

In substance, the same requirements of necessity and proportionality are also held to govern the just exercise of force. In *bellum justum*, it is

___

65. The issue of proportionality arose in the Suez crisis in 1956. In attacking Egypt, Israel justified her action as a legitimate measure of self-defense, taken in response to a continuous series of armed raids on Israeli territory by fedayeen bands based in Egypt and in anticipation of what was alleged to be an impending attack on Israel by Egyptian forces. Quite apart from the issue of anticipatory self-defense raised by the Israeli action, the obvious and acknowledged intent of the Israeli action was to destroy the fedayeen bases in Egypt—that is, to remove this particular source of danger. At the time, the action was generally condemned because, among other reasons, it was considered unreasonable and disproportionate to the acts provoking the Israeli attack. In defense of the Israeli position, however, it may be contended that the action was without purpose or reason unless directed to removing this source of danger. In this respect, it is interesting to compare the position taken by Israel in 1956 and the position taken by the U.S. in the Cuban crisis in 1962. Much has been made of the proportionality and reasonableness of the Cuban "quarantine" in view of the considerable danger allegedly posed by the presence of Soviet missile bases in Cuba. It should be noted, however, that the declared policy of the American government was not only to stop the further shipment of missiles to Cuba but to compel the withdrawal of such weapons as were already on the island, and to do so by any and all means that might prove necessary. The proportionality and reasonableness of the American position can hardly be judged exclusively in terms of the measures that were actually taken; it must also be judged in terms of the measures threatened if the quarantine proved ineffective and the missiles were not removed.

true, the requirement of proportionality possesses a broader meaning than does the requirement of proportionality in international law. In the latter, the proportionality required is little more than what may be termed a proportionality of effectiveness. In the former, the proportionality required is both a proportionality of effectiveness and a proportionality of value. In *bellum justum* it is not enough that the use of force is proportionate, though no more than proportionate, to the effective protection of endangered interests or values. To this proportionality of effectiveness must be added a proportionality of value, requiring that the values preserved through force are proportionate to the values sacrificed through force. Indeed, it is the proportionality of value rather than of effectiveness upon which primary emphasis is placed in *bellum justum*. At the same time, the requirement of a proportionality of value can hardly be regarded as a meaningful restraint, however great the emphasis placed on it. Devoid entirely of the element of specificity, it is—as earlier observed[66]—a prescription that can readily be adjusted to the most varied of actions. It is not surprising that the requirement of a proportionality of value has been invoked with an apparent plausibility on all sides of the nuclear issue by Christian moralists. It illustrates that a prescription the converse of which is manifestly absurd can tell us very little that is meaningful about how men ought to behave.[67]

66. Cf. pp. 233–34.

67. Once again it must be emphasized that the principle of proportionality (of value) does not of itself confer a distinctive quality on *bellum justum*. This principle is implicit in almost every conceivable justification of force. Not only does it express what may be termed the "logic of justification," it is compatible with almost every justification—or condemnation—of force men have ever given. It is frequently assumed that the difficulty in applying the principle of proportionality, and the limited utility of the principle when it is applied, result from men's inability to know all the facts of a situation and, above all, from men's inability to foresee the consequences of their actions. This is certainly true, but it is by no means the whole truth. Even if all the relevant facts were known, and all of the consequences of action (or abstention from action) foreseen, the application of the principle of proportionality would give rise to uncertainty and, in consequence, to disagreement. This is so for the apparent reason that the principle of proportionality is devoid of substantive content. Nor is there any real consensus among theorists of the just war with respect to the values that should form the content of the principle of proportionality. To be sure, there is agreement that the state, though it is considered an important value, cannot be considered the supreme value. Hence, the application of the principle of proportionality by theorists of *bellum justum* may lead to results that are different from the results of applying this principle by those who impute supreme value to the state and, accordingly, to the state's necessities. But this difference is scarcely sufficient to establish a meaningful consensus among the former with respect to the values that should form the content of the principle of proportionality. Moreover, even if we assume that men can know all of the consequences of their actions and can achieve meaningful agreement on the plurality of values the preservation of which may justify war, there is still no objective way of determining (cal-

8

If we are to find a distinctive quality in *bellum justum*, a quality that sets clear and meaningful limits to the necessities of the state, that quality cannot be found simply in the causes and ends of war. Nor can it be found in the general principles governing the conditions of war. If this quality is to be found at all, it must be in the restraints placed on the conduct or means of war. To say this is not to imply that the doctrine of *bellum justum*, whether in its classic or in its modern versions, has indeed made the means of warfare the center of moral gravity.[68] On the contrary, it is in the causes and ends justifying war that

culating) whether the evil attendant upon the waging of war is justified in terms of the good obtained through war; reasonable men can, and will, reach quite disparate conclusions. Of course, the requirement of proportionality would give a distinctive character to *bellum justum* if it afforded a distinctive method of determining (calculating) a proportionality of value and one that somehow avoided these difficulties. This is admittedly not the case. The scales used by the theorists of the just war are the same scales used by others (though the weights are presumably different), and the results are quite as uncertain and subject to controversy. With respect to the manner of establishing either proportionality or disproportionality in war, then, there is little, if indeed anything, that is distinctive in *bellum justum*.

68. Whether the theory of the just war *should* always have made the conduct of war the center of moral gravity is another matter. In this connection Paul Ramsey has written: "Since at least everyone seeks peace and desires justice, the ends for which war may legitimately be fought are not nearly so important in the theory of the just war as is the moral and political wisdom contained in its reflection upon the conduct or means of warfare. Unless there is a morality applicable to instruments of war and intrinsically limiting its conduct, then we must simply admit that war has no limits—since these can hardly be derived from 'peace' as the 'final cause' of just wars." "The Case for Making 'Just War' Possible," *Nuclear Weapons and the Conflict of Conscience*, ed. John C. Bennett, pp. 146–47. Although Ramsey's latter assertion is an exaggeration, neglecting as it does the moderating effects limited ends in war may have on the conduct of war, even if it were accepted as true it would not follow that his former assertion must also be true. Nor can imaginative reconstructions of the *bellum justum* doctrine, such as Ramsey's (cf. *War and the Christian Conscience*), prove more than what the theory of the just war should perhaps have always had as its central emphasis, given the premises from which it starts. In fact, it is surprising how little emphasis was placed on the means of warfare by expositors of the traditional doctrine. It is this relative neglect along with the emphasis placed on the interpretation of war as an act of vindicative justice undertaken for the punishment of the wicked that has prompted critics to conclude that far from leading to greater restraint in the conduct of war the traditional doctrine had the contrary effect. Whatever the merit of this criticism, it is a matter of record that the greatest progress in the mitigation of war came in a period when the idea of the just war was in eclipse. No doubt, this progress cannot be attributed simply to the decline of *bellum justum*. Other and more important factors were at work in the eighteenth and nineteenth centuries which explain the limited wars of the period and the growing observance in war of the immunity of the civilian population. Even so, a persuasive case may be made for the position that the interpretation of war as a duel between equals significantly contributed to the humanization of warfare. There are perhaps no logical reasons why the interpretation of war as a

we must find the principal focus of the doctrine. It is true that in many contemporary analyses of the just war, the means permitted in war have been given markedly increased attention. Even so, it would be rash to conclude that at present primary emphasis is placed on the manner in which war must be conducted. In this respect, as in many others, the evolution of *bellum justum* appears to parallel the evolution of international law. In both, it is the *jus ad bellum*—or, perhaps more accurately, a *jus contra bellum*—rather than a *jus in bello* that has formed the primary emphasis. Moreover, to the extent that the manner of warfare has been increasingly emphasized, the significance of this emphasis must largely be seen in the effects it has had in redefining the *jus ad bellum*.[69]

Despite these considerations, it is over the issue of the means permitted in war or to deter war that we must find, if anywhere, a significant conflict between the necessities of the state and the demands of *bellum justum*. The general nature of that conflict is clear enough. Whereas reason of state must reject the claim that there are any inherent limits on the means that may be threatened or employed to preserve the state, *bellum justum* must insist that there are such limits and that they may never be transgressed, whatever the circumstances.[70] The argument of necessity must reject the claim of inherent limits on the means of war, not because it is informed by an "ethic of responsibility" and therefore requires the statesman to calculate and to weigh the possible consequences of alternative courses of action but because it presupposes as an ultimate end the preservation and continuity of the state. The doctrine of *bellum justum* evidently cannot share this presupposition, else it could not insist that there are means that may never be employed. At the same time, there is no denial here of the need to calculate and to weigh possible consequences of alternative courses of action. There is simply the insistence that whatever the results of calcu-

---

duel between equals, rather than as the punishment of the wicked, should lead to greater restraint in the conduct of war, but there are very persuasive psychological reasons which suggest this result. These reasons are scarcely offset by the claim that the wicked are to be punished for love's sake, for the sake of a love that comprises the enemy but at the same time does not preclude—in St. Augustine's words—"a benevolent severity." For all his realism, Augustine's insistence upon the loving killer, or the loving avenger, who would vindicate justice though without passion and self-assertion was not very realistic.

69. That is, in restricting the circumstances or occasions in which the resort to armed force is considered justified.

70. It must be made clear that this conflict is not over the proportionality or disproportionality of means, in terms of their effects, but over the means themselves. The distinction is a critical one, since it is only over the issue of means, per se, that a clear conflict may arise between reason of state and *bellum justum*.

lation, certain limits must be imposed on the means permitted the statesman, limits that may never be transgressed.[71]

To the degree that *bellum justum* has a distinctive quality, then, this
quality is to be found not merely in the significance given to the means
of action but above all in the insistence that *bellum justum* is an "ethic
of ultimate means." This quality is blurred, if not lost, if the problem of
means is itself reduced to what is, in effect, another form of calculation.
Thus it is not enough to argue that one may never do evil so that good
may come because the good will not come (only the evil), or that the
evil act will corrupt the actor and thereby defeat his ends (however
desirable in themselves), or that the means cannot be separated from the
ends but are themselves the ends in the very process of coming into
existence. It is not enough to argue in this manner if only for the reason
that each of these familiar contentions is open to question. Whether the
use of evil means will always and necessarily defeat the ends of action,
if only by corrupting the actor, is not an issue that can be decided in

71. The position taken in the text is at variance with what is perhaps the prevailing view of this conflict, a view that reflects the position taken by Max Weber
in his now classic essay, "Politics as a Vocation" (cf. *From Max Weber: Essays in
Sociology*, ed. H. H. Gerth and C. Wright Mills [New York: Oxford University
Press, 1958], pp. 77ff.). In this essay Weber wrote: "We must be clear about the
fact that all ethically oriented conduct may be guided by two fundamentally differing and irreconcilably opposed maxims: conduct can be oriented to an 'ethic of
ultimate ends' or to an 'ethic of responsibility.' This is not to say that an ethic of
ultimate ends is identical with irresponsibility, or that an ethic of responsibility is
identical with unprincipled opportunism. Naturally nobody says that. However, there
is an abysmal contrast between conduct that follows the maxim of an ethic of
ultimate ends—that is, in religious terms, 'The Christian does rightly and leaves
the result with the Lord'—and conduct that follows the maxim of an ethic of
responsibility, in which case one has to give an account of the foreseeable results of
one's actions." In contrasting an "ethic of responsibility" with an "ethic of ultimate ends," Weber presumably implies that an ethic of responsibility is *not* an
ethic of ultimate ends. But this is not true—at any rate, it is not necessarily true.
The statesman has as his highest moral imperative the preservation of the state
entrusted to his care. If we say that he must act responsibly we mean that he must
take all possible care to estimate the results or consequences of his actions. In saying
this, however, we do not mean that the statesman has no ultimate end. Although
the statesman must act prudently in preserving the state entrusted to his care, he
must nevertheless preserve the state whatever the means. We might just as well say
then that Weber's ethic of responsibility is an ethic of ultimate ends precisely because the statesman must—if necessary—subordinate the means to the ends of
action. On the other hand, we might just as accurately call Weber's ethic of ultimate ends an "ethic of ultimate means." The statement that the Christian does
rightly and leaves the results with the Lord means, if anything, that certain acts
(means) are never to be employed whatever the consequences that may follow from
their nonemployment. The Christian does not feel "irresponsible" for the consequences any more than the statesman feels "irresponsible" for the means. It is
simply a question of whether one accepts absolute restraints on action, whatever
the ends sought, or whether one does not do so.

the abstract. No doubt, the task of the moralist would be greatly simplified if it could be so decided. He would then enjoy the best of both worlds. If certain means are never to be employed or threatened, it is not only because they are in and of themselves evil but also because they are, after all, imprudent, a form of mistaken calculation. Unfortunately, experience shows that good may come of evil, that the use of evil means does not always corrupt the actor, and that it is much too simple to conceive of means as themselves the ends of action in the very process of coming into existence.[72] If certain means are to be absolutely forbidden, they must be forbidden quite apart from these considerations. If certain means are to be absolutely forbidden, they must be so forbidden because of their intrinsic evil. If one may never do evil that good may come, it is not—or not primarily—because the good probably will not come but simply because one may never do evil.

Taken by itself, however, the bare assertion that there are absolute restraints on the means permitted even in war does not tell us what it is that is absolutely forbidden. Nor are we appreciably enlightened with respect to that conduct absolutely forbidden when we are told further that we may never do evil, or threaten to do evil, so that good may come. If evil signifies that which is absolutely forbidden, we have simply been told what we already knew or should have known: that which is absolutely forbidden is evidently that which may never be done. The position that certain means may never be employed or threatened, even to preserve the independence and continuity of the state, does clearly mean that the state cannot be considered a supreme value for men. Moreover, if the survival of the state cannot serve to justify certain means, it follows that those values the state, and perhaps only the state, may serve

72. Were the means employed by the Allies in World War II little more than the ends of action in the very process of coming into existence? Did they corrupt, as presumably they invariably must corrupt, the actors? It requires a very perverse reading of contemporary history to answer these questions affirmatively. Yet there are many Christian moralists who continue to insist that these questions must be answered affirmatively. To affirm the former is not of course to justify the means employed in World War II. It is simply to say that the moralist who condemns certain means as intrinsically evil cannot expect to support his argument on every occasion by absolutizing what are in reality no more than prudential maxims. The temptation to do just this, however, is very great. Thus in recent years the condemnation by Christian moralists of policies of deterrence has often proceeded not only, and not even primarily, from the position that such policies imply the intent to do evil, and are accordingly to be considered in the same proscribed category as the doing of evil, but from the position that they are ultimately a form of bad calculation (i.e., either that they will issue in catastrophic conflict, or that they will corrupt the actors even if they do not issue in such conflict, etc.). As the age of deterrence progresses, the latter argument becomes less and less persuasive—even, one suspects, for those who advance it.

to protect also cannot be considered supreme. But these conclusions, however significant they may be, still do not afford us much guidance with respect to that conduct which is absolutely forbidden.

It is another matter to identify the one restraint that in some form must be observed in war if this activity is to prove amenable to substantive limitation. Apart from the limitation the ends of war may impose on the conduct of war, it is apparent that this conduct can be significantly limited only by limiting those individuals who may be made the objects of attack. It is equally apparent that the only viable basis of the distinction to be drawn between those who may be made the objects of attack and those who may not be so made must rest upon the degree of involvement or participation in warlike activities. Historically, the importance of this distinction for the law of war is generally acknowledged. The development of a body of rules regulating and limiting the conduct of war has been largely synonymous with the development of the principle that distinguishes between the armed forces (combatants) and the civilian population (noncombatants) of belligerents and requires belligerents both to refrain from making the civilian population the deliberate object of attack and to safeguard this population from injuries not incidental to operations undertaken against combatant forces and other legitimate military objectives. The decline in this century of the practices traditionally regulating the manner of warfare has also been largely synonymous with the decline of this principle.

It is the same principle that forms the main limitation on the just conduct of war. In the doctrine of *bellum justum*, however, the norm forbidding the direct and intentional attack on noncombatants represents an absolute injunction. At any rate, it is only with those versions of *bellum justum* which do so regard this norm that we are here concerned. For it is only where the prohibition against the deliberate killing of noncombatants is considered absolute that a clear conflict may arise between the necessities of the state and the requirements of an ethic that presumably sets limits to these necessities. In the theory of the just war, the distinction in question is held to define the essential difference between war and murder—that is, the essential difference between the permitted and the forbidden taking of human life. It is the deliberate killing of the innocent that is always to be avoided, that may never be justified even as a reprisal measure taken in response to similar measures of an adversary. This is, in substance, the evil that may never be done, or threatened, so that good may come.

Despite the absolute character given it, whether and to what extent the norm forbidding the direct and intentional attack upon the innocent does set significant limits to the necessities of the state are not self-answering questions. Restraints may be absolute in character yet innocuous in terms of the specific behavior they are interpreted to forbid. In forbidding the deliberate attack upon the innocent, we must still determine who are the innocent and what constitutes a deliberate attack upon them. The answer to the first question does not present considerable difficulties provided only that the innocent are equated with noncombatants and the latter identified—as, indeed, they have been traditionally identified—by the remoteness of their relationship to warlike activities. Difficulties may of course arise and persist over the precise characteristics requisite for noncombatant status, but unless the very concept of noncombatant status is itself suppressed these difficulties are not likely to prove intractable.[73] The answer to the second question does pose very considerable difficulties, however, and it can scarcely be said that these difficulties have been any more satisfactorily resolved by theorists of *bellum justum* than by international jurists. That the former attribute an absolute character to the norm forbidding the direct and intentional attack upon the innocent only serves to accentuate rather than to resolve these difficulties.

In the practice of states the principle distinguishing between combatants and noncombatants has never been interpreted as giving the latter complete protection from the hazards of war. It has always been

73. Even so, these difficulties do at least indicate that the absolute prohibition against attacking the innocent rests on a distinction that is far more relative and pragmatic in application than is commonly admitted. Theorists of *bellum justum* regularly point out that the concept of "innocence" corresponds to the concept of "noncombatancy" and, indeed, use these presumably corresponding terms interchangeably. In state practice, however, the distinction between combatants and noncombatants has always had a relative character in the sense that at the very least its application has been dependent both on the manner in which states organize for war and on the technology with which they conduct war. To this extent, then, it has always been true that the scope of noncombatancy could vary, and has varied, considerably; hence the scope of innocence could also vary, and has varied, considerably. Moreover, the relative character of the concept of noncombatant status is unavoidably a function as well of the degree of remoteness from warlike activities that is held to constitute this status. It is no doubt true that if the concept of noncombatant status is to be granted in principle, remoteness from warlike activities cannot be pushed beyond certain limits. Yet it must be admitted that what these limits are in practice is an issue over which reasonable men may differ and have frequently differed. Theorists of *bellum justum* sometimes assume that because the concept of innocence, like the concept of noncombatancy, depends upon objective behavior and not a subjective state of mind (i.e., personal innocence or guilt) this concept is thereby susceptible to objective determination. But this is not true. Though the status of noncombatants, as well as the status of innocents, depends on objective behavior, the determination of either depends on a subjective appreciation of this behavior. In the subjective interpretation of this behavior there is no apparent reason for according greater weight to the insights of Christian moralists than to the insights of others.

accepted that if war is to prove at all possible the immunity of non-combatants must be qualified, and substantially so. Thus the investment, bombardment, siege, and assault of fortified places, including towns and cities, have always been recognized as legitimate measures of warfare, even though such places may contain large numbers of peaceful inhabitants. More generally, belligerents have never been required to cease military operations because of the presence of noncombatants within the immediate area of these operations or to refrain from attacking military objectives simply because of the proximity of military objectives to the noncombatant population. These qualifications to the principle of noncombatant immunity are to be explained in terms of military necessity, which permits belligerents to take those measures required for the success of military operations and not otherwise forbidden by the law of war (in this instance, not forbidden by some rule other than the principle distinguishing between combatants and noncombatants). To this extent, then, the scope afforded to the principle of noncombatant immunity has always been dependent upon the scope afforded to military necessity.

The same dependence upon military necessity is apparent in considering the concept of military objective. Time and again the attempt has been made to limit the concept of military objective by freeing it from the uncertainty and potential expansiveness of military necessity. Time and again the attempt has failed and has served only to emphasize the dependence in practice of the meaning given to military objective on the meaning given to military necessity. The essentially indeterminate character of the concept of military objective therefore reflects the essentially indeterminate character of the concept of military necessity, dependent as the latter is in any given period upon the manner in which societies organize for and conduct war, the technology with which war is waged, and the ends for which war is undertaken. No doubt, it is true that if the principle of noncombatant immunity is to be retained at all in war there must be *some* limits placed on this relationship of dependency. Whatever the meaning given to military necessity, noncombatants cannot as such be considered a military objective. But short of the clear negation of the principle of noncombatant immunity, what these limits must be in practice has never been clear. All that can be said with assurance—all that could ever be said with assurance—is only that the scope of the immunity accorded the civilian population is largely dependent upon the meaning given to the concept of military objective and that the concept of military objective varies as the character of war, hence the character of military necessity, varies. Moreover, even if it were possible to resolve the uncertainty that marks the concept of military objective, there would still remain the problem of determining the extent of the incidental or indirect injury that may be inflicted upon the civilian population in the course of attacking military objectives. The answer to this latter problem, however, remains as uncertain and controverted as does the answer to the problem of what constitutes a legitimate military objective. To the extent the attempt has been made to answer it, the basis of that attempt has largely been through recourse to the very principle—military necessity—that accounts for the uncertainty attending the scope of military objective and that, in consequence, gave rise to the problem in the first place.

The general import of these considerations is clear enough. However critical the principle distinguishing between combatants and noncombatants may be for the regulation and limitation of war, this principle has always had a relative and contingent character in state practice as well as in the law that emerged from this practice. As such, the scope afforded it has always been subject to the imperious claims of necessity, the manifestations of which in the conduct of war are to be found in the claims of military necessity and of reprisal. Indeed, so pervasive is this subjection that belligerents have been able in practice to reduce the effective scope of the principle of noncombatant immunity almost to a vanishing point while nevertheless affirming the continued validity of this principle. Even where the attack upon noncombatants is openly avowed as direct and intentional, the continued affirmation of the principle of noncombatant immunity may be given a semblance of plausibility if the action is represented as a reprisal taken in response to similar behavior of an adversary.

In giving the principle of noncombatant immunity an absolute and unconditioned character, the doctrine of *bellum justum* presumably rejects this subordination to the claims of necessity. Since it may clearly do so only at a very high price, however, the temptation is understandably great to pose a rejection which, in terms of the specific consequences that may be drawn from it (hence the practical limits it imposes on military necessity), is more apparent than real. If *bellum justum* requires that the innocent never be made the deliberate object of attack, the question nevertheless remains in what circumstances this absolute prohibition is deemed to have been transgressed. In answering this question the theorists of the just war have very little to say that is distinctive or instructive with respect to what constitutes a legitimate military objective. Apart from being told what we already knew—that noncombatants cannot as such be considered a legitimate military objective—we are left in quite as uncertain a position as before over what does constitute a legitimate military objective. Moreover, it must be made clear that no more than international law does *bellum justum* require a belligerent to refrain from attacking military objectives simply because of the proximity of these objectives to the civilian population. What *bellum justum* does require is that in attacking military objectives the death and injury done to noncombatants be beside the intention—at any rate, beside the direct or positive intention—of the attacker, that this death and injury done to noncombatants not constitute a means for achieving an otherwise legitimate military end, and that, finally, the evil effect of the action not prove disproportionate to the good—or, at any rate, the morally sanctioned—effect.[74]

These requirements constitute the essential contribution of *bellum justum* to the vital issue of means. That they fail to provide a clear let alone a satisfactory solution to this vital issue is perhaps less a criticism of them than a testimony to the intractability of the issue to which they are addressed. Nor is it the essential indeterminacy of intent that compels this conclusion, since *bellum justum* plainly requires more than subjective intention in judging the quality of action. Not only does it emphasize along with intent the objective consequences of action; for the most part it deduces intent from these consequences. Whether or not the actor is deemed to have intended to do evil is determined, in the absence of acknowledged intent to do evil, by inquiry into the means he has chosen. The character of the means he has chosen is in turn determined by inquiry into the action itself, above all by inquiry into the consequences following from or the consequences that might reason-

74. The general principle involved here, and which comprises the above conditions, is commonly termed the principle of double effect. There are some variations in the formulation of these conditions. Thus it is often said that of the two effects of a permitted action, the first, and good, effect is directly or positively intended, while the second, and evil, effect must be beside the actor's intention or only indirectly intended. In any event, the evil effect cannot be a means to the good effect. Hence, in the chain of consequences or in the order of causality—though not necessarily in order of time—the good effect must either precede or be immediate with the evil effect, else the evil effect would presumably cause, or be a means to, the good. The principle of double effect therefore attempts to reconcile the injunction against doing evil that good may come with the taking of certain acts that are known, and even known with certainty, to entail evil effects. In the case of war it is evident that this attempted reconciliation is mandatory if war is to be sanctioned at all, since evil effects of varying magnitude—i.e., the death and injury of the innocent—form an unavoidable effect of war. Of the three conditions set out in the text, only the first two are examined in succeeding pages. The third requirement, that of proportionality, has already been discussed in relation to the justice of war in general. The indeterminacy of this test in a narrower context is almost as great as it must prove to be in a broader context, even though some writers attempt to reduce this indeterminacy by insisting that the effects, both evil and good, must be the "immediate" effects. No useful purpose is served by raising once again those considerations brought forth in earlier pages. Even so, the extreme limits to which the test of proportionality has been pushed by some moralists are significant and will be noted in a later connection.

ably have been expected to follow from the action. Yet it is precisely this dependence on the objective—indeed, on the quantitative—character of action to which just war theorists are ultimately driven that lays bare the largely relative nature of the judgments they must make.[75] In practice, whether the death and injury done to the innocent is directly intended or is beside the intention of the actor is determined by the scope of this death and injury. But there are no objective criteria for determining how much death and injury may be done to the innocent while still preserving the right intention, or, conversely, when such death and injury must establish the wrong intention. In the absence of such criteria, it is clear that the judgments men make will be influenced in varying degree, whether consciously or unconsciously, by the claims of necessity. What was apparently excluded at the front door is therefore admitted in large measure through the back door.

Nor is this all. The attempt to reconcile the necessities of war—of any war—with the injunction against doing evil that good may come can be undertaken only by virtue of an implausible, or, at any rate, an artificial, notion of means. If it is known with certainty that in attacking a military objective death and injury will be inflicted upon the innocent, if it is known that two effects will follow inevitably from the action, the destruction of the military objective and the death and injury of noncombatants, is it still plausible to assert as theorists of *bellum justum* do assert that the one effect is a means while the other effect is not?

75. It is not enough to admit this dependence without drawing the full consequences from that admission. Thus Paul Ramsey writes: "It is the virtue, and perhaps the irrelevance, of modern formulations of the rule of double effect in the theory of the just war that, by requiring more than subjective intention, by requiring that objectively also the intrinsically evil effect of the slaying of innocent people be not a means to whatsoever military advantage, we are brought close to the rejection of all modern warfare." *War and the Christian Conscience*, p. 64. But how can we tell whether or not this slaying is a means rather than a second or indirect effect? Surely we cannot do so through analyzing intentions as such, since the indeterminacy of intent gave rise to the problem in the first place. Nor can we do so through study of the sequence or order of action. The second effect need not come later in time. Ramsey goes on to note: "It is a question of which effect is, in the objective order, incidental to which, even when both effects are produced at the same time from a single action." But this is clearly a matter of quantity then—of objective consequences. Another writer, discussing the principle of double effect in much the same terms as Ramsey, declares: "It is nonsense to pretend that you do not intend to do what is the means to your chosen end. Otherwise there is absolutely no substance to the Pauline teaching that we may not do evil that good may come." G. E. M. Anscombe, "War and Murder," in *Nuclear Weapons and Christian Conscience*, ed. Walter Stein (London: Merlin Press, 1961), p. 59. This statement leaves in abeyance the critical issue: What are the means you take to your chosen end? Are they determined by inquiry into the intention of the actor or by inquiry into the nature of the end the actor seeks and the character of the measures without which this end cannot be achieved?

Ordinarily, we regard a certain effect as a means to an end if that end cannot be secured without this effect, if the realization of the one is dependent, and is known to be dependent, upon the occurrence of the other. If this view is accepted, the death and injury inflicted on the innocent in the course of attacking a military objective is as much a means as is the destruction of the military objective. Whereas the one effect, destruction of the military objective, is a means to the end of victory in war, the other effect, the death and injury of noncombatants, is indirectly a means to the same end and directly a means to the end of destroying the military objective. Both effects, however, must be considered as means. It is true that one may avoid this conclusion, and thereby deny that the effect of inflicting death and injury on noncombatants is a means, by equating the notion of means with the question of intent. On this latter view, the one effect is a means because it is intended while the other effect, although it is foreseen, is not a means because it is presumably not intended, at least not directly intended, only reluctantly permitted. But this view not only must raise those difficulties attending the determination of intent considered above, it must also impute a meaning to intent that is very questionable. If it is known that an act will have certain evil consequences, and the act is nevertheless taken, it is plausible to contend that some of these consequences were not intended only if intent is made synonymous with wish or desire. This equation, however, accords neither with ordinary usage nor with common sense. We may not wish or desire something to happen, yet we may intend it to happen. The reason for this distinction is simply that to intend means to have in mind as something to be done or brought about. Thus we may not wish or desire a certain consequence of action and consider this consequence as tragic or as an evil. Even so, we intend this consequence if we know that it will result from a certain action and we nevertheless take this action.[76]

76. There is a further point to be made in this connection. To say, as do the theorists of *bellum justum*, that an act must "positively intend only the good effect and merely tolerate the evil effect" is to give a moral significance to the notion of intent without resolving the real difficulty. Objectively, we still intend the one effect just as much as we intend the other effect. It does not alter matters to characterize the one effect as positively intended and the other effect as merely tolerated. Moreover, even the moral significance implied thereby is not without difficulty. When a military objective is attacked, death and suffering always result if only for combatants. Do we "positively intend" this, is it a "good effect"? To the Christian moralist it would hardly seem so. From his point of view what we should "positively intend" is to repel injustice. The "good effect" is the repelling of injustice or perhaps the vindication of justice. The death and suffering inflicted on combatants is not as such a good effect. It, too, is an evil that is tolerated, though only tolerated, in order to achieve a good end (effect). Of course, it is an evil that is far more tolerable than other evils—e.g., the death and suffering of noncombatants. Once again,

It is altogether understandable that theorists of *bellum justum* have been so insistent upon tying an implausible notion of means to an equally implausible notion of intent, in view of the critical purpose this association serves. Once it is abandoned the attempt to reconcile the necessities of any war with the injunction that evil may not be done must also be abandoned. Yet to abandon this vain reconciliation is not also to abandon the position that means must remain limited; to acknowledge that it is not possible to wage war without doing evil is not thereby to open the door to any and every evil. There are still means and means, just as there is still evil and evil. If the issue that must be faced and somehow resolved is not whether one may do evil that good may come but rather how much evil one may do that any good may come, it is not for this reason without significance. There is surely a very important difference between the destruction of a city in order to destroy a military objective within or near the city and the destruction of the military objective, although destruction of the military objective inevitably involves inflicting some death and injury on noncombatants. There is still a very important difference even if we acknowledge that in both cases the death and injury done to the innocent is a means to the desired effect (end) and that in both cases this death and injury is intended. Whereas in the one case the death and injury done to noncombatants is, or may be, itself desired, in the other case it is not. If the one means is compatible with warfare that still retains significant limits, the other means is either not compatible or much less so. Above all, perhaps, is simply the difference in the objective consequences, the quantitative effects, of the two actions.

There is no compelling reason, then, why we must accept the contention that if it is once accepted that evil must be done in war, the issue of means is dissolved and any behavior sanctioned. This result may follow. The assumption that it must follow is no more compelling than the assumption that if men only believe that evil may never be done their behavior will thereby be restrained. Instead of restraining their behavior, the belief that evil may never be done may only strain their ingenuity. If evil may never be done, the practical significance of this injunction will still depend on the manner in which doing evil is

---

the point must be stressed that at issue here is not whether one evil is greater than, or less tolerable than, the other evil but whether both evils (effects) must be considered as means. This issue cannot be resolved by endless, and inconclusive, discussion of the question of intent. Even if we were to concede that what is "indirectly intended" or "reluctantly permitted" is somehow different from what is "directly intended" or "positively permitted," it does not follow that the effect only indirectly intended is not a means. It, too, is a means, though it is a means that may be distinguished from the means that is directly intended or positively permitted.

conceived. Given sufficient ingenuity of conception, war takes on the character of an event in which ever-greater evil effects may result yet apparently through no evil acts. In the most recent, and perhaps the most impressive, example of this ingenuity of conception it is argued that even the waging of a thermonuclear war need not imply the doing of evil so long as belligerents employ their weapons only against counter-force targets and other legitimate military objectives. The death and injury suffered by civilian populations would admittedly constitute a very great evil, but these evil effects might still be justified. At any rate, these evil effects, so long as they could somehow be reconciled with the requirement of proportionality, would still not be the doing of evil. And if this use of nuclear weapons is not the doing of evil, it seems clearer still that the threat to use nuclear weapons against military objectives need not be considered forbidden. Moreover, in order to remove lingering doubts about an intent to do evil, the threat to use nuclear weapons against military objectives may be attended by the express renunciation of an intent ever to use these weapons directly against a civilian population. In view of the magnitude of the expected destruction that would still be indirectly inflicted on the civilian population in the course of a direct attack on military objectives, deterrence would in all likelihood remain effective. Finally, however frequent and vehement the disclaimer of an intent directly to attack the civilian population of a potential adversary, even as a measure of reprisal in response to a similar attack, the character of nuclear weapons is such that an adversary can never be assured the weapons will not be used in this manner. This residual uncertainty results not only from the inherently ambiguous character of these weapons; it also, and perhaps more importantly, results from men's inability to predict with any real confidence what the consequences will be of using nuclear weapons and, indeed, whether their use can be reasonably controlled at all. This residual uncertainty forms the capstone of the deterrent system; it cannot be removed from this system short of the dismantling of the system through destruction of the weapons themselves.[77]

77. The position summarized above has been articulated at length by Paul Ramsey, *The Limits on Nuclear War* (New York: Council on Religion and International Affairs, 1963) and "More Unsolicited Advice to Vatican Council II," in *Peace, the Churches and the Bomb* (New York: Council on Religion and International Affairs, 1965). What makes Ramsey's writings of particular interest is not only the ingenuity with which he develops the argument for a just deterrent strategy and a just nuclear war strategy, should deterrence fail, but that he does so while remaining firmly committed to the more general position that the distinctive quality of *bellum justum* must be found in the restraints on the means of warfare, that there are certain means which because of their intrinsic evil may never be justifiably employed and that a largely teleological view of the Christian ethic, in refusing to place abso-

lute limits on means, leads to the suspension—indeed, to the ultimate perversion—of an essential part of that ethic. This general position Ramsey set out in detail in his earlier study, *War and the Christian Conscience*. In the two later essays, cited above, he is concerned to show, first, that if war is to be a "rational" and "politically purposive activity" it must be predominantly a "trial of strength" rather than a "test of resolve" or "battle of wills" and, second, that if war is so conceived it is possible to fashion a just—*and effective*—deterrent strategy as well as a just policy for waging nuclear war. Ramsey assumes that if war is a trial of strength it must thereby have limited (and objective) purposes; accordingly, it must also be conducted by limited means. If, however, war is a test of wills it must have essentially unlimited (and subjective) purposes; accordingly, it very probably must also be conducted by unlimited means. In terms of nuclear strategies, the former concept of war will go no higher than counterforce warfare whereas the latter concept may—and probably will—go to city exchanges (*The Limits on Nuclear War*, pp. 17–20). The argument is unpersuasive, however, because the essential distinction on which it rests is untenable. Will, or resolve, is a decisive ingredient in any "trial of strength." It is indeed difficult to imagine the character of a trial of strength that at the same time would not also be a trial of will or test of resolve. Of course, it is another matter to argue that the measures taken in war should be roughly commensurate or proportionate to the purposes of war and, accordingly, that war *both* as a trial of strength and as a test of will should reflect this commensurability. This counsel of perfection, which in practice men have seldom been able to meet, still says nothing about the nature of the purposes men should entertain in war. Instead, it merely says that whatever these purposes may be, the measures taken in war should be commensurate to them. Even so, one apparent qualification to this counsel is the sometimes advantageous tactic of attempting to obtain one's purposes either without a trial of strength altogether or with a minimum trial of strength by appearing more determined (resolved) than an opponent. If there are obvious limits to this tactic, they are very difficult to fix with any precision if only for the reason that the worth men set on the purposes or interests for which they fight, and consequently the lengths to which they are prepared to go in order to obtain or to defend these purposes or interests, are difficult to fix with any precision. It is no adequate answer to this consideration to insert the antidote of common sense and to insist that some interests are still more important than other interests, which is undoubtedly true, or that an opponent cannot be persuaded that all your interests are equally vital to you simply because you insist they are equally vital, which is also true. Despite these necessary, though obvious, limitations the fact remains that in most major conflicts there is a significant, and persistent, area of uncertainty in which one may obtain one's purposes by appearing more determined, and by being more determined, than an opponent. Moreover, there is the critically important consideration that the temptation to substitute a trial of wills for a trial of strength is roughly commensurate to the prospect of horrendous consequences issuing from a trial of strength. The relevance of this consideration in the case of almost any trial of strength between nuclear powers need not be labored. Indeed, to the extent that this prospect appears so horrendous as to render increasingly incommensurable the relation between the consequences of employing nuclear arms and the purposes or interests to be secured through such employment, to that extent the temptation, amounting almost to a compulsion, arises to substitute a trial of wills for what was heretofore a trial of strength and a trial of wills. In other terms, the trial of wills to which we give the name deterrence increasingly becomes the modern analogue of the wars of former periods; instead of "acting" out their conflicts, men are increasingly driven to "play" them out. In a nuclear age, then, the "spiritualization" of war appears inevitable unless nuclear powers are to abandon war altogether (i.e., in spirit and in form) in their mutual relations or to "conventionalize" nuclear wars. Ramsey's argument provides no persuasive considerations that the latter wars may prove feasible. Despite his sometimes all-too-

It is roughly in this manner that the attempt has been made to bring both nuclear deterrence and even the waging of thermonuclear war into apparent conformity with the requirements on means laid down by *bellum justum*. The cumulative effect of that attempt is to reduce to a hollow shell the injunction against doing, or intending to do, evil that good may come. Not only does it strain the notion of doing evil beyond reasonable limit, but even on the basis of its own presuppositions it must rely on the threat to do evil. That this threat is for the most part implicit rather than explicit, that it largely inheres in the nature of the weapons themselves and men's inability to predict the consequences of using these weapons rather than in the overt threat to use them in a certain manner, does not alter matters. The expectations men entertain of the way in which nuclear weapons would be used if deterrence failed form as much a part of the reality of deterrence, so long as these expectations persist, as do the weapons on which such expectations rest. In consequence, whatever the express articulation of deterrent strategies, so long as men continue to entertain these expectations the effectiveness of the deterrent threat will continue to rest largely on what is interpreted as a threat to do evil. And given the novelty of the weapons that form the basis of deterrent systems, there is, after all, quite as much to be said for the view that the use of nuclear weapons would not and could not be confined to military objectives as there is to be said for the con-

---

confident statements about "limited counterforces warfare," his argument that just deterrent strategies are possible rests in part precisely on the uncertainty—indeed, the skepticism—that nuclear war can be so limited. Finally, in drawing a distinction between trials of strength and trials of wills, Ramsey neglects altogether the consideration that in any conflict, nuclear or otherwise, the importance of will depends upon the stakes of conflict. Thus in what is primarily a hegemonial conflict will becomes supremely important precisely because what is at stake is not whose will is to prevail in order to secure some other, and perhaps limited, objective but whose will is to prevail in order to prevail. Now one may refuse to consider this case, one may dismiss it out of hand as Ramsey is disposed to do simply by excluding it from the realm of "concrete policy," but in doing so one also dismisses the most important conflicts that arise among men. An analysis that declares in effect that it will not consider hegemonial struggles, that it will not deal with conflicts in which the motives of vainglory and of survival are inextricably mixed yet all-important, is largely irrelevant to the present period of state relations, not to speak of other periods. Nor can one get around this criticism by using such question-begging terms as Ramsey's *"political* limits," "controlling objectives," "choiceworthy political effects," etc. If these terms are intended to rule out of order conflicts in which the desire to be first or in which the desire to survive are paramount, what point can they have when these are precisely the critical conflicts with which we must deal? And even if we take these terms seriously, to argue, for example, that hegemony or survival are not "choiceworthy political effects" is, to say the least, a rather curious reading of history. If, however, we read history more normally, they are not only the effects men have most desired, but also the effects that render the element of will supremely important.

trary view. To be sure, it may be argued that even if deterrent strategies rely on the threat to do evil, that threat still does not necessarily imply an actual intent to do evil. If what is evil to do must also be evil to intend to do, however small the chance that this intent will have to be carried out, it does not follow that what is evil to intend to do must also be evil to threaten to do. Nuclear strategies may therefore rely, it is argued, on a threat to do evil that still need not betray an actual intent to do evil. And even if the moralist may question the justification of threatening to do evil, though not intending to do evil, there is still a difference between a threat of action that carries no intent to act and a threat that does do so. But all this argument succeeds in establishing is a distinction that no one would care to deny: that is, that a threat to act may be distinguished from an intent to act. It does not indicate how the threat on which deterrence is based, if only by implication, can be effectively maintained without also maintaining the intent to carry out the threat if necessary. Still less does it indicate how, in practice, an intentless threat may be distinguished from an intentful threat without putting the threat to the one and only reliable test. In the absence of this test, however, it must be admitted that the argument cannot be conclusively disproved. All that can be said, though it seems quite enough, is that in the absence of very strong evidence to the contrary, there is no reason to assume that a threat to do evil does not also imply an intent to do evil.[78]

78. These remarks ought not to be interpreted as an acceptance of the view that what is evil to do is also evil to threaten to do, and to intend to do, whatever the consequences of refusing to threaten evil and however small the chance that the threat will ever have to be acted on. It is not self-evident why what must be evil to do must also be evil to threaten to do, quite apart from the circumstances attending and the consequences following this threat. The view that if an act would be evil to do it must also be evil to intend to do may take several forms. In its pure form, one must never intend to do evil simply because one ought never to entertain an evil intent, and this quite apart either from the prospect that the intent will have to be acted on or from the consequences the intent (not the action) may have for those who entertain it. In its less than pure form, one must never intend to do evil because of the possibility that at some time, in some circumstances, one will do evil. Finally, there is the argument that even if the intent may never have to be acted on, one ought never to intend to do evil in view of the debilitating consequences that entertaining this intent will have for its possessor. In its pure form, then, the injunction against intending evil is evidently independent of calculation and consequence, whereas in its impure forms this injunction is just as evidently dependent on calculation and consequence. Moreover, in its impure forms this injunction is open to question when applied to a given situation precisely because it is dependent on calculation and consequence. Thus the condemnation of strategies of deterrence which are based on these impure, or less than absolute, versions of the injunction against doing evil are open to challenge and to possible rejection on their own chosen grounds. It may well be, for example, that the possibility of deterrent strategies breaking down is so small as to be negligible. And if this possibility is negligible, or

The conclusion to which these considerations lead is that if we are not deliberately to press *bellum justum* into the mold of reason of state, there is an irreconcilable conflict between the requirements of *bellum justum* and the requirements of deterrent strategies. This conclusion is not prompted in the first place by the unpersuasive character of the attempts that have been made to reconcile possible deterrent strategies with the requirements on means laid down by *bellum justum*.[79] Even if these attempts were more persuasive than they are, they would fail in what must be their fundamental purpose, which is to show that in principle as well as in practice such reconciliation is possible. It is not enough to demonstrate that a hypothetical deterrent strategy or an equally hypothetical strategy for waging thermonuclear war may just possibly be

---

is believed to be negligible, the consequences of holding this intent may not prove debilitating at all for the holders. Even if this possibility is not believed to be negligible, it may not prove debilitating. Indeed, we have already noted that what evidence there is seems to point to the conclusion that, on the whole, deterrent strategies have not proven debilitating for those societies maintaining them (cf. pp. 284ff.). At any rate, the argument from consequences is dependent on an examination of consequences, so far as we are in a position to do so, and a weighing of these consequences against the possible consequences of abandoning a deterrent strategy. By implication, it also involves a comparison of the values gained and sacrificed by each set of consequences and the making of a choice. But this must mean that the values involved, including the value of avoiding the intent to do evil, are only relative in character. In marked contrast, the Christian moralists who insist on the pure form of the injunction against intending to do evil must unreservedly condemn deterrent strategies, if the considerations put forth in the text above are sound. Even if deterrence is acknowledged as a means to a very desired end (world peace), and even if deterrence is acknowledged to operate with something akin to certainty, particularly if the threat is made sufficiently horrendous, it must nevertheless be condemned if it implies the intent to do evil. Given the consequences that would probably follow from the condemnation of deterrence, if such condemnation were acted upon, the understandable reluctance on the part of many moralists to avoid that result has been productive of ingenious efforts toward condoning deterrence yet insisting upon the pure form of the principle that evil may never be intended that good may come. The "psychology of deterrence" of course encourages such efforts. Thus, in addition to the distinction drawn between threat and intent, discussed above, it has been urged that deterrence requires us to distinguish between an interim and a final or ultimate intention. According to this argument, there is no ultimate evil intention involved in deterrence, only an interim intention to do evil. Paradoxically, one's ultimate intention can be free from evil only if one's interim intention is evil. If I really intend to do evil, and the adversary knows I really intend to do evil, I will never have to do evil. My interim intent not only saves me from having to carry out this intent; the knowledge of this permits me ultimately not to intend to do evil at all.

There is no end to this sort of casuistry. However much these efforts may elicit our admiration, and even sympathy, they fail to persuade.

79. We must emphasize the term "possible." It is ludicrous to speak of reconciling "actual" deterrent strategies with the requirements on means laid down by *bellum justum*, since these strategies are expressly based on the threat of attacking civilian populations if necessary. We have no reason to suppose that this threat does not correspond to real intent.

made compatible with *bellum justum*. What must instead be shown is that the limiting conditions that may just possibly establish this compatibility can also be made, as a matter of principle and of practice, politically effective yet remain self-contained. No one has shown this, however, and it is altogether unlikely that anyone will be able to show this. All that can be shown is that the principal, and apparently the indispensable, sanction for the limits required of the just war, nuclear or otherwise, remains the meaningful threat of nuclear war, which clearly exceeds these limits.[80]

80. A very different view of the possibility of reconciling the requirements of *bellum justum* with the requirements of nuclear deterrence is taken by Paul Ramsey in *The Limits of Nuclear War* and "More Unsolicited Advice to Vatican Council II." Ramsey believes such reconciliation is possible if we distinguish with sufficient clarity between a "declared" and a "real" intention and if we assess correctly the "shared deterrence in the collateral damage inflicted by use of nuclear weapons over legitimate targets only." Although both points have been dealt with in the text, some additional remarks on the second point are in order. Ramsey's collateral damage is mainly the damage inflicted on noncombatants in the course of attacking military objectives. It is, in his view, not only an effective form of deterrence ("mutual and enough, without ever thinking of executing city-hostages") but a just form of deterrence ("Legitimate deterrence is the indirect effect of the unavoidable indirect effects [collateral civil damage] of properly targeted and therefore justly intended and justly conducted war in the nuclear age."). "More Unsolicited Advice," pp. 46–47. We must ask, however, if purely counterforce deterrence has been "mutual and enough," why haven't nuclear powers been satisfied with it? The answer, it would appear, is that whereas the statesman knows that the limitation of violence is ultimately dependent on the threat of unlimited violence, Ramsey refuses to acknowledge this dependency. Besides, how limited is the nuclear war, hence the deterrent intent, Ramsey does consider compatible with *bellum justum*? Expert testimony indicates that between major nuclear powers a nuclear war limited to counterforces may still be expected to result in the deaths of perhaps a majority of the population of the participants. Even if we were to accept the view that this "indirect effect" of killing half a population would not be indiscriminate, there would remain the question of the proportionality of the action. Ramsey has correctly pointed out the indeterminacy of the test of proportionality. But if we are to retain this test at all, and we can scarcely discard it, the admitted indeterminacy of proportionality cannot be simply caricatured. If there is a point beyond which the sheer destruction of nuclear war becomes disproportionate to any good sought, where does Ramsey draw this line? To answer by declaring that the line cannot be drawn in advance is to permit, if only by implication, the death and injury of any portion of an adversary's noncombatant population so long as this death and injury is the presumed indirect effect of properly targeted weapons. Finally, and perhaps most importantly, the question arises whether Ramsey's use of "collateral" effects, in terms of indirect civil damage, is not a clear abuse of the principle of double-effect, in the sense that this principle is understood by Ramsey as well as by other Christian moralists. In a critique of Ramsey's position on collateral damage, Walter Stein correctly identifies this abuse: "The decisive flaw in Ramsey's position is the dependence of his supposed 'collateral deterrence' upon effects essential to the purpose of nuclear strategy, directly indispensable, radically wanted—and yet to be sanctioned as 'side-effects.'" "The Limits of Nuclear War: Is a Just Deterrence Strategy Possible," in *Peace, The Churches and The Bomb*, p. 81.

There is no way, then, by which the present circle can be squared, no way by which the necessities of the nuclear power can be acknowledged yet the measures by which these necessities may be preserved always limited. In principle, there has never been a way by which the state's necessities can be acknowledged yet the measures by which these necessities may be preserved always limited. Nuclear weapons have not created this dilemma; they have simply illuminated it as never before and given it greater poignancy than men ever thought possible. Even so, whether and to what extent the requirements of *bellum justum* are reconcilable in practice with the necessities of the state has always been conditioned by circumstance. When circumstance has permitted a reconciliation in practice, the reconciliation has nevertheless been made possible by the meaningful, if perhaps unobtrusive and unoppressive, prospect of conflict that must exceed the limits of the just war. The age-old institution of reprisal is but the most obvious illustration of this truth that the possibility of restraint in men's behavior has been ultimately grounded in the possibility of a lack of restraint, or, in the terms of *bellum justum*, that the possibility of not doing evil has been ultimately grounded in the possibility of doing evil. Nevertheless, it is true that in the case of strategies of nuclear deterrence, the threat to do evil is more obtrusive and oppressive than ever before. It is also true that the dilemma which in practice could once be left in abeyance by those who insist that the state's necessities must always remain limited can no longer be left in abeyance. If the Christian moralist is not to empty *bellum justum* of all meaningful content, he has little choice but to condemn this most recent expression of necessity.

Thus it is particularly in the nuclear age that it is the fate of *bellum justum* either to risk political irrelevance or to risk sacrificing its distinctive claim in order to remain politically relevant. If the injunction against doing evil that good may come is taken seriously, the price is political irrelevance. If *bellum justum* is to remain politically relevant, the price is the erosion of the significance of "doing evil." For political relevance can be ultimately insured only by acceptance of the constituent principle of statecraft, which is that of reciprocity or retribution. Given the circumstances in which statecraft is conducted, the rejection of this principle is tantamount to the rejection of statecraft itself. Yet it is precisely this principle that *bellum justum* must reject if it is to set limits to the necessities of the state. That the point in practice at which the latent antagonism between the injunction against doing, or threatening, evil and the principle of "like for like" must become overt cannot be determined in the abstract and with certainty does not mean that it cannot be determined at all. That it depends upon circumstance and a judgment that may always prove fallible does not warrant the conclusion that it is therefore nonexistent. Whoever takes this position must refuse to acknowledge that in practice it is scarcely possible to identify the doing of evil at all.[81]

81. These general conclusions find significant illustration, it would seem, in the recent statement on war and deterrence adopted by the second Vatican Council. Cf. Second Vatican Council, *Pastoral Constitution on the Church in the Modern World, December 7, 1965* (National Catholic Welfare Conference, 1966), pp. 84–91. It is true that at the outset of its statement the Council places great emphasis on the "permanent binding force of universal natural law and its all-embracing principles." Moreover, it declares that "actions which deliberately conflict with these same principles, as well as orders commanding such actions are criminal, and blind obedience cannot excuse those who yield to them." When applied to the conduct of war these principles are interpreted by the Council to condemn, and to condemn absolutely, "total war" as well as "any act of war aimed indiscriminately at the destruction of entire cities or extensive areas along with their population. . . ." In this most solemn declaration the Council has insisted that there are at least some necessities that can never be justified, some means that are never permitted, and, accordingly, some evil that may never be done. But if the acts the Council condemns may express, and in certain circumstances clearly do express, the necessities of a nuclear power, it is equally clear that these acts do not express the most important necessities of a nuclear power. Nuclear war is a possibility and increasingly in the view of most observers only a remote possibility. Deterrence is the reality in which we live at present and the reality in which we are very likely to continue living for a considerable time. The necessities of the nuclear power do not find their principal manifestation today in that dreaded, but hopefully remote, possibility of nuclear war. They do find their principal manifestation in deterrence. It is clear, then, that the significance of this most recent expression of the Christian response to the ancient plea of reason of state must be found in the Council's position on deterrence. That position, however, is one of studied ambiguity. The Council declares that "many regard" the accumulation of arms for immediate retaliation against aggressive attack "the most effective way by which peace of a sort" can presently be maintained. Does the Council share this regard? It will not say so. Yet it does say that this accumulation of arms serves as a deterrent "in a way heretofore unknown." Does this imply indirect acceptance of what "many regard"? One cannot be sure. The Council disavows knowledge of the facts of deterrence ("whatever be the facts about this method of deterrence"). Yet it declares that "men should be convinced that the arms race . . . is not a safe way to preserve a steady peace." Why should men be so convinced, whatever be the facts? Again, the Council implies that "this method of deterrence" prevents war while aggravating the causes of war, that deterrence both lessens and increases the dangers of war. This analysis may very well be true, though one may still seriously question whether sums spent on new weapons prevent an "adequate remedy" for the "multiple miseries afflicting the modern world," just as one may question whether these multiple miseries constitute a significant cause of the war men hope to avoid. But how can the Council know all this without also knowing the facts about "this method of deterrence"? It is not the ambiguities marking the Council's analysis of deterrence that are of primary concern here, however, but its judgment of the morality of deterrence. Whatever the facts about this method of deterrence, what is the Council's position on the legitimacy of this method? In refusing to condemn the possession of nuclear weapons, does the Council thereby approve, however reluctantly, the possession of these weapons for deterrent purposes? It would seem so. Nor is this all. In failing to condemn strategies of deterrence that rest, and that are known to rest, in the ultimate resort, upon the

threat of destroying "entire cities," does the Council thereby approve, however reluctantly, these deterrent strategies? Again, it would seem so. If this is the most reasonable interpretation of the Council's position on the morality of deterrence, the substance of this position is that the means that may never be employed and the evil that may never be done may nevertheless be threatened. Thus does the Council attempt to reconcile the irreconcilable: the requirements of *bellum justum* and the necessities of a nuclear power.

4

THE CONQUEST OF FORCE

1

It cannot occasion surprise that many resist the argument developed in preceding pages. The principal conclusion to which that argument must lead has always given rise to unease and never more so than today. Now as in the past, its acceptance affords a justification for any measures deemed essential to the preservation and continuity of the state. In response to the demand that limits must somewhere be placed on the means permitted the statesman, however noble his professed ends, it asserts that, prudence apart, there are no limits the validity of which is independent of circumstance. As against the injunction that evil must not be done that good may come, it responds that not only may evil be done but that no determinate limits may be drawn to the evil that may be threatened, or done, if necessary for the preservation and continuity of the state. To the charge that the state is thereby made the source of value, it replies that the state, though not the source of value, indeed remains the indispensable condition of value.[1] In strategies of nuclear deterrence may be found only the latest, though in many respects the most striking, expression—one is even tempted to say the perfect

---

1. This statement should perhaps read: "though not necessarily the source of value." Even in this form, however, the qualification is significant. It is ignored by Carl Friedrich, who concludes his study of reason of state by declaring: "The fundamental problem of politics is how to organize the community for the purpose of making such final decisions [i.e., between conflicts of value]. The idea of reason of state represents one possible answer. This answer involves necessarily the assertion of a highest value. The highest value it asserts to be the life of the political community to which we belong. If we do not accept this decision, if we wish to assert another highest value, we cannot escape from rejecting the state and the idea of its ratio." *Constitutional Reason of State*, p. 127. Our analysis has tried to show that the issue is not so simple as Friedrich portrays it, that one may well reject the state as the highest value yet accept, and accept for very good reasons, the idea of the state's *ratio*.

expression—of a principle of action which has often given rise to unease but which has seldom prompted men to respond to this unease by insisting that there are limits to the necessities of the state and that, whatever the circumstances, these limits may never be transgressed.

Have recent developments altered the conditions of this argument and thereby invalidated the conclusion to which it has heretofore led? Is the appeal to reason of state no longer persuasive even when considered on its own chosen grounds? The view that finds an affirmative response to these questions must rest, in the main, on the conviction that the state can no longer effectively perform its traditional protective functions. In consequence, the state is presumably deprived of what has always been its principal justification. That justification was, in any event, ambiguous. If the state has been justified as the indispensable condition of value, it has also been a constant threat to those values the preservation of which has provided its principal justification. On this view, modern weapons have finally resolved the ambiguity that has always characterized the argument of necessity. The state, even the great nuclear state, can no longer effectively perform its traditional protective functions. Instead, it has become a threat—indeed *the* threat—to individual and cultural values.

If this view is once accepted it seems only reasonable to conclude that if men have not yet forsaken the idol of the sovereign state, they must become increasingly aware of the spurious nature of the state's continued claim to be the indispensable condition of value. When we examine the contemporary world, however, what we find is not the state in atrophy but, if anything, the state triumphant. This triumph of the state is not simply a matter of the state's universalization consequent upon the dissolution of empire. It is also a triumph of the state in depth, that is, a triumph of the state's persistent claims to men's loyalties. What seems characteristic of the present period is surely not a widespread and growing skepticism toward the state but the faith with which so many peoples have accepted the state, or the nation-state, as the principal institution for achieving a hoped-for destiny.

How are we to account for this apparent triumph of the state when, on the above view, objective developments must make the state increasingly obsolete? Is it plausible to contend that this apparent triumph is only apparent? It would not seem so. If the state has attained a role and significance it never before possessed, it seems far more plausible to attribute this result not to the persistence of an illusion but to the effectiveness with which the state continues to perform its traditional protective functions while enormously expanding the scope of its other activities. This effective expansion of the range of state activities must in part explain the heightened expectations the state evokes today and the emotional significance men attach to that institution.[2] In part, however, the significance men attach to the state must be found simply in the sense of strength and well-being they continue to derive from identification with a society, the nation, the preservation of which is considered indistinguishable from the preservation of the state.

It is only by concentrating on the limiting case of thermonuclear war that the view can be persuasively maintained that the state may no longer be considered a condition, let alone an indispensable condition, of value. Short of this limiting case, the assertion that the state can no longer fulfill its protective functions is evidently unfounded. Not only does it continue to fulfill these functions, but for the most part it fulfills them more effectively than in the past. It is quite true, as noted earlier,[3]

2. Nor is this effective expansion of the range of state activities offset by a growing interdependence of states. The fashionable theme of state interdependence today often confuses fact with norm, reality with aspiration. And even when it avoids this confusion, it draws too optimistic conclusions from interdependence. It is very questionable whether the interdependence of states has grown over-all since the period prior to World War I. In a number of important respects, interdependence appears to have diminished rather than increased. Thus the economic interdependence of the major European states at the beginning of the present century was greater than the economic interdependence of the major states is today. A similar conclusion must be drawn when comparing the economic relationship during these two periods between the advanced states and the underdeveloped areas. If states have not grown more interdependent economically, have they nevertheless become more interdependent militarily? Elsewhere in the text it is argued that the answer to this question must be negative. For their possessors, at least, nuclear-missile weapons have not made states more dependent on others for their security. On the contrary, these weapons have made states less dependent, if security is identified with physical security. And although it is true that in the extreme situation of thermonuclear war the state can no longer effectively perform its traditional protective functions, it is also true that in the extreme situation no amount of interdependence can compensate for this ineffectiveness. Modern weapons may have given rise to a "community of fate." It is a confusion, however, to identify this community of fate with the actual interdependence of states today. These considerations apart, it is not enough to point to the increased interdependence of states in isolation from concomitant domestic developments. What must instead be shown is that this interdependence has been relatively more significant than the parallel growth in state activities. When this relative comparison is drawn, however, the evidence clearly does not point to the triumph of interdependence. Finally, even if it could be shown that the interdependence of states has steadily grown at the expense of the independence of states, this would not in itself lead to optimistic conclusions. Kenneth Waltz rightly points out: "Interdependence that locks national interests so closely together that separation is self-evidently destructive of all good things may increase the chances of peace. Short of that threshold, the new form of the old argument that war will not occur because it does not pay brings little comfort. If interdependence is growing at a pace that exceeds the development of central control, then interdependence may increase the occasions for war." "Contention and Management in International Relations," *World Politics* (July, 1965), pp. 733–35.

3. Cf. pp. 277–80.

that nuclear-missile weapons have dealt a decisive blow to the territorial "impermeability" of the state. Even so, the security effects of these weapons have not been consistently negative. On the contrary, short of the extreme situation they have markedly improved the security problem for their possessors. Although the "hard shell" or "impermeability" that characterized the state in the past has vanished, in the case of nuclear states it has been succeeded by a new kind of shell, a new kind of impermeability. This new shell is no less "real" than the old simply because the old was rooted in the material quality of territoriality whereas the new is rooted in the psychological quality of deterrence. If "reality" is but a synonym for effectiveness, we have reason to believe that the hard shell of deterrence is far more real than its predecessor. The extreme situation apart, modern weapons have indeed resolved the ambiguity that has always characterized the argument of necessity, provided that security is identified with physical security, though they have done so in a manner precisely contrary to the view considered above.

The limiting case of thermonuclear conflict is, of course, another matter. But if in this case the state must become the unqualified destroyer rather than the ambiguous protector, the question remains: What is the alternative to a strategy of deterrence, with its potentially unlimited threat and its attendant risks, that does not at the same time abandon the ends of statecraft? Obviously, an "alternative" must abandon the means distinctive to statecraft in general and to a strategy of deterrence in particular. Is there such an alternative that can do so, however, without abandoning most of the ends of statecraft as well? The issue of means may be resolved simply by abandoning the *ultima ratio* of statecraft. To this extent, at least, pacifism has always formed an alternative, and continues to form an alternative today. In condemning war, for whatever reasons, pacifism abandons the means distinctive to statecraft. In refusing to threaten a potential aggressor with retributive measures, in refusing to confront an adversary with the prospect of returning like for like, pacifism abandons the constituent principle of statecraft. At the same time, it must abandon most of the ends of statecraft as well. For these reasons, pacifism cannot be regarded as an alternative political strategy. Nor has it been so regarded, whether by the few who have advocated it or by the many who have rejected it. In abandoning not only the means but most of the ends of statecraft as well, pacifism must be regarded as an alternative to statecraft per se.

There is nothing novel in contemporary pacifism insofar as it acknowledges that the rejection of war, and the threat of war, are synonymous with the rejection of statecraft, whether defined in terms of means or of ends.⁴ What is presumably novel is the claim that the renunciation of the threat and use of armed force, though not of nonviolent forms of resistance, represents a new kind of statecraft. Whereas nonviolent resistance is at one with traditional pacifism in renouncing war, the advocacy of nonviolence has frequently been marked by the refusal to draw the consequences from this renunciation pacifists have commonly drawn. Instead, the rejection of war has been seen not as the rejection of statecraft, but only as the rejection of a particular kind of statecraft. Nonviolence is represented as a new kind of statecraft, as an alternative not to statecraft per se but to the old kind of "violent" statecraft and, indeed, in the nuclear age, as the only realistic statecraft.⁵

There is little, if anything, in the experience to date with nonviolence to support this claim that the abandonment of the distinctive means of statecraft for the methods of nonviolence need not also imply the abandonment of the ends of statecraft. The circumstances that have attended the successful employment of nonviolence evidently bear little relation to the circumstances normally characterizing interstate conflicts and no relation at all to the circumstances marking great power conflicts. Indeed, the circumstances attending the latter conflicts can only serve to accentuate to the point of caricature the known limitations of non-violent methods. It is a commonplace that where methods of nonviolent resistance have been successfully employed, they have been employed by groups that have had little or no prospect of achieving their ends primarily through the threat or use of violence. Whatever the philosophy

---

4. It is another matter to contend that the experience with war in this century and, above all, the prospects held out by a thermonuclear conflict have given to pacifism a new persuasiveness. Even so, this does not make of pacifism a relevant political strategy today, in contrast to the past.

5. This contrast between so-called traditional pacifism and contemporary advocacy of nonviolent resistance cannot be taken too literally. It is useful only in the sense that it is indicative of general tendencies. There are advocates of nonviolent resistance who do not stress its workability, who do not represent nonviolence as a new kind of statecraft. Moreover, there have been pacifists who have stressed the workability of pacifism. Thus the contrast between vocational pacifism and prag-matic (political) pacifism, or between a Christian pacifism of renunciation and a secularist pacifism of prudence. Even this contrast may prove misleading in implying that the only possibility of a "pure" pacifism is one which is informed by the Chris-tian faith. This need not be the case, however, since a so-called secular pacifism may be "pure," in the sense that it, too, is a commitment taken in obedience to an ultimate ideal and taken quite independently of concern for practical consequences. This issue apart, prior to the present century, pacifism, whether Christian or secular, tended to be a pacifism of renunciation. It is the experience with war in this century, and the reaction to this experience, that have at once given an impetus to pacifism and altered its traditional outlook from a pacifism of renunciation to one of prudence. Nonviolent resistance may be seen as the most significant result of this alteration.

that has informed strategies of nonviolence, in practice they have in-variably been the means of the materially weak. Experience indicates that for the great majority of followers the attractiveness of nonviolence is inversely proportionate to the strength of the group with which they are identified.[6] Moreover, the effectiveness of nonviolent methods ap-pears dependent upon face-to-face contact; at any rate, they have been successfully employed only when the protagonists have been in this relationship. Equally important for the success of nonviolence is the moral vulnerability of the strong to the appeals of the weak. If the oppressed are in a position to appeal to the oppressors in terms of values the oppressors themselves profess, though in practice deny, a significant though incalculable advantage is thereby enjoyed. Even then, there does not appear to be an instance of a nonviolent campaign which has not been conditioned in significant measure by the prospect that at some point violence would be employed. The purity of nonviolence has been, at best, a matter of a few men's convictions and not of most men's calculations and expectations.[7]

6. To be sure, philosophies of nonviolence consistently emphasize the spiritual strength required of the commitment to nonviolence, a strength that is presumably to compensate for material weakness. But this emphasis carries conviction only for the very few, not for the many. It is only the few who are neither demoralized nor debased by material weakness, not the many. This is one reason why the state, and particularly the strong state, remains so significant a factor in the lives of most men. These observations evidently do not hold for saints. But the world is not made up of saints. This is not to say that philosophies of nonviolence are consistently based on a radically optimistic view of men's potentialities. In part, of course, they clearly are so based, though they can hardly be said to be consistent in this bias. Thus advocates of nonviolence never seem quite able to decide whether nonviolence is a necessity because man is so bad or a meaningful possibility because man is apparently so good. Similarly, they can never quite decide whether the presumed effectiveness of nonviolence stems from the fear it creates in the adversary or the decency it inspires in him.

7. What has been earlier observed in the analysis of *bellum justum* (cf. pp 304–5) must prove equally applicable here. The purity of nonviolence, its distinctive quality, is to be found not merely in the significance given to the means of action but above all in the insistence that nonviolence is an "ethic of ultimate means." This distinc-tive quality is blurred, if not lost, if the problem of means is itself reduced to what is, in effect, a form of calculation. Thus it is not enough to argue that one may never use violent means on behalf of good ends because the ends escape one, or that the means cannot be separated from the ends but are themselves the ends in the very process of coming into existence. To the extent that nonviolence is an "ethic of ultimate means," its purity must be found in its refusal to employ violent methods quite apart from these considerations, which may or may not be true but which cannot be decided in the abstract. It can come as no surprise that the rank and file comprising nonviolent movements have not found in nonviolence an "ethic of ultimate means" but a strategy pursued primarily for expediential reasons. Indeed, what has broadly marked these movements has clearly not been a devotion to means, a conviction that, in Gandhian terms, "nonviolence is truth-creating," but a com-mitment to certain ends that has been sufficiently intense to sustain the employment

Thus the experience of nonviolent methods would appear to have almost no relevance to interstate conflicts.[8] Nonviolence is admittedly not a strategy for preserving the state's independence; indeed, it can scarcely become a meaningful strategy in any sense until that independence has been lost. It is equally apparent that the sacrifice of the state's independence must imply the sacrifice of still other values as well. The significance of this sacrifice is not altered by the curious, and misleading, insistence that the values so sacrificed are merely material in contrast with the spiritual, and presumably higher, values embodied in the commitment to nonviolence. Political freedom may be considered a value that ought to be sacrificed rather than defended by violence, and particularly if its defense entails the risk of nuclear war. But no useful purpose is served by characterizing this choice as a sacrifice of the material on behalf of the spiritual.

---

of nonviolent methods, though even then in circumstances where violent methods were almost always inexpedient. In the case of the Indian independence movement it is a matter of record that most of Gandhi's followers refused to consider nonviolence as a matter of principle—an ethic of ultimate means—though they did justify and practice nonviolence largely on grounds of expediency. Gandhi, it is true, found in nonviolence an ethic of ultimate means. It is not true, however, that the Gandhian method of *Satyagraha* relied on pure persuasion. Not only were the means it sanctioned coercive—nonco-operation, boycotts, strikes—but their almost inevitable effect was to cause injury to the adversary. To this extent, the purity of the Gandhian doctrine, with its insistence on never causing harm or injury to the opponent, can only be a purity of intention and not of action. For these reasons Gandhi's insistence, and the insistence of sympathetic interpreters, that his method of testing or finding the "truth" amounted simply to "action based on the refusal to do harm" is no more acceptable than the contention that the ethic of the Gandhian philosophy is identical with the ethic of Jesus. In fact, between the nonresistance of the latter and the nonviolent resistance of the former there is an unbridgeable gulf, as Reinhold Niebuhr pointed out many years ago. Moreover, it is significant that in Gandhi's case the element of calculation was never entirely absent. One of his recent interpreters quotes Gandhi to the following effect: "It is not because I value life low that I can countenance with joy thousands voluntarily losing their lives for *Satyagraha*, but because I know that it results in the long run in the least loss of life, and, what is more, it ennobles those who lose their lives and morally enriches the world for their sacrifice." Joan Bondurant, *The Conquest of Violence* (Princeton: Princeton University Press, 1958), p. 27. A sharp distinction must be made between this concern for consequences and the disinterestedness that marks Jesus' ethical ideal.

8. Nor are there any instances of the attempted application of nonviolence to interstate conflicts. And it seems almost superfluous to add that since achieving independence India has acted in no way that would in this respect somehow distinguish her from other states. From the armed seizure of Hyderabad in 1948 to the conflict with Pakistan in 1965, Indian governments have failed to give even modest encouragement to the hope that nonviolence may be relevant to statecraft. In this respect, many observers found in the position taken by India toward Pakistan during the 1965 hostilities a strong desire to disabuse the outside world that India remains in any sense the "land of nonviolence."

Whether we define statecraft in terms of the means employed or the ends sought, nonviolence must therefore be seen as the abandonment of statecraft rather than as a new kind of statecraft. To this extent, there is no essential distinction between contemporary versions of nonviolence and traditional pacifism. Nor is this all. It is clear that nonviolence, if it is to prove more than merely a prudential strategy the weak may in certain circumstances successfully employ against the strong, must assume not merely a change of sorts in men but something akin to their moral transformation. Men are not only expected to forego employing a means that has hitherto been central to social and political life, they are expected to forego the many ends this means has secured, and may still secure, for them. The latter point is critical though commonly neglected in discussions of nonviolence. The central issue nonviolence must raise is not so much whether it is compatible with the nature of man but whether it is compatible with the ends of man. We may well conclude that the evidence does not support the view that war is a biological necessity and that men are accordingly compelled by instinct to perpetuate this institution. It does not follow, however, that the disappearance of war is therefore primarily a matter of devising, by some "leap in our thinking," new methods or techniques of conflict resolution. Nor does it follow that the disappearance of war is primarily a matter of reversing the "learned link," if it be that, between violence and masculine courage. At the root of these and similar arguments is the common assumption that if man is not compelled by his nature to perpetuate the institution of war, he may resolve his conflicts by other and less destructive methods. If this assumption is unexceptionable, it is also rather beside the point in considering the prospects of a warless world. Of course, men may resolve their conflicts by methods other than war. But the decisive issue is whether they can always secure the ends they desire by methods other than war. For the past, at any rate, the evidence is overwhelming that war, the organized use of armed force, has been a means for securing a variety of desired ends, ends that could not be secured other than through war.

Expectations of a warless world may be entertained, then, either under the condition that war—or the threat of war—can no longer secure the ends men desire or under the condition that men no longer desire these ends—at least, no longer desire these ends to the degree that they are willing to threaten or to employ armed force on their behalf. The advocacy of nonviolence may rely, and in practice frequently does rely, rather indiscriminately on both conditions; the appeal to nonviolence is at once an appeal to men's lower and higher faculties, to their faculty for sacrifice as well as to their faculty for calculation. It is not surprising that this should be so; the coalescence of the two appeals yields the strongest possible position. Nevertheless, a clear distinction must be drawn between these two conditions. If neither the use nor the threat of armed force can any longer secure the ends men desire, there is no need to appeal to his sense of sacrifice. There is only a need to educate him to this "new fact." But if the threat or use of armed force may still secure for men ends they could otherwise not secure, then the acceptance of nonviolence does indeed presuppose men's moral transformation. It is only by denying, whether implicitly or explicitly, the ends men have sought through war, or by minimizing the significance of the ends that have often prompted men to war, that proponents of nonviolence can largely ignore the supreme difficulties in replacing war with nonviolent methods of conflict resolution.[9]

These considerations indicate that if a commitment to nonviolence is nevertheless represented as an alternative to the predicament in which men presently find themselves, it is an alternative only in the sense that every vision of a "new beginning" in history is an alternative. We do not for this reason dismiss nonviolence. We simply do not find it very useful to speculate on such new beginnings.

2

If it does not seem useful to speculate on new beginnings that require the transformation of man, is it nevertheless useful to speculate on new beginnings that presumably require the transformation of the system rather than of man? Many would appear to think so. While the serious advocacy of nonviolence remains confined to a very few, the goal of general disarmament has attracted a much larger and more impressive following. The appeal of comprehensive disarmament is further reflected by the commitment on the part of governments to the goal of a disarmed world. That this commitment is of itself without immediate

9. And it is only by denying, whether implicitly or explicitly, the ends men have sought through war, or by minimizing the significance of these ends, that proponents of nonviolence—and not only proponents of nonviolence—can pose the almost rhetorical question: If men have rid themselves of slavery, why not of war? If we assume that war, or the threat thereof, may still obtain for men what they otherwise might not obtain, the answer is clear. Men will rid themselves of war when they no longer desire, or sufficiently desire, the things war may secure for them. In fact, however, they still desire certain things sufficiently to use, or to threaten the use of, armed force. Of course, the comparison of slavery and war is also vulnerable on other grounds. Whereas slavery could be, and was, given up "incrementally," as it were, the same cannot be said of war. A society that abandoned slavery did not thereby place itself at the complete mercy of others that retained slavery. But a nation that abandons war does clearly place itself at the mercy of those nations that do not do so.

and practical consequence does not detract from the significance govern-ments apparently attach to efforts that are intended to convey at least the appearance of serious commitment. In recent years proposals for general disarmament have acquired a status they never before possessed.

If general disarmament represents a possible alternative to the present system of self-help, in the sense that it is seen as leading to the trans-formation of this system, it does so only if attended by measures that go far beyond disarmament as such. For the abandonment of arms, even though accompanied by effective procedures of inspection and verifica-tion, would not thereby transform the present system. Without the development of supranational institutions for ensuring peace and security, and peaceful change, there would remain the possibility that states could at any time break the disarmament agreement and rearm. The threat of military force would therefore remain one of the instruments of diplomacy. Moreover, in the absence of effective collective procedures, war itself would remain the *ultima ratio* of diplomacy, though at one stage removed.[10]

A distinction must be drawn, then, between proposals for disarma-ment that are limited to the disarmament process itself and proposals that place general disarmament within the broader framework of other and more comprehensive measures for the organization of peace and security.[11] Whereas the former assume the continued reliance of states

10. It is quite true that states would not undertake general disarmament unless they were disposed at the time to resolve their conflicts by other means than war. Moreover, comprehensive disarmament, whatever the reasons that might prompt it, could be expected to result in a number of other significant changes in the inter-national system, quite apart from such peacekeeping institutions states might estab-lish for ensuring peace and security in a disarmed world. It is surely not unreasonable to assume that some of the causes of conflicts in the present world would be sub-stantially mitigated, if not altered, in a disarmed world. Thus even if the argument is granted that security is a condition of disarmament, it remains true that dis-armament is also a condition of security. At the same time, there are limits to the assumptions that may reasonably be made respecting both the factors that might prompt general disarmament as well as the effects of general disarmament. If gen-eral disarmament, though unattended by the establishment of effective supranational institutions, is nevertheless expected to result in the transformation of the present system of self-help, it may do so only if we assume as well the transformation of man. How else may we entertain the expectation that in a disarmed world men would no longer threaten or use armed force? Is it because of the expectation that serious conflicts of interest would not arise? Or is it because of the expectation that even if such conflicts were to arise they would not be resolved by the threat or use of force? Either expectation, however, must assume man's moral transformation.

11. The "disarmament process" may be understood to comprise the procedures agreed upon for reducing and restricting arms, as well as the means of disclosure and verification. It does not include those arrangements that may be provided, in addition to disclosure and verification, for ensuring that the arms agreement is observed and to which the term "peacekeeping" generally refers.

upon the traditional instruments of diplomacy, the latter assume that these instruments must be supplanted by new methods of resolving conflict and ensuring peace. Whereas the former assume the continuance by and large of the institution of self-help, in which each state remains at liberty to protect its interests as best it can with the means at its disposal, the latter assume that the scope of self-help will be severely restricted. Whereas the former necessarily assume that states may break the disarmament agreement and rearm, and that the threat of rearmament will therefore remain one of the instruments of diplomacy, the latter assume that effective peacekeeping institutions of a supranational character must ensure that states are not able to break the disarmament agreement and rearm. Whereas, finally, the former may accord only a modest role to law, the latter must give to law a central role. For the latter type of proposal is dependent upon the creation of a centralized security system within which states would be deprived of their traditional freedom not only to resort to armed force in the last resort but also to threaten seriously the security of their neighbors through other forms of coercion. Yet it is precisely because a centralized security system would have to be created for a society comprising very disparate and conflicting groups that these restraints on coercion would have to take a predominantly legal form and would have to be clearly defined. They would have to take a predominantly legal form because the forces other than law that normally operate within stable and cohesive domestic societies to restrain contending groups would remain—at least for a considerable time—weak and undeveloped.[12] They would have to be very clearly defined because of the weakness of those forces other than law which in domestic societies serve both to restrain contending groups and to give meaning to the law itself. In the absence of those social forces other than law which largely give to the law its effectiveness while at the same time reducing the dependence upon law, "peace through law" can be attained only by giving to law a role of importance that it has rarely possessed in domestic society. And since the rule of law is still always the rule of men, this can only mean conferring an extraordinary power on those who are competent to apply and enforce the law. It is chiefly for these reasons that the recurrent demand of "peace

12. It is, of course, the vitality of the forces other than law that makes possible the "rule of law," that term being used in its broader sense. "The essence of the rule of law ideal," Julius Stone remarks, "lies . . . not in technical rules as such, but rather in the supremacy of certain ethical convictions, certain rules of decency prevalent in the community, and in the psychological fact that those who are at the apex of power share those convictions and feel bound to conform to them." *Quest for Survival: The Role of Law and Foreign Policy* (Cambridge: Harvard University Press, 1961), p. 4.

through law" either appears impossible to satisfy or seems to hold out novel dangers if, by some miracle, it were suddenly to be satisfied.

The evident virtue of comprehensive disarmament proposals that are limited to the disarmament process itself is that the international society they presuppose still largely corresponds to the present international society. To this extent, the obstacles to be overcome in achieving general disarmament do not seem unmanageable. The order of a disarming and disarmed world appears very much like the order of the present world. Not only does the nation-state retain its paramount position in a disarmed world, not only does it continue to perform on the whole its present functions and continue to lay successful claim to men's loyalties, but the character of the international order continues to depend, as it has always depended, principally upon the disposition of the great powers.[13] Disarmament is to be undertaken, if at all, within the context of great power relations and despite the conflicts that presumably will continue to mark these relations. It follows that what the great powers may do they may also undo if the circumstances prompting their initial agreement should change.[14]

13. This statement obviously assumes that in a disarmed world the great powers will remain great powers. Nor does there seem to be persuasive reason for assuming otherwise, although a number of observers do dispute this assumption. It should be made clear that this assumption does not rest simply on the identification of military power with other forms of power, hence of influence, although a rough correspondence does generally obtain between military power and other forms of power. A much more important reason for making this assumption is the strong probability that in a disarmed world of the kind discussed here, potential military power will play very largely the same general role that actual military power plays in the present world. If so, the great powers will not only remain great powers but will continue to determine, as they have always determined, the degree and kind of order that the international society may at any time possess. There is no persuasive reason for believing, then, that a disarmed world without supranational institutions would be thrown into disorder and chaos. There is no persuasive reason for believing this because there is no persuasive reason for believing that a disarmed world would confront us with the task of fashioning an "order without force."

14. An illustration of this type of disarmament proposal may be seen in the Soviet Union's draft treaty of March, 1962, on general and complete disarmament. Throughout, the draft treaty is addressed almost entirely to the disarmament process itself and reflects the general position on disarmament consistently maintained by the Soviet Union since the 1920s. In substance, the peacekeeping measures contained in the Soviet proposal scarcely go beyond a reaffirmation of the United Nations Charter. The Soviet plan therefore acknowledges, and even presupposes, the prospect that in most of the present conflicts of interest between the great powers they shall retain their traditional freedom of action—a freedom symbolized by their right of veto in the Security Council. On this view, if nations are ever to abandon their arms, though most of the basic conflicts that gave rise to these arms remain, it will only be through the present system and not as a result of its deliberate transformation. It follows from the Soviet position that, apart from denying themselves the capacity to resort directly to armed violence, states in a disarmed world will con-

The evident defect of comprehensive disarmament proposals that are limited to the disarmament process itself is not that they represent a covenant without a sword; it is rather that the sword—though at one stage removed—is the traditional sword for maintaining covenants between states. Thus the system of self-help with its attendant hazards is left essentially unaltered.[15] Moreover, these proposals require us to assume that despite the persistence of profound divisions, the threat of thermonuclear war, or perhaps the experience with a less-than-catastrophic thermonuclear conflict, will prompt nations to disarm and to remain disarmed while continuing to rely upon methods of self-help, including the threat of military force (a threat that is implicit in the threat to rearm). This assumption, however, represents a break from almost the whole of our past experience. There may be no logical reason for assuming that, in the absence of those institutions and conditions that have brought peace and security to some domestic societies, nations will not disarm or, even if they do disarm, will not remain disarmed

tinue to rely upon the traditional instruments of diplomacy. States may always break the disarmament covenant and rearm. The threat of military force therefore remains one of the instruments of diplomacy. Hence war itself remains the *ultima ratio* of diplomacy, though at one stage removed. It is important to note that this interpretation of the general disarmament proposal discussed in the text, and of which the Soviet draft treaty is considered representative, assumes that a reliable system of verification can be devised and accepted by the parties to the disarmament agreement. This is, admittedly, a very large assumption. If it is invalid, however, this type of disarmament proposal makes very little sense. It is *possible* to argue that in a disarmed world nations might continue to rely upon methods of self-help if it is assumed that the illegal accumulation of arms could not be undertaken surreptitiously. It is equally possible to argue that, given certain kinds of arms, the absence of a reliable inspection system and the consequent possibility of cheating would not prove incompatible with a system of self-help. But it is scarcely possible to employ the latter argument with respect to nuclear weapons, for the nature of these weapons is such that their sole possession by a nation, though only in limited quantity, may well confer upon the possessor what is in effect a virtual monopoly of force. If there is no reliable way of ensuring that the parties to a general disarmament agreement have carried out their obligations, the risks of disarming in a world where nations continued to rely upon methods of self-help would be inordinately great. These risks could be reduced to acceptable proportions only by a very large and all-powerful centralized force.

15. Nor is this all. Although the system is left essentially unchanged, the fact that the sword is one stage removed may, and in the opinion of some does, represent an added source of danger and even a quite considerable one. If in a disarmed world the means of self-help other than military power were to prove inadequate for defending one's vital interests, the principal alternative, as already emphasized, would be to rearm. But it is quite possible that the new arms race would prove more unstable and less controllable in its effects than the present situation, if only for the reason that we have come to know a good deal about the present arms race and the means required for keeping it under reasonable control. In an arms race beginning from a condition of general disarmament, however, we would very likely be confronted with an essentially novel situation and one much less amenable to control.

despite the persistence of profound conflicts of interest. If history is at all relevant in this respect, however, there is good reason to expect they will do neither.

Quite different considerations apply to proposals for general disarmament within the context of supranational institutions that would severely restrict the scope of self-help permitted to states. In substance, such proposals are scarcely distinguishable from the more conventional proposals for world government. Illusions nevertheless persist on this simple, though vital, point. Thus the authors of what have perhaps become the best-known proposals for achieving "world peace through world law" are at pains to emphasize that their proposals, which entail comprehensive disarmament and the establishment of supranational institutions to prevent the recourse to force by states, deal only with the "limited field of war prevention."[16] The structures and powers thereupon prescribed for dealing with this "limited field," however, contain the essential features of world government. It could scarcely be otherwise since the prevention of armed conflict is anything but a limited field, involving as it does—directly or indirectly—most of the essential attributes of governance. The same must be said of proposals for comprehensive disarmament which represent themselves as clear alternatives to the present system of self-help. Although their focus of interest is comprehensive disarmament, the indispensable concomitant of disarmament is an international society that has succeeded in establishing effectively centralized institutions for maintaining peace, ensuring security, and providing for just and peaceful change.[17] These functions are the principal functions of the state everywhere, although they are not performed with equal effectiveness everywhere and although they are nowhere performed by the state alone.

If the difficulties of disarmament proposals requiring the transformation of the international system are apparent, are the virtues of these proposals any more apparent? If these proposals are not feasible, nor

16. Grenville Clark and Louis B. Sohn, *World Peace Through World Law* (2d ed. rev.; Cambridge: Harvard University Press, 1960), pp. xv, xvi.

17. An illustration of this type of disarmament proposal may be seen in the U.S. "Outline of Basic Provisions of a Treaty on General and Complete Disarmament in a Peaceful World" of April, 1962. The essence of the peacekeeping proposals in the U.S. "Outline" is disarmament within a transformed—and, ultimately, a radically transformed—system of international security. Although there is very little indication as to the actual design of the supranational institutions that are to operate in a disarmed world, the basic principle is clear: Comprehensive disarmament can occur only within an international society that has succeeded in establishing effective collective procedures for maintaining peace, ensuring security, and providing for just and peaceful change. The institution of self-help must be replaced by a central authority possessed of an effective monopoly of legitimate force and otherwise bearing the essential attributes of government.

likely to become so in the foreseeable future, do they still represent a desirable utopia? In part, the answer to these questions depends upon the actual design of the supranational institutions that are to operate in a disarmed world. In part, however, the answer depends upon the assumptions one makes about the world in which this transformation would occur. Indeed, it is the latter assumption that must prove critical, since the kind of world one assumes must largely determine the character of the institutions adequate to maintain peace.

If one assumes a world that, though still comprised of states, no longer is deeply divided by antagonistic social and political systems, no longer is marked by great disparities in political and economic development, and no longer is beset by hegemonial rivalries, then the answer to the above questions must almost surely be affirmative. In such a world the state, with its traditional insistence upon the right of self-help, can no longer find persuasive justification, for the state no longer remains the indispensable condition of value. In such a world the state may still not wither away of its own accord, but the desirability of disarming it and ensuring its disarmament can hardly be gainsaid. It can hardly be gainsaid not only because in such a world the state is no longer the indispensable condition of value, but also because the basic conditions requisite for the transformation of international society already largely exist. This being so, the design of the institutions requisite for effecting this transformation and for maintaining it need not pose insoluble problems and, of equal significance, need not hold out novel dangers. Their design need not pose insoluble problems because they are not expected to accomplish impossible tasks. They need not hold out novel dangers because what is expected of them is at least roughly comparable to what is expected of institutions with which we have had experience.[18]

18. Even here, however, we are left with an ultimate doubt. Even for this benign, though purely imaginary, world there must remain a final uncertainty. If the peace that the limited societies of the past and of the present have enjoyed has resulted in large measure from a consciousness of community, from a consensus that is always far more the creator than the creature of law, we must recall that this cohesiveness that facilitates the peaceful composition of conflicting interests has been developed within the context of a hostile external environment. It is impossible to determine how important the existence of the external foe has been in promoting internal unity. But there is no doubt that it has been a significant factor in the development of all historical societies that have achieved lasting political unity. Raymond Aron points out that the expansion of political units in the past and present has never signified more than a change of form of the "tribal conscience," a "change of scale within history, the nature of which remains the same." *Paix et Guerre*, p. 583. A world federation, he observes, would signify the abandonment of the "tribal conscience" and would represent a "conversion of history." Is such a conversion possible, if only in principle, Aron asks, or is it contrary to the nature of man to conceive of a society without enemies? (p. 741.)

The apparently self-evident quality of these conclusions disappears if one assumes instead a world that by and large retains the antagonisms, disparities, and rivalries of the present world. It is not necessary in this context to speculate how, given the persistence of these conditions, a sudden break-through to a disarmed world, attended by supranational institutions, might occur.[19] It is only necessary to speculate how desirable this break-through would be if, by some unexpected event, it were to occur. What kind of supranational institutions would be required to ensure peace in a world still marked by the huge disparities and still torn by the deep conflicts of the present world? Obviously, the question can be usefully considered only in a very general way. Even so, the attempt to answer it, if only in a very general way, is not without a certain value.

It is reasonably clear, to begin with, that in considering the kind of authority required to ensure peace and security in a world that resembles the present world, we cannot safely rely on our past experience with the state, and particularly our experience with Western liberal regimes. We cannot do so because we have no experience of a state presiding over a society even remotely comparable to international society. We have no experience of a state that has suddenly been brought into being principally by a shared fear of catastrophe, in much the same manner that Hobbes conceived of the creation of the Leviathan. Nor do we have any relevant experience of a state presiding over a society the cohesiveness of which must depend, at least for a substantial period, almost entirely on the fear of catastrophic war resulting from the disruption of society and the consequent breakdown of the central authority. In the absence of a consensus that grows out of, and reflects, shared traditions and common values, it is this fear that would provide the "consensus" of the new society. It is this same fear, together with the threat of sanctions by the central authority, that would have to be relied on for effecting such change as the central authority might deem necessary and just.

If these considerations are well-founded, we could expect the supranational authority to endure, and to prove effective in maintaining a warless world, only if it were endowed with very considerable powers.

19. The favored line of speculation is that of a break-through occurring as a result either of a near-disaster or, even more persuasive, of an actual—though limited— disaster. Thus John Strachey writes of the "agonizing view that some such unforgettable experience as the destruction of a city or a country, in a nuclear war which was then, somehow arrested, may, though heaven forbid it, have to be endured before men will face the necessities of survival in the nuclear age." *On the Prevention of War* (New York: St. Martin's Press, 1963), p. 312.

To the objection that a society with so restricted and so negative a "consensus" cannot be expected to create a central authority with very considerable powers, the answer must be that it is precisely because a society has so restricted and so negative a "consensus" that it must have an all-powerful central authority if peace is to be ensured. It is precisely the absence of those social forces, other than the state, which give stability and cohesiveness to many domestic societies and which facilitate the compromise of conflicts that necessitates endowing a central authority with very considerable powers in order to ensure peace. Given the kind of society over which a supranational authority must be expected to preside, peace, if it is to be maintained, can be maintained only by heavy reliance upon the authority's power of armed coercion. Against recalcitrant and aggressive states possessed of large power potential, order can be ensured only if the central authority disposes of an armed force of sufficient magnitude as to leave little doubt over the outcome of any challenge.[20] It is only by assuming what clearly cannot be assumed that many advocates of comprehensive disarmament, attended by supranational peacekeeping institutions, manage to avoid this central conclusion. It is only by assuming either that the major groups comprising the new society will no longer have deep conflicts or, better yet, that these major groups—the nation-states—will themselves quickly atrophy

20. In his examination of contemporary thought on world government, Inis Claude observes that the concept of the state's monopoly of power tends to be taken too literally: ". . . the assumption that this monopoly is the key to the effectiveness of the state as an order-keeping institution may lead to an exaggerated notion of the degree to which actual states can and do rely upon coercion, and thus to a distorted understanding of the basis for a hypothetical world state." *Power and International Relations* (New York: Random House, 1962), p. 234. Claude argues that theorists of world government are not mistaken in looking at domestic experience for clues to the problem of achieving world order, but that they misread the lessons of that experience. "The prevention of civil war is the function of national government most relevant to the problem of ordering international relations . . . governments cannot and do not perform this function by relying primarily upon either police action against individuals or military action against significant segments of their societies . . . governments succeed in this vitally important task only when they are able to operate an effective system of political accommodation." (p. 269.) Although Claude underestimates the significance of the state's "monopoly of power" in maintaining domestic peace, he is surely correct in his criticism of the oversimple and apolitical view of the order-keeping role of the state entertained by advocates of world government. But given the society we assume a world government would preside over, a monopoly of power must be the key to the effectiveness of the world authority's order-keeping role if there is to be a key at all. Advocates of world government may and do misread the significance of domestic experience; ironically enough, this misread experience is not mistaken when applied to the circumstances of international society. That is why the prospect of effective world government, given these circumstances, is not one that can be easily endorsed.

in importance that visions of a world authority that is effective though possessed of quite modest powers can be entertained.[21]

There are, it is true, limits to the powers of a central authority that states would almost certainly insist upon in drawing up the social contract for the new society. It is only reasonable to expect that the wealthier among them would insist upon certain safeguards against the extreme prospects of a compulsory redistribution of the world's wealth. It is clearer still that all states would insist that the integrity of their territory and of their political institutions be guaranteed. Even if it is assumed that some catastrophe, or near-catastrophe, suddenly converted men to belief in the need of transforming the present system, and therefore to agreement in principle upon these guarantees, it must nevertheless remain very doubtful whether they would be, and could be, honored in practice. In part, the reason for this skepticism is that these guarantees would extend to the very issues that presently occasion, and that may be expected to continue to occasion, the most serious conflicts among states. A supranational legislative authority denied the competence to deal with these issues would thereby be denied the competence to deal with the most significant causes of conflict. It is difficult to believe that such an authority would in fact abstain from dealing with these issues. Moreover, in one important respect it could not refrain from doing so if comprehensive disarmament is to be effectively supervised and maintained. At the very least, decisions would have to be made with respect to the levels of internal security forces permitted to states, levels that must be expected to vary considerably from one state to the next and, within the same state, from one period to the next. Yet the power to determine the internal security requirements of states is, in effect, the power to determine the legitimacy of regimes.[22]

21. These assumptions almost invariably mark the writings of advocates of world government. Thus Clark and Sohn believe that once a world authority is established, states will quickly diminish in importance. Challenges to the order of the new society will presumably come mainly from individuals. In a discussion of enforcing disarmament they write: "It is reasonable to assume that in most instances the government of a nation in whose territory a violation occurs would not be involved in it and that such violations could be adequately dealt with by prompt action against the individuals responsible for them." *World Peace Through World Law*, p. 306. Given this assumption it is entirely reasonable to think that the world authority can be of modest dimensions.

22. What Charles B. Marshall writes with respect to the U.S. government's conception of general and complete disarmament is equally applicable in the present context. "The collective authority, with its irresistible coercive instrument, would become arbiter of questions of legitimacy touching the regime in every land. To its jurisdiction would come questions of enlarging quotas of force permitted to particular governments for internal security. . . . In an extremity involving a regime's inability to counter a domestic challenge with its permitted quota of internal security

There is no need to pursue the inquiry further. The moral it suggests is clear enough. If disarmament proposals requiring the transformation of the international system are not feasible, nor likely to become so in the foreseeable future, one must also question whether they represent a desirable utopia. For the same considerations that make impossible the sudden break-through to a disarmed world, attended by effective supranational institutions, also place in serious question the desirability of this break-through, if one assumes the persistence of conditions that presently characterize international society. To be sure, this question does not arise if one assumes a very different world from the present world. But in this very different world the question does not arise because the principal conditions that make it meaningful have simply been assumed away. Men may disarm because the principal reasons for maintaining arms have largely disappeared. They may accept the subordination of the state to a world authority because the principal justification of the state no longer obtains. A new beginning of sorts will already have been made and men need only have the wisdom to consolidate it.

3

Has a new beginning already been made, though a new beginning that bears little or no relation to the visions we have considered? Is the prospect of large-scale interstate violence already sufficiently remote that we have no need to anguish over impossible alternatives? Has the break-through so devoutly wished for already been achieved? To put these questions so openly and so starkly cannot but elicit a negative response, particularly from "responsible participants" and "sober observers." This response would prove misleading, however, to the extent it served to obscure the significant change in expectations that has occurred in recent years. Whereas only a few years ago anxiety over the prospects of avoiding nuclear war was general and pronounced, today no such anxiety dominates men's thoughts to anywhere near the same degree that it did at the end of the last decade. Within the space of a very few years the specter of a nuclear apocalypse has markedly receded and men have drawn new confidence in the future. Anxiety over the prospects of avoiding nuclear war has increasingly given way to confidence that the dreaded contingency can be avoided indefinitely, and with its avoidance the avoidance of other large-scale interstate conflict as well. Although

---

forces, it would fall to the world collectivity to lend or not to lend a hand with a fraction of its irresistible components—a political question of sweeping import." "Character and Mission of a United Nations Peace Force," in Arnold Wolfers *et al.*, *The United States in a Disarmed World* (Baltimore: The Johns Hopkins Press, 1966), p. 189.

the system of self-help will otherwise remain essentially unaltered, the ultimate hazards that have attended the system will henceforth be avoided.[23]

The manifestations of this new-found optimism are many and varied. They may be seen in the growing confidence that man can control the new technology that but a short time ago appeared so constricting and so oppressive. The fears of an earlier period, that the new technology must frustrate and defeat the ends men seek to attain, have clearly not disappeared, but they have just as clearly diminished. Thus the problems of maintaining effective command and control over the great deterrent systems no longer prompt the once widely held view that these complex and automated systems have, as it were, a life and a will of their own—that "their" errors rather than human errors may precipitate an accidental or an inadvertent war. If this view was always misleading, it nevertheless was indicative of the anxiety with respect to the more narrowly technical problems of controlling modern weapons in time of peace, an anxiety shared by both governments and their publics. In the space of a very few years, however, this anxiety has progressively given way to a confidence that the technical problems of command and control of strategic weapons systems, at least when these problems are confined to the purposes of deterrence, have been successfully resolved.

More significant than a sense of mastery over the narrowly technical problems of controlling weapons for the purposes of deterrence is the growing confidence in the ability to control crisis situations, particularly those crises involving the great powers and in which the possibility of employing nuclear weapons arises.[24] There is, of course, nothing novel in the aspiration, as such, to manage diplomatic crises. What is novel in contemporary "crisis management" is the intensity of aspiration to exercise a far greater measure of control over those critical junctures in state relations than men have exercised in the past and the confidence that this may indeed be done through exhaustive analysis, imaginative speculation, and careful planning for future actions.[25] Whereas in the

23. The nuclear utopia described in these pages is thus a rather hard utopia. It does not literally follow the maxim that "the more things change the more they remain the same" but alters this piece of wisdom to read: "The more some things change the more other things remain the same." There are, of course, moderate and not so moderate versions of the nuclear utopia. We are concerned principally with the former.

24. As between the great powers this possibility must probably be considered a *conditio sine qua non* of a crisis.

25. It is not without some irony, however, that the most notable case of crisis management in recent years—the Cuban missile crisis—was preceded neither by exhaustive analysis nor by imaginative speculation nor by careful planning for future actions.

past crises all too often "broke" on men who, being unprepared and having no time, were made the prisoners of events, crisis management would reverse this ancient and today most dangerous form of servitude and make men the masters of events. Moreover, as between the great powers at least, a confidence in crisis management almost of necessity implies a confidence in the avoidance of large-scale conflict. In an earlier period the successful management of crises may not have been incompatible with the recourse to major war. In the nuclear age, such recourse must form the salient feature of a mismanaged crisis.[26]

A growing confidence in the ability of men to manage crises has been accompanied by a growing confidence that force may be employed in a regulated—indeed, in a highly regulated—manner. The concept of a controlled strategic nuclear war, a war in which the great nuclear powers might still lose several million in casualties, is only the most spectacular, though also the most debatable, manifestation of this confidence in men's ability to regulate violence. Less spectacular, though far more significant, is the concept of controlled escalation—that is, of the controlled competition in risk-taking or resolve by means of the step-by-step expansion of the scope and intensity of war.[27] Nothing shows in a more striking way the change that has occurred, particularly in the U.S., in scarcely more than a decade. As late as the middle 1950s the nation's President, and one of its most distinguished soldiers, could still declare that force has no limitations save those imposed "by the limitations of

26. These statements may be questioned for the reason that the ideal, or norm, of crisis management remains in part ambiguous. This ambiguity reflects both a divergence of value and a divergence of opinion over the possibility of controlling large-scale conflict, particularly if such conflict involves the use of nuclear weapons. When are crises resolved in a favorable manner? The unexceptionable answer, of course, is that a crisis is resolved favorably when one's interests are preserved, though without the use of violence. Is the outcome of a crisis necessarily unfavorable, however, if its resolution leads to violence? Unless crisis management is defined as the nonviolent resolution of crises the answer is evidently negative. The difficult issue, then, is this: At what point on the scale of violence is the outcome of a crisis unfavorable? This issue may be put in still another way: At what point on the scale of violence is the outcome of a crisis unfavorable for the reason that other interests are not preserved? Clearly, this point is reached with general thermonuclear war not only because we assume that we cannot control it but also because we assume it will be destructive of our interests. It is another matter to determine at what point short of this crisis management must be deemed to have failed. In part, this determination will depend upon the interests men hold and, more specifically, upon the manner in which they order these interests. Thus, even if a large-scale conflict can be controlled, it may still represent a failure of crisis management if a high enough value is attached to the avoidance of such a conflict. In part, however, this determination will depend upon whether a large-scale conflict, even a nuclear conflict between the great powers, can be controlled and over this issue a sharp divergence of opinion persists.

27. Cf. pp. 185–90. A controlled strategic nuclear war is itself one of the steps on the escalation ladder, though it is a very high step and thus a very debatable one.

force itself."[28] In thus articulating the conviction that once force is employed man has moved from the realm of freedom to a world of necessity, General Eisenhower no more than generalized a widely held view. This view may still find expression among the general public. It would come as a shock, however, if expressed today by a high government official. A view that appeared almost unchallenged only a short time ago is now regarded by those who are concerned with military-strategic issues as dangerously naïve. From the conviction that force, once employed, imposes its own limits we have turned almost full circle to the conviction that man remains throughout the master and may impose whatever limits he disposes. Apprehension over the uncontrollable character of force has suddenly given way to a marked confidence in man's ability to control force.

It is in the increased confidence in nuclear deterrence, however, that we must find the principal manifestation of, and basis for, the new optimism. It is quite true that expressions of this confidence in the stability and reliability of the balance of terror between the nuclear superpowers and their allies are regularly attended by cautionary qualifications.[29] What stands out, however, are not the qualifications but the expressions of confidence in an arrangement that has been fully operative for only a very few years. Even so, during this brief period men have either grown tired of or have simply learned to accommodate themselves to the well-known paradoxes and persisting uncertainties of deterrence, although these paradoxes and uncertainties are no less apparent today than when they were first laid bare. Nor is this surprising, since it is clear that the paradoxes are insoluble and the persisting uncertainties irremediable, both being rooted in weapons that invalidate the traditional continuity between deterrence and the overt use of the weapons on which deterrence rests.[30] The attempt at a partial restoration of this continuity, through the concept of a limited strategic nuclear war, has if anything served only to underscore the very great difficulties attending all such efforts. In fact, there is no way to restore in a meaningful and reliable manner the former continuity between deterrence

28. Remarks made by President Eisenhower at a press conference, January 12, 1955 (*The New York Times*, January 13, 1955).

29. Cf. pp. 142–79 for an extended discussion of these qualifications.

30. Thus we have the paradox that the effectiveness of deterrence is attributed both to the willingness of states to employ nuclear force and to the unwillingness of states to employ nuclear force, to the belief that there are no interests over which states are prepared to initiate thermonuclear war and to the belief that there are interests over which states are prepared to initiate thermonuclear war. Or we have the uncertainty that must attend a threat that is never acted on, and that would in all probability be self-defeating to act on.

and the overt use of the weapons on which deterrence rests without at the same time weakening the deterrent quality of these weapons. Given sufficient confidence in the effectiveness of nuclear deterrence, the failure to restore a continuity that once made the carrying out of the deterrent threat a rational instrument of policy has not given rise to unease. Instead, it has reinforced men's conviction that nuclear deterrence will not fail.

These are the more apparent manifestations of the belief that major war may now be avoided even though the international system remains otherwise essentially unchanged. The optimistic conviction that a new beginning has already been made can be placed in a broader perspective and its persuasiveness thereby enhanced. In an earlier chapter of this work the principal developments leading to the expansion of the state's power before the nuclear age were examined.[31] It was seen that a sudden and radical expansion of state power gave the military machines of major states a potential mass, scope, and intensity, as well as a dynamism and volatility, that greatly complicated the control of force as an instrument of policy in war and short of war. As events turned out, the requisite methods of control and restraint to balance this sudden and radical expansion of power did not emerge concomitantly with the state's expanded power. Instead, the relations of states were characterized during most of the period in question by an almost chronic instability, an instability that appeared largely inseparable from the effects of the sudden expansion of power. Moreover, when instability eventuated in war, the result of the state's new-found power was to make wars far more intense and destructive than before. Indeed, once in war the problem of controlling and restraining the new sources of power seemed beyond the abilities of governments. Were these results somehow inevitable? Did the new sources of power somehow ensure that once war had broken out it would escape men's control? Did the new sources of power constitute in themselves a principal cause of war, though a cause the significance of which would of course vary according to the other characteristics of the international system?[32] Even so, did they create anxieties and give rise to ambitions that made prudent and moderate statecraft increasingly difficult?[33]

31. Cf. pp. 41–120.

32. And above all the number and character of the great powers dominating the international system.

33. An earlier, and pessimistic, response to these questions was given by the German historian, Friedrich Meinecke, in closing his study of the development of reason of state. Writing under the impact of the first World War, Meinecke declared: "The very restrictedness of the power-resources had been the means of salvation to European humanity and ultimately even to the state itself, and had

From the vantage point of the present, an optimistic response to these questions—optimistic because it supports the outlook elaborated in these pages—need not attempt to minimize the effects of the state's tremendously increased power resources in making the wars of the first half of this century far more intense and destructive than they would otherwise have been. Nor, for that matter, need an optimistic response minimize the generally destabilizing effects of this sudden increase in state power, and particularly when conjoined with other destabilizing developments. These effects may be acknowledged and at the same time considered as transient. They may be seen as the accidental rather than as the necessary effects of the state's new power position. Even when seen as necessary effects, they may still be seen as necessary only for the period through which we have already passed. For the future, however, the effects of the state's radically increased power may prove—and, to the optimist, will prove—very different, and for the reason that the significance of this expansion of power was always ambivalent. The same general developments that in an earlier period contributed to an almost chronic instability and, when war occurred, that led to unprecedented destruction, also contained the prospect of promoting an unparalleled stability and of deterring major war altogether.[34]

Thus if the centralization and rationalization of state power gave late nineteenth- and twentieth-century governments a control over the forces of society their predecessors had never enjoyed, if this development permitted governments to channel and to direct the energies of society to a degree unknown to previous governments, the effect might just as well have been to limit violence rather than, as the case turned out, to have permitted it almost uncontrolled sway. And if it is assumed that the machinery of the modern state will nearly always be dominated by prudent and conservative bureaucracies, the former effect seems all the more plausible. It is true that this effect did not characterize the period from the late nineteenth century to the close of World War II. Although the professionalization and modernization of military power made the problem of the political control of force critical, in

---

constantly warded off the hypertrophy of power. Now its apparent unrestrictedness became destiny. . . . War in general, that last and strongest instrument of *raison d'état*, was no longer what it had been calculated to be; it had become a daemonic force which scorned the rein of *raison d'état* and threw its rider in the abyss. Power had overflowed its banks. The passions and ambitions of the people were united with the tempting new military resources to create the ominous atmosphere in which the pure and cautious type of statecraft could no longer flourish." *Machiavellism*, pp. 418, 422.

34. See, for example, F. H. Hinsley, *Power and the Pursuit of Peace* (Cambridge: Cambridge University Press, 1963), pp. 275–88, 346–67.

peacetime as well as in war, governments all too frequently did not exercise the requisite degree of control. The consequence of this failure was to permit military planning and the conduct of war to follow a logic of their own. That logic was the inflexible logic of military efficiency held by the general staffs, and it required, once war came, the earliest military defeat of the enemy through the application of maximum offensive force. Given this logic, which remained almost entirely within the narrow bounds of military necessity, not only did the peacetime exploitation of military power for deterrent purposes remain relatively undeveloped, but, more importantly, the possibility of exercising effective political control over military power, once this power was set in motion, was severely restricted. Yet there was nothing inevitable in the failure of governments to control the professional managers of the new military potential. On the contrary, the centralization and rationalization of state power provided the opportunity of doing so more effectively than governments had ever been able to do in the past. That opportunity has now been substantially realized. In the period following World War II, and particularly in the years following the middle 1950s, nothing seems more apparent than the determination and effectiveness with which the governments of the nuclear powers have politicized a realm that was once widely considered as governed by a logic of its own.

Similarly, if the popularization of the state provided governments with a source of power they never before possessed, if the growing identification of society and state permitted governments to exploit human resources in an unprecedented manner, the change that occurred in the relation between rulers and ruled also imposed upon governments constraints that were novel. These new constraints, imposed by an increasingly assertive public opinion, clearly have not always been pacific in disposition. In the years prior to World War I it would be difficult to make out a persuasive case for the pacific disposition of public opinion. If anything, public opinion in this period was bellicose rather than pacific. In the period following World War I the reverse was clearly true for the public opinion of some states, though the fact that it was true—or that it was more true—only for the public opinion of some states significantly contributed to international instability and, ultimately, to war. Moreover, whatever the disposition of public opinion prior to war, once in war it has not generally operated to restrain the actions of governments. Instead, public opinion in time of war has tempted governments, and has often compelled them, to abandon restraints they might otherwise have observed and to seek more ambitious ends than they might otherwise have sought. These considerations evidently must qualify a simple faith in the pacific influence of public opinion on the actions of governments. Even so, these considerations need not be taken to invalidate the view that public opinion may and increasingly does restrain governments from the pursuit of policies that carry the risk of war. They need not be taken to invalidate the view that the propensity of public opinion, particularly in industrialized democratic societies, is to react with increasing disfavor to policies that require sacrificing some of the benefits of even an abundant economy. This reaction need not, and probably should not, be interpreted as evidence of an inherently pacific disposition of mature industrial societies. It may be interpreted simply as evidence of a marked preference for domestic over foreign concerns. Governments cannot be unresponsive to this normal public preference which requires that they act with caution and circumspection in foreign affairs. And if public opinion is still prone to become more bellicose than governments once crises arise or war is undertaken, this consideration is also a source of restraint on governments in the pursuit of policies that may eventuate in war. The prospect that effective control over policy must prove increasingly difficult once force is employed, because of the rising pressures of public opinion, is itself a considerable deterrent to the initiation of force.

Finally, the modernization of military power, the tremendous increase of potentially destructive energy that accompanied the outburst of industrial growth and scientific-technological advance, though evidently bringing with it novel dangers also contained the promise of novel opportunities. For the same increase of destructive power that afforded novel incentives for war also provided novel deterrents to war. If the record of the first half of this century appears dominated by the former rather than the latter, the reasons for this dominance may themselves be seen to provide cause for optimism with respect to the future. Whereas at the beginning of the century governments of major states had little appreciation of, and even less experience with, the problems of controlling the new power placed at their disposal, a very different judgment must be made today when reviewing the persistent and sophisticated efforts of the most powerful states to subordinate force to political limitations in a systematic and calculated manner. Whereas the pace of technological innovation injected a new factor of uncertainty into warfare and military planning, complicated the calculation of relative military power, and made the control and prediction of war's outcome more difficult, thereby promoting instability through sharpening both the ambitions and the fears of governments, the prospect of yet another, and potentially decisive, technological break-through now appears sufficiently remote, and the mutual destructiveness of nuclear war sufficiently certain, to promote an unparalleled degree of stability. Whereas the prenuclear military technology, though increasingly destructive, could still be actively employed by the ambitious as a rational instrument of policy and thus remained an imperfect deterrent to major war, nuclear technology, by virtue of its assured destructiveness, has decisively removed this remaining imperfection.

It is roughly in this manner that the present juncture may be seen as the culmination of a great transformation the apparent ambiguity of which is finally resolved only after the advanced stages have been reached. If the instability that marked this transformation was greater than the instability of earlier periods, to the extent that this instability resulted from the expansion of power it was that very expansion which would eventually give rise to stability once it had progressed beyond its initial stages and once men had begun to assimilate its evident lessons. If the wars that attended this transformation were more intense and destructive than preceding wars, it was principally because the very force that increasingly served to deter resort to major war also ensured that war between the great powers would become more intense and destructive once it did break out. But even if these wars are seen as somehow inherent in the transformation, even if they are considered as necessary rather than as accidental, they form only a provisional necessity. At least, they do so unless we are to assume that man is unable to assimilate the evident lessons of his history.

4

The view that a new beginning has already been made is not implausible. At any rate, it is not implausible when given moderate and qualified expression. It is not implausible if only for the reason that it does not require us to assume the sudden and deliberate transformation either of man or of the state system. There is little, if any, reliance on a "leap" in our thinking and on the devising of "new methods" of conflict resolution. There is little, if any, expectation that the peril in which nuclear weapons have placed mankind will prompt men to rise above their partial interests. Still less is there the expectation of man's transformation through a sudden and radical extension of his faculty of sympathy. If men are expected to behave reasonably, if they are expected to eschew action that must prove or that is very likely to prove self-defeating, they are not expected to abandon statecraft. They are not expected to forego either the means that has hitherto been central to international political life or most of the ends this means has secured, and may still secure, for them. Hence the central issue nonviolence must raise—that is, whether nonviolence is compatible with the ends of man—does not arise here.

To be sure, men are expected to limit their actions and to pursue the ends of statecraft within the area bounded by these limits. To this extent, it must be assumed that at least some of the ends men have heretofore sought to obtain through force must be moderated, if not abandoned. Even so, within these limits they remain free to pursue most of the ends they have pursued in the past. Moreover, the principal foundation on which the restraints rest that are now expected of men remains substantially the same foundation as that on which past restraints have ultimately rested. Now as in the past, it is the threat and expectation of retribution that must be relied on to induce men to set limits to their behavior.

Similarly, the view that a new beginning has already been made presents us with a readily discernible state system. The international society it postulates is not an imaginary construct but, in substance, the present international society with its antagonistic social and political systems, its great disparities in political and economic development, and its many and deep rivalries. In this society the nation-state does not hold out the foreseeable prospect of withering away, to be replaced by effectively centralized supranational institutions, but remains the principal institution for achieving a hoped-for destiny. In this society, therefore, the state remains the indispensable condition of value. Accordingly, the system of self-help remains essentially unaltered and armed force continues to form the *ultima ratio* of diplomacy, though an ultimate means that is employed with increasing caution and restraint.

The optimism that informs the view that a new beginning has already been made may, and frequently does, take an unqualified expression. If the ultimate hazards of statecraft are henceforth to be avoided, if the prospect of a nuclear apocalypse and even of large-scale interstate violence may now be confidently dismissed, it is not because men have grown wiser and still less because they have grown better. It is simply that circumstances have changed. These changed circumstances, however, presumably have little, if anything, to do with men's deliberate efforts. But if the circumstances conditioning the conduct of statecraft have not changed through any deliberate effort of men, it is still the case that men must adjust their behavior to the changes that have occurred. An unqualified optimism over the prospects of avoiding catastrophe is thus the handmaiden of a markedly deterministic outlook. Nor is this surprising. If the avoidance of a nuclear catastrophe depends in substantial measure on the restraint men choose to exercise, if the prospect of a new beginning depends largely on men acting more wisely in the future than they have often acted in the past, then optimism cannot but be qualified. For the wisdom gained by one generation may be neglected by the next, and the restraints observed by one generation may be abandoned by the next.

In its most plausible form, however, a qualified optimism characterizes the view under consideration. Man is not simply being drawn along by great, though—as it turns out—ultimately benign, forces that he can at best comprehend but can neither materially alter nor control. The principal developments that have led to the radical expansion of state power appear as "givens," but even these developments are not literally seen as foreclosing the future; they present men with novel opportunities as well as with novel risks. If in the assessment of opportunities and of risks the former are found to outweigh the latter, this optimism does not stem from an unbounded faith in the ultimately benign character of the major developments of contemporary history. In large measure it stems, as indeed it must stem, from the belief that men can and do learn from experience and that given the experience of this century they have grown wiser. Thus even a qualified optimism must, and regularly does, find in nuclear weapons a cause of a transformation of sorts in men, although this transformation is clearly not the transformation expected, or hoped for, by the proponents of nonviolence. A qualified optimism does not find this transformation to rule out the possibility that men may still miscalculate or that they may still act unreasonably. It merely insists that nuclear weapons make their possessors much more cautious in employing force, that these weapons afford the strongest possible incentive for men to behave reasonably.[35]

However plausible the qualified optimism that men have already made a new beginning, the general analysis on which this optimism rests can only point to probabilities and not to certainties. That limitation, while entirely justified, must nevertheless severely limit the practical relevance

35. The effects of nuclear weapons on men form a pervasive theme in the literature on deterrence and on the prospects of stability in the present international system. Although there is a broad consensus that the possession of nuclear weapons has the effect of sobering their possessors, of making them more cautious, of inducing them to behave more "responsibly," there are significant variations in the estimates made of these effects. To the question whether Hitler would have been more cautious and moderate had he been confronted with the prospect of thermonuclear war, an unqualified optimism answers by posing the rhetorical question: Would Hitler have remained Hitler had he been confronted with the prospect of thermonuclear war? A qualified optimism, however, simply insists that these weapons do impel men to greater caution in employing force, that they do prompt men to greater restraint in pursuing the ends of statecraft. Of course, the prospect that men will behave sensibly also depends on other circumstances as well, and particularly on the clarity of the pressures to which a response is required. Thus the significance of the respective merits of bipolar and multipolar international systems, when considered in terms of the opportunities each affords men to behave reasonably—that is, to avoid a mutually destructive war. Cf. pp. 142–50, 169–79.

of the analysis. In considering the future of international conflict we are not interested simply in probabilities. Given the possibly fatal consequences of a thermonuclear war, we are also interested in a specific event that may well prove to be nonrepetitive. Indeed, we are above all interested in a specific event precisely because it may prove to be nonrepetitive. At best, a qualified optimism can assert that this event is highly improbable, that its occurrence may now be regarded as increasingly exceptional. Is this sufficient when the exception may well turn out to be fatal? Of the prenuclear age it has often been said that although wars were inevitable, no particular war was inevitable. In the nuclear age it may be true that wars—at least, major wars—are not only no longer inevitable but highly improbable. Even so, the catastrophic specific event remains possible. From inevitable though recoverable events we have therefore "progressed" to the improbable though still possible fatal event.

Thus even if a qualified optimism that a new beginning has already been made is accepted, it not only is of limited practical relevance but must also prove less than comforting. Even if the dreaded event may now be considered so unlikely as to constitute an historical aberration, it must remain of critical significance in view of its possibly fatal character. Even if men have recently achieved a rather remarkable and unexpected mastery of force, that mastery is not so perfect, and in a system that remains one of self-help does not afford the prospect of becoming so perfect, as to preclude the possibility of thermonuclear war. Moreover, the war no one wants may still occur so long as the order of international society continues to rest in so large a measure on the possibility of its occurrence. A point that has been emphasized in earlier pages of this work must once again be emphasized here.[36] The peace of deterrence is a peace that rests on the possibility of thermonuclear war. Once men were persuaded that they could with confidence remove that possibility from their calculations, one of the principal inducements to restraint would thereby disappear. With its disappearance would also disappear one of the principal bases of such order as international society presently enjoys. It scarcely needs observing that an order dependent upon the possibility, hence the threat, of thermonuclear war is not the most desirable of orders. In the absence of an alternative basis of order, however, there are severe limits to the optimism that men may with prudence entertain of the future.[37]

36. Cf. pp. 19–21, 185–92.
37. The above considerations would seem to point to the greater utility of concentrating on the more specific factors affecting the short—or shorter—term pros-

Is it possible to strengthen the peace and order of deterrence? Beyond this, is it possible to move, however modestly, toward a peace and order that do not rest so centrally upon the threat of nuclear violence? What is novel and oppressive about the peace of deterrence is not that it rests upon the threat of violence but that it rests upon a threat of violence which, if ever carried out, might make a future peace impossible. What is novel and oppressive about the order of deterrence is not that it rests upon the threat of disorder but that it rests upon a threat of disorder which, if ever carried out, might make the building of a new order impossible. Previously, the threat of disorder has always carried within it the vision of a new order. Now, however, the threat of disorder—of nuclear disorder—is such that it no longer permits men to entertain with any real assurance the vision of a new order. Nuclear weapons have not created the apparent paradox that the possibility of restraint in men's behavior is ultimately grounded in the possibility of a lack of restraint, for that paradox is indeed as old as human history. But modern technology has magnified that paradox to the nth degree, and it is largely for this reason that the peace and order of deterrence, despite what presently appears as a high degree of stability, are both novel and oppressive.

These considerations merely point to the urgency of the questions posed above. They afford no persuasive reason for believing that these questions may be answered affirmatively, unless the optimistic assumption is granted that what men need to do they will somehow do. In fact, the need to strengthen the peace and order of deterrence, and perhaps in time even to move modestly beyond, is no more apparent than the imposing obstacles in the way of realizing that need. Given these obstacles, it is not surprising that most prescriptions for strengthening world order tend to take on either a self-evident or a problematic character. Whereas the former amount in substance to little more than the general admonition that men take to heart the common peril in which

---

pects of avoiding major international violence. The difficulty with this alternative, however, is that if we once go beyond the very specific factors and the most immediate prospects we are confronted with substantially the same uncertainty characterizing the view that a new beginning has already been made. Thus, as an earlier discussion has indicated (cf. pp. 142–79), the principal developments affecting international stability during the next two or three decades—continued bipolarity or a gradually emerging multipolarity, the proliferation of nuclear weapons, the evolving relationships of the developed states to the underdeveloped countries—are all marked by a considerable uncertainty. Their effects on the prospects of avoiding thermonuclear conflict are largely indeterminate. Then, too, it is characteristic of most of these more modest analyses that they also place a considerable reliance on the prospect—or hope—that men will behave reasonably and that a major incentive to reasonable behavior will be the fear of nuclear war.

modern technology has placed them and act with greater caution and restraint, the latter attempt to lay down the more specific norms that must presumably comprise a strengthened international order. Whereas the former urge what is obviously immanent in the very meaning of order, even an "order" that is marked by the practice of self-help and that has little more than the modest objective of co-existence through the avoidance of major violence, the latter necessarily go well beyond this residual meaning of order and, by defining the further restraints on coercion, indicate those other values that are to be protected by an improved, though still a structurally unchanged, international order.[38]

It is as easy to criticize either type of proposal as it is difficult to conceive of a more promising alternative. The principal criticism to be made of the former is its tendency to accept the status quo and thus to fall—however unconsciously—into complacency or resignation. Although the peace and order of deterrence are to be strengthened, and eventually perhaps even to be displaced, the methods for accomplishing these ends are, after all, by and large the same methods that are presently employed, the difference being that henceforth they must be employed with still greater caution and restraint. Given this position, the temptation readily arises not only to find in deterrence the best of all *possible* orders but to consider deterrence—once attended by the requisite, though not exorbitant, degree of prudence—as a self-sustaining order. This attitude has all too frequently been the nemesis of past orders; it could also prove to be the nemesis of deterrence.

This criticism does not imply the superiority of prescriptions that would go substantially beyond the admonition of "politics as usual but with a much greater dose of caution."[39] Proposals that would go sub-

38. We do not consider here proposals that require the sudden and explicit transformation of the present system—that is, a transformation entailing the abandonment of the system of self-help and the establishment of effectively centralized supranational institutions. Cf. pp. 331–41. Instead, the proposals considered in these pages look toward an improvement of the present system. To be sure, these proposals may, and frequently do, project the eventual transformation of the system of self-help. Even so, this transformation is to come, if it does finally come, only as a consequence of the progressive improvement of the present system.

39. In these words Stanley Hoffmann, *The State of War* (New York: Frederick A. Praeger, 1965), p. 52, summarizes the conclusion reached by Raymond Aron in *Paix et Guerre.* Hoffmann goes on to observe: "I wonder whether the formula ought not to be amended for both the philosopher and statesman: 'Act so that traditional politics, the necessary framework of and starting point for action, bring about through prudence the coming of the postwar age—supposing this age were ever possible.'" Elsewhere (pp. 154–59), Hoffmann examines the actions—indeed, the norms or restraints—that might not only strengthen but eventually move men beyond the oppressive peace and order of deterrence. It can scarcely be said, however, that his attempt to open the door at least on Aron's world, condemned as it

stantially beyond this admonition, yet at the same time stop short of urging the structural transformation of the international system, must invariably encounter two formidable obstacles. Even if states are not expected to surrender the right of self-help, they are expected to agree on the scope of this right. Even if states are not expected to surrender their claim to vindicate justice with the means at their disposal, they are expected to agree on the meaning of the justice they may still vindicate. There have been periods when such agreement was at least a meaningful prospect. The same cannot be said of the present period. It is quite true that deterrence has given rise to an order of sorts, however minimal that order may be. But the order of deterrence remains essentially an order without legitimacy.

Moreover, even in periods when the internal structures of states and the concepts of justice on which those structures rested have not been so disparate as to preclude the possibility of meaningful agreement among states on the essential attributes of a legitimate international order, the difficulty of translating such agreement into clear and reliable restraints on the regulation and control of force has been notorious. In a system dominated by self-help the possibility of achieving an effective agreement on the use of force, on the scope and meaning of the right of self-help, is, and is of necessity, very low. It is very low primarily because the conditions of security can seldom, if ever, be foreseen with the clarity and assurance that are necessary to induce a commitment even on

---

is to the "antinomies of action," is a very successful one. It is instead indicative of the intractability of the issues involved that the brilliance of Hoffmann's analysis of the contemporary "state of war" appears in striking contrast to the rather vague and inconclusive attempt to improve upon this state. In substance, we are told that states must have a greater concern for order, that their aim must be to make the game safer and ultimately even to transform it, and that their actions must reflect—in however modest a manner—this concern for and aspiration toward greater order. Thus the principal prescription that in the choice of means "states select the one that appears to them less dangerous—if not for the international system (which some nations have good reasons to want to change to their benefit)—at least for needed world order." If this advice is unexceptionable, it still does not carry us very far. The difficulty, of course, is that while states may well appreciate the need for greater order—and above all the need to avoid a nuclear holocaust—they also continue to entertain aspirations that can be satisfied only by means that threaten even a minimal kind of order. If "less dangerous" means will give them what they want, they can be expected to choose these means. If not, they can be expected to abstain from "more dangerous" means only at the cost of surrendering their aspirations. To expect them to do so on behalf of a needed world order is, however, to presuppose a transformation that clearly has not occurred and that shows little prospect of occurring in the foreseeable future. Aron's "antinomies of action" thus remain, moderated only by a hoped-for greater dose of caution. Hoffmann resists this conclusion because he is less optimistic than Aron over the prospects that men will behave reasonably even though the game remains essentially unchanged.

the part of those states generally satisfied with the status quo. The proverbial reluctance of states to define not only the present but the future conditions of their security, at least their reluctance to do so in terms that go beyond generalities, is not simply due to an innate perversity or to unavowed, and expansionist, intentions. Nor is it the result of a paranoia presumably bred by long training in the tortuous logic of reason of state. Instead, it is only the expected—indeed, the "natural" —response to the basic condition in which all states find themselves. It is this condition that must largely explain the historic reluctance of states to permit international law to qualify the "right" of self-preservation.[40] It is the same condition that must largely explain the present controversies and consequent uncertainties arising from divergent interpretations of the norms of the United Nations Charter which pertain to the regulation of force.[41] Quite apart, then, from the revolutionary character of the present international system, it is important to appreciate the difficulties that have always and necessarily attended attempts to regulate the use of force by states. Where security has not been effectively collectivized, where self-help remains the principal mode of defense and of redress, these attempts either prove entirely abortive or give rise to "restraints" states may accept without undue fear of being restrained.

Thus as between the critical need for greater order and the imposing obstacles in the way of realizing this need the outcome remains uncertain. It is scarcely surprising that this should be so. The uncertainty that marks the issue of order is but the final uncertainty of the many uncertainties that characterize contemporary world politics. The sudden expansion of the state system, together with the heterogeneous character of the universal system that has resulted from this expansion, must evidently account for a substantial measure of the uncertainty that impresses both observer and actor. Even in the absence of other changes, the capacity of the international system to absorb new states without resultant instability and conflict has always been limited. Not only is the present expansion without precedent; it has occurred together with other changes that are also without precedent and the effects of which are equally uncertain.

Among these other changes, it is, of course, the change in the technology of war that has given rise to greatest uncertainty. The persisting uncertainty over the consequences of nuclear weapons for international order would be reduced, if not altogether resolved, only if it could be

40. Cf. pp. 271–76.
41. Cf. pp. 296–99.

demonstrated either that war—or the threat of war—can no longer secure the ends men desire (or can secure these ends only at prohibitive cost) or that men no longer desire these ends—at least, no longer desire these ends to the extent that they are willing to threaten or to employ armed force on their behalf. Provided that either or both of these propositions were true, it would only remain for all governments to adjust their behavior accordingly.[42] In fact, neither of these propositions has been persuasively demonstrated. It may be true that some of the ends for which men have been willing to employ force are now placed in doubt, that some of the purposes deemed sufficient to sanction force as recently as the beginning of this century are no longer so considered. Thus it may be true, as many now argue, that in the future territorial conquest will no longer form one of the ends for which governments are willing to employ force and that even now this change is apparent. In part, the expected disappearance of one of the age-old ends of war is attributed to the diminished value—economic and military—of territorial conquest. In part, it is attributed to the sharply rising costs—moral and material— of territorial conquest. Even if this argument is accepted (and it is really persuasive only when applied to highly developed countries) there are other objectives that are equally significant, if not far more significant than territorial conquest, and for which governments evidently remain willing to threaten or to employ force. These other objectives are, for the most part, as old as the history of state conflict.

It is clearer still that the experience of the recent past does not bear out the extreme argument that military power has lost its former utility. Nor does this experience even support the more moderate view that the utility of military power has substantially declined. Whether in its extreme or in its modest version, the view that military power is at an ever-increasing discount in state relations ultimately rests on at least one of the following assumptions: that if force cannot do everything (or nearly everything) it can do nothing, that if force is not visibly (overtly) used it is useless (or very nearly so), and that if force is once employed (particularly as between nuclear powers) its use is virtually uncontrollable. None of these assumptions is true, as the analysis presented in preceding pages of this study has sought to show. Although there are many things military power cannot do, and has never been able to do, there are a number of things it can still do and they are very important. Nor is the utility of military power exhausted by its active employment. On the contrary, the utility of military power is greatest where it does

---

42. We are not arguing that this adjustment would necessarily take place. Institutions may persist even though they have lost their utility.

not have to be actively employed, or even threatened, yet deters those actions the absence—or repression—of which affords its principal justification. Whether the active employment of force, even as between nuclear powers, must lead to its virtually uncontrolled use is not an issue that can be decided simply by appeal to some metaphysic of force which decrees that war, being a "thing in itself," suffers no limitations save those limitations imposed by war itself. The view that if war cannot be abolished the conduct of war can still be controlled and its effects moderated is no more absurd than the view that although man cannot control the manner in which war is conducted he can nevertheless abolish war itself. And if it is argued that it is precisely because man cannot control the conduct of war that he will ultimately be driven in the nuclear age to abandon war itself (and ultimately, it must be added, the threat of war), the question remains: Will he also abandon the ends he has sought through war or the threat of war? If not, and we have no persuasive reason for believing that he will abandon these ends, he has no alternative (other than self-destruction) but systematically to cultivate the limitation and regulation of force.

Once again, then, we must put the question: Has a new beginning already been made? And, if so, what assurance do we have that it will continue? Have technological and political developments in the nuclear age put the particular utopia of a world of tolerably regulated force within the realm of likelihood? We cannot answer these questions with any real degree of assurance. We cannot do so if only for the reason that our experience with the new technology remains limited. In the history of state relations a decade is a very brief period. Yet it is only within this brief period that we have experienced a balance of terror. That nuclear weapons have made their possessors more cautious in the employment of force, that these weapons have made their possessors anxious to avoid direct military confrontations, that they have generally provided their possessors with a novel and powerful incentive to subordinate force to political limitations in a more systematic and calculated way than in the past—all this may be accepted without affording satisfactory answers to the questions put above. For nuclear weapons impel men to want a kind of assurance they cannot have from an experience that is of brief duration and indicative only of general trends. Moreover, even the small comfort that may be drawn from this recent experience is qualified by the appreciation of the principal foundation on which it apparently rests. If nuclear weapons have effected a transformation of sorts in men, if these weapons have impelled men to act with greater caution and restraint, we have no persuasive reasons for believing that this transformation results from a new morality and not simply from considerations of expediency and utility. The view that a new beginning has already been made is plausible largely for the reason that it does not require us to go beyond these considerations and to postulate man's moral transformation. May it not be argued, however, that there is a point beyond which the very strength of this view becomes a source of weakness? Is there not a point beyond which reliance on considerations of expediency and utility—even to sustain an order limited to the modest objective of preventing major violence—is not only inadequate but dangerous? These considerations may prove adequate in dealing with the expected, the known. Are they adequate to deal with the unexpected? If they are not, or if they are of doubtful adequacy, we can only hope for an eventual transformation of attitudes toward force that strikes deeper roots than the recent transformation described in this study.

INDEX

Abel, Elie, 154
Acheson, Dean, 225, 299
Afghanistan, 85
Africa, 164, 165, 166
Agadir, 89
Aggression: instinctual basis of, 5–6; definition of, 24, 110, 126, 230; by Germany before World War II, 68, 69, 92–96 *passim*; collective security against, 95, 109–10; Soviet, 130, 131, 143, 210; massive retaliation against, 131, 249; limited war against, 132; counterforce strategy against, 135; escalation against, 138; in Asia, 162; in *bellum justum*, 292, 293, 294; mentioned, 23, 33, 171, 187, 196, 199, 255
Aggression, indirect: by China, 159; public opinion of, 229–30; legal definition, 231
Agincourt, Battle of, 57
Airpower: in World War I, 65, 67; role short of war, 89, 90, 91–92, 128; use against Japan, 94; German development of, before World War II, 113–14; in disarmament negotiations, 113–15, 116–17; use in Asia, 162, 186; mentioned, 55, 59, 66, 68, 262. *See also* Disarmament; Strategic bombing; Vietnamese War
Algeciras, 89
Algeria, 142, 161, 163
Alliances: flexibility of, in classical balance of power system, 70, 71–75, 99–104 *passim*, 144, 177; secrecy of, 73, 74, 84; offensive role of, 80, 82; defensive role of, 81–82, 83–85, 107; Bismarck's system of, 82–85, 98, 106; restraining role of, 83–84, 87, 175; pre-World War I consolidation of, 84–88, 104, 105, 106; pre-World War II failure of, 88, 94–95; as cause of war, 88, 106–7, 117–18; polarized by arms races, 91; role in nuclear age, 172–78 *passim*, 109–10, 143, 144, 170; of United States, in Asia and the Pacific, 162, 176; mentioned, 45, 76, 79, 281, 282. *See also* Balance of power; NATO; Warsaw Treaty Organization
Alsace–Lorraine, 82

Angell, Norman, 16
Anglo-French Entente, 85
Anglo-Japanese Alliance, 58, 85, 111
Anglo-Polish Treaty, 96
Anglo-Russian Entente, 85, 86
Anscombe, G. E. M., 311
Antiballistic missiles, 125, 146
Ardrey, Robert, 33
Arendt, Hannah, 19
Argentina, 91, 111, 112
Arms control. *See* Disarmament
Arms race: in eighteenth century, 46; development as form of power politics, 56–62; before World War II, 88, 107; as cause of conflict, 88, 107, 112, 180; United States-Soviet, 121, 123, 146–47; as dynamic element in balance of power, 143; dangers of, 146, 261, 287, 321; control of, 182, 183, 184; mentioned, 21, 84, 89, 90, 91, 111. *See also* Nuclear weapons; Rearmament; Strategy; Technology
Aron, Raymond, 17, 66, 137, 138, 145, 204, 207, 266, 281, 290, 337, 354, 355
Asia: Japanese expansion in, 93; Chinese expansion in, 158, 159, 162; containment in, 158; use of tactical nuclear weapons in, 158; multipolarity in, 170, 172, 176. *See also* Third World
Asia Minor, 14
Athens, 201, 270
Augustine, Saint, 303
Austria: in World War I, 56, 64; in eighteenth century system, 70–76 *passim*; in Bismarck's system, 80–85 *passim*, 106; in Balkan wars, 90, 172; Germany's "blank check" to, 86, 143; mentioned, 49, 53, 54, 78, 79, 103
Austrian Succession, War of, 51, 71, 73, 74
Austro-Prussian Alliance, 80, 84
Austro-Prussian War, 53
Austro-Russian Alliance, 73, 103

Bacteriological weapons, 113, 168, 217–18
Balance of interests, 148–57 *passim*. *See also* Crises

361